In the next volume...

Light Shining Upon Darkness

Lag arrives at the town of Lament, only to discover that Noir has been stealing letters. Realizing that the town's convent hides a secret, he hatches a plan to infiltrate it. But he has no idea what—or who—awaits him inside!

Available February 2012!

Route Map

Finally, I am including a map indicating the route followed in this volume, created by the mapmaker at Lonely Goatherd Map Station of Central Yuusari.

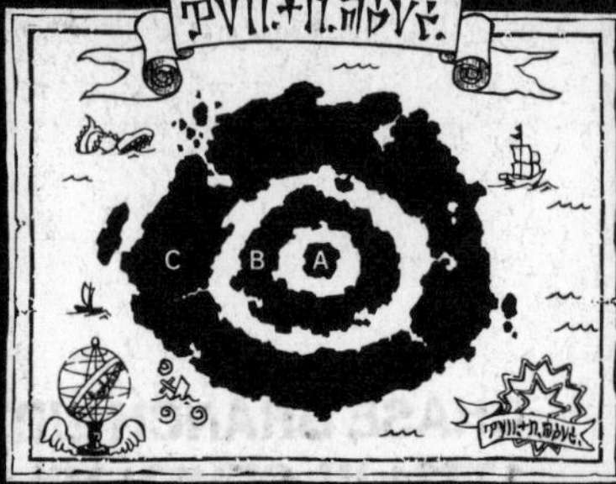
C
B
A

A: Akatsuki B: Yuusari C: Yodaka

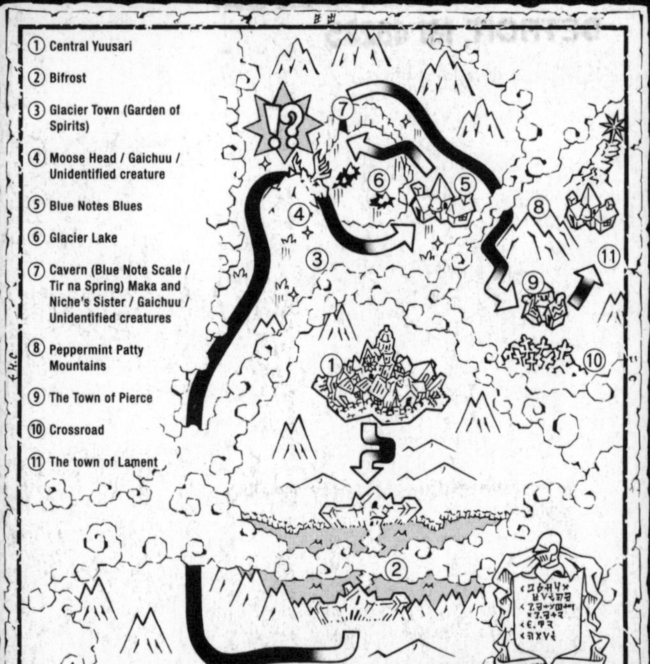
① Central Yuusari
② Bifrost
③ Glacier Town (Garden of Spirits)
④ Moose Head / Gaichuu / Unidentified creature
⑤ Blue Notes Blues
⑥ Glacier Lake
⑦ Cavern (Blue Note Scale / Tir na Spring) Maka and Niche's Sister / Gaichuu / Unidentified creatures
⑧ Peppermint Patty Mountains
⑨ The Town of Pierce
⑩ Crossroad
⑪ The town of Lament

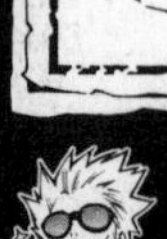

There? Have I had my revenge? Will you no longer ignore my plight? I'm not asking for much here—just pay attention to me! And maybe put me in the book! And...a cover spread wouldn't hurt either, now that I think about it. Can't you just picture it? Me in full color, leaping into action? Just give me a chance here!

Ah, Lag! Please save me as well! Bring me back to reality! Me too, me too, me too!!

■ GAICHUU

In the far distant past, "Spirit Insects" were born—ordinary insects that had absorbed the spiritual energy of the land. When such an insect dies, its *heart* gradually vanishes. The body that is left turns into a Gaichuu. Spirit Insects that turn into amber while they still have some *heart* left become Spirit Amber, which is used to aid Amberground...and Lag and the other Letter Bees. Amazing! I should team up with my son, Junior, for immediate further research!!

Whoa! This means I've got to get my turn at last! I'm going to actually appear in the book!! I am, aren't I? Noir awakened a Gaichuu no one had seen before. What could he be planning? It's me! Time for my science team to take the stage! My existence will save Amberground, everyone! Oh, dear! I'm tearing up!! Waah!!

■ THE TOWN OF LAMENT

nb: lament (English), *lamentazione* (Italian) / deep sorrow and regret, or a poem, song or musical piece expressing sorrow.

■ VERITY CONVENT

Huh? There's more? Well, this is a convent for those who believe in the Empress of Amberground. They believe that "work is prayer," so they live mostly self-sufficiently. They earn their living by selling the wine, beer and herbal brews that they make...and convent cookies. But what is Roda doing there? That's right... The Man Who Could Not Become Spirit said they had hideouts everywhere. Could this convent be one of their hideouts? Well, you can leave this mystery to me, don't you think? Ha ha ha...

nb: Verity / the unmistakable truth.

nb: Celica / A line of Toyota sedans (1970–2006). The name is derived from the Latin for "heavenly" or "celestial."

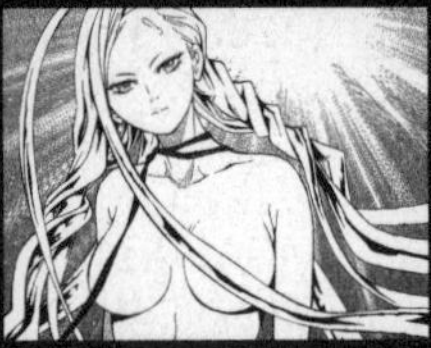

■ CHILD OF MAKA

They were really children of humans, but the tears of the Maka must have had an effect on them. Perhaps it's a kind of "Maka extract." But never mind that! Niche's sister, please refuse to wear pants!! Er...this is just my own personal suggestion.

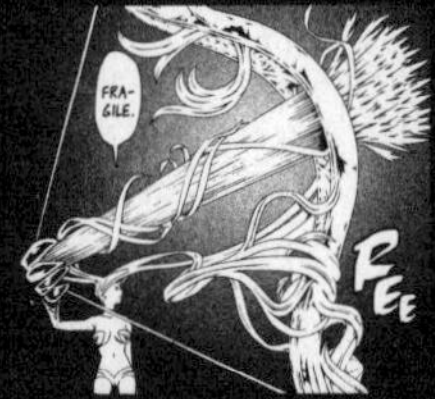
FRA-GILE.
FEE

I thought Niche was tremendously powerful, but her sister is even scarier. I guess that's what Niche would have grown into if she hadn't met up with Lag. She doesn't really get humans...and she has a vast repertoire of blade action. She and Niche have a lot in common, I think, but the Children of Maka have such inscrutable faces. They don't seem to sweat much either.

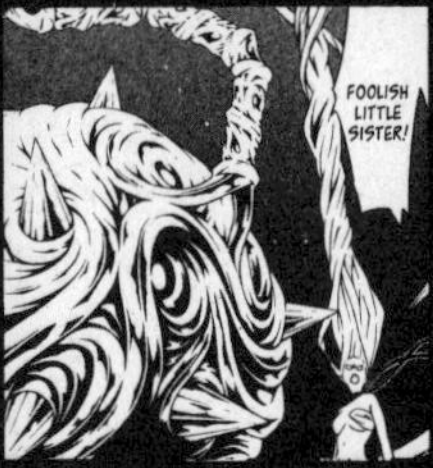
FOOLISH LITTLE SISTER!

But when Niche's sister's emotions run high, she has trouble talking. When she first saw Niche, her face remained impassive, but judging from her speech I think she was a little excited. If that's the case, I suppose there's something endearing about her...although she still terrifies me. Now that Niche is with Lag, I wonder if she'll grow up to be more like a human than a Maka. And I wonder if she'll ever develop emotionally to the level of a mature human.

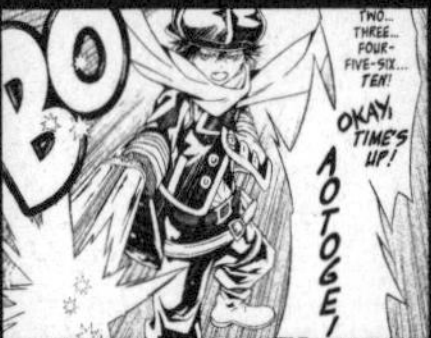
TWO... THREE... FOUR-FIVE-SIX... TEN!
OKAY, TIME'S UP!
AOTOGE!
BO

■ SHINDAN

Zazie may be a little indiscriminate about spreading ill will. Zazie's an easier one to understand. On the other hand, Noir is complex and shoots dangerous *heart*. When Wasiolka got shot, he became gloomy and dull. In addition to the restoration shindan, there are shindan that give people bitterness and pain, like Noir's. What's more, there are shindan that can cause not just emotional pain, but physical injury...but I'll get to those in due time.

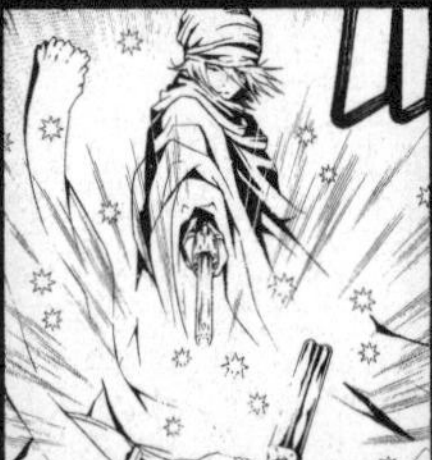

This is the first time Lag has willfully shot a human with a shindan, isn't it? That is, of course, if Niche's sister can be considered human. But he did it not to hurt her, but to show her the feelings for Niche that were in his *heart*. Perhaps Lag will remember this incident if he ever gets the chance to shoot Noir with the Letter Bullet, his only hope of restoring Gauche's *heart*.

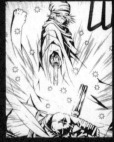

■ TIKITIKI

A simple animal (or is it?), the tikitiki first appeared in volume 1. They say it's delicious broiled, grilled or sautéed. At least once in your life, you should have it prepared raw...with soy sauce, sashimi-style. But it's a little scary when served live. You have to swallow it while it's still twitching. Bottoms up!

■ GLACIAR LAKE AND BLUE NOTE SCALE

Travel from the cavern of ice pillars containing Gaichuu, and you come to a huge underground lake. In the past, many "Maka Paths" led from the cavern up to the icebergs; they seem to be the paths the Maka took to fly up to the sky. As the mayor said, the cavern is filled with a thick fog, making it impossible to enter. I believe Lag and Niche were only able to reach the underground lake because the Maka wanted to allow Niche in.

nb: The Blue Note Scale is used in jazz and blues music. In it, the notes of the major scale are altered by adding flattened third, fifth and seventh notes, called "blue notes."

■ TIR NA SPRING

nb: Tir na Nog / in Celtic mythology, the world where fairies dwell.

■ MAKA

So the Maka really does exist! But that stupid mayor... The stories passed down in the village, including the one about the "Child of Maka," are not exactly myths, just made-up stories. Dr. Cezanne, who transmitted the words of the mayor's great-grandfather, must be turning over in his grave. It seems the Maka are able to expel freezing air from their bodies to freeze the Gaichuu. Who could have imagined there were thousands of them? The Maka could be protecting not just this land, but the whole world. And could it really have been alive since ancient times?

The Maka's biology and abilities are still unknown, but it's definitely an amazing creature. Maybe someday this discovery will help Lag and his friends. But listen... If the Maka exists, then I might really exist too, right? There's hope for me after all! Bwa ha ha! Somebody hurry up and find me! Look for me in Hachinosu! I bet I'm there! I'm sure I am!

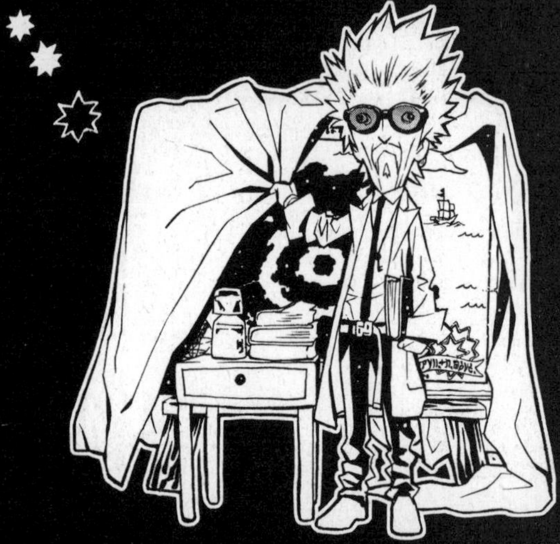

Dr. Thunderland's Reference Desk

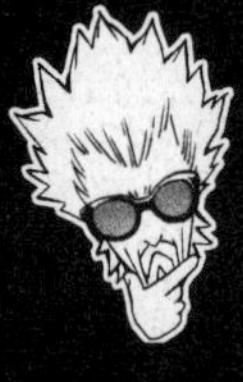

I am Dr. Thunderland.

Or am I? Recently a dark fragment of suspicion has been growing within me. I wonder if I really am Dr. Thunderland. Am I? Am I…?

Do I really exist in this world? Do I have substance? I seem to work at the Yuusari Post Office and carry out assorted experiments from day to day. But what do I really do?

As we review the details of my world that were revealed in this volume, won't you please double-check my existence?

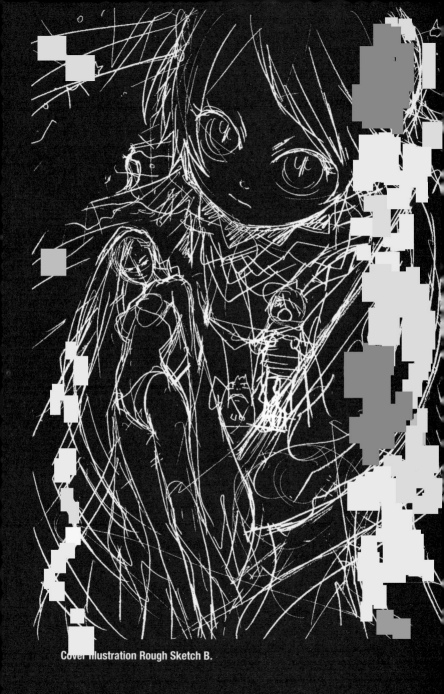

Cover Illustration Rough Sketch B.

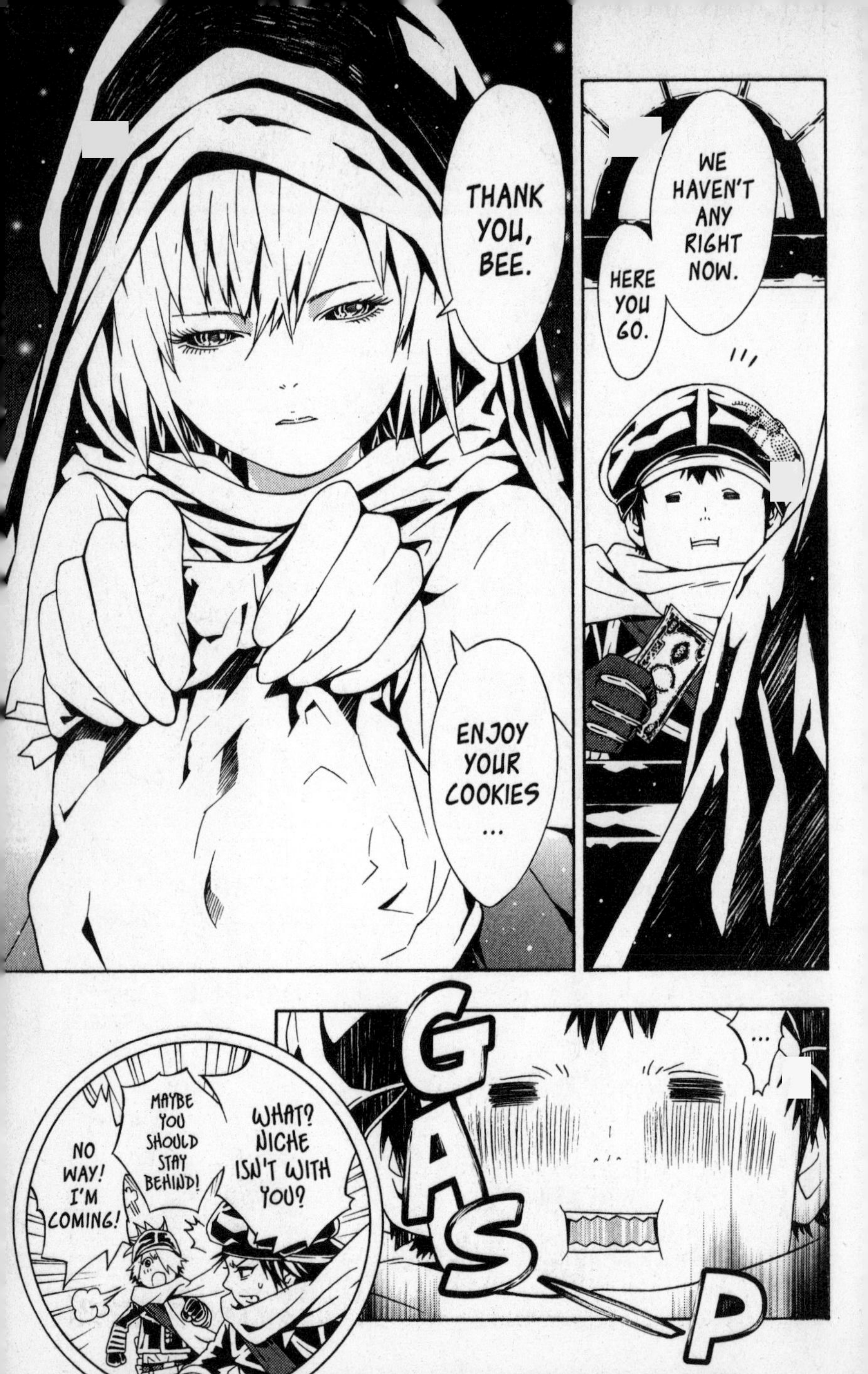
WE HAVEN'T ANY RIGHT NOW.
HERE YOU GO.
THANK YOU, BEE.
ENJOY YOUR COOKIES ...
...
GASP
WHAT? NICHE ISN'T WITH YOU?
MAYBE YOU SHOULD STAY BEHIND!
NO WAY! I'M COMING!

VOLUME 7: BLUE NOTES BLUES (THE END)

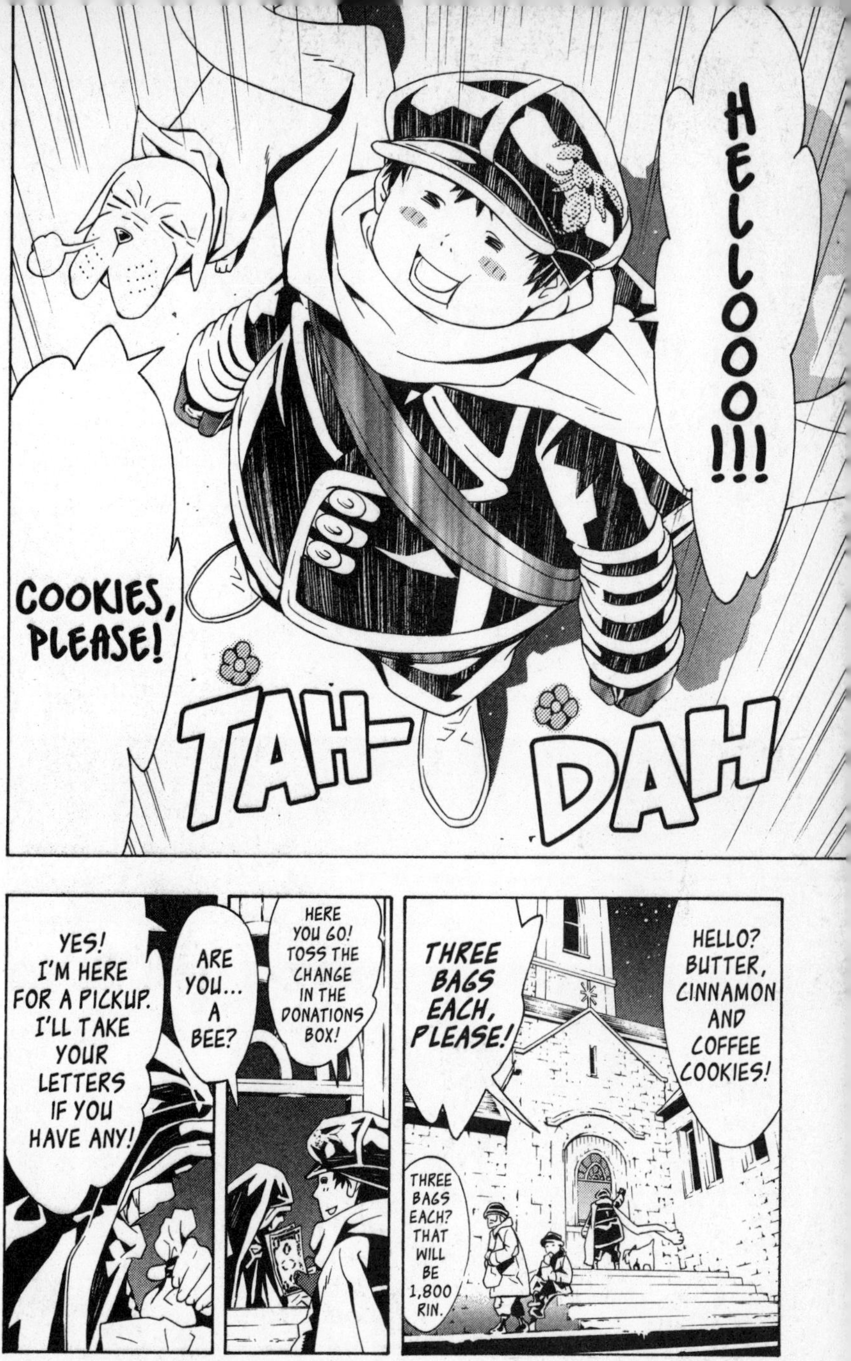
HELLOOO!!!
COOKIES, PLEASE!
TAH-DAH
HELLO? BUTTER, CINNAMON AND COFFEE COOKIES!
THREE BAGS EACH, PLEASE!
THREE BAGS EACH? THAT WILL BE 1,800 RIN.
HERE YOU GO! TOSS THE CHANGE IN THE DONATIONS BOX!
ARE YOU... A BEE?
YES! I'M HERE FOR A PICKUP. I'LL TAKE YOUR LETTERS IF YOU HAVE ANY!

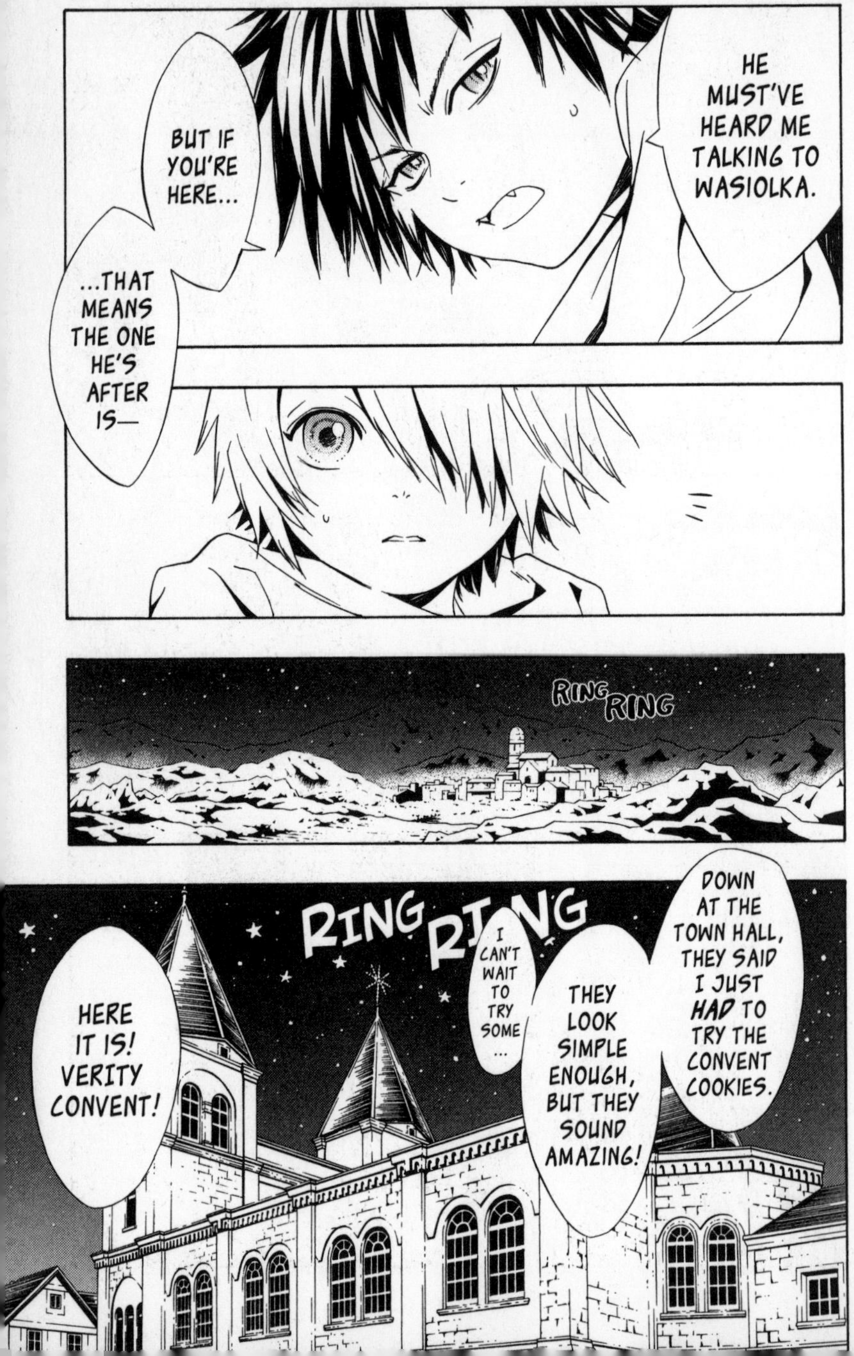
HE MUST'VE HEARD ME TALKING TO WASIOLKA.
BUT IF YOU'RE HERE...
...THAT MEANS THE ONE HE'S AFTER IS—
RING RING
RING RING
DOWN AT THE TOWN HALL, THEY SAID I JUST *HAD* TO TRY THE CONVENT COOKIES.
THEY LOOK SIMPLE ENOUGH, BUT THEY SOUND AMAZING!
I CAN'T WAIT TO TRY SOME...
HERE IT IS! VERITY CONVENT!

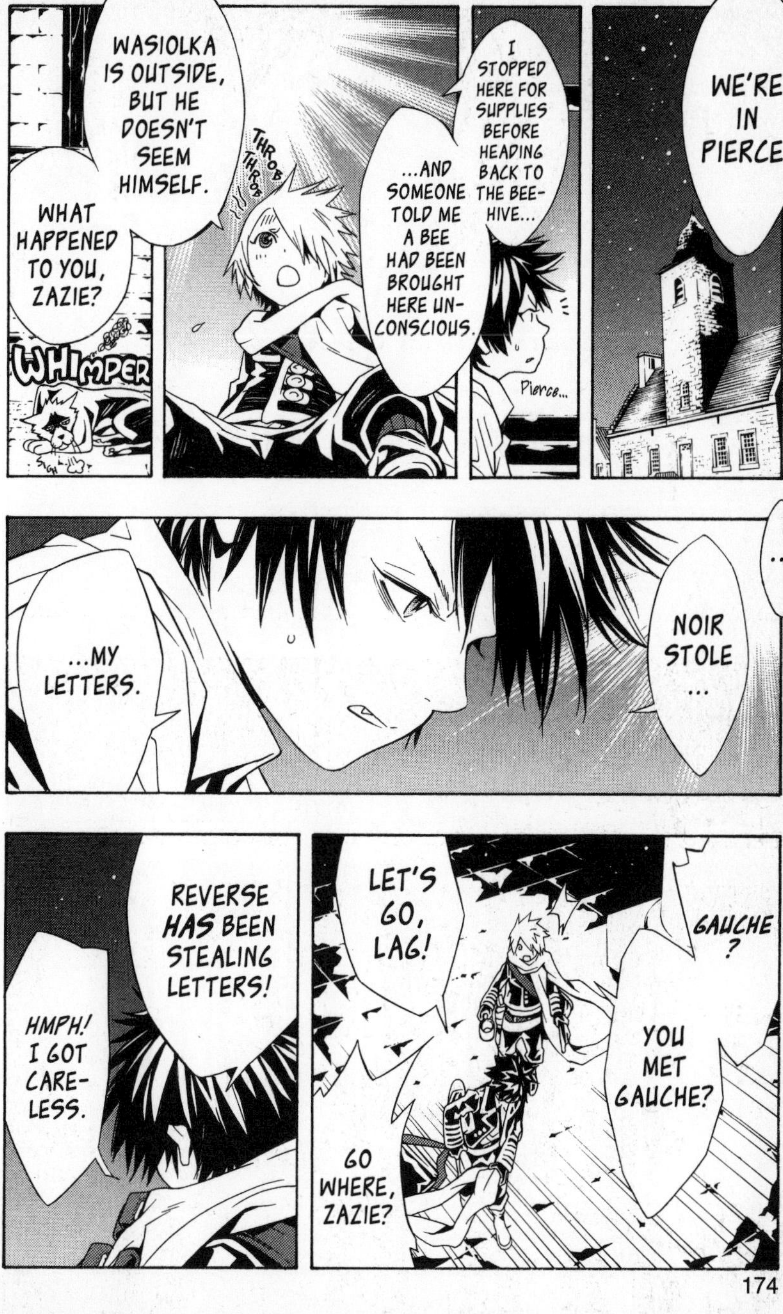
WE'RE IN PIERCE.
Pierce...
I STOPPED HERE FOR SUPPLIES BEFORE HEADING BACK TO THE BEE-HIVE...
...AND SOMEONE TOLD ME A BEE HAD BEEN BROUGHT HERE UNCONSCIOUS.
THROB THROB
WASIOLKA IS OUTSIDE, BUT HE DOESN'T SEEM HIMSELF.
WHAT HAPPENED TO YOU, ZAZIE?
WHIMPER
SIGH
...
NOIR STOLE ...
...MY LETTERS.
GAUCHE?
YOU MET GAUCHE?
LET'S GO, LAG!
GO WHERE, ZAZIE?
REVERSE HAS BEEN STEALING LETTERS!
HMPH! I GOT CARELESS.

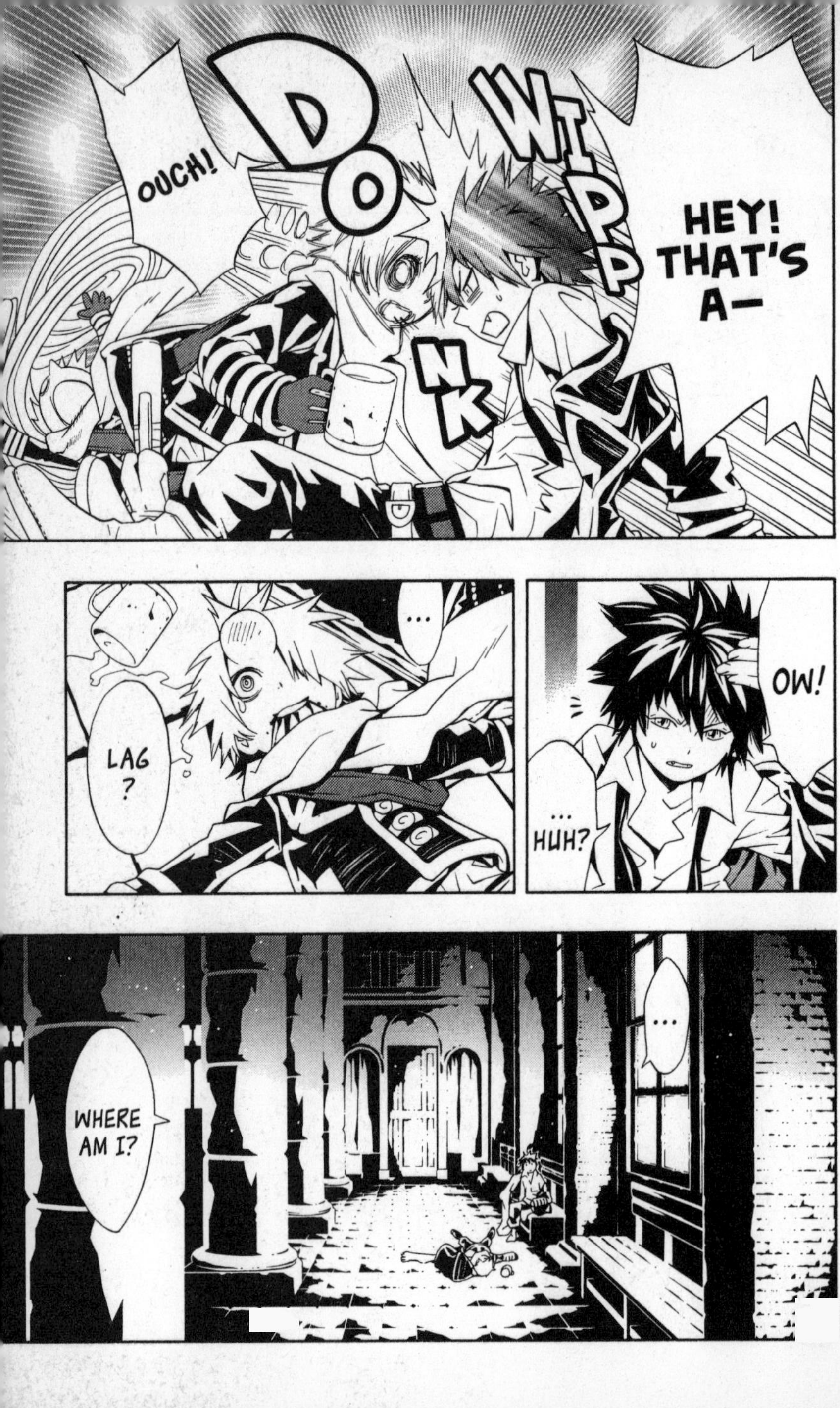
HEY! THAT'S A—
WHIPP
DONK
OUCH!
OW!
... HUH?
...
LAG?
...
WHERE AM I?

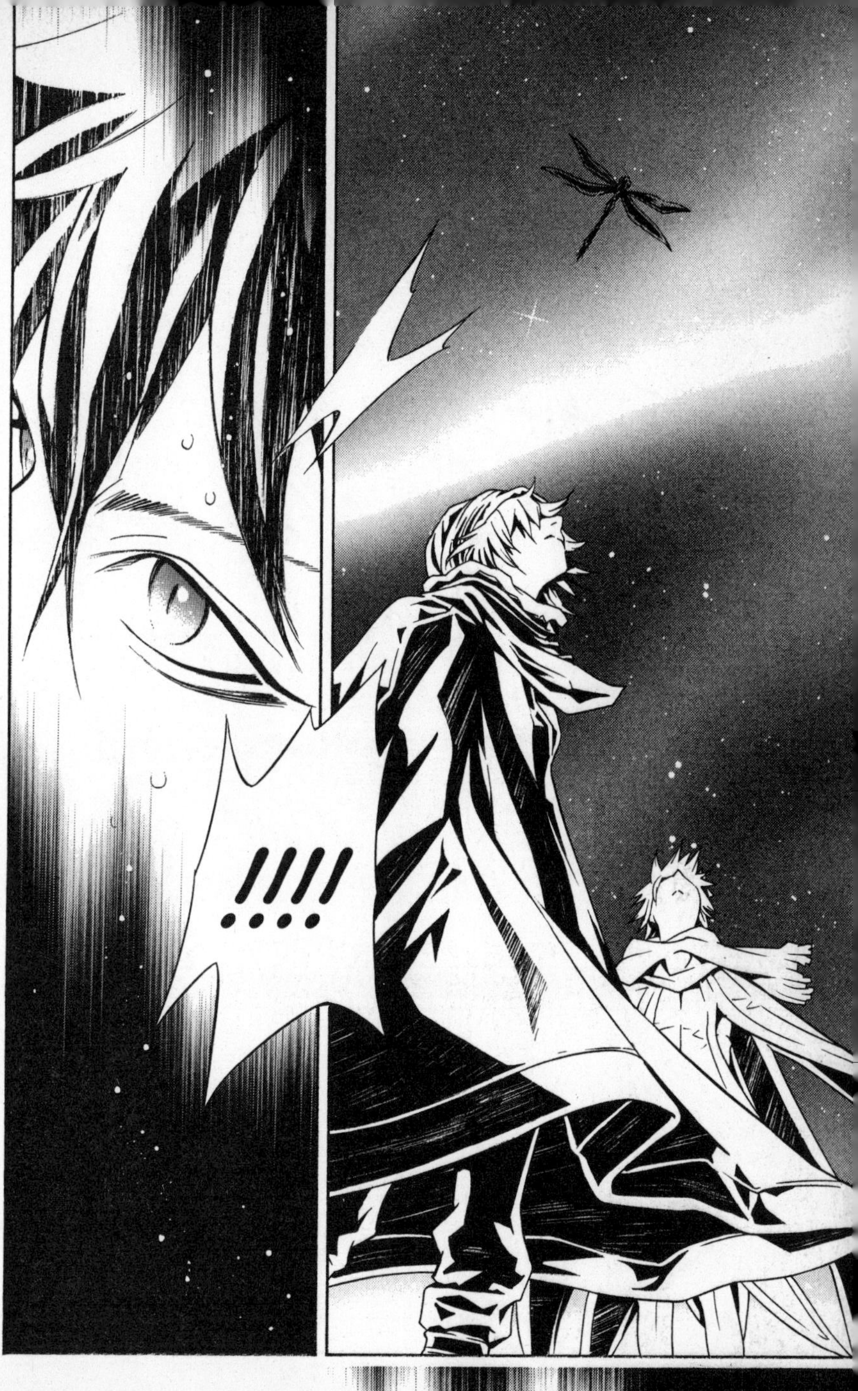
!!!!

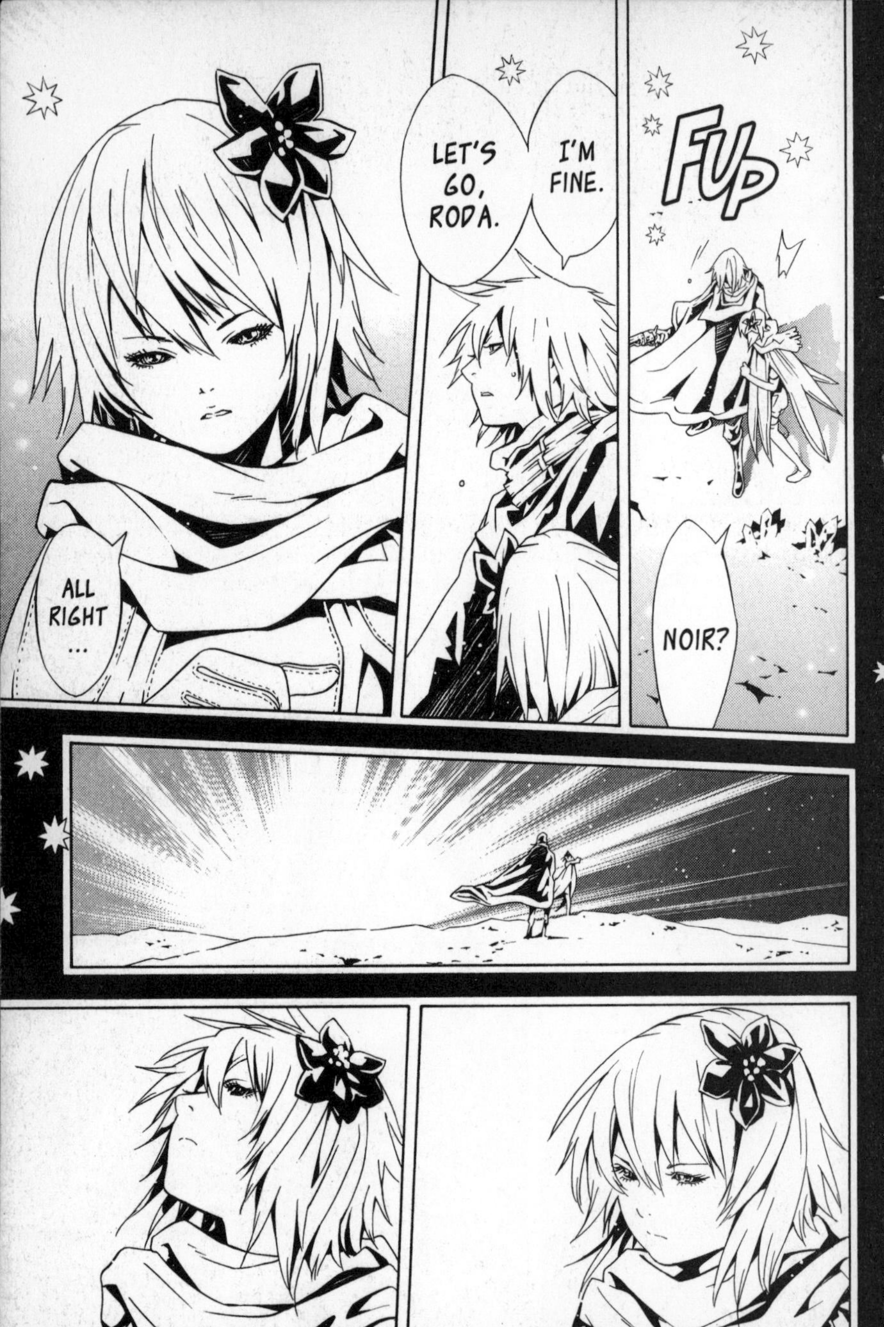
FUP
NOIR?
I'M FINE.
LET'S GO, RODA.
ALL RIGHT ...

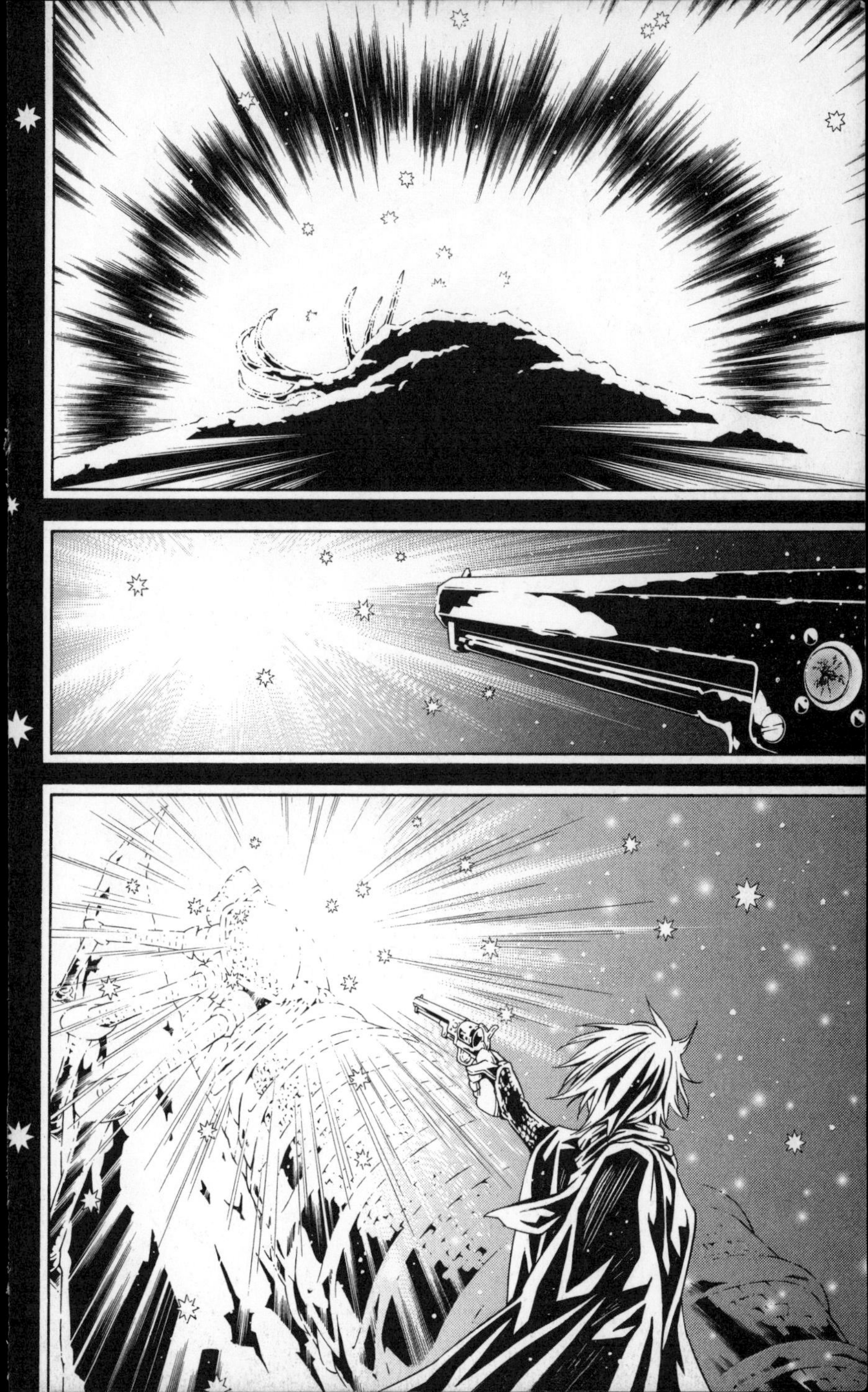

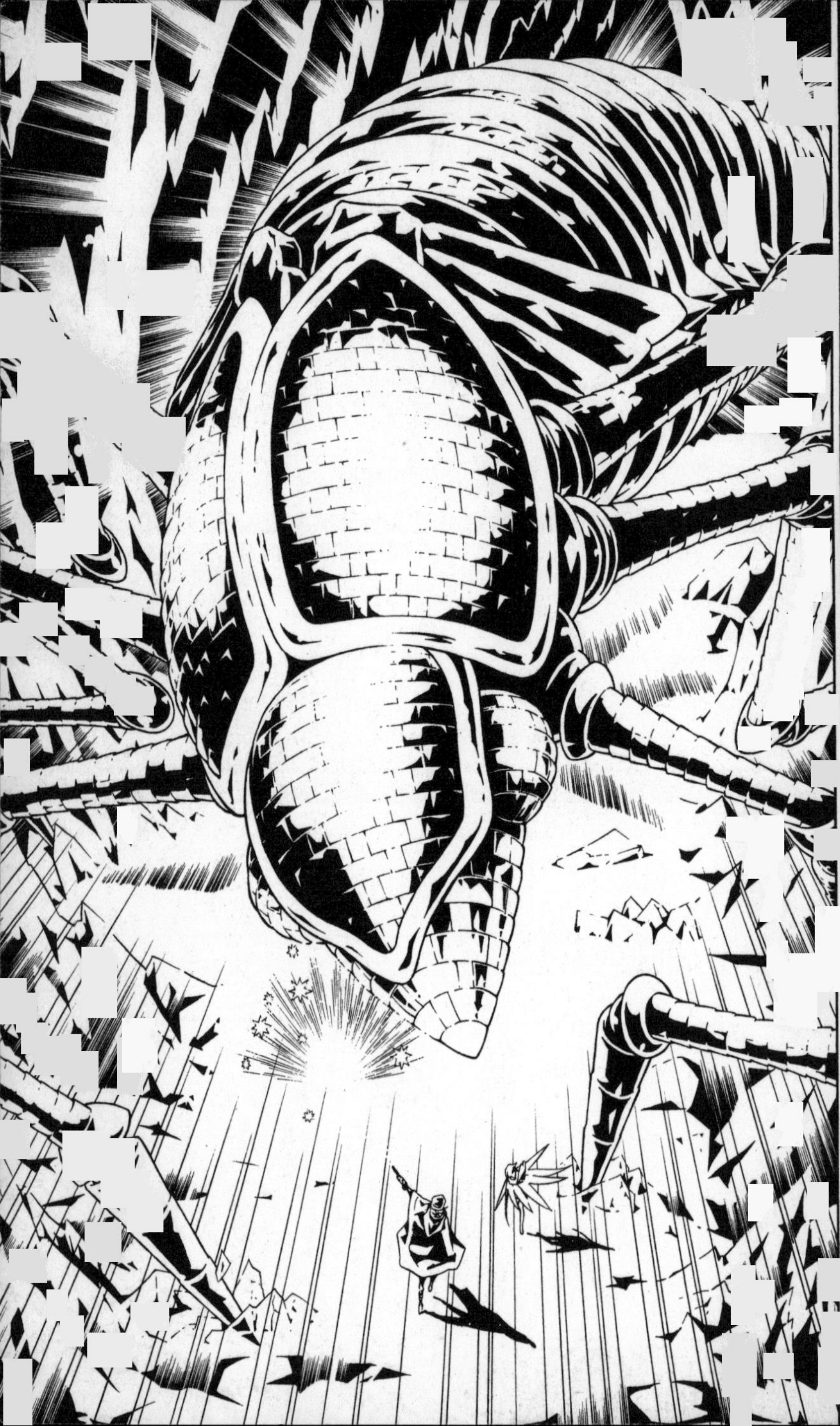

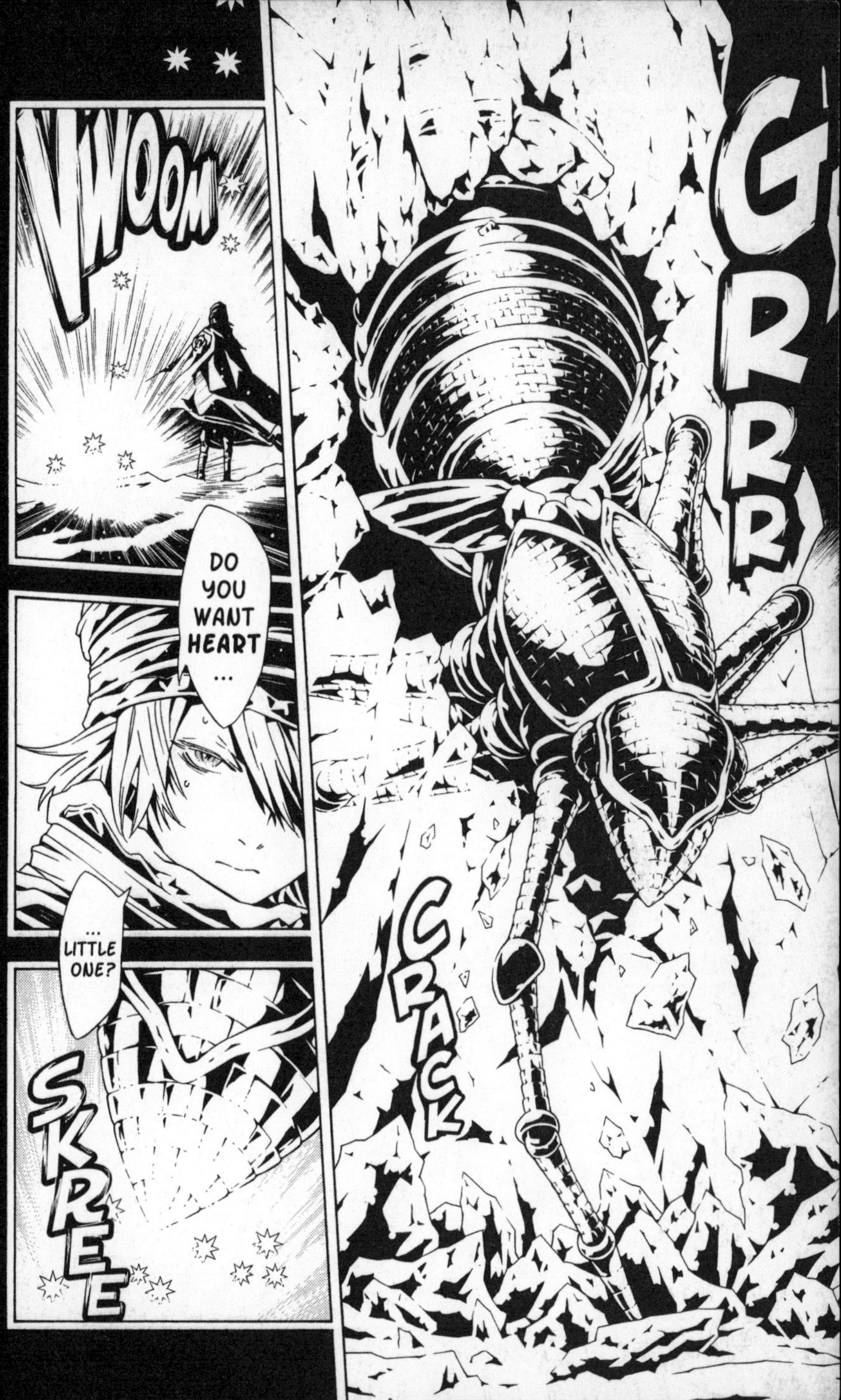
GRRR
CRACK
VWOOM
DO YOU WANT HEART ...
... LITTLE ONE?
SKREE

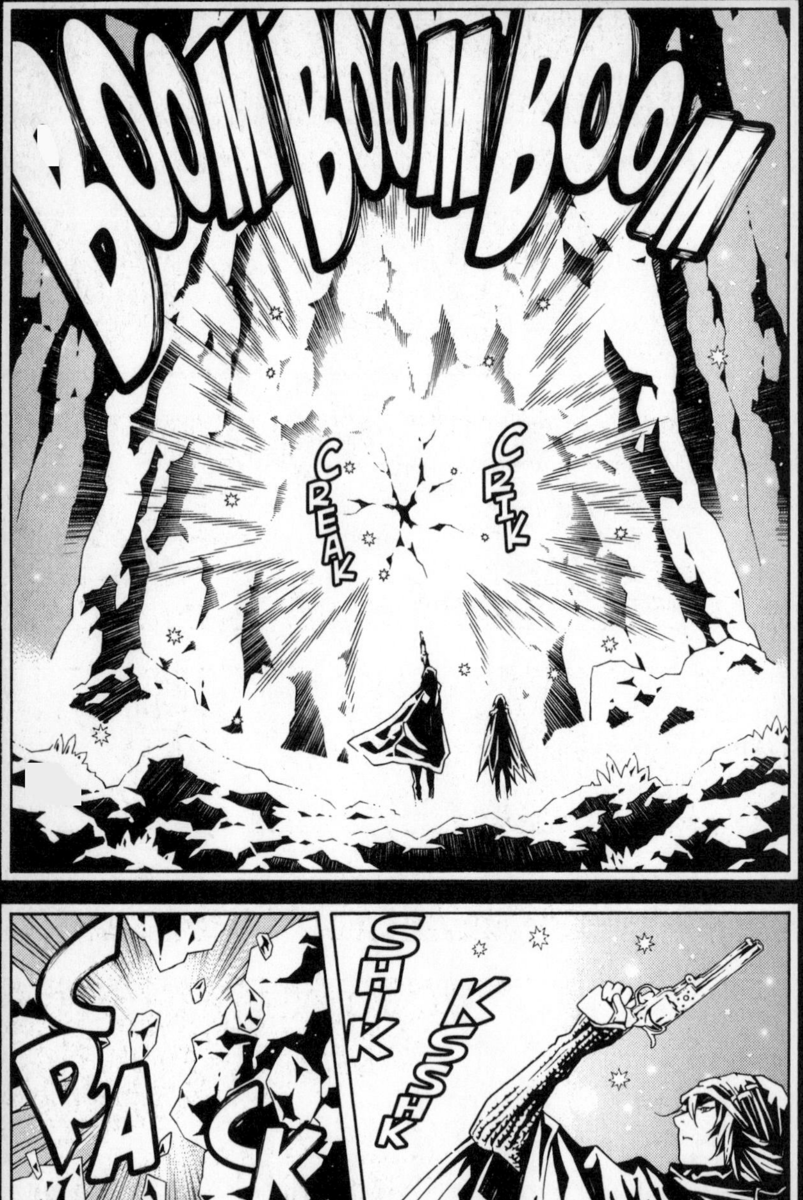
BOOM BOOM BOOM
CRIK
CREAK
SHIK
KSSHK
CRACK

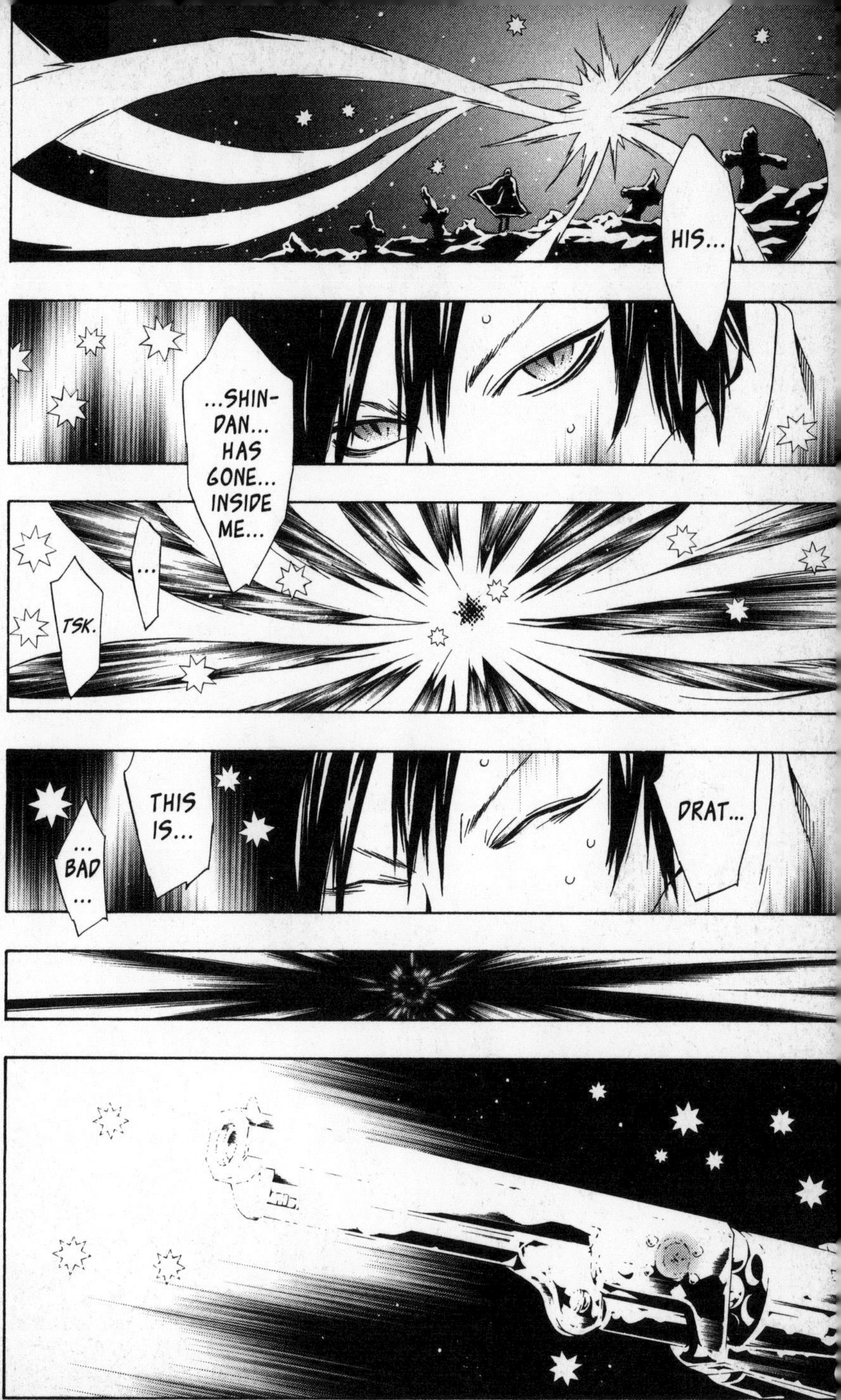
HIS...
...SHIN-DAN... HAS GONE... INSIDE ME...
...
TSK.
DRAT...
THIS IS...
...BAD...

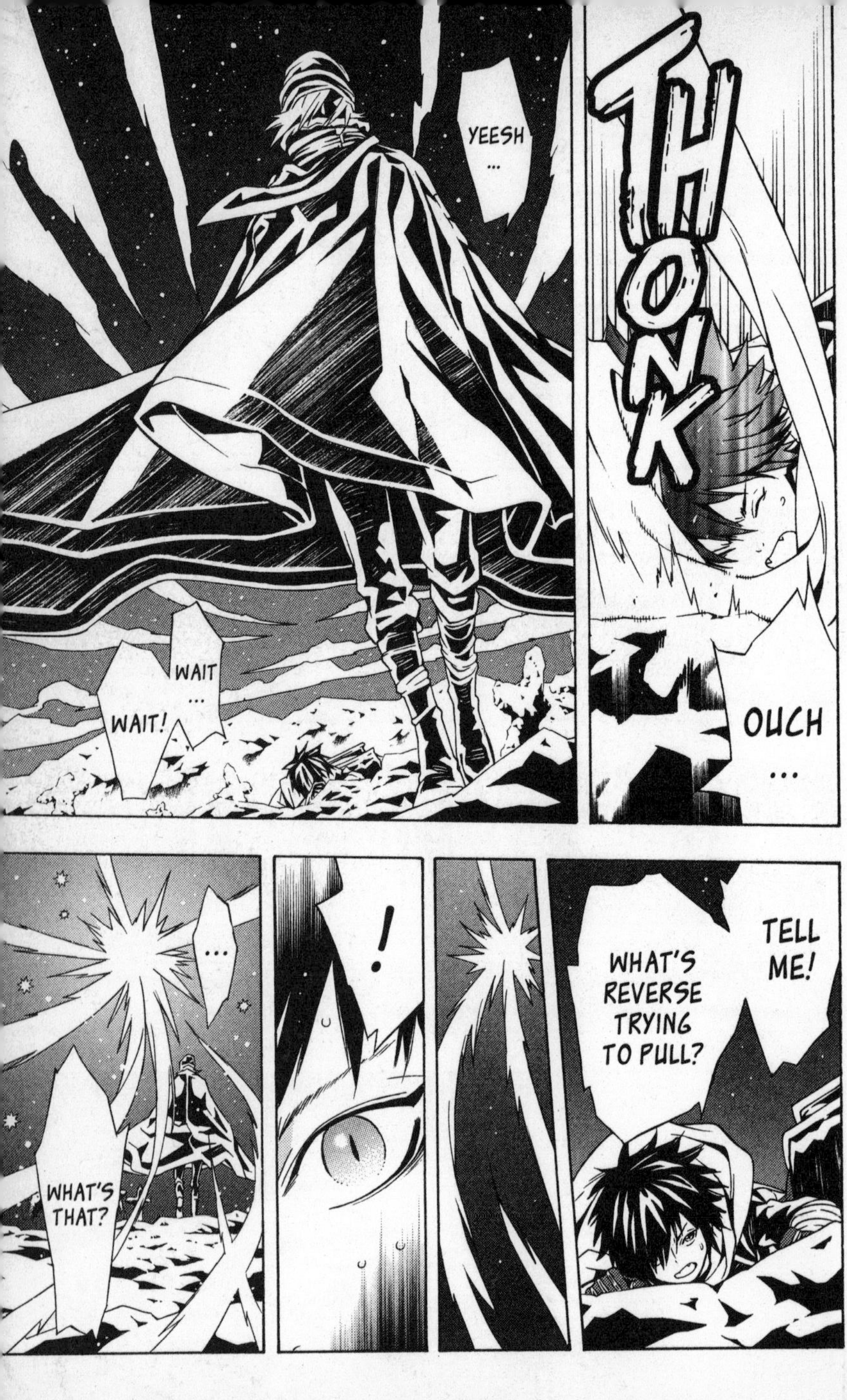
THONK
OUCH ...
YEESH ...
WAIT ...
WAIT!
TELL ME!
WHAT'S REVERSE TRYING TO PULL?
!
...
WHAT'S THAT?

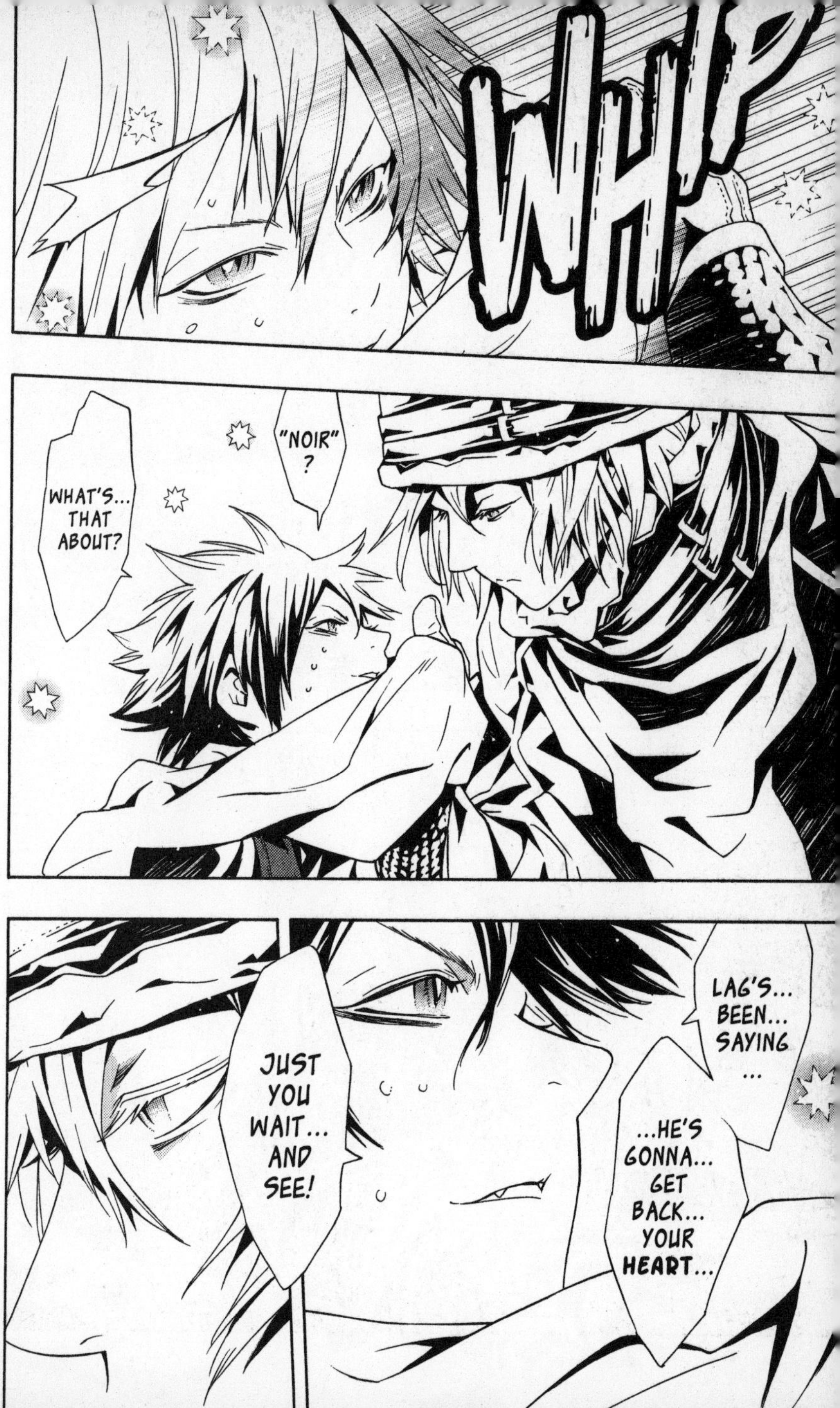
WHY?
"NOIR"?
WHAT'S... THAT ABOUT?
LAG'S... BEEN... SAYING...
...HE'S GONNA... GET BACK... YOUR HEART...
JUST YOU WAIT... AND SEE!

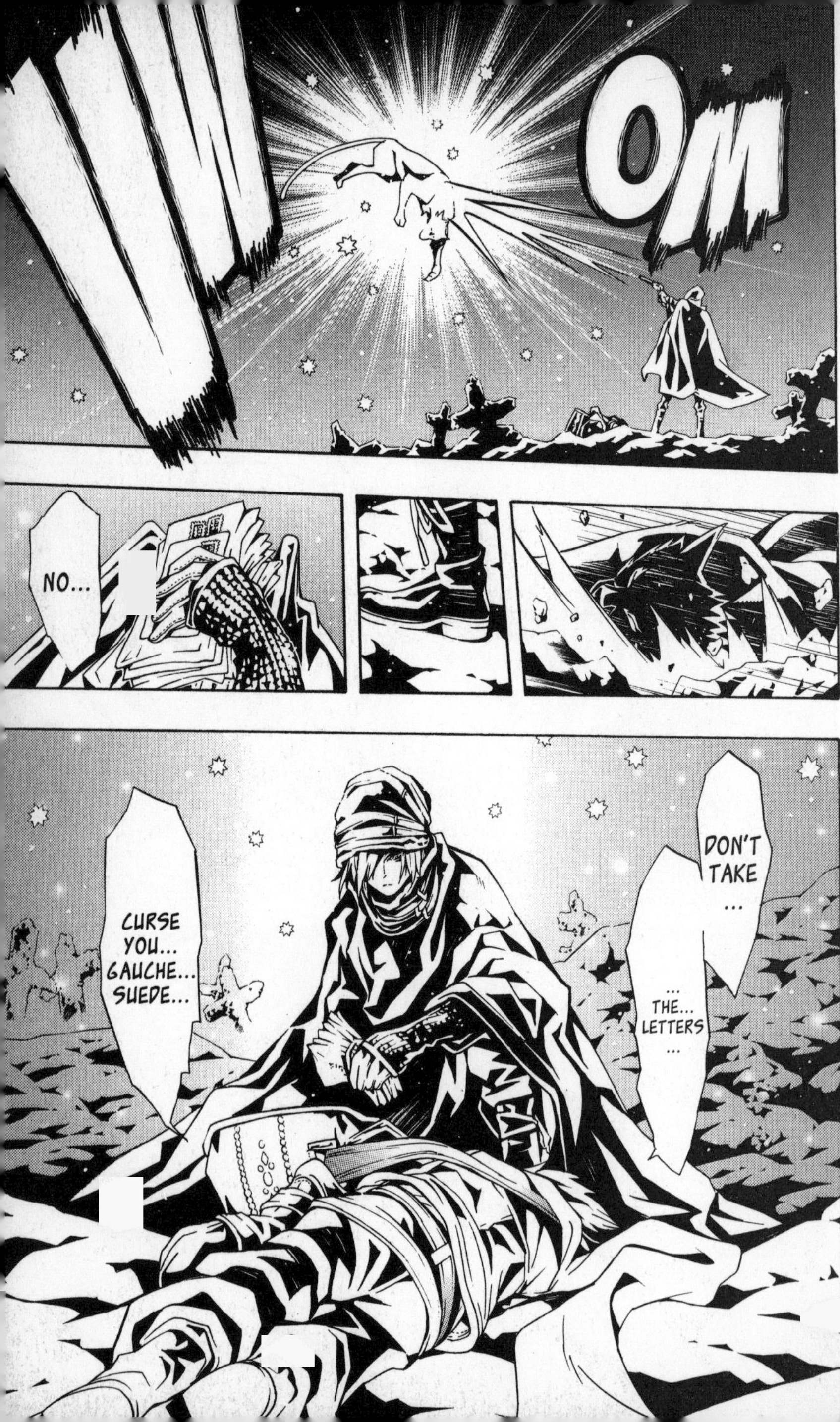
NO...
DON'T TAKE ...
... THE... LETTERS ...
CURSE YOU... GAUCHE... SUEDE...

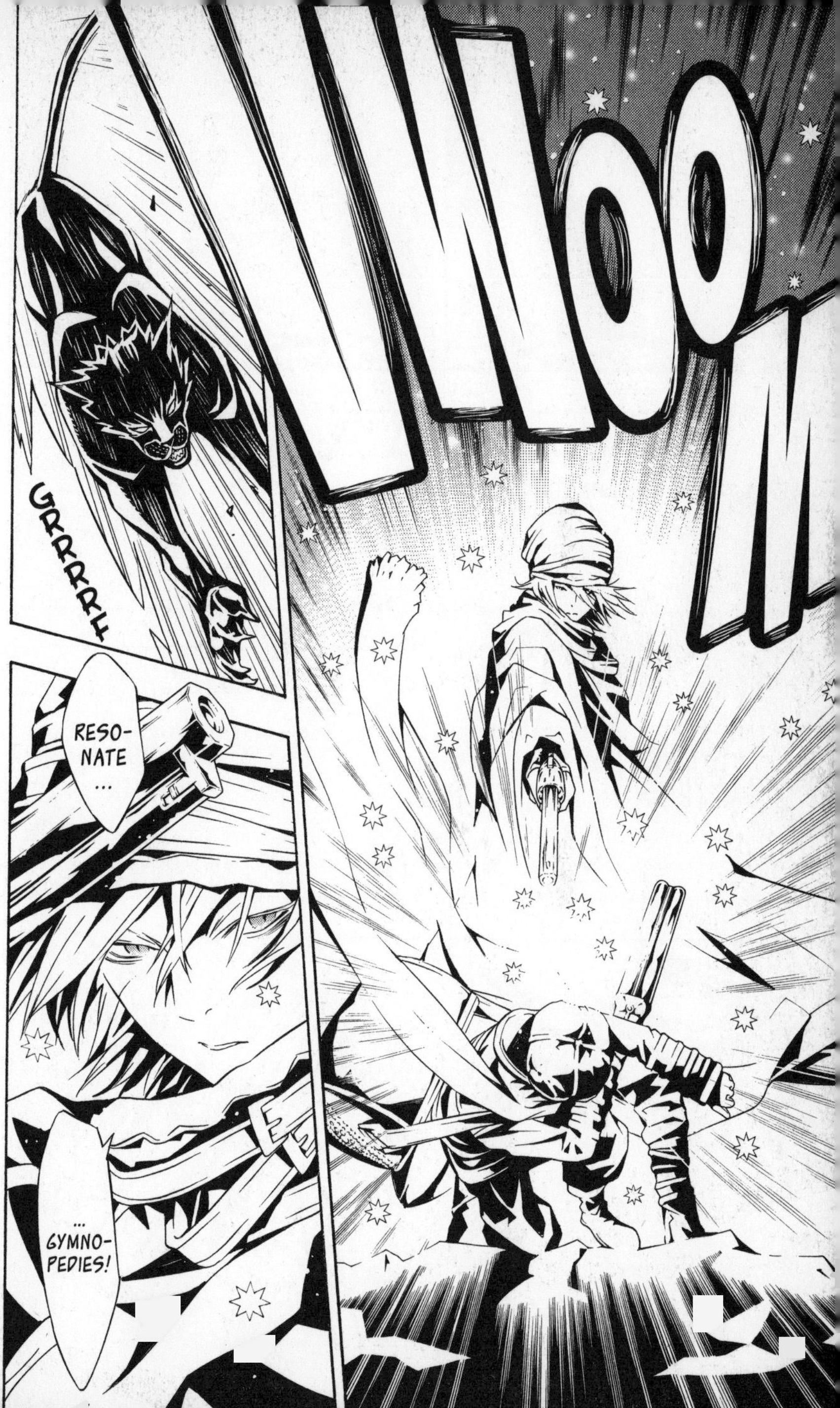
WHOOM
GRRRRRF
RESO-NATE ...
... GYMNO-PEDIES!

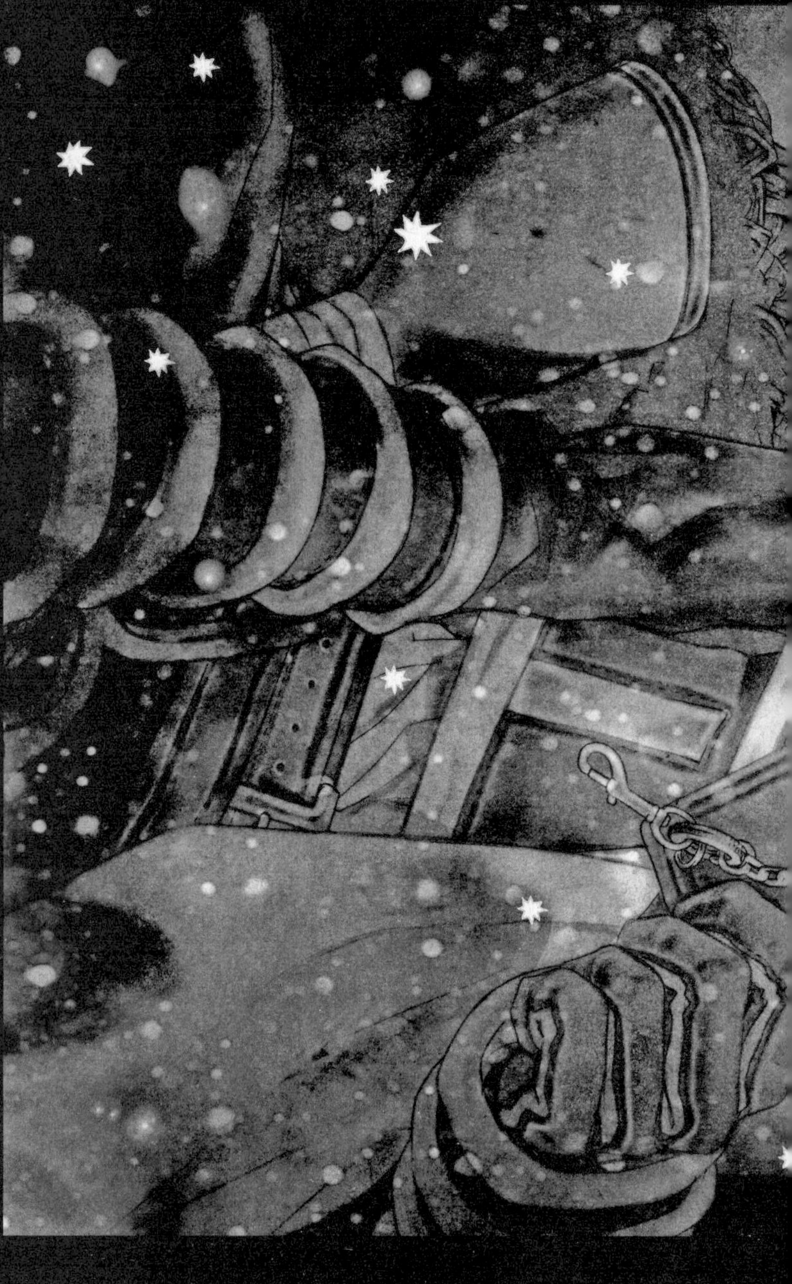

Volume 7

SHONEN JUMP Manga Edition

Story and Art by Hiroyuki Asada

English Adaptation/Rich Amtower
Translation/JN Productions
Touch-up & Lettering/Annaliese Christman
Design/Frances O. Liddell, Amy Martin
Editor/Shaenon K. Garrity

TEGAMIBACHI © 2006 by Hiroyuki Asada. All rights reserved.
First published in Japan in 2006 by SHUEISHA Inc., Tokyo. English
translation rights arranged by SHUEISHA Inc.

The rights of the author(s) of the work(s) in this publication to be so
identified have been asserted in accordance with the Copyright, Designs
and Patents Act 1988. A CIP catalogue record for this book is available
from the British Library.

The stories, characters and incidents mentioned in this publication are
entirely fictional.

Printed in the U.S.A.

Published by VIZ Media, LLC
P.O. Box 77010
San Francisco, CA 94107

10 9 8 7 6 5 4 3 2 1
First printing, November 2011

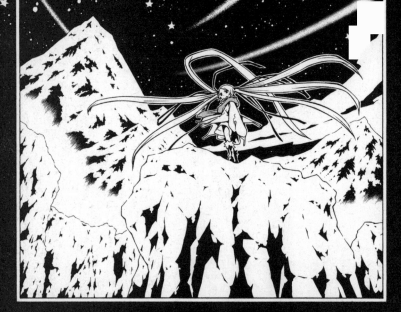

Tegami Bachi

LETTER BEE

VOLUME 7

Blue Notes Blues

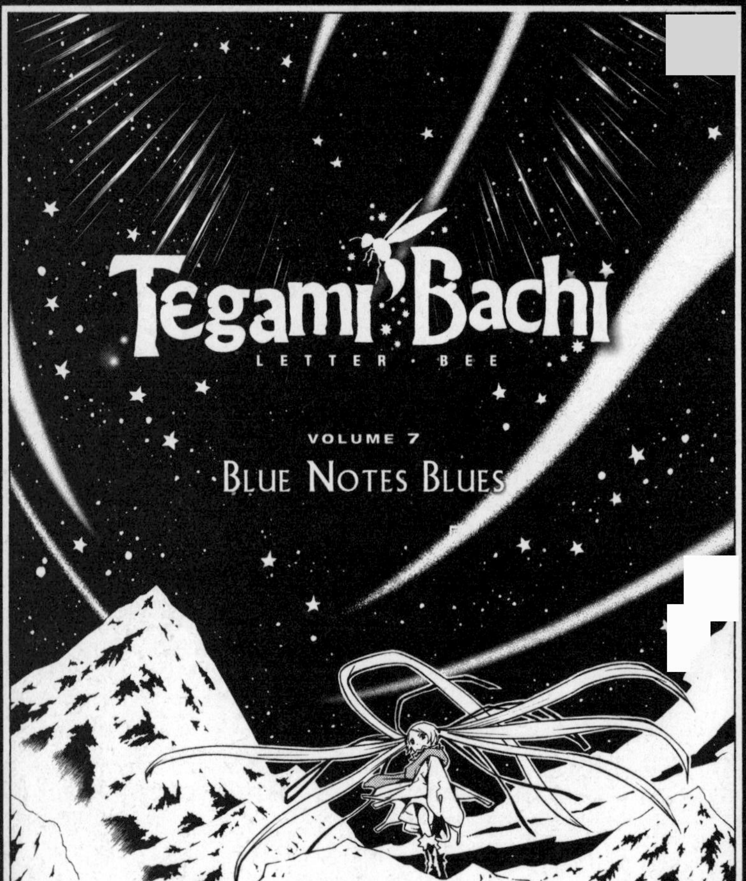

STORY AND ART BY

HIROYUKI ASADA

This is a country known as Amberground, where night never ends.

Its capital, Akatsuki, is illuminated by a man-made sun. The farther one strays from the capital, the weaker the light. The Yuusari region is cast in twilight; the Yodaka region survives only on pale moonlight.

Letter Bee Gauche Suede and young Lag Seeing meet in the Yodaka region—a postal worker and the "letter" he must deliver. In their short time together, they form a fast friendship, but when the journey ends, each departs down his own path. Gauche longs to become Head Bee, while Lag himself wants to be a Letter Bee, like Gauche.

After his interview, Lag learns from Zazie, the observer for his test, that Gauche is no longer a Letter Bee. Lag seeks out Sylvette, Gauche's sister, only to discover that Gauche was dismissed from his post and vanished after losing his *heart*.

A Letter Bee at last, Lag visits Honey Waters, a town in northwest Yuusari, in hopes of finding the missing Gauche. And find him he does—but the Gauche he meets has lost his *heart* and become a marauder named Noir. Their meeting is brief, and Gauche vanishes once more. In despair, Lag puts all of his hopes into a Shindan called Letter Bullet. Whether this Shindan will open Gauche's *heart*, Lag can only hope...

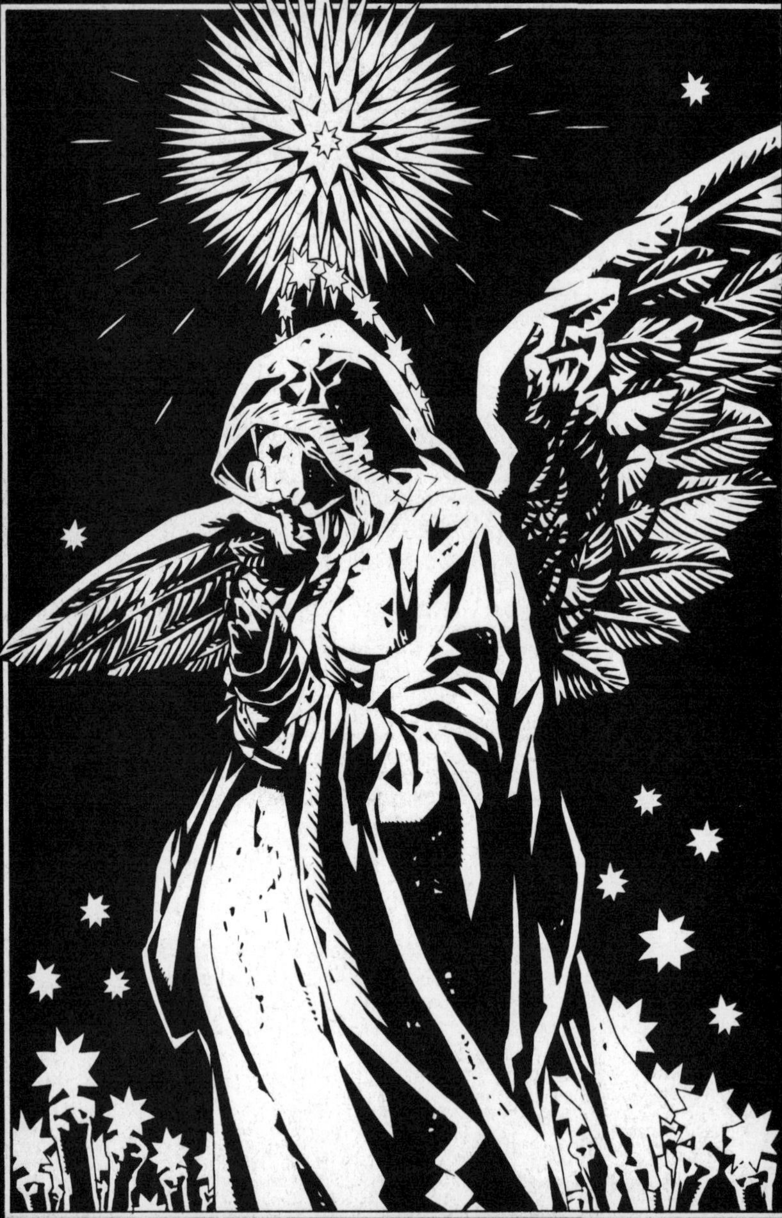

List of Characters

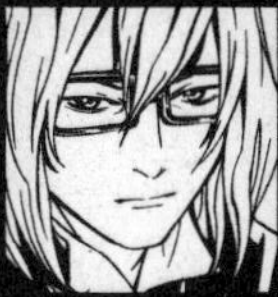

LARGO LLOYD
Beehive Director

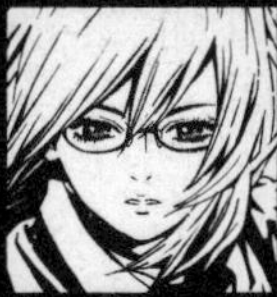

ARIA LINK
Beehive Assistant Director

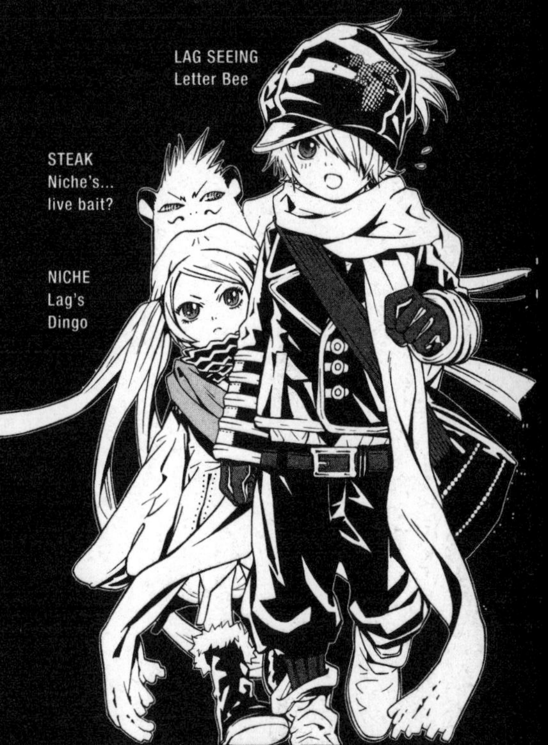
LAG SEEING
Letter Bee
STEAK
Niche's... live bait?
NICHE
Lag's Dingo

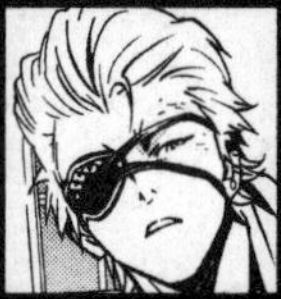

DR. THUNDERLAND, JR.
Member of the AG Biological Science Advisory Board, Third Division and head doctor at the Beehive

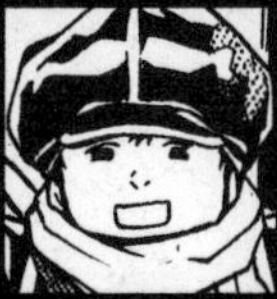

CONNOR KLUFF
Letter Bee

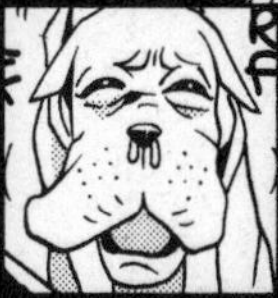

GUS
Connor's Dingo

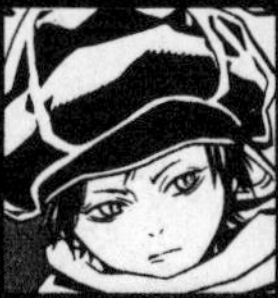

ZAZIE
Letter Bee

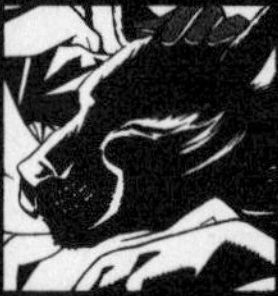

WASIOLKA
Zazie's Dingo

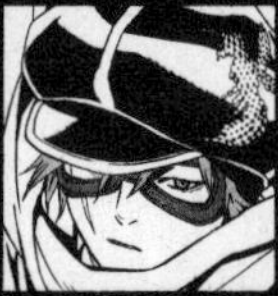

JIGGY PEPPER
Express Delivery Letter Bee

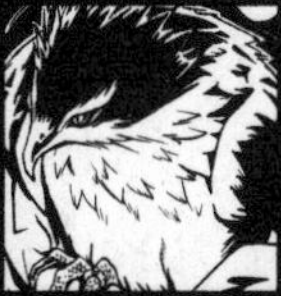

HARRY
Jiggy's Dingo

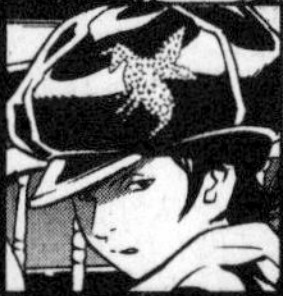

MOC SULLIVAN
Letter Bee

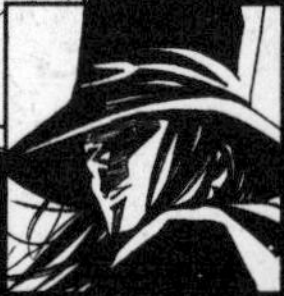

THE MAN WHO COULD NOT BECOME SPIRIT
The ringleader of Reverse

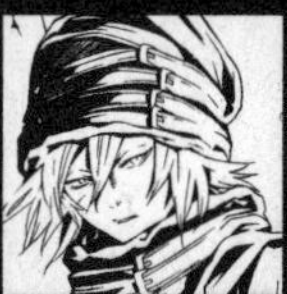

NOIR (FORMERLY GAUCHE SUEDE)
Marauder for Reverse and an ex-Letter Bee

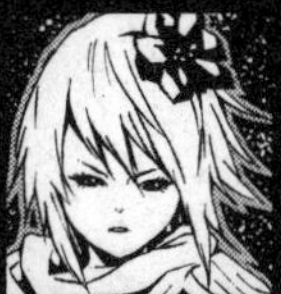

RODA
Noir's Dingo

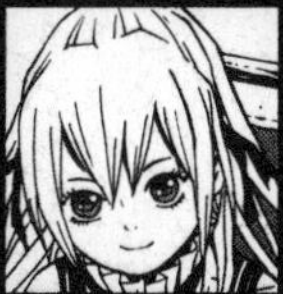

SYLVETTE SUEDE
Gauche's Sister

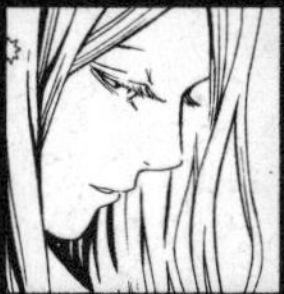

ANNE SEEING
Lag's Mother (Missing)

Tegami Bachi
LETTER · BEE

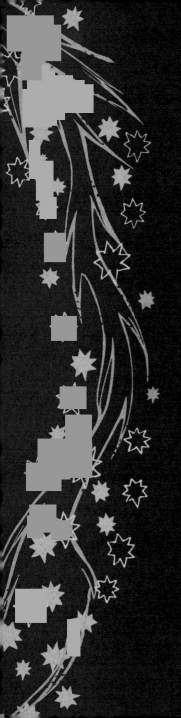

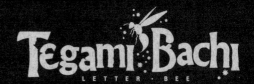

VOLUME 7
Blue Notes Blues

In all things...

the heart must take precedence.

The heart rules over all things...

...and all things come from the heart.

—THE SCRIPTURES OF AMBERGROUND, 1st verse

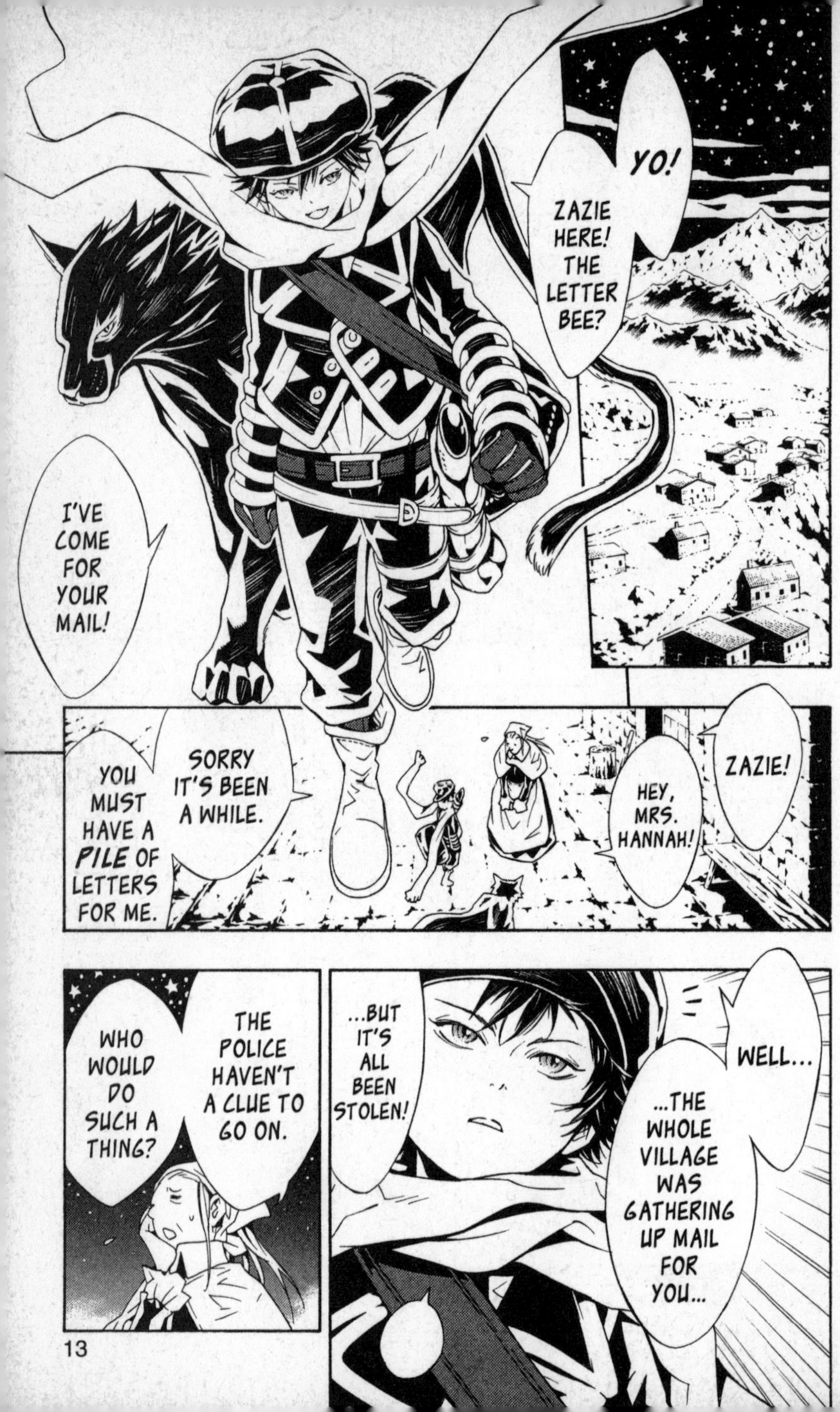
YO!
ZAZIE HERE! THE LETTER BEE?
I'VE COME FOR YOUR MAIL!
ZAZIE!
HEY, MRS. HANNAH!
SORRY IT'S BEEN A WHILE.
YOU MUST HAVE A *PILE* OF LETTERS FOR ME.
WELL...
...THE WHOLE VILLAGE WAS GATHERING UP MAIL FOR YOU...
...BUT IT'S ALL BEEN STOLEN!
THE POLICE HAVEN'T A CLUE TO GO ON.
WHO WOULD DO SUCH A THING?

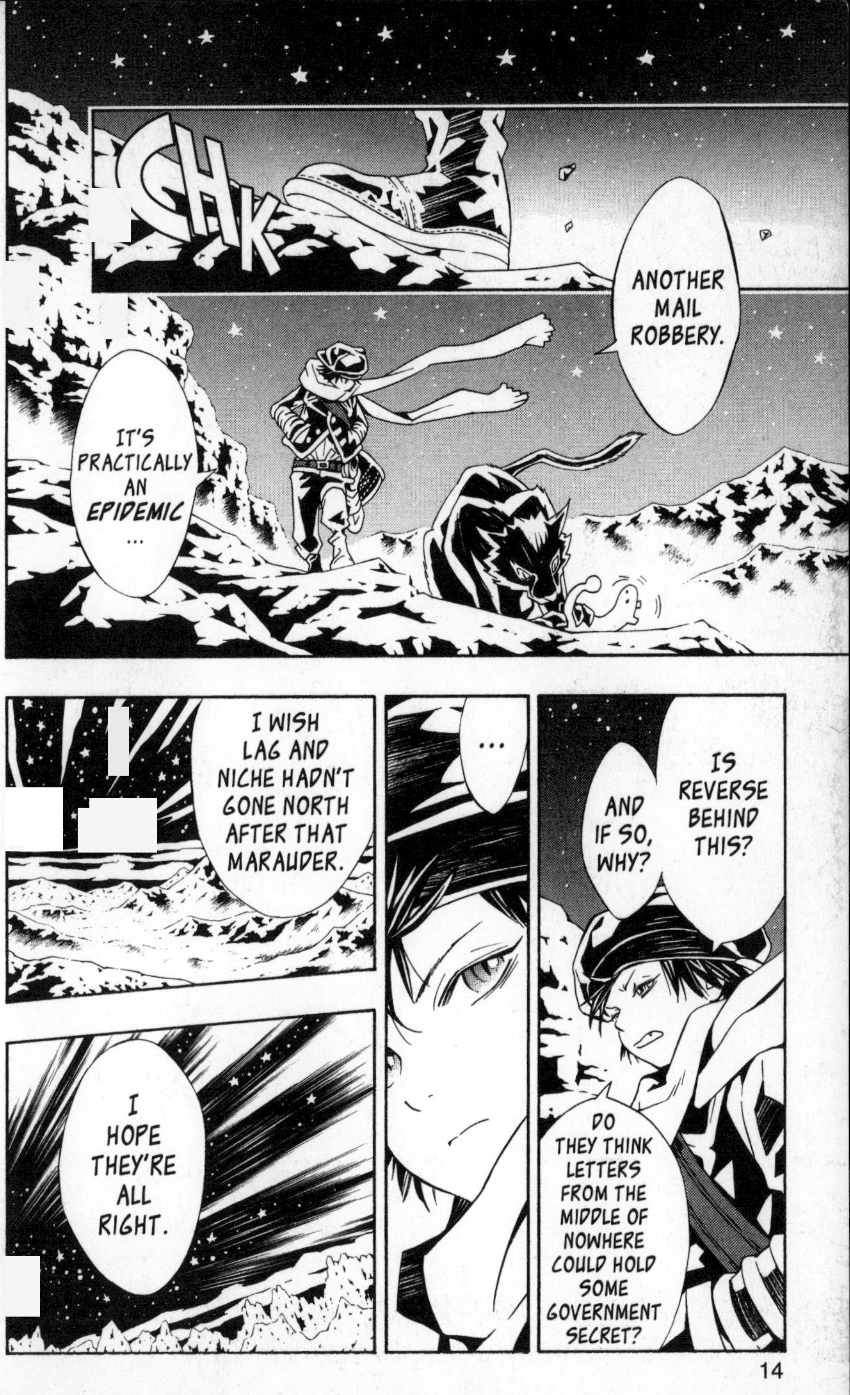
CHK
ANOTHER MAIL ROBBERY.
IT'S PRACTICALLY AN EPIDEMIC...
IS REVERSE BEHIND THIS?
AND IF SO, WHY?
DO THEY THINK LETTERS FROM THE MIDDLE OF NOWHERE COULD HOLD SOME GOVERNMENT SECRET?
...
I WISH LAG AND NICHE HADN'T GONE NORTH AFTER THAT MARAUDER.
I HOPE THEY'RE ALL RIGHT.

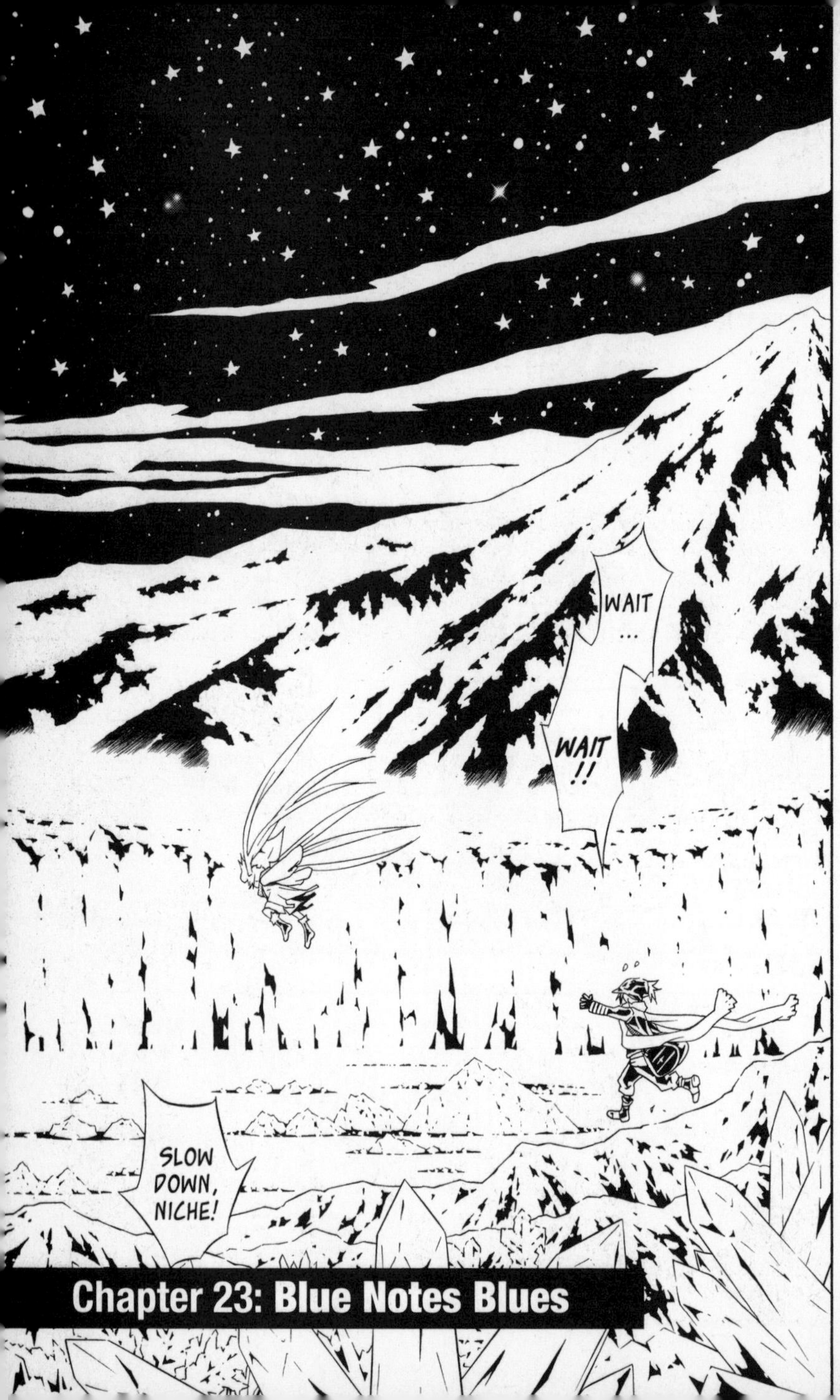
WAIT...
WAIT!!
SLOW DOWN, NICHE!

Chapter 23: Blue Notes Blues

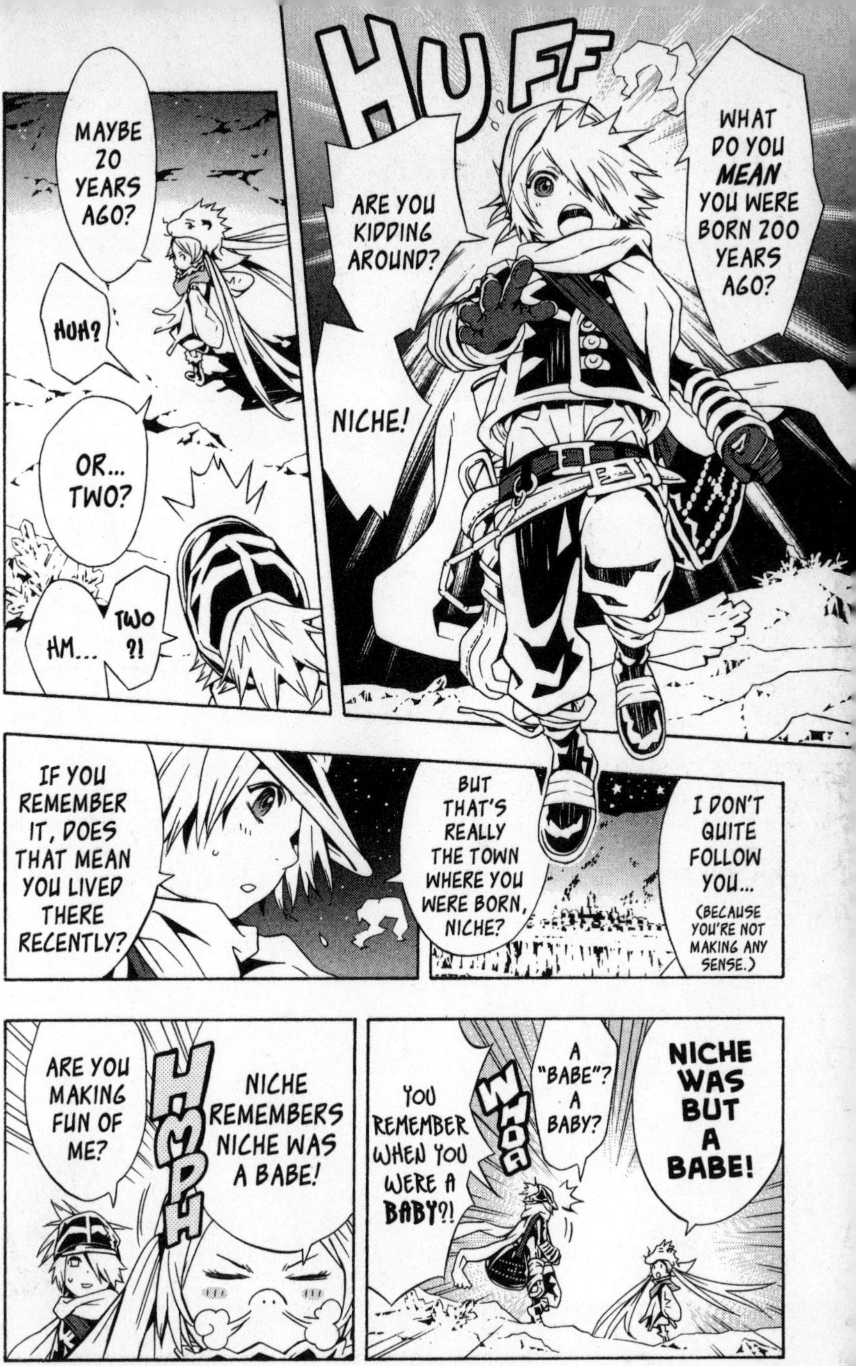
HUFF
WHAT DO YOU MEAN YOU WERE BORN 200 YEARS AGO?
ARE YOU KIDDING AROUND?
NICHE!
MAYBE 20 YEARS AGO?
HUH?
OR... TWO?
TWO ?!
HM...
I DON'T QUITE FOLLOW YOU... (BECAUSE YOU'RE NOT MAKING ANY SENSE.)
BUT THAT'S REALLY THE TOWN WHERE YOU WERE BORN, NICHE?
IF YOU REMEMBER IT, DOES THAT MEAN YOU LIVED THERE RECENTLY?
NICHE WAS BUT A BABE!
A "BABE"? A BABY?
WHOA
YOU REMEMBER WHEN YOU WERE A BABY?!
NICHE REMEMBERS NICHE WAS A BABE!
HMPH
ARE YOU MAKING FUN OF ME?

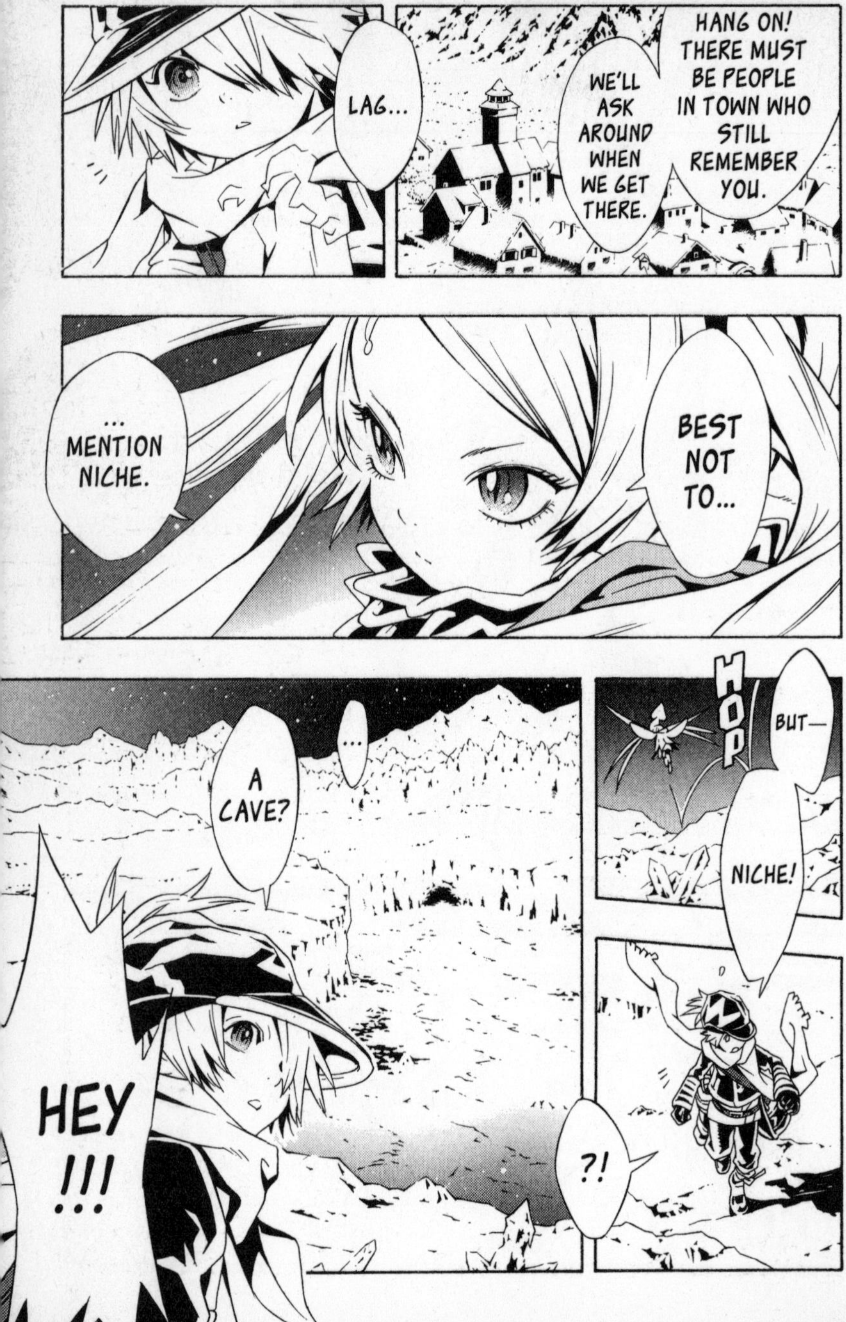
HANG ON! THERE MUST BE PEOPLE IN TOWN WHO STILL REMEMBER YOU.
WE'LL ASK AROUND WHEN WE GET THERE.
LAG...
BEST NOT TO...
... MENTION NICHE.
HOP
BUT—
NICHE!
?!
...
A CAVE?
HEY!!!

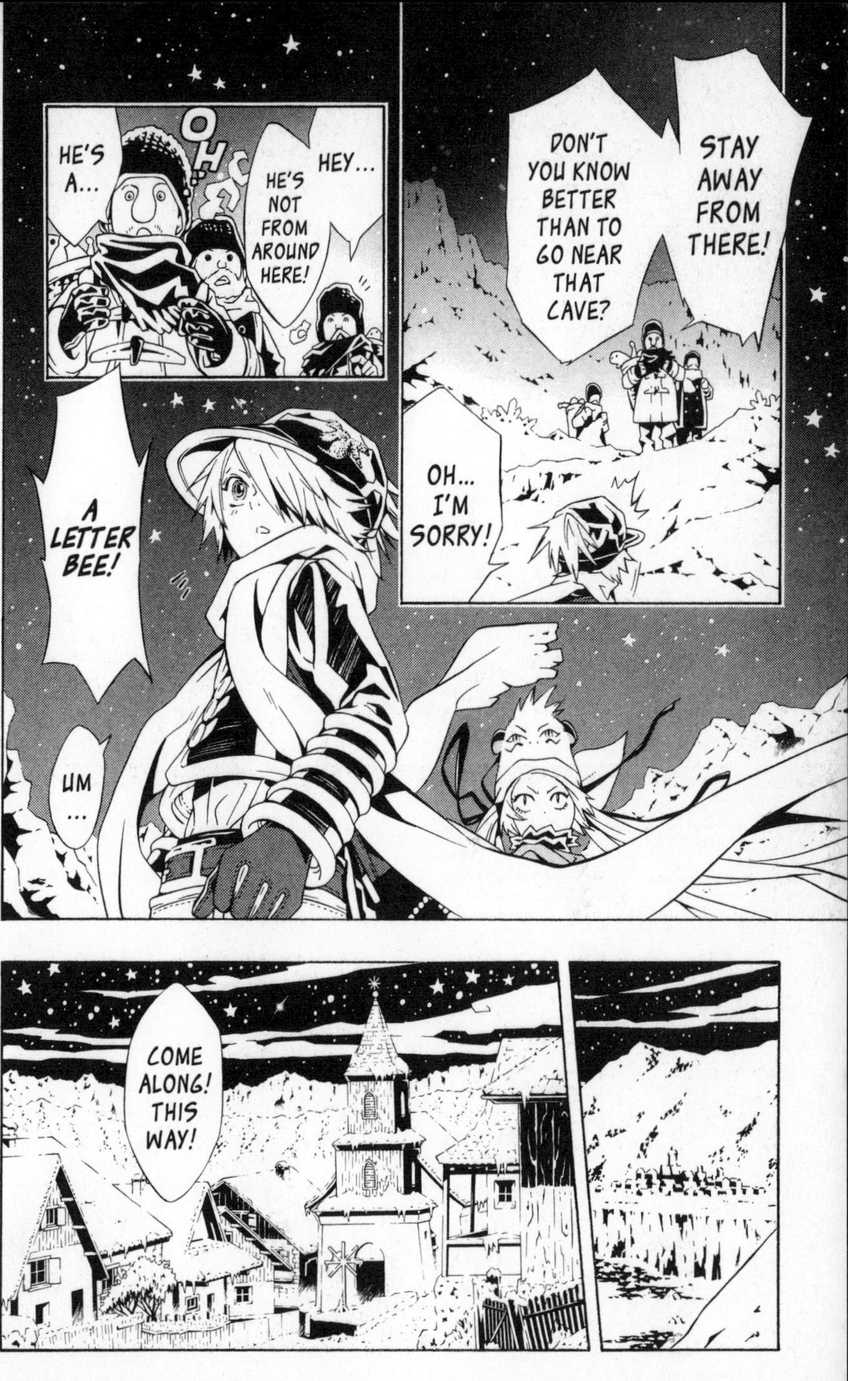
STAY AWAY FROM THERE!
DON'T YOU KNOW BETTER THAN TO GO NEAR THAT CAVE?
OH... I'M SORRY!
HEY...
HE'S NOT FROM AROUND HERE!
OH
HE'S A...
A LETTER BEE!
UM...
COME ALONG! THIS WAY!

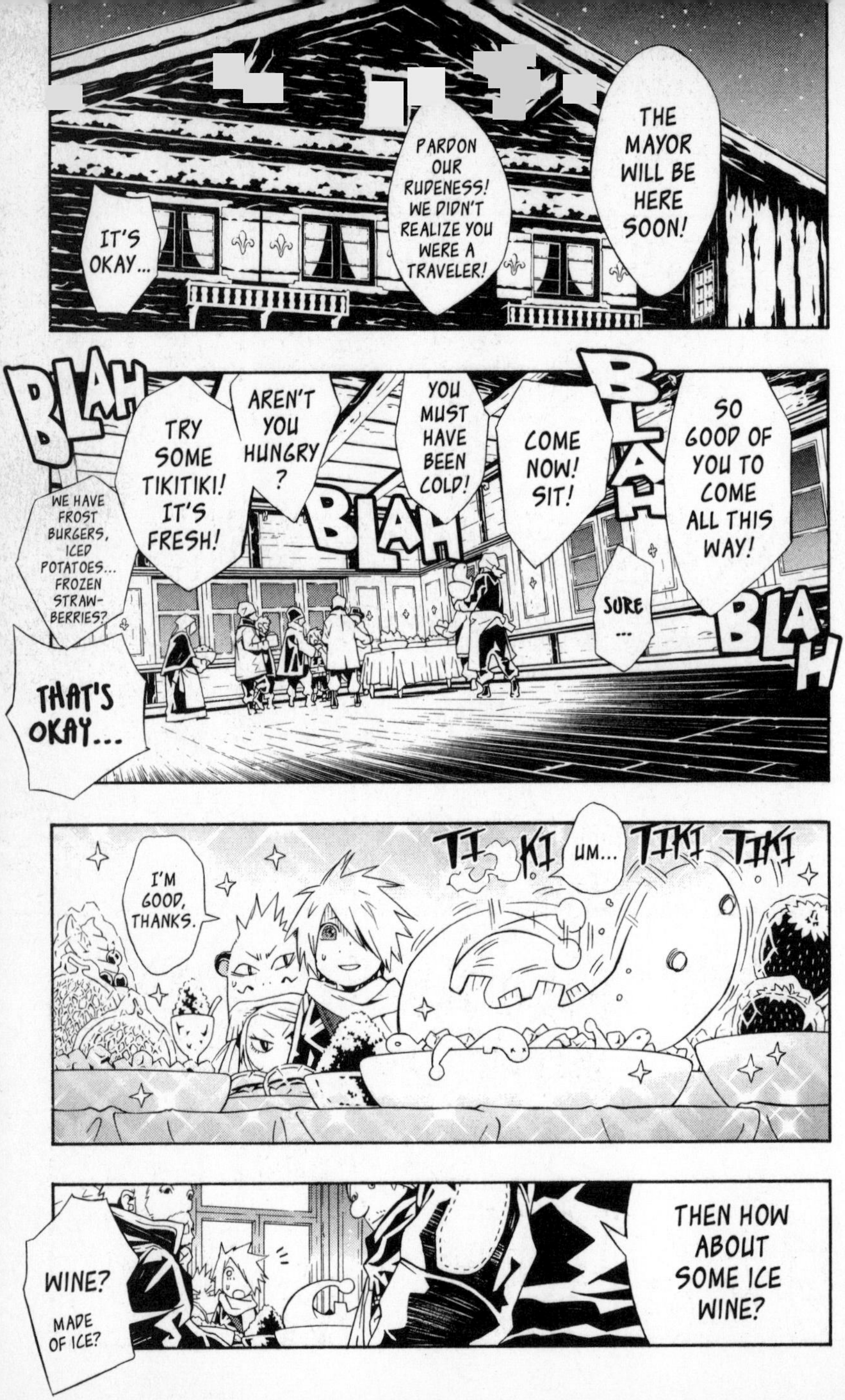
THE MAYOR WILL BE HERE SOON!
PARDON OUR RUDENESS! WE DIDN'T REALIZE YOU WERE A TRAVELER!
IT'S OKAY...
BLAH
SO GOOD OF YOU TO COME ALL THIS WAY!
BLAH
SURE ...
COME NOW! SIT!
YOU MUST HAVE BEEN COLD!
BLAH
AREN'T YOU HUNGRY?
TRY SOME TIKITIKI! IT'S FRESH!
BLAH
WE HAVE FROST BURGERS, ICED POTATOES... FROZEN STRAW-BERRIES?
THAT'S OKAY...
TIKI TIKI
UM...
TI KI
I'M GOOD, THANKS.
THEN HOW ABOUT SOME ICE WINE?
WINE?
MADE OF ICE?

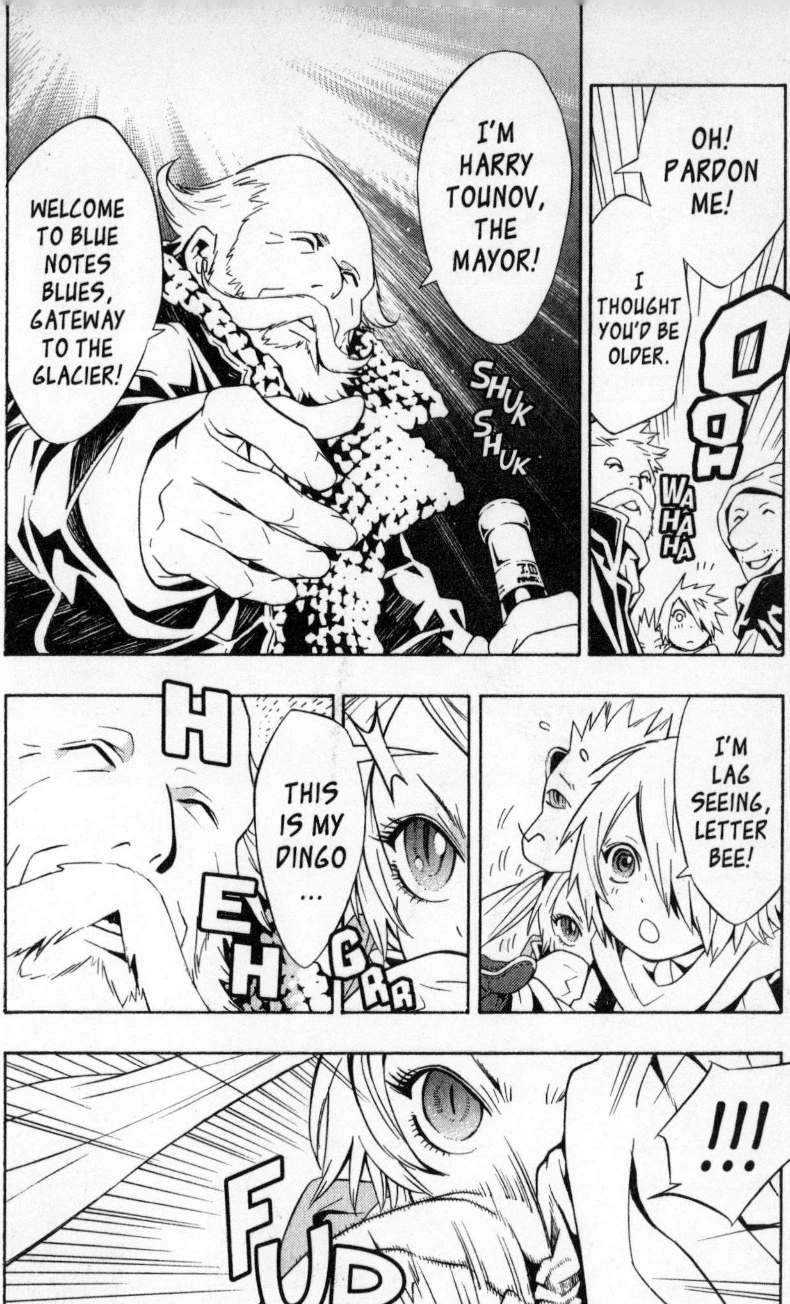
OH! PARDON ME!
I THOUGHT YOU'D BE OLDER.
OOH
WAHAHAHA
I'M HARRY TOUNOV, THE MAYOR!
WELCOME TO BLUE NOTES BLUES, GATEWAY TO THE GLACIER!
SHUK SHUK
I'M LAG SEEING, LETTER BEE!
THIS IS MY DINGO ...
GRR
HEH
!!!
FUP

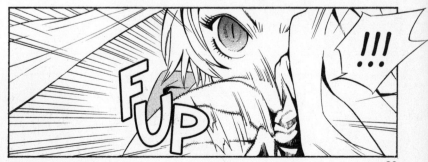

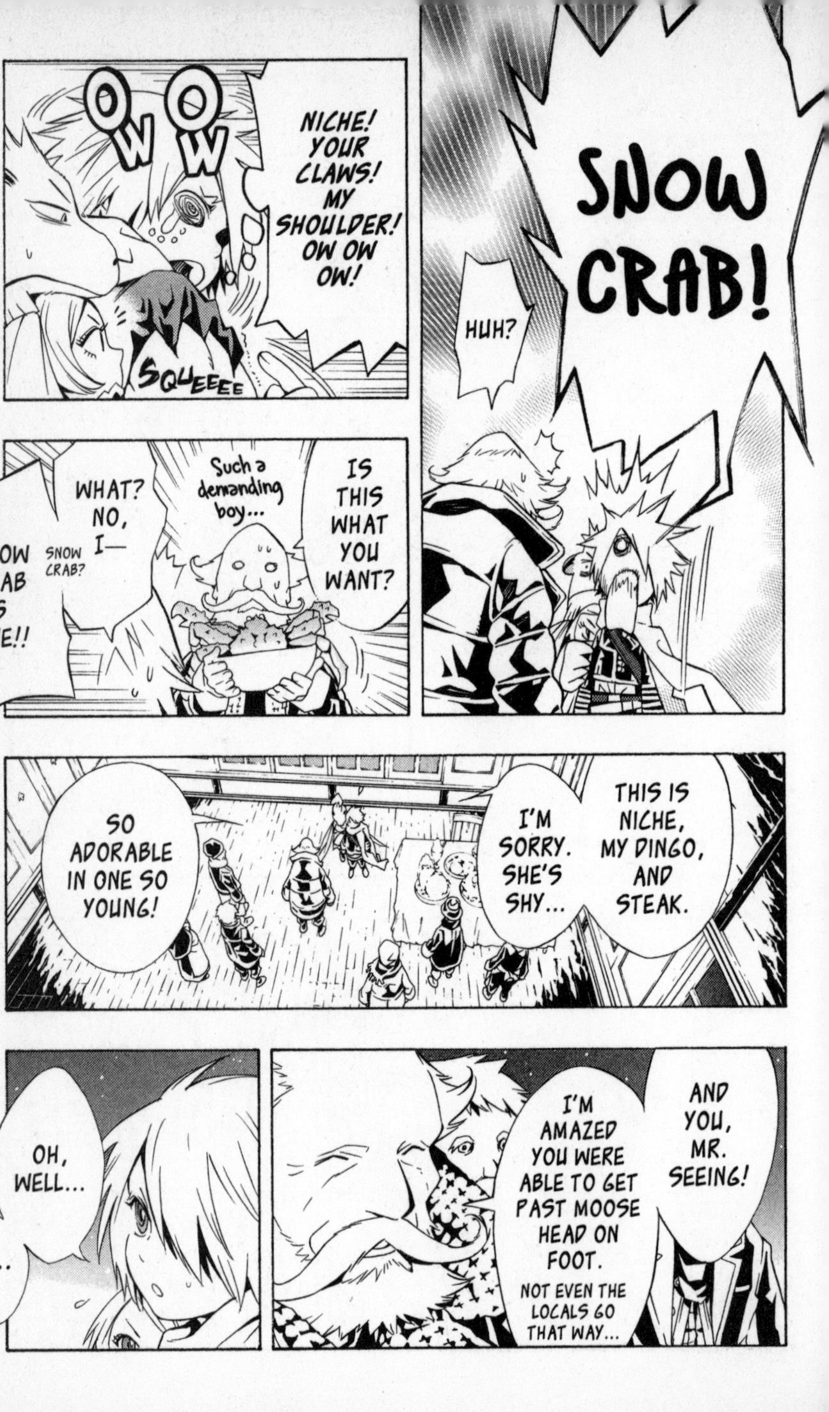
SNOW CRAB!
HUH?
OW OW
NICHE! YOUR CLAWS! MY SHOULDER! OW OW OW!
SQUEEEE
IS THIS WHAT YOU WANT?
Such a demanding boy...
WHAT? NO, I—
SNOW CRAB?
SNOW CRAB IS FINE!!
THIS IS NICHE, MY DINGO, AND STEAK.
I'M SORRY. SHE'S SHY...
SO ADORABLE IN ONE SO YOUNG!
AND YOU, MR. SEEING!
I'M AMAZED YOU WERE ABLE TO GET PAST MOOSE HEAD ON FOOT.
NOT EVEN THE LOCALS GO THAT WAY...
OH, WELL...
...

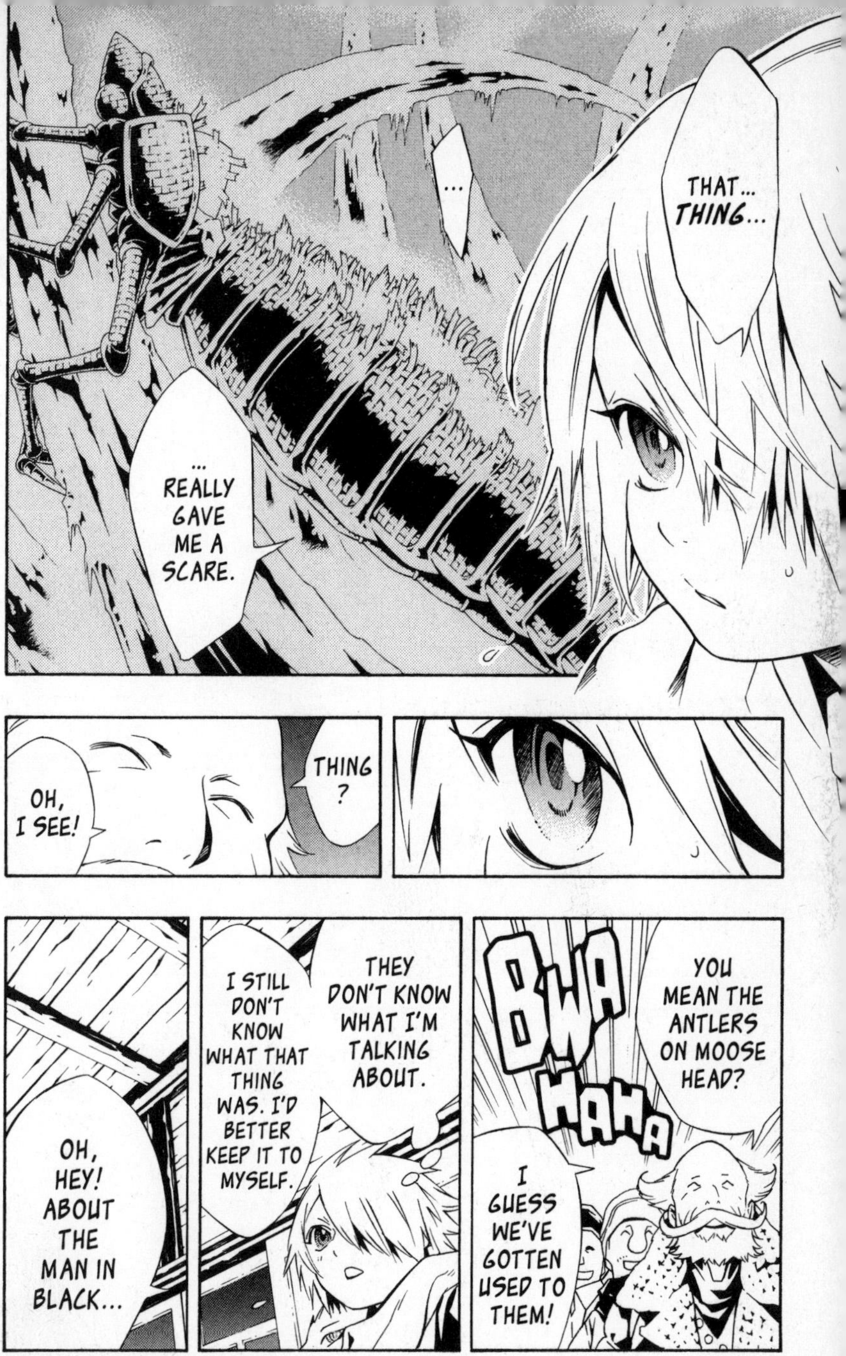
THAT... *THING*...
...
... REALLY GAVE ME A SCARE.
THING?
OH, I SEE!
YOU MEAN THE ANTLERS ON MOOSE HEAD?
BWA HAHA
I GUESS WE'VE GOTTEN USED TO THEM!
THEY DON'T KNOW WHAT I'M TALKING ABOUT.
I STILL DON'T KNOW WHAT THAT THING WAS. I'D BETTER KEEP IT TO MYSELF.
OH, HEY! ABOUT THE MAN IN BLACK...

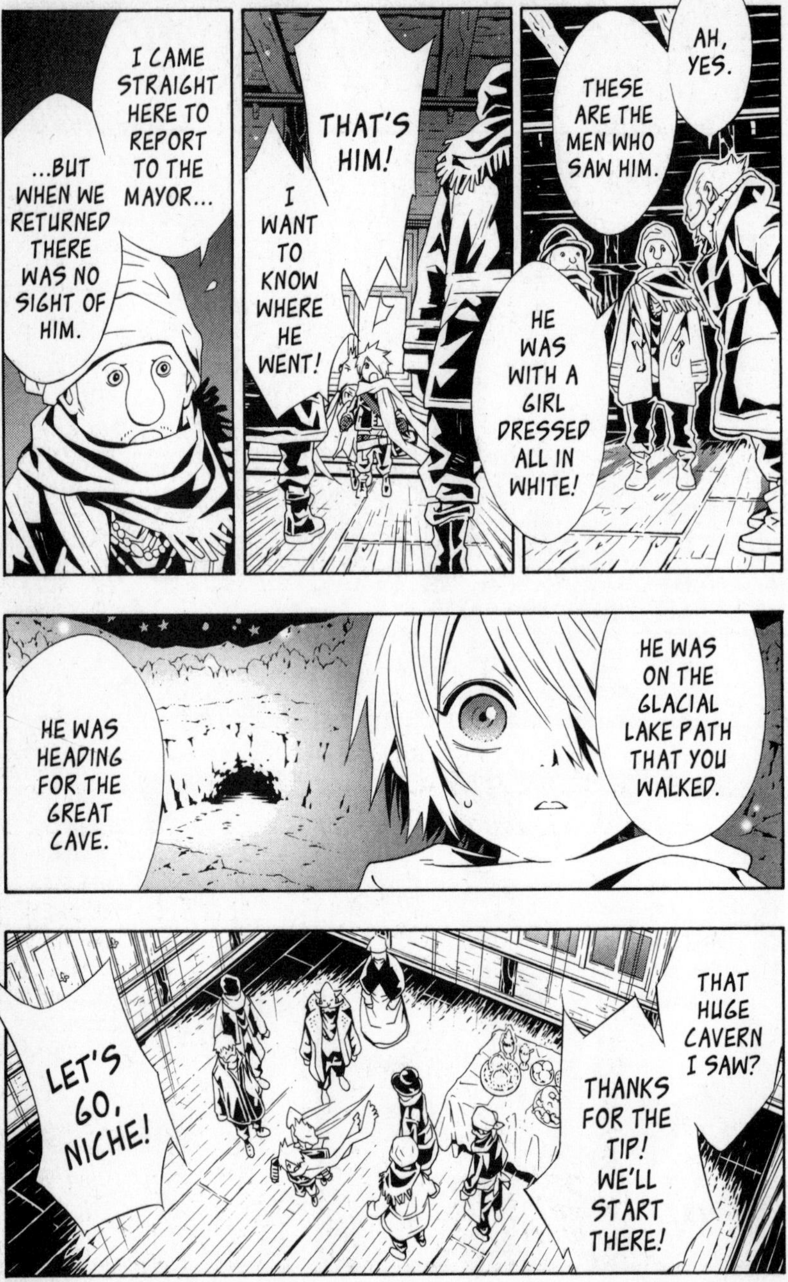
AH, YES.
THESE ARE THE MEN WHO SAW HIM.
HE WAS WITH A GIRL DRESSED ALL IN WHITE!
THAT'S HIM!
I WANT TO KNOW WHERE HE WENT!
I CAME STRAIGHT HERE TO REPORT TO THE MAYOR...
...BUT WHEN WE RETURNED THERE WAS NO SIGHT OF HIM.
HE WAS ON THE GLACIAL LAKE PATH THAT YOU WALKED.
HE WAS HEADING FOR THE GREAT CAVE.
THAT HUGE CAVERN I SAW?
THANKS FOR THE TIP! WE'LL START THERE!
LET'S GO, NICHE!

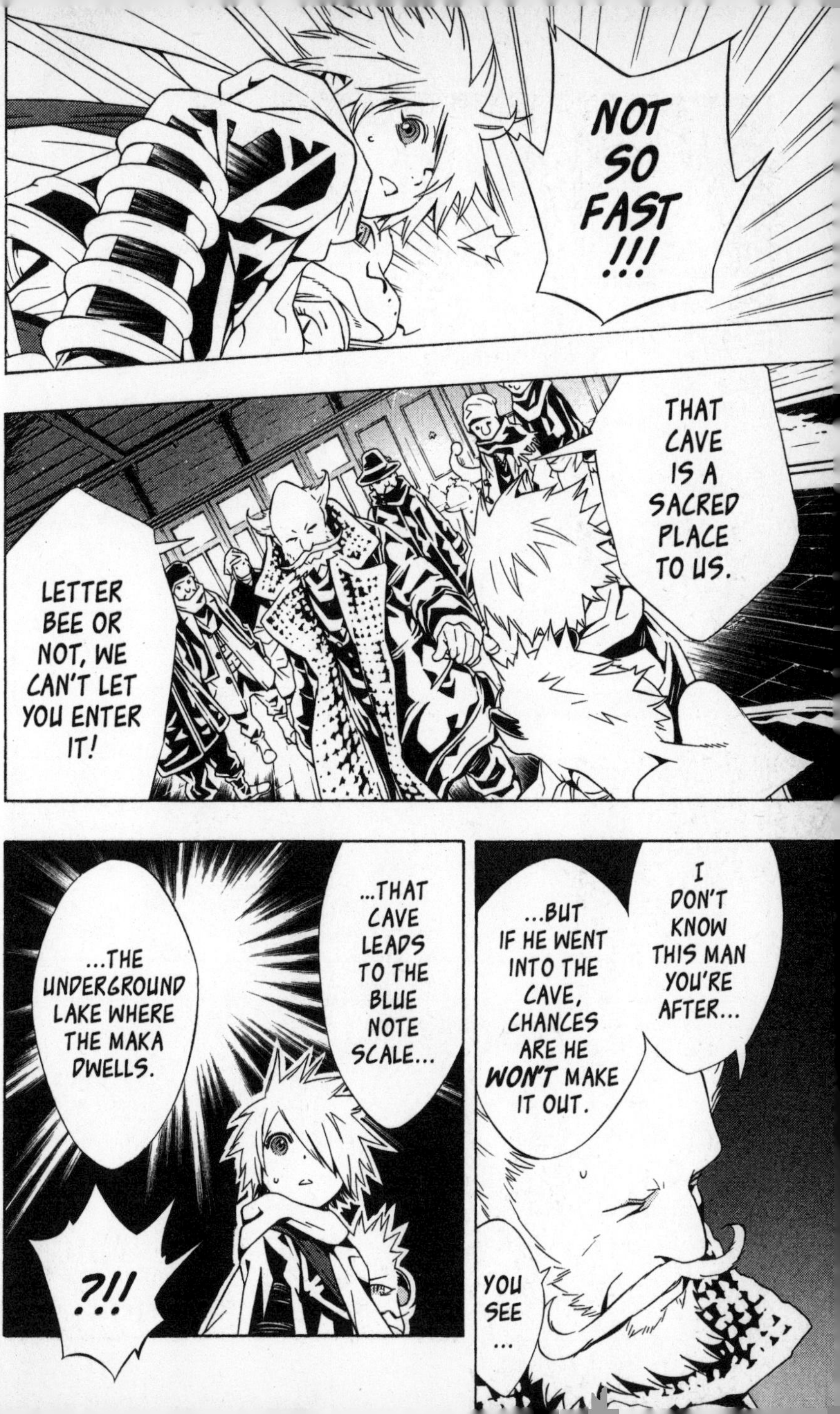
NOT SO FAST!!!
THAT CAVE IS A SACRED PLACE TO US.
LETTER BEE OR NOT, WE CAN'T LET YOU ENTER IT!
I DON'T KNOW THIS MAN YOU'RE AFTER...
...BUT IF HE WENT INTO THE CAVE, CHANCES ARE HE WON'T MAKE IT OUT.
YOU SEE ...
...THAT CAVE LEADS TO THE BLUE NOTE SCALE...
...THE UNDERGROUND LAKE WHERE THE MAKA DWELLS.
?!!

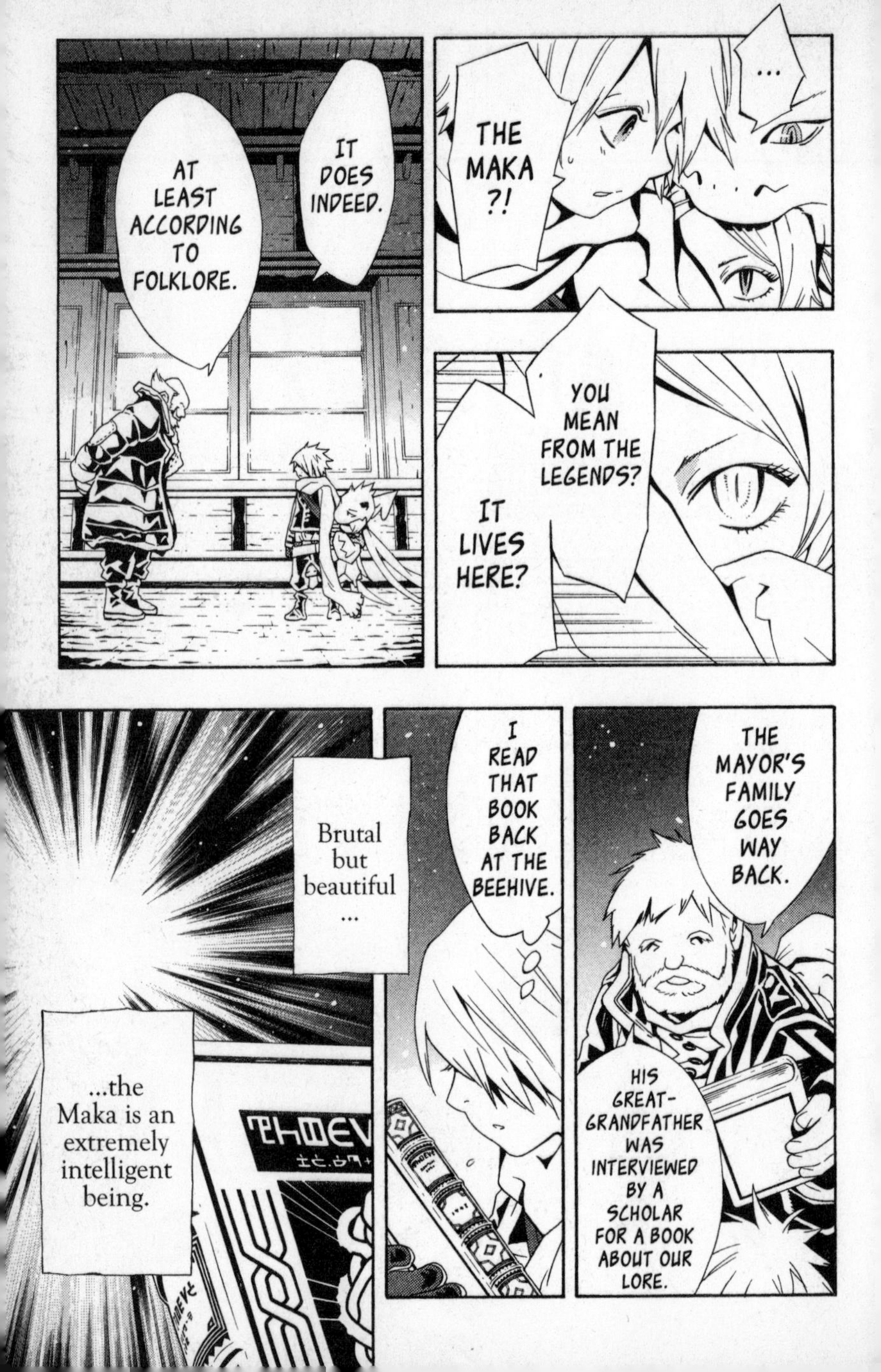
...
THE MAKA ?!
YOU MEAN FROM THE LEGENDS?
IT LIVES HERE?
IT DOES INDEED.
AT LEAST ACCORDING TO FOLKLORE.
THE MAYOR'S FAMILY GOES WAY BACK.
HIS GREAT-GRANDFATHER WAS INTERVIEWED BY A SCHOLAR FOR A BOOK ABOUT OUR LORE.
I READ THAT BOOK BACK AT THE BEEHIVE.
Brutal but beautiful ...
...the Maka is an extremely intelligent being.

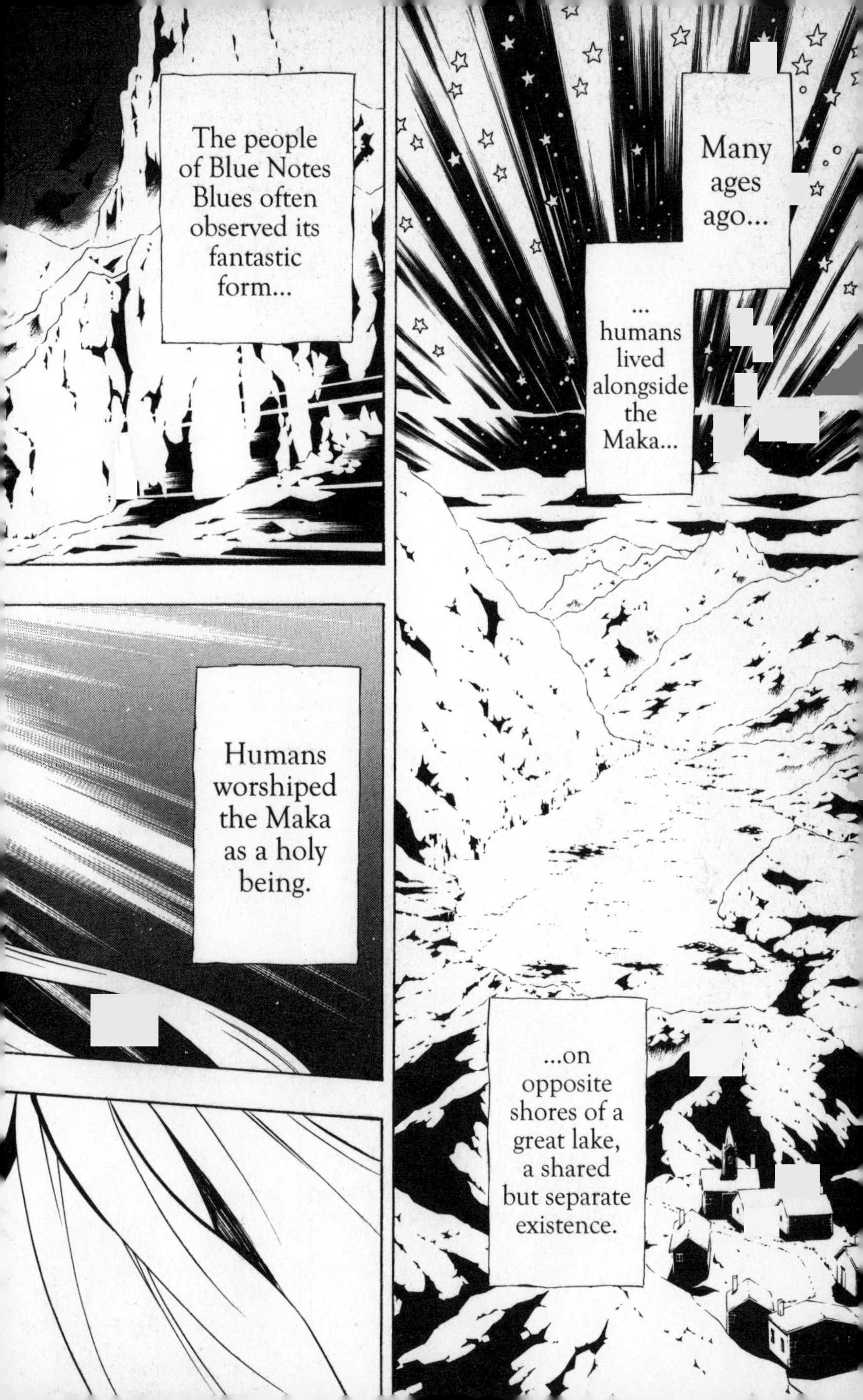

Many ages ago...
... humans lived alongside the Maka...
...on opposite shores of a great lake, a shared but separate existence.
The people of Blue Notes Blues often observed its fantastic form...
Humans worshiped the Maka as a holy being.

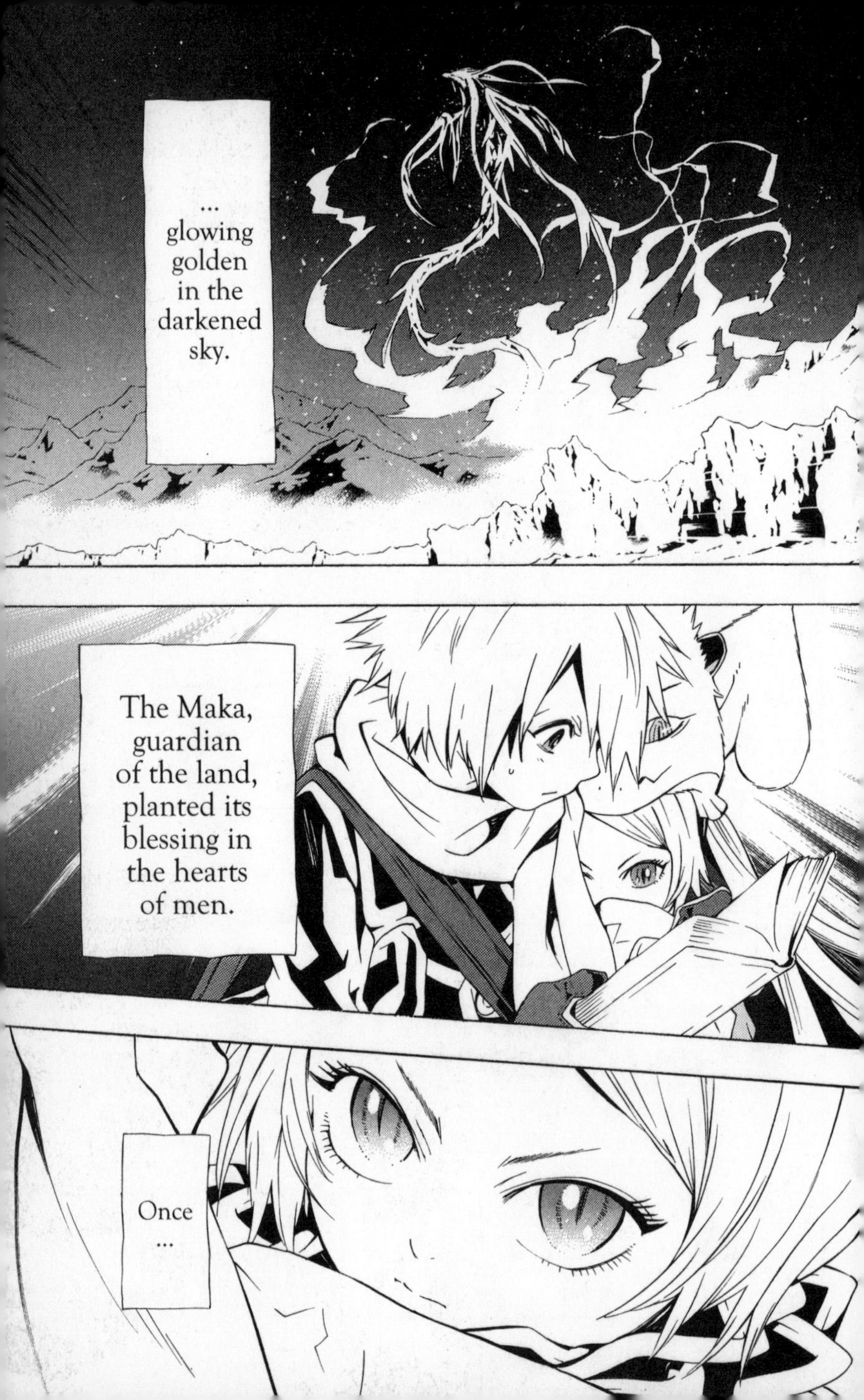
... glowing golden in the darkened sky.
The Maka, guardian of the land, planted its blessing in the hearts of men.
Once ...

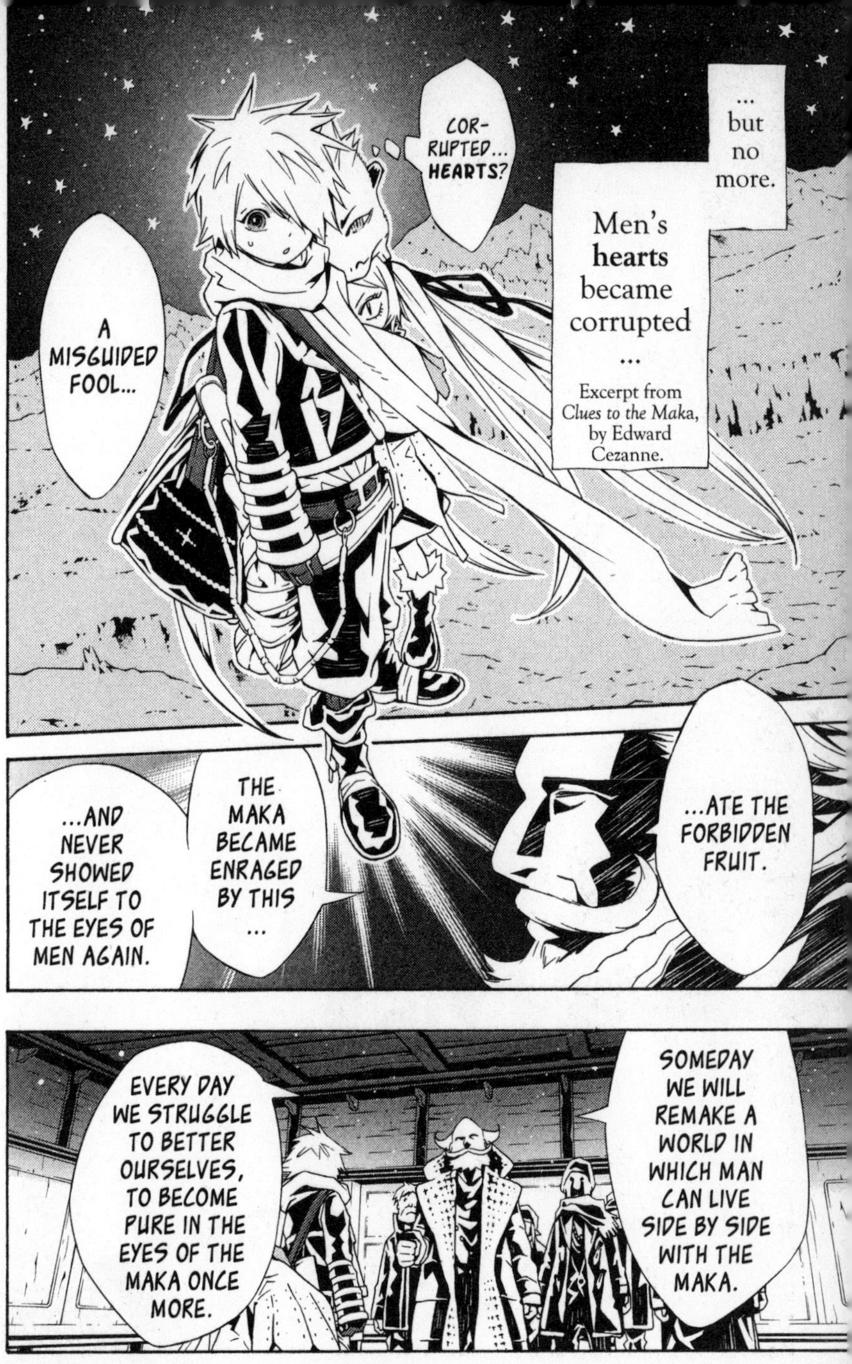

... but no more.
Men's **hearts** became corrupted ...
Excerpt from *Clues to the Maka*, by Edward Cezanne.
COR-RUPTED... HEARTS?
A MISGUIDED FOOL...
...ATE THE FORBIDDEN FRUIT.
THE MAKA BECAME ENRAGED BY THIS ...
...AND NEVER SHOWED ITSELF TO THE EYES OF MEN AGAIN.
SOMEDAY WE WILL REMAKE A WORLD IN WHICH MAN CAN LIVE SIDE BY SIDE WITH THE MAKA.
EVERY DAY WE STRUGGLE TO BETTER OURSELVES, TO BECOME PURE IN THE EYES OF THE MAKA ONCE MORE.

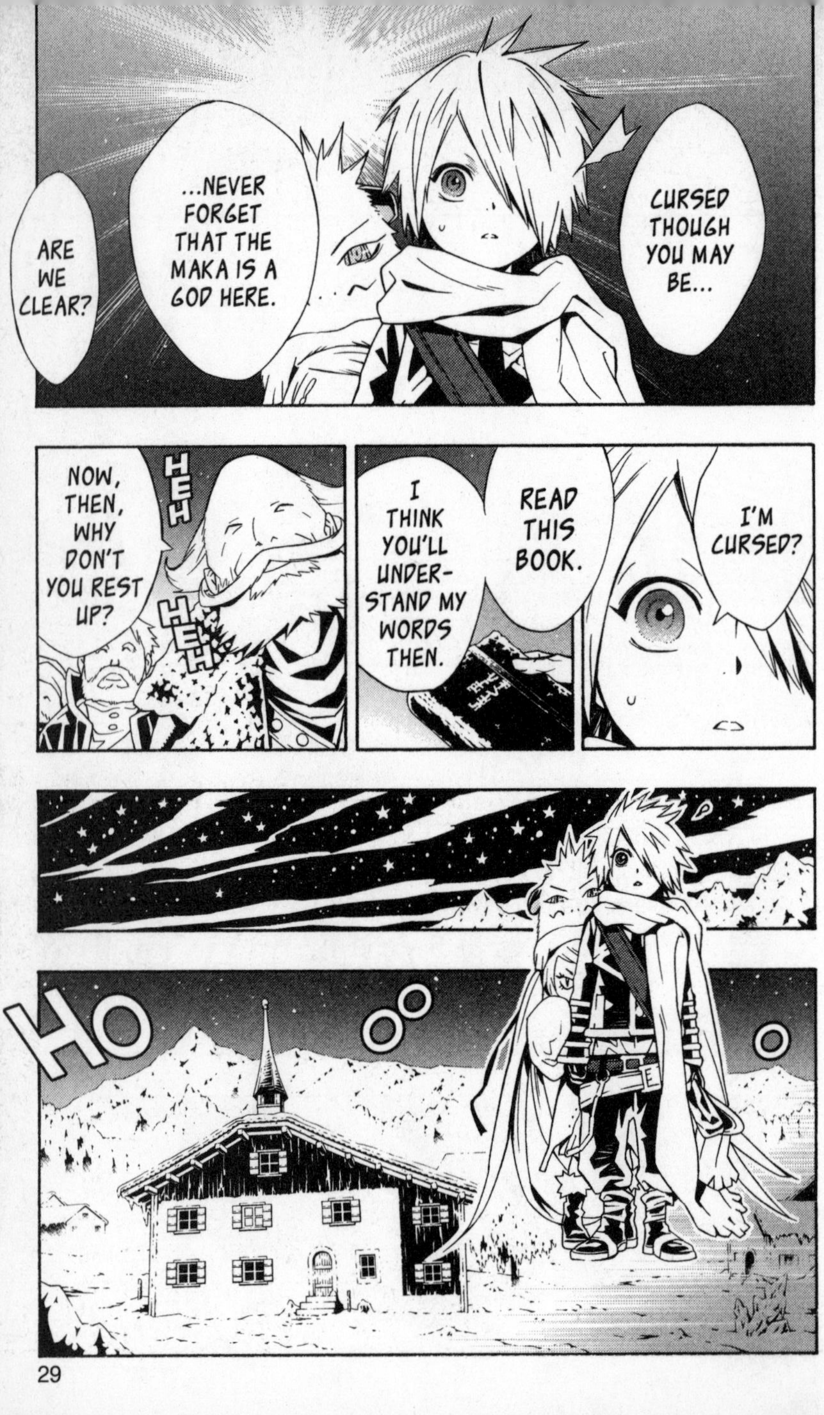
CURSED THOUGH YOU MAY BE...
...NEVER FORGET THAT THE MAKA IS A GOD HERE.
ARE WE CLEAR?
I'M CURSED?
READ THIS BOOK.
I THINK YOU'LL UNDER-STAND MY WORDS THEN.
HEH
NOW, THEN, WHY DON'T YOU REST UP?
HEH HEH
HOOOO

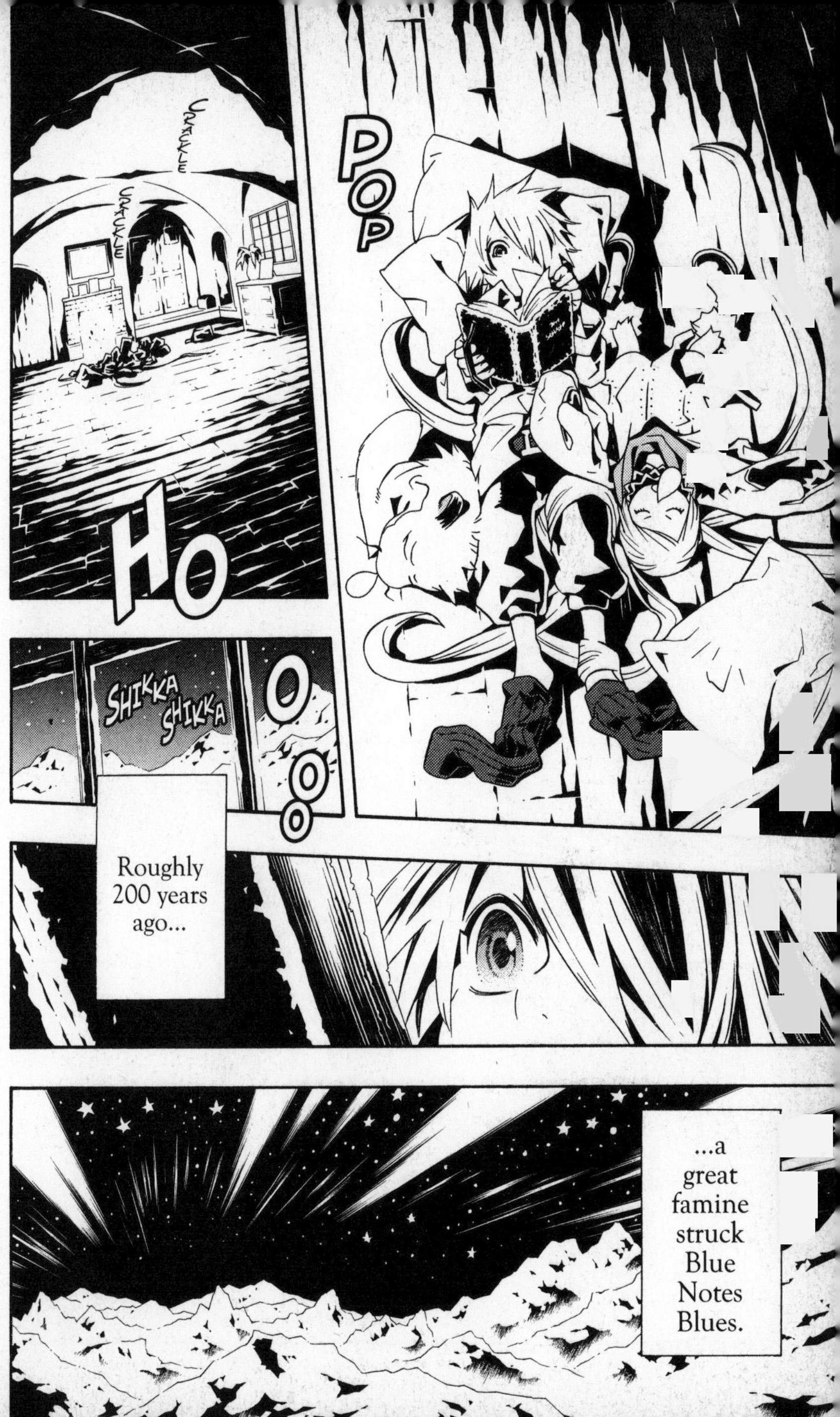
POP
CRACKLE
CRACKLE
HO
OOO
SHIKKA SHIKKA
Roughly 200 years ago...
...a great famine struck Blue Notes Blues.

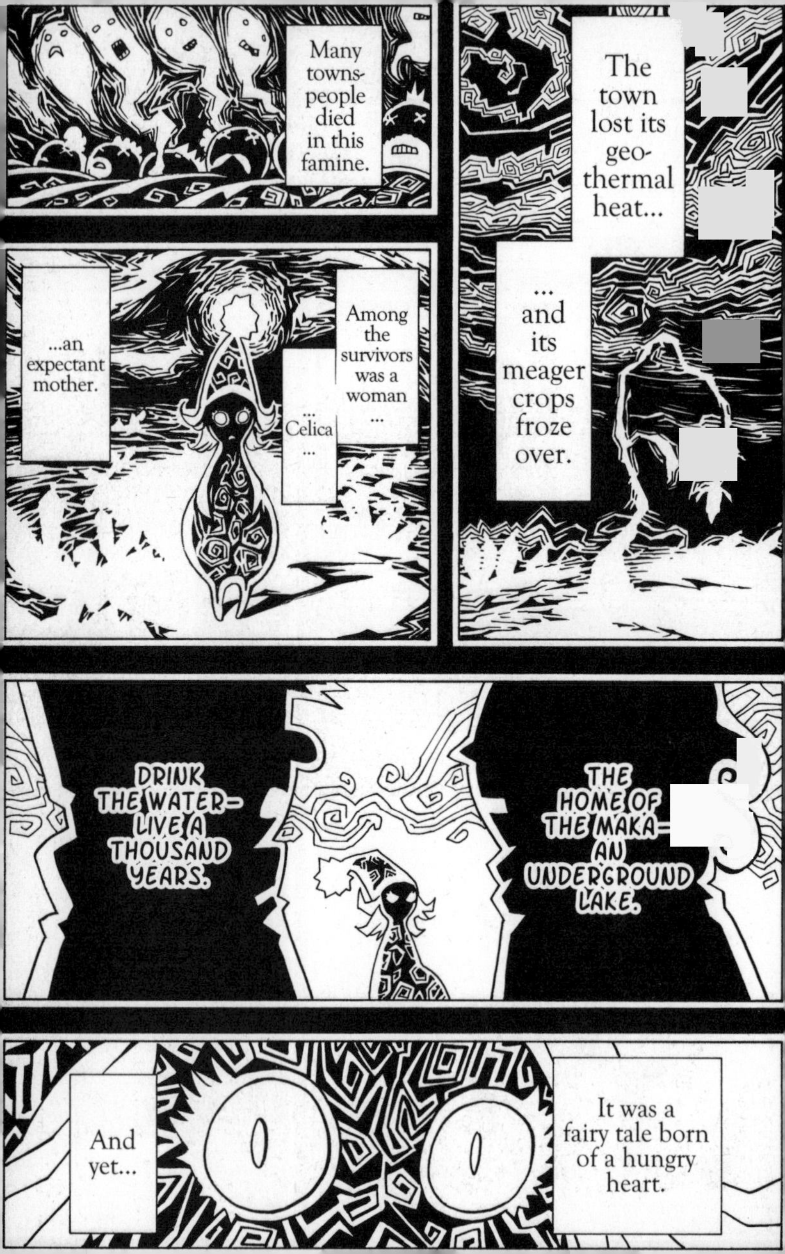
The town lost its geo-thermal heat...
...and its meager crops froze over.
Many towns-people died in this famine.
Among the survivors was a woman...
...Celica...
...an expectant mother.
THE HOME OF THE MAKA—AN UNDERGROUND LAKE.
DRINK THE WATER—LIVE A THOUSAND YEARS.
It was a fairy tale born of a hungry heart.
And yet...

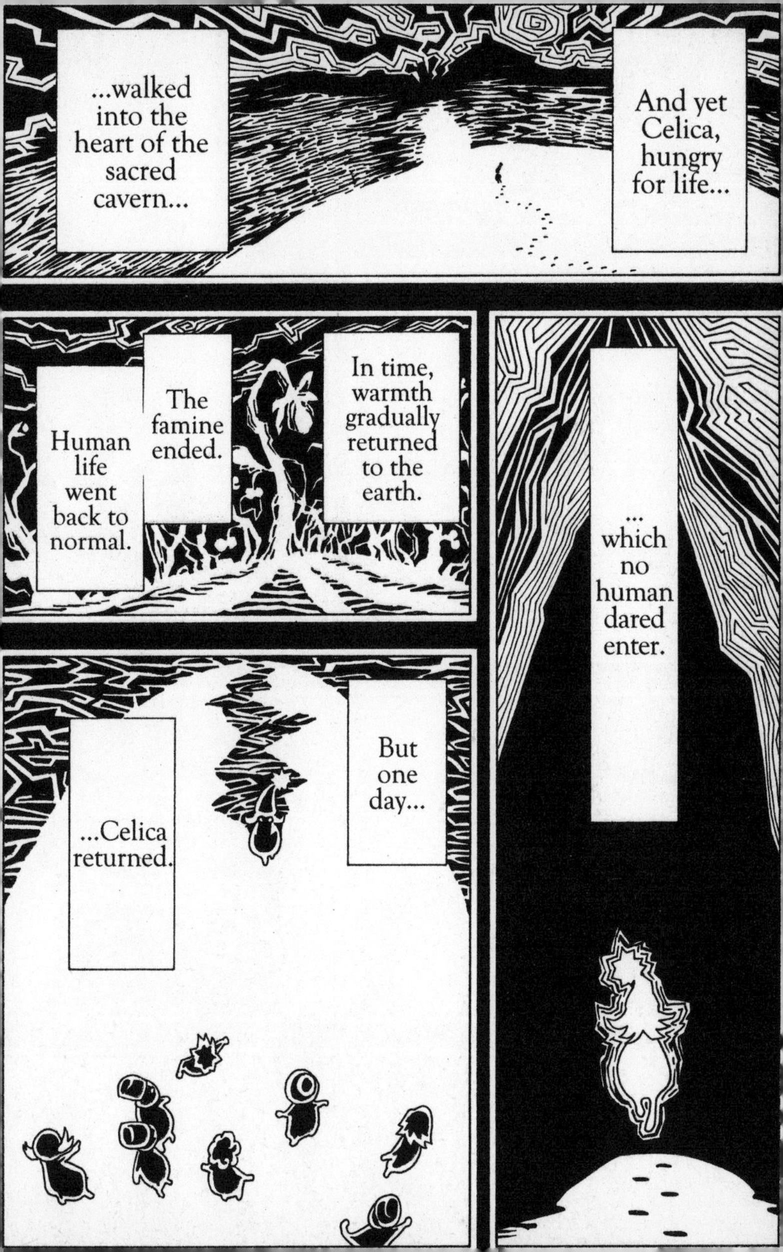
And yet Celica, hungry for life...
...walked into the heart of the sacred cavern...
...which no human dared enter.
In time, warmth gradually returned to the earth.
The famine ended.
Human life went back to normal.
But one day...
...Celica returned.

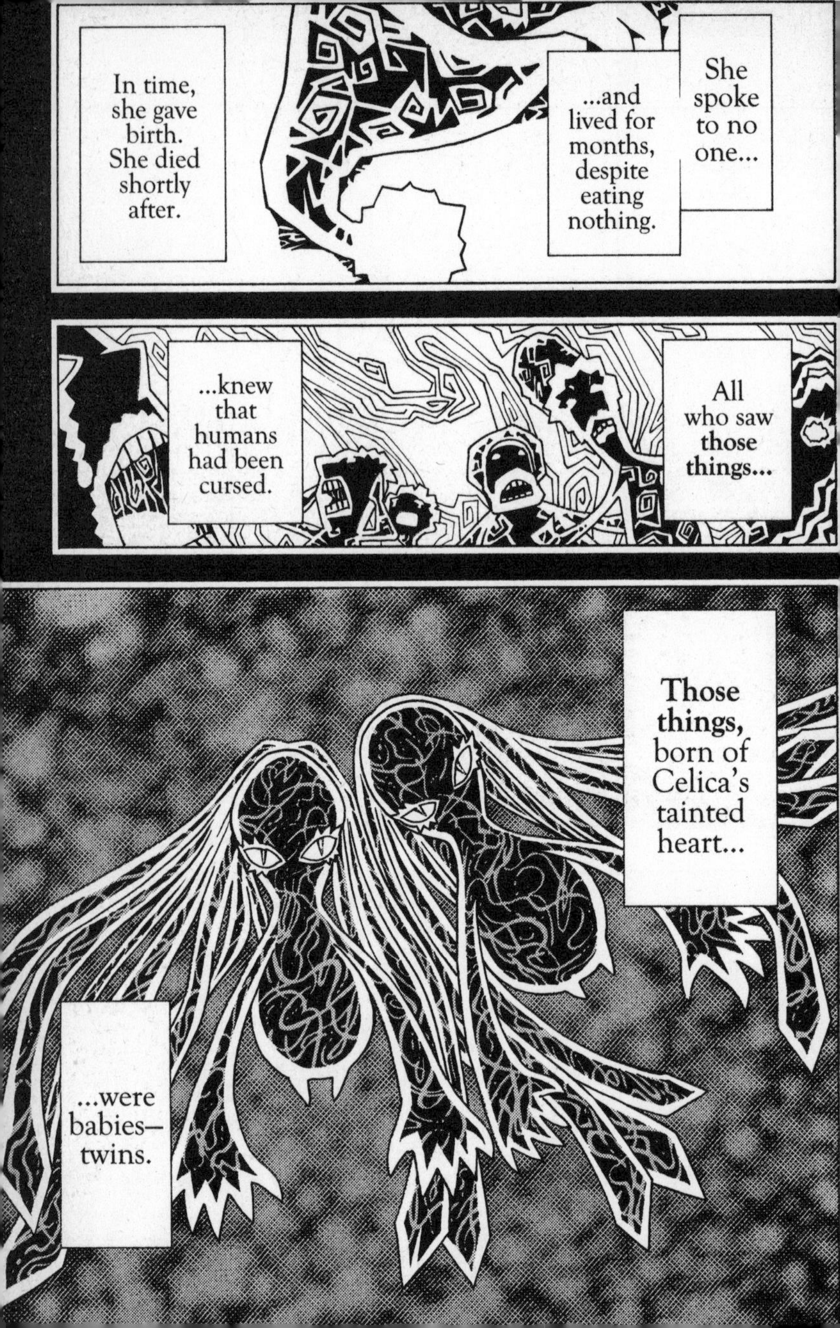

She spoke to no one...
...and lived for months, despite eating nothing.
In time, she gave birth. She died shortly after.
All who saw **those things...**
...knew that humans had been cursed.
Those things, born of Celica's tainted heart...
...were babies—twins.

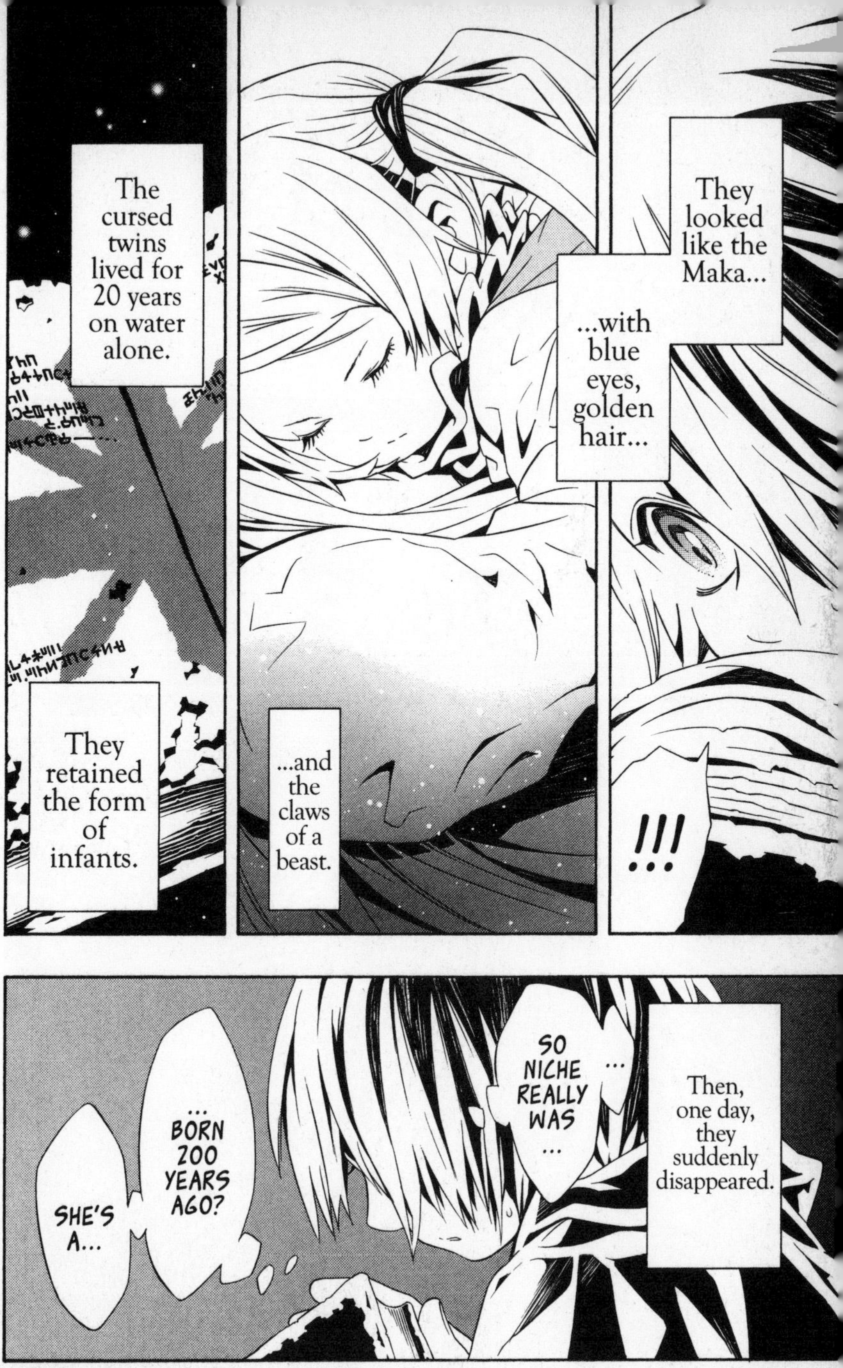

They looked like the Maka...
...with blue eyes, golden hair...
!!!
...and the claws of a beast.
The cursed twins lived for 20 years on water alone.
They retained the form of infants.
Then, one day, they suddenly disappeared.
...
SO NICHE REALLY WAS ...
... BORN 200 YEARS AGO?
SHE'S A...

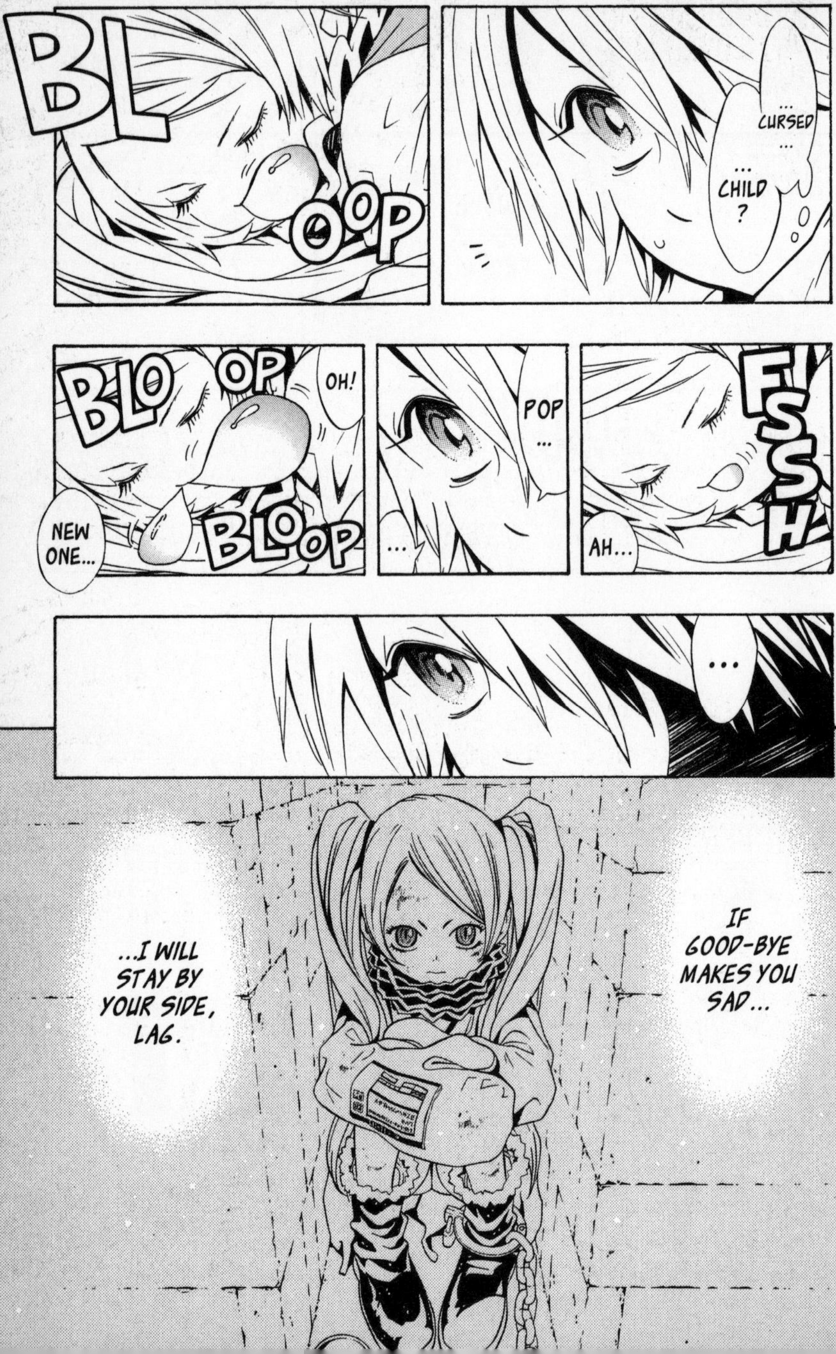
... CURSED ...
... CHILD ?
BL OOP
FSSH
AH...
POP ...
...
OH!
BLO OP
NEW ONE...
BLOOP
...
IF GOOD-BYE MAKES YOU SAD...
...I WILL STAY BY YOUR SIDE, LAG.

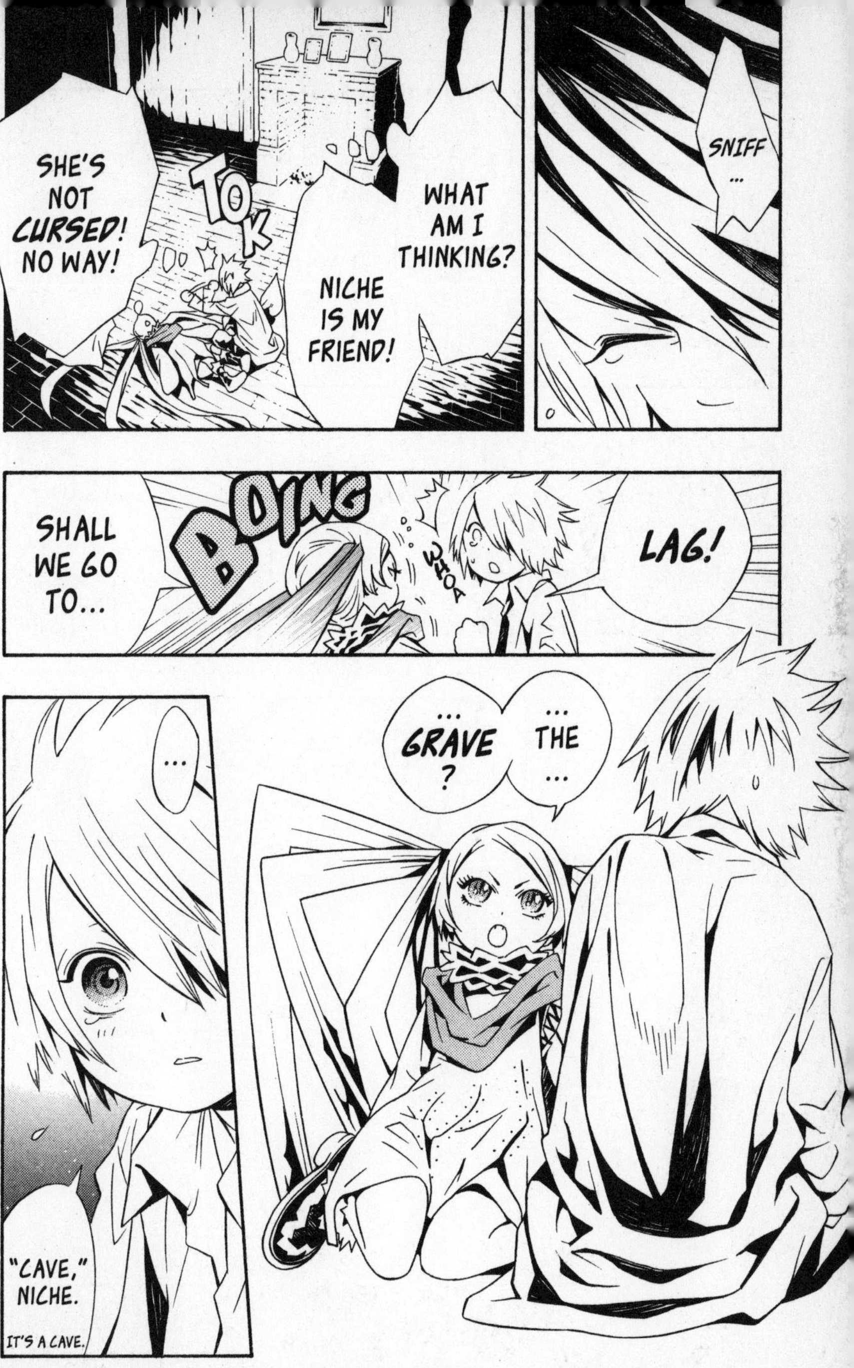
SNIFF ...
WHAT AM I THINKING?
NICHE IS MY FRIEND!
TOK
SHE'S NOT CURSED! NO WAY!
LAG!
WHOA
BOING
SHALL WE GO TO...
... THE ...
... GRAVE ?
...
"CAVE," NICHE.
IT'S A CAVE.

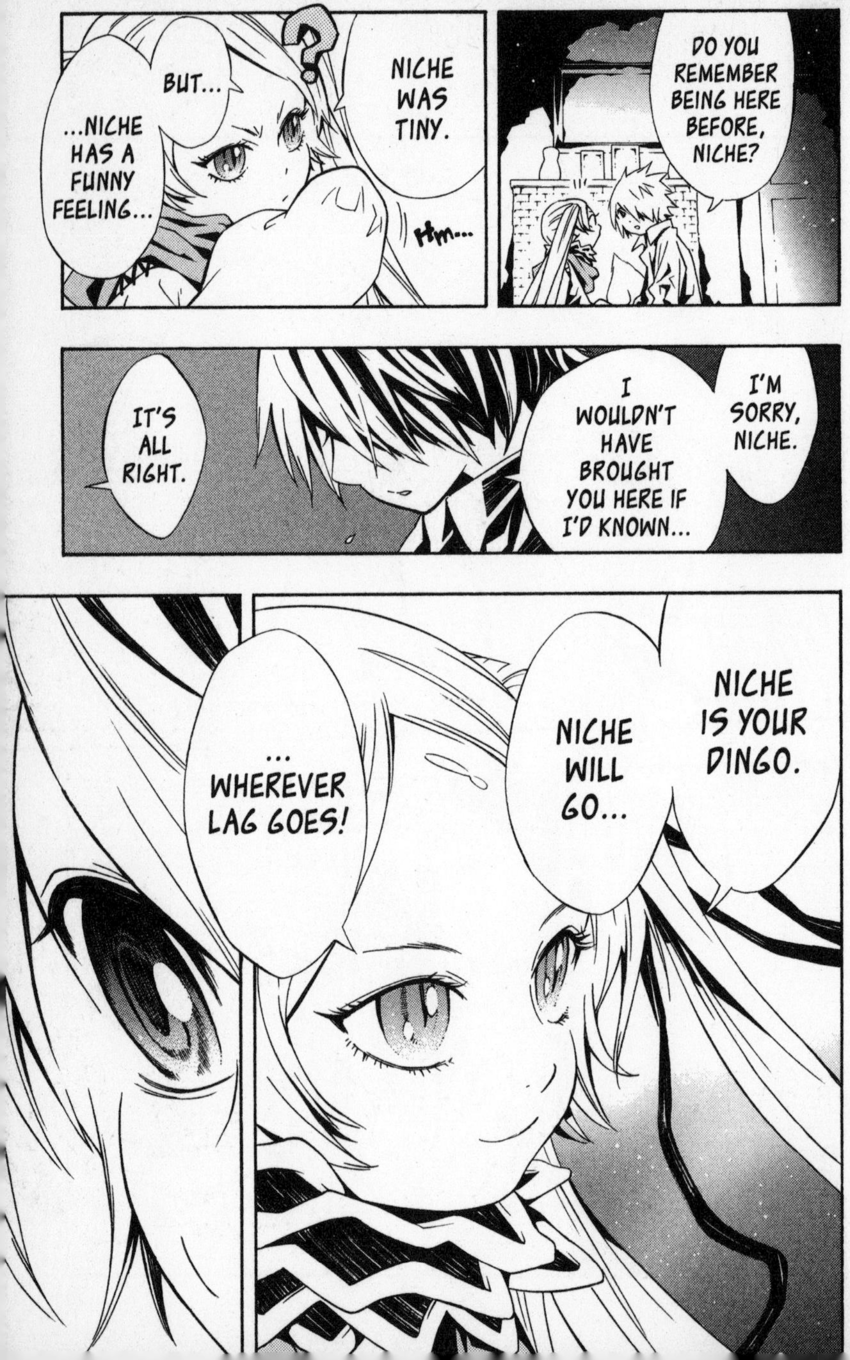
DO YOU REMEMBER BEING HERE BEFORE, NICHE?
NICHE WAS TINY.
BUT...
...NICHE HAS A FUNNY FEELING...
Hm...
I'M SORRY, NICHE.
I WOULDN'T HAVE BROUGHT YOU HERE IF I'D KNOWN...
IT'S ALL RIGHT.
NICHE IS YOUR DINGO.
NICHE WILL GO...
... WHEREVER LAG GOES!

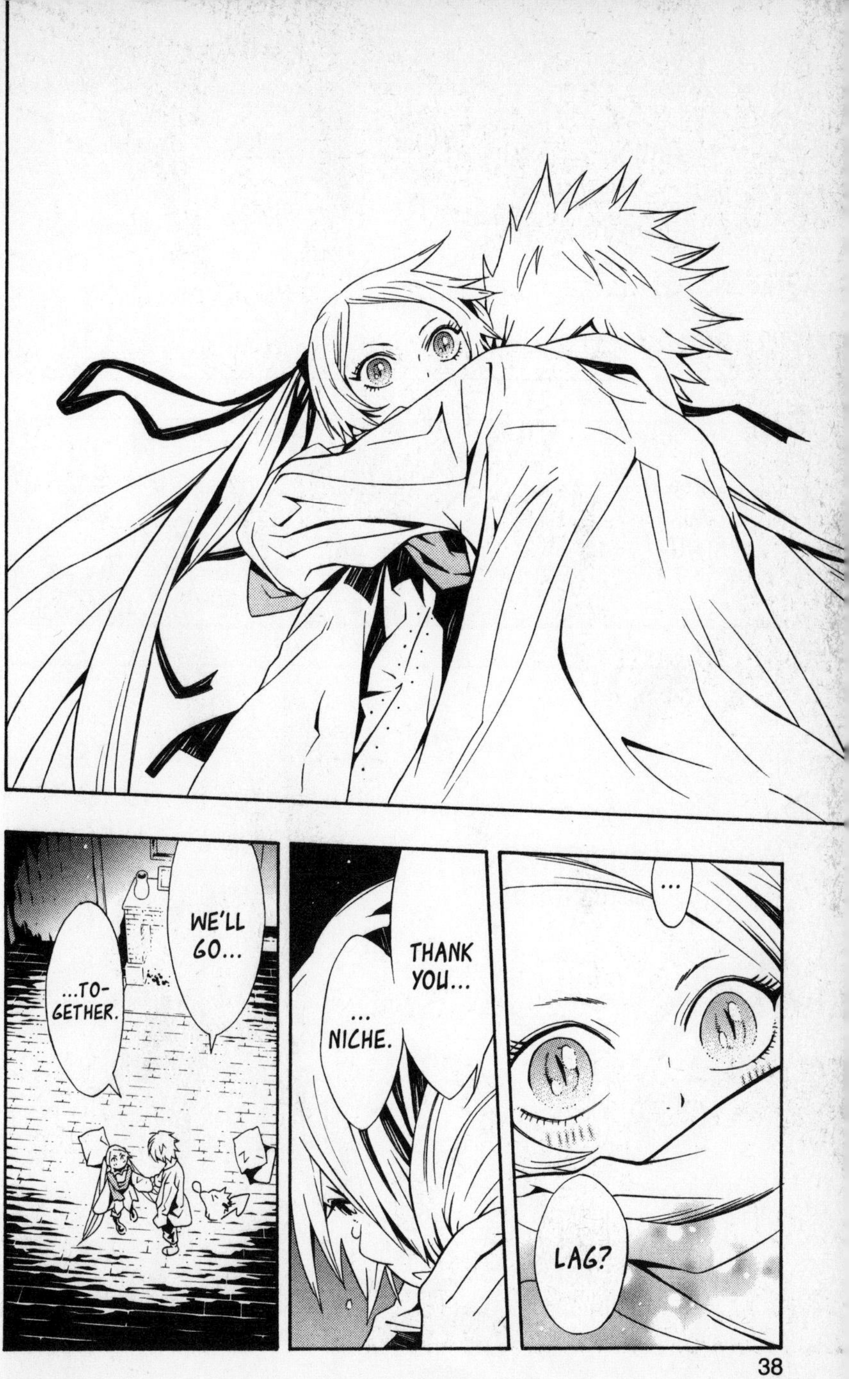
...
LAG?
THANK YOU...
... NICHE.
WE'LL GO...
...TO-GETHER.

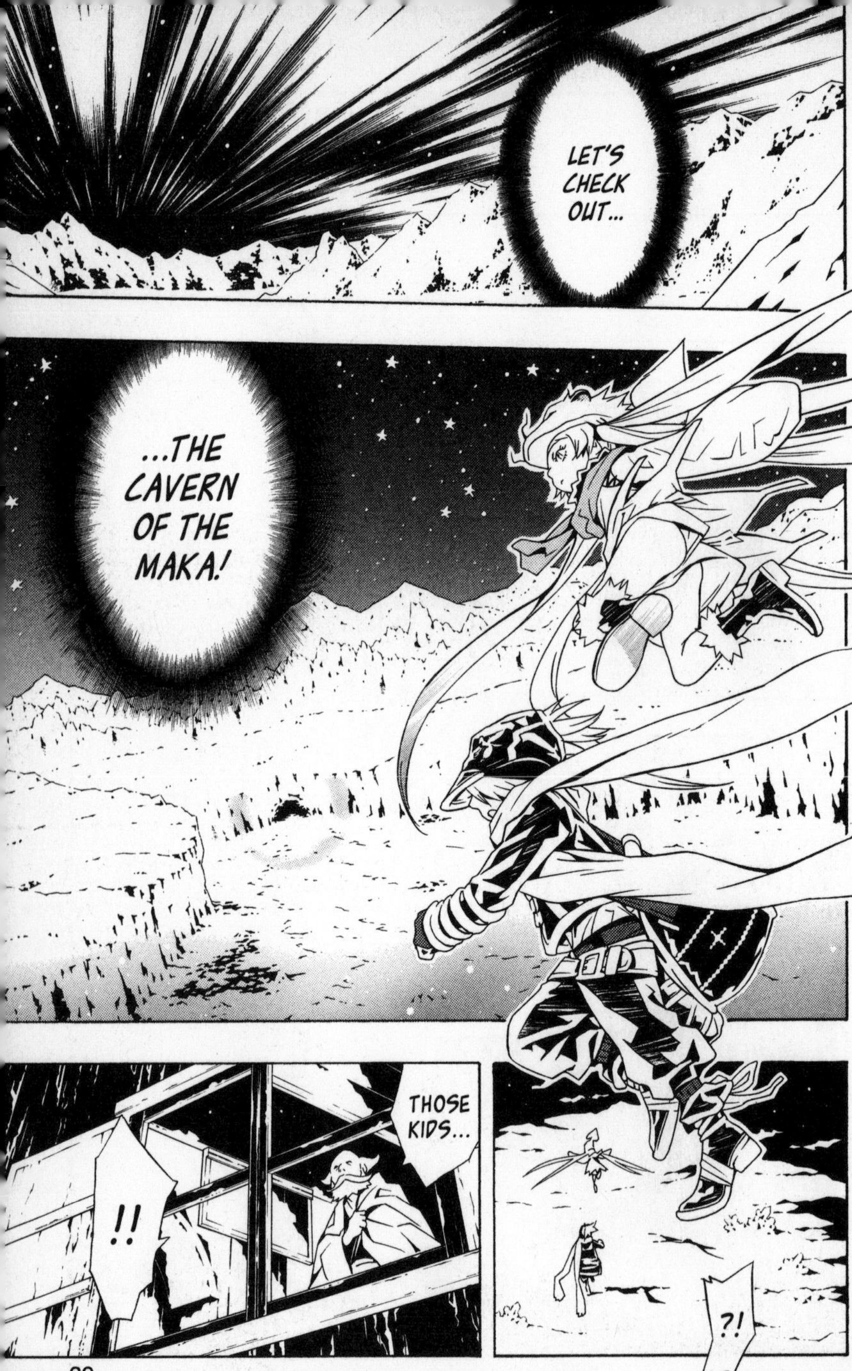
LET'S CHECK OUT...
...THE CAVERN OF THE MAKA!
?!
THOSE KIDS...
!!

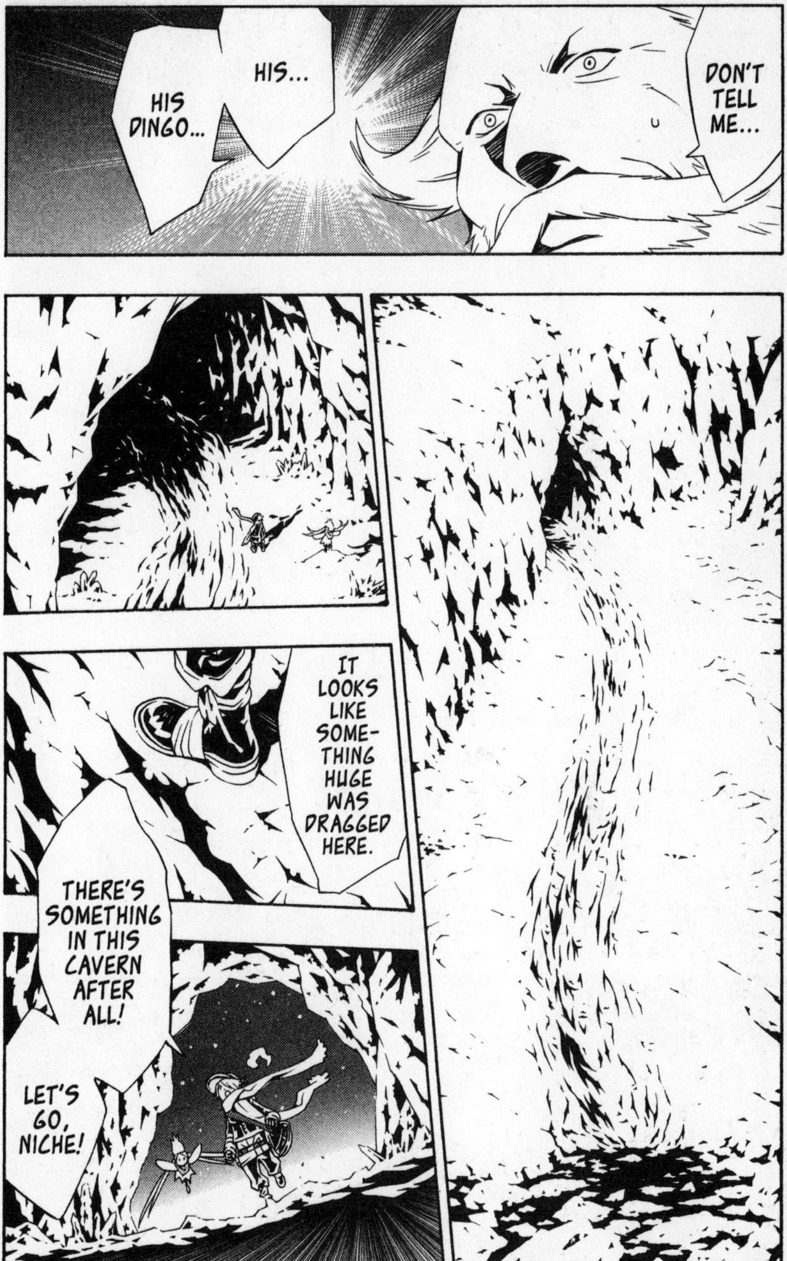
DON'T TELL ME...
HIS...
HIS DINGO...
IT LOOKS LIKE SOMETHING HUGE WAS DRAGGED HERE.
THERE'S SOMETHING IN THIS CAVERN AFTER ALL!
LET'S GO, NICHE!

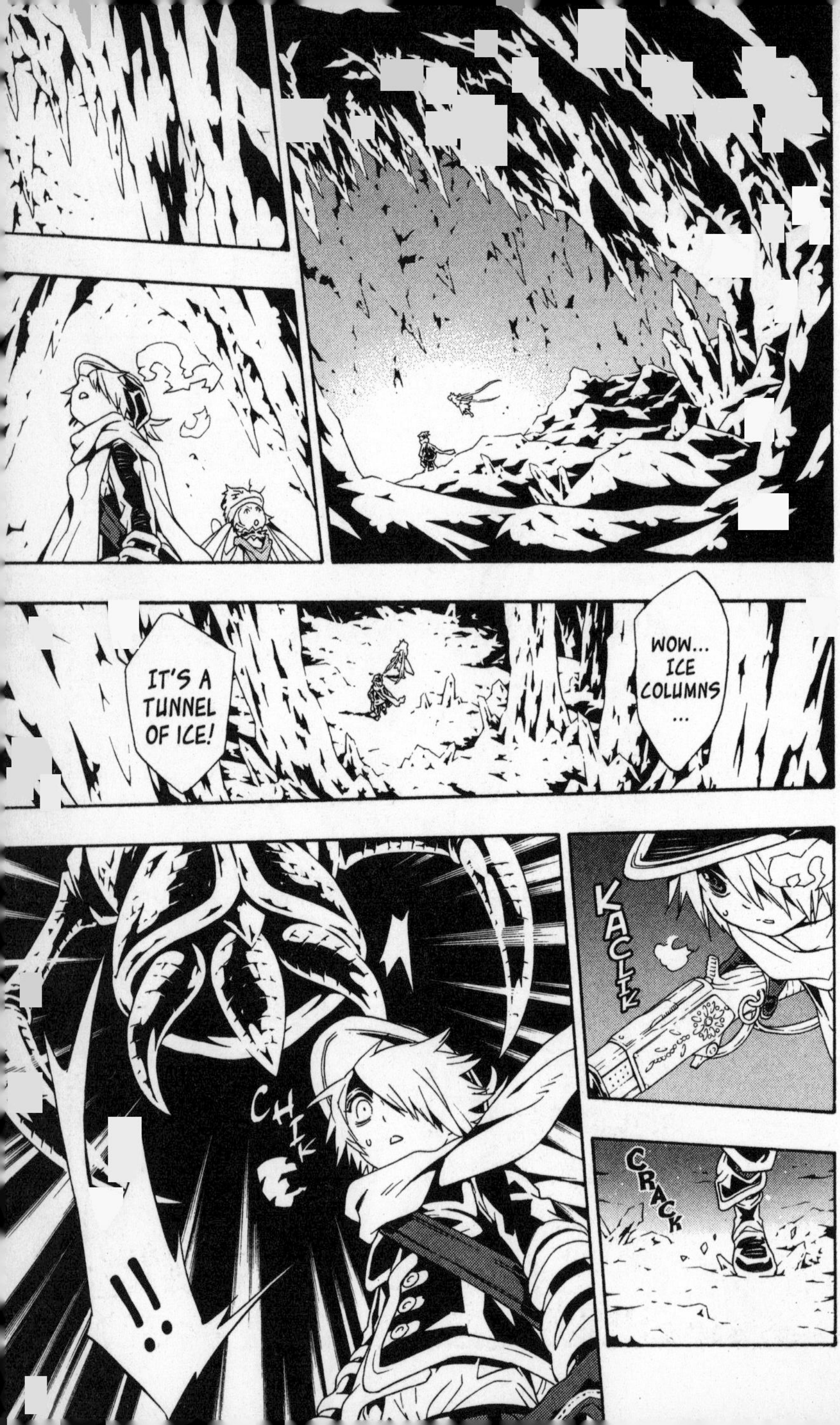
WOW... ICE COLUMNS ...
IT'S A TUNNEL OF ICE!
KACLIK
CRACK
CHIK
!!

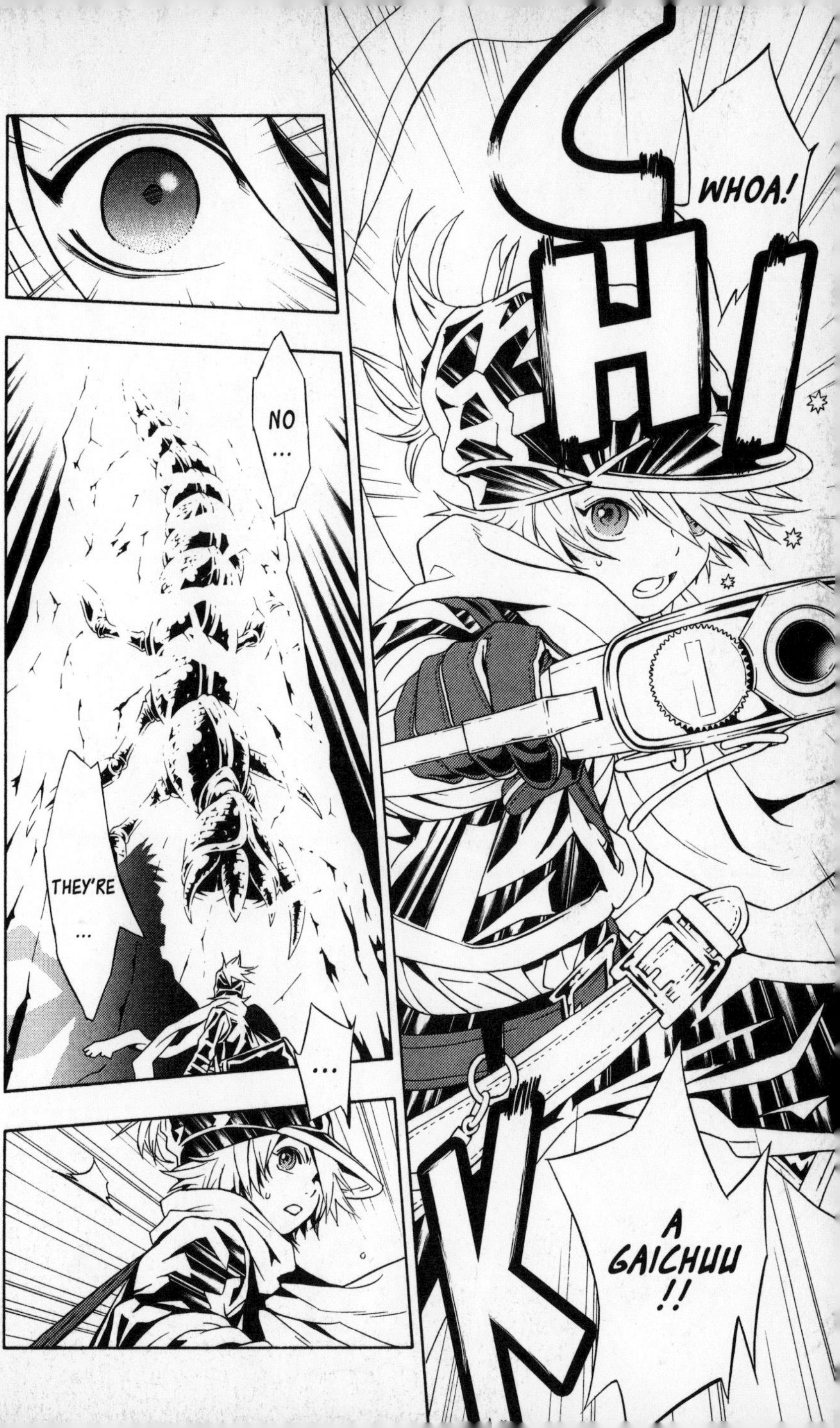
WHOA!
CHIK
A GAICHUU !!
NO ...
THEY'RE ...
...

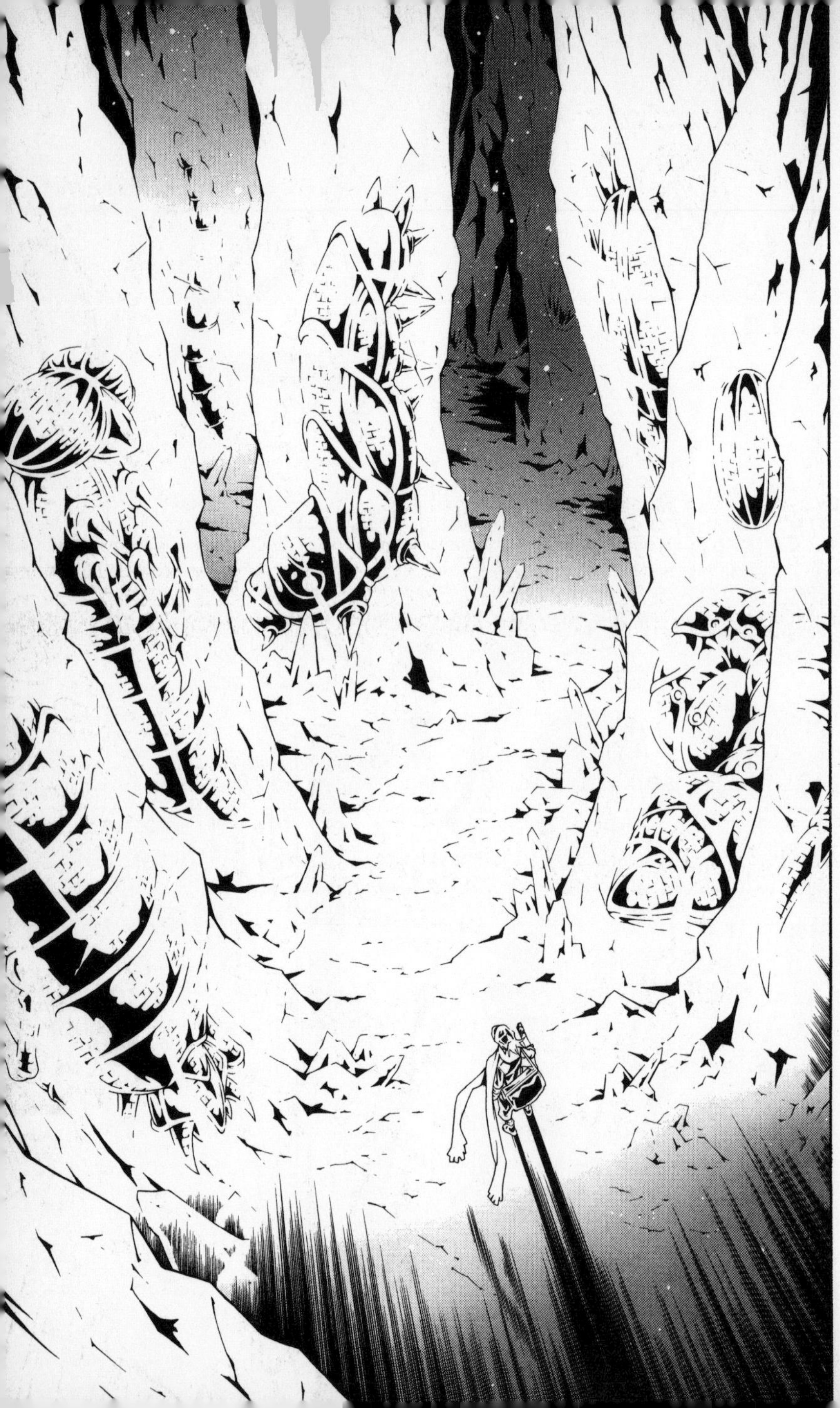

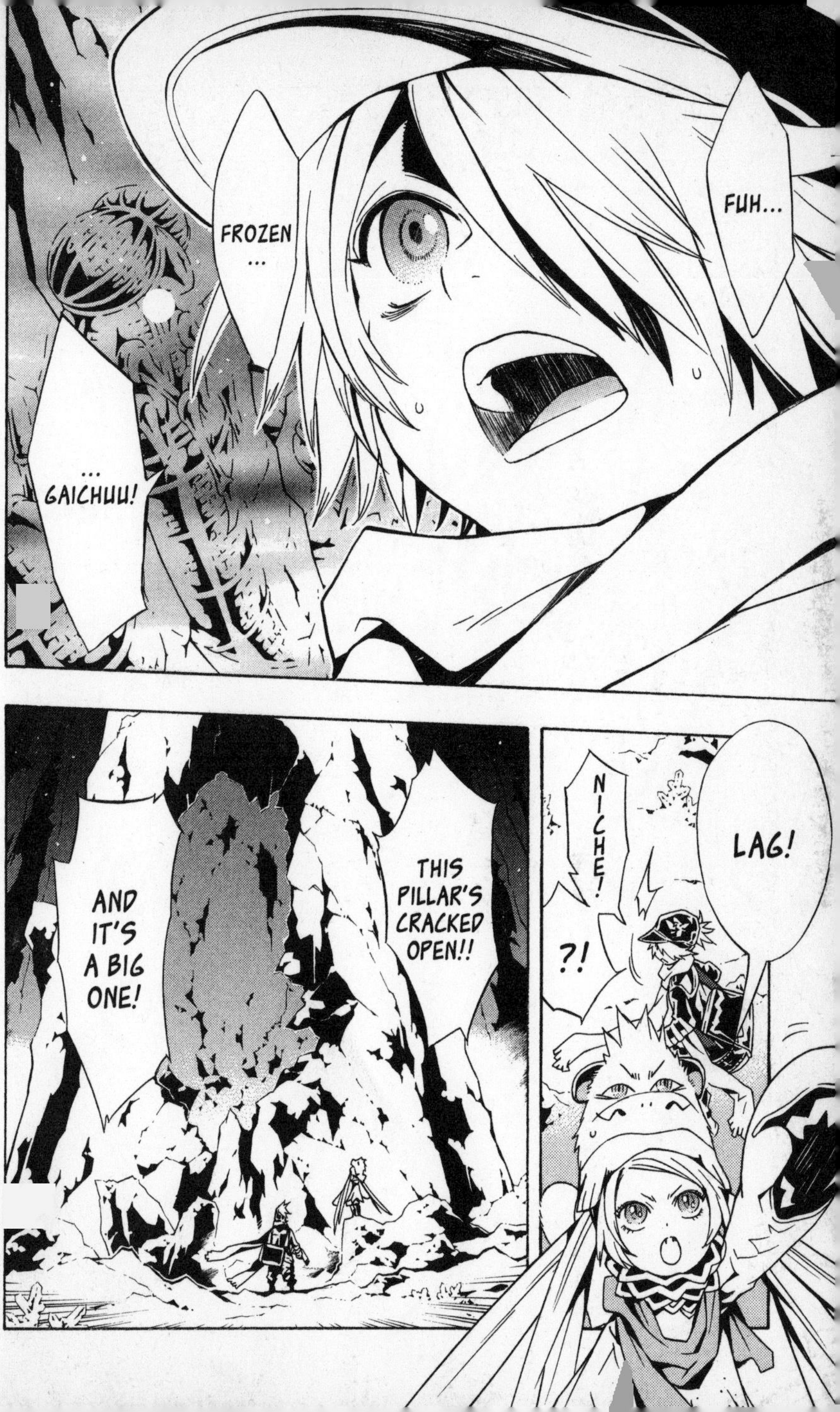
FUH...
FROZEN ...
... GAICHUU!
LAG!
NICHE!
?!
THIS PILLAR'S CRACKED OPEN!!
AND IT'S A BIG ONE!

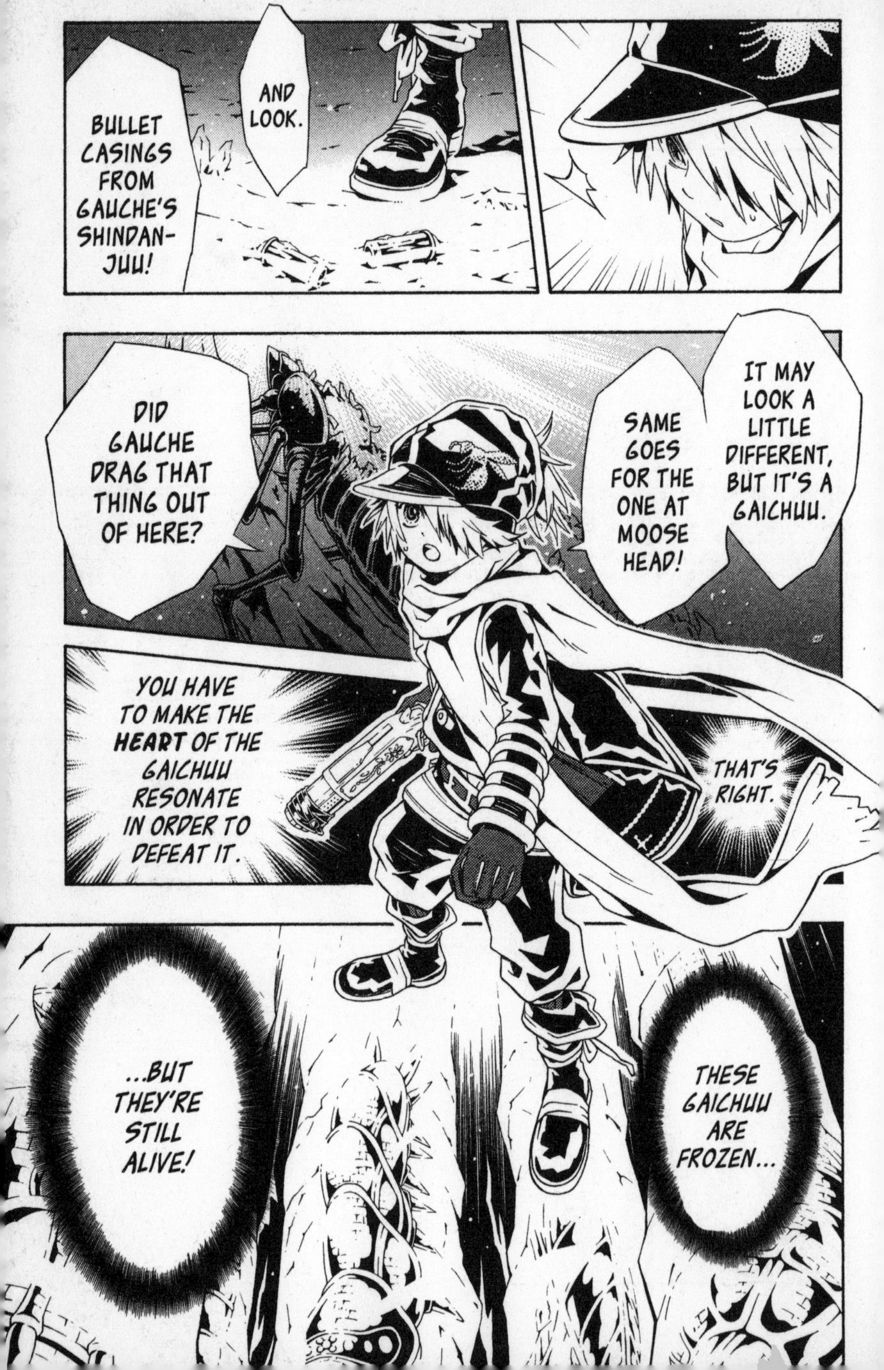
AND LOOK.
BULLET CASINGS FROM GAUCHE'S SHINDAN-JUU!
IT MAY LOOK A LITTLE DIFFERENT, BUT IT'S A GAICHUU.
SAME GOES FOR THE ONE AT MOOSE HEAD!
DID GAUCHE DRAG THAT THING OUT OF HERE?
THAT'S RIGHT.
YOU HAVE TO MAKE THE **HEART** OF THE GAICHUU RESONATE IN ORDER TO DEFEAT IT.
THESE GAICHUU ARE FROZEN...
...BUT THEY'RE STILL ALIVE!

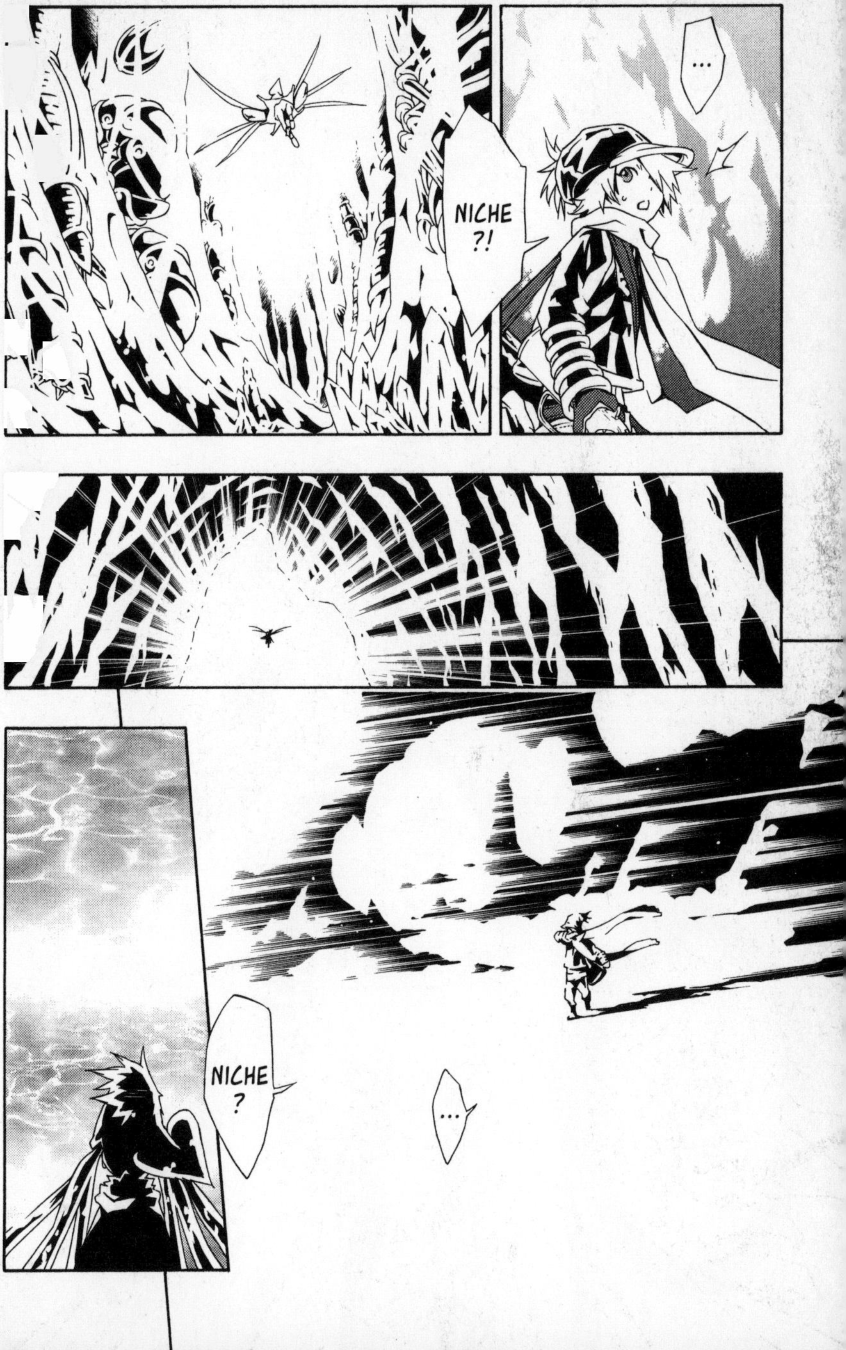
...
NICHE ?!
NICHE ?
...

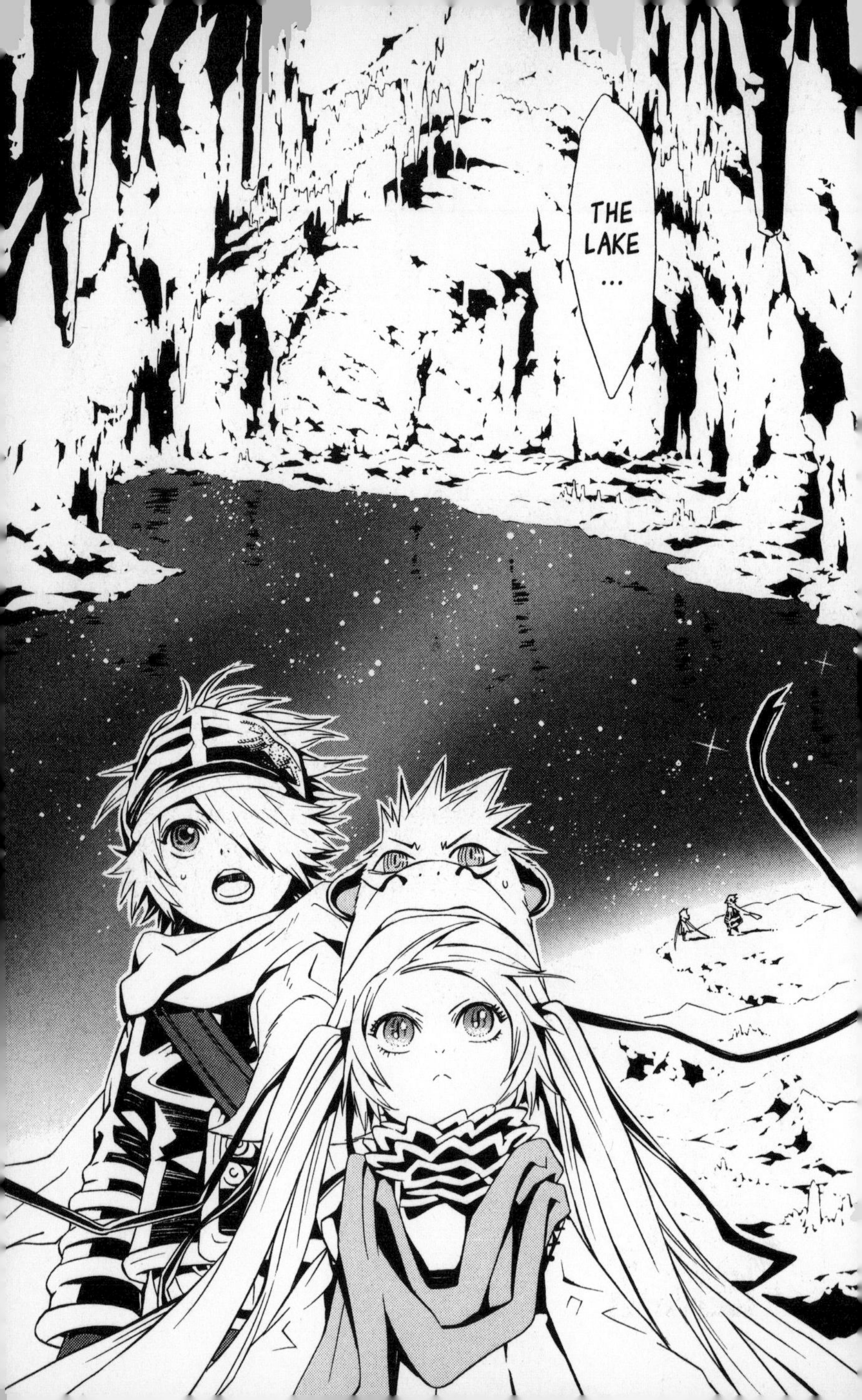
THE LAKE ...

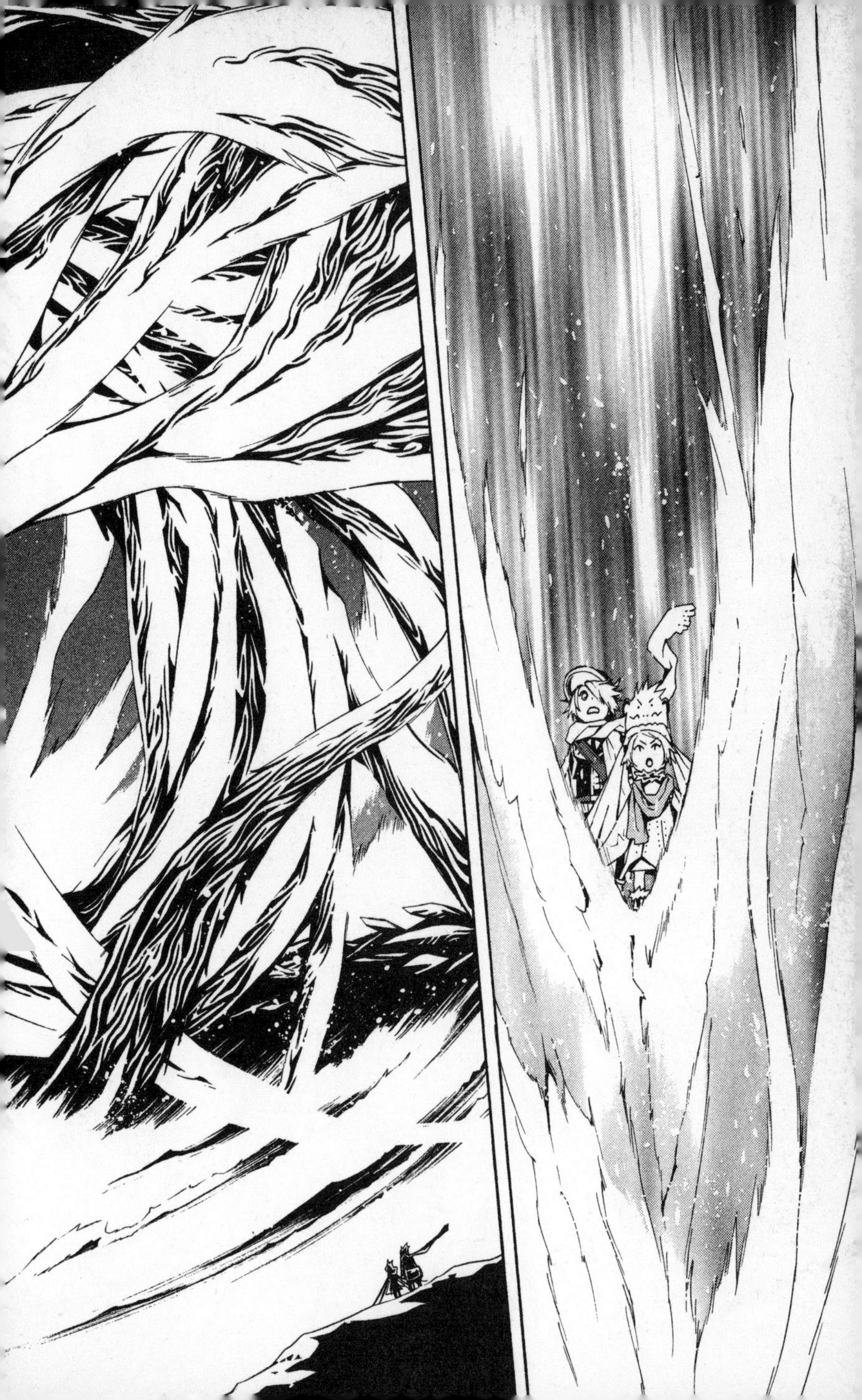

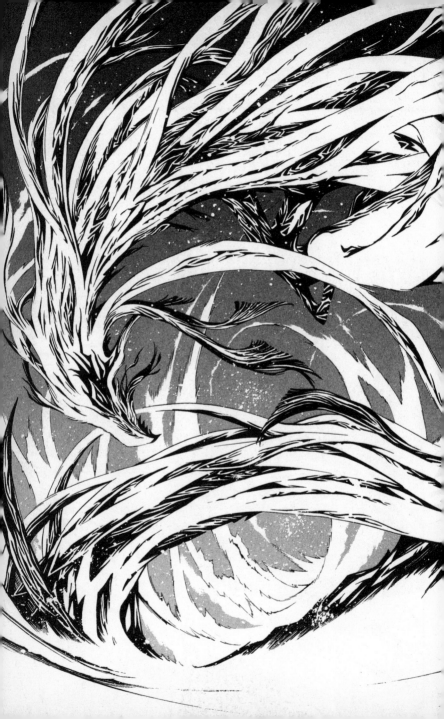

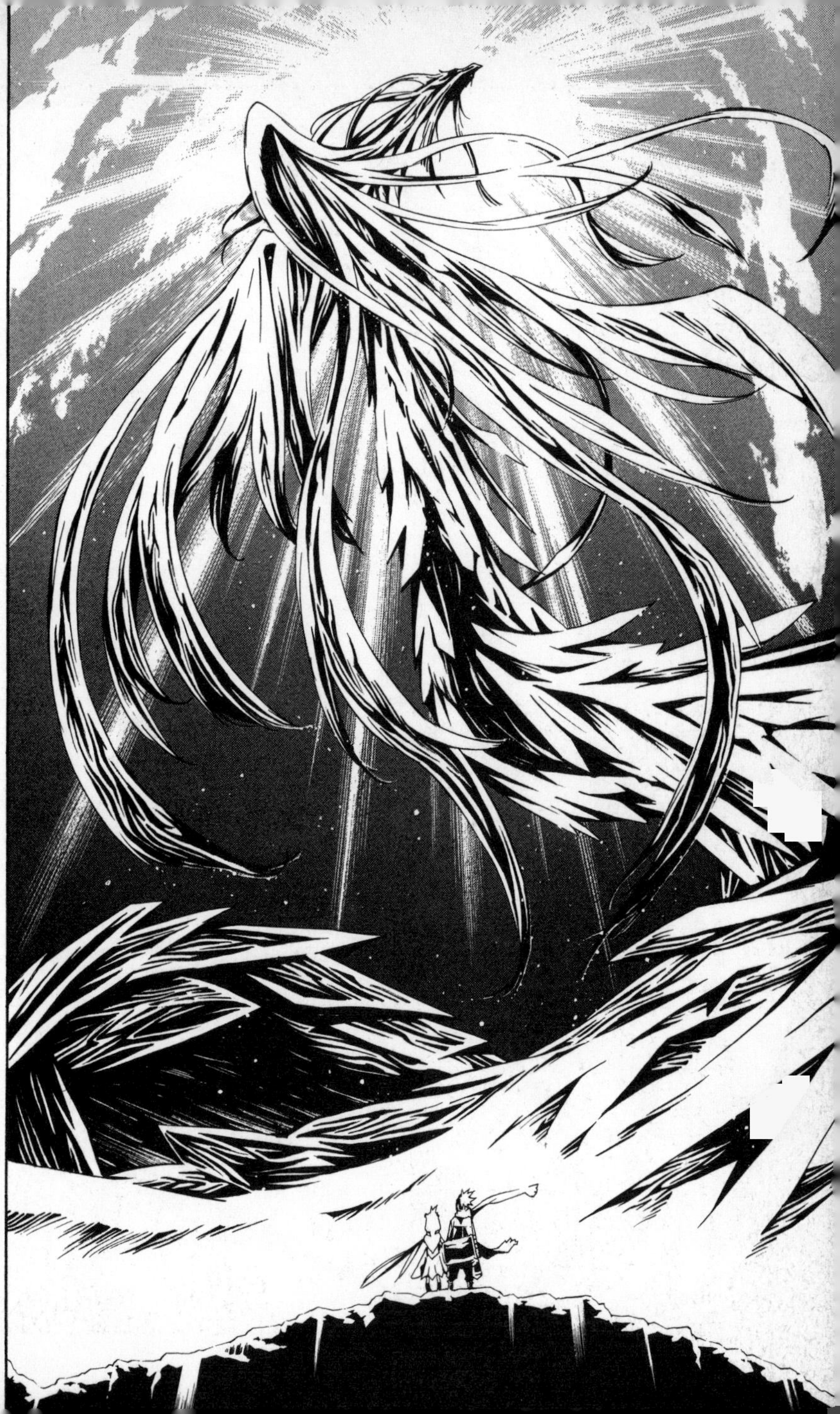

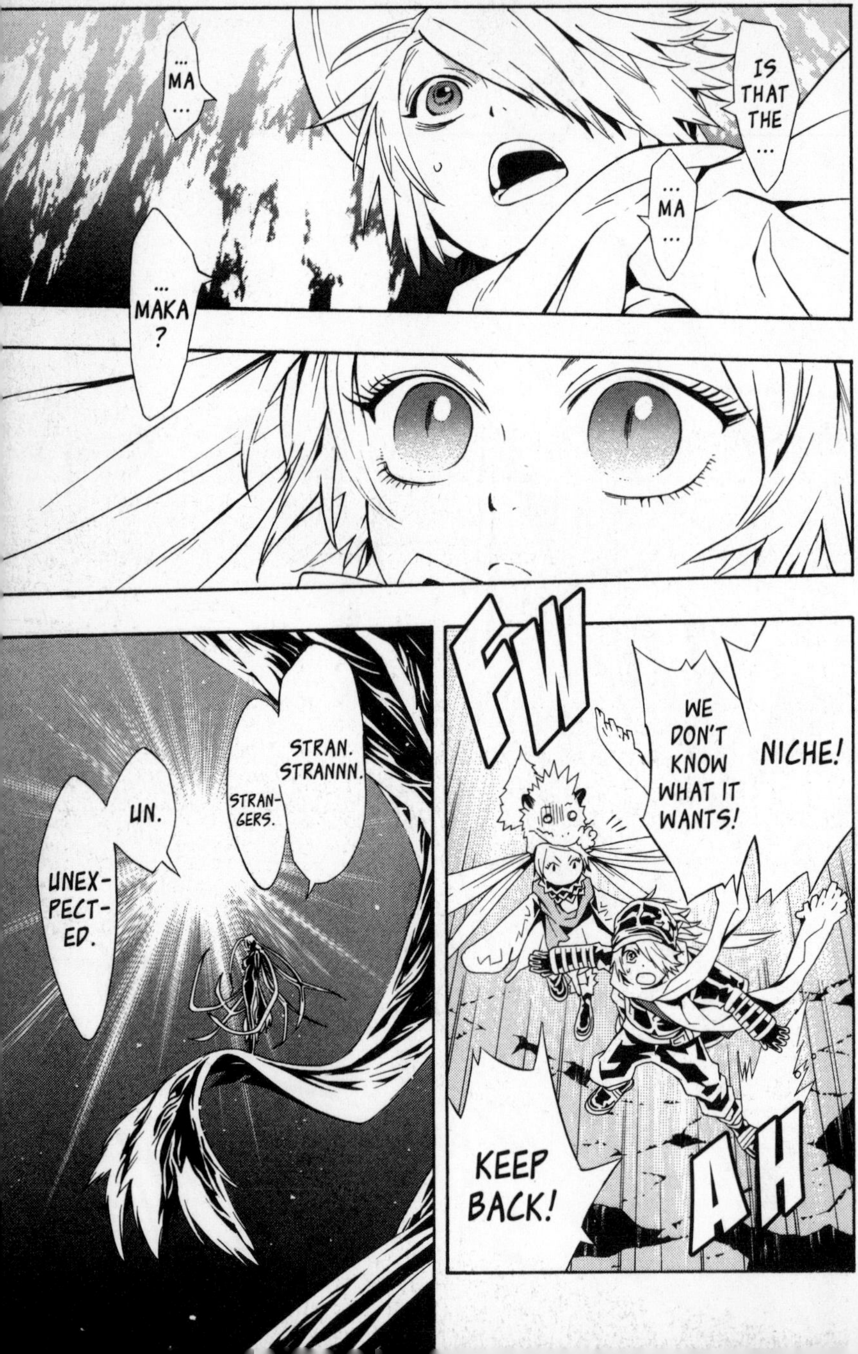
IS THAT THE ...
... MA ...
... MA ...
... MAKA?
NICHE!
WE DON'T KNOW WHAT IT WANTS!
FW
AH
KEEP BACK!
STRAN. STRANNN.
STRAN-GERS.
UN.
UNEX-PECT-ED.

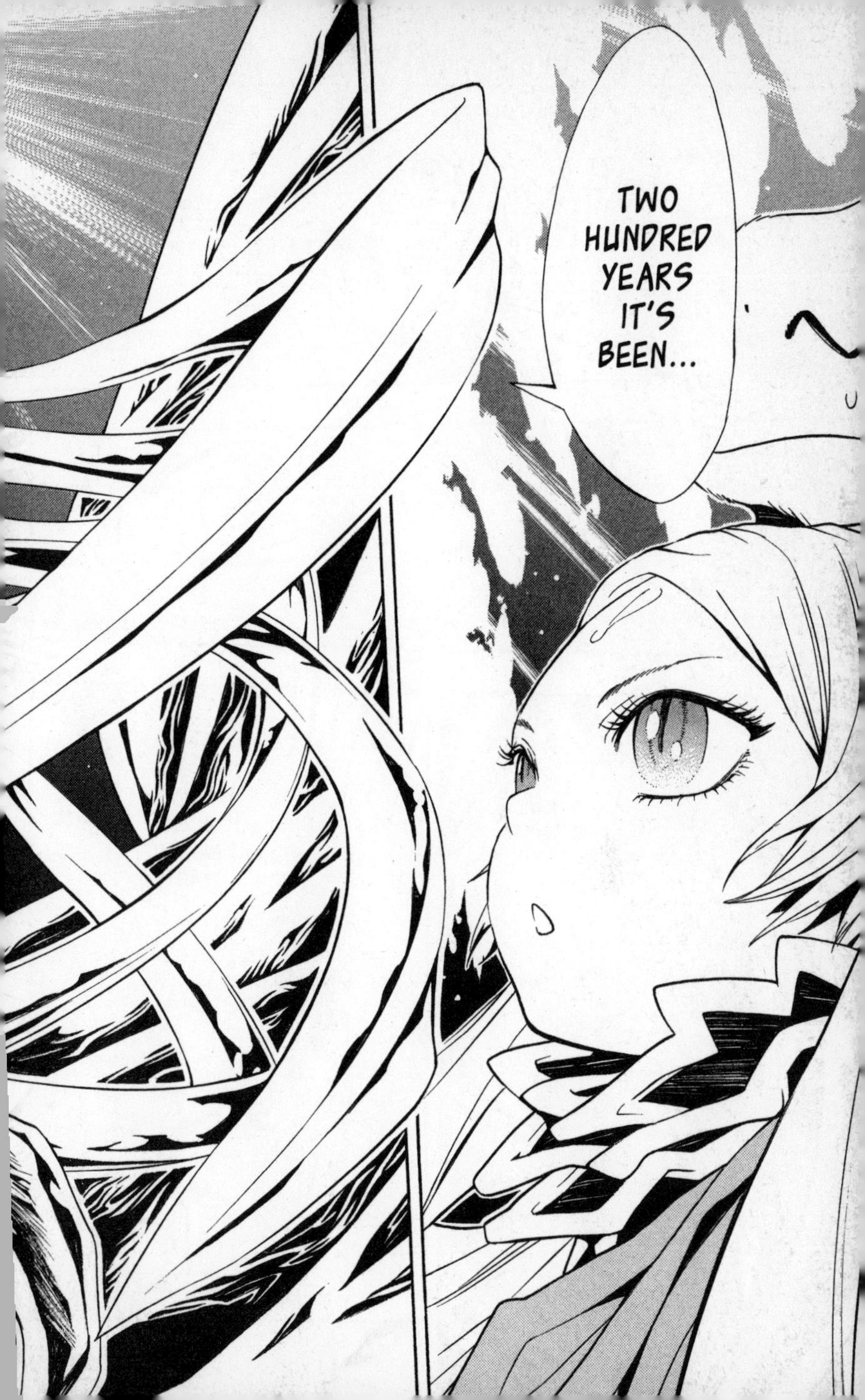
TWO HUNDRED YEARS IT'S BEEN...

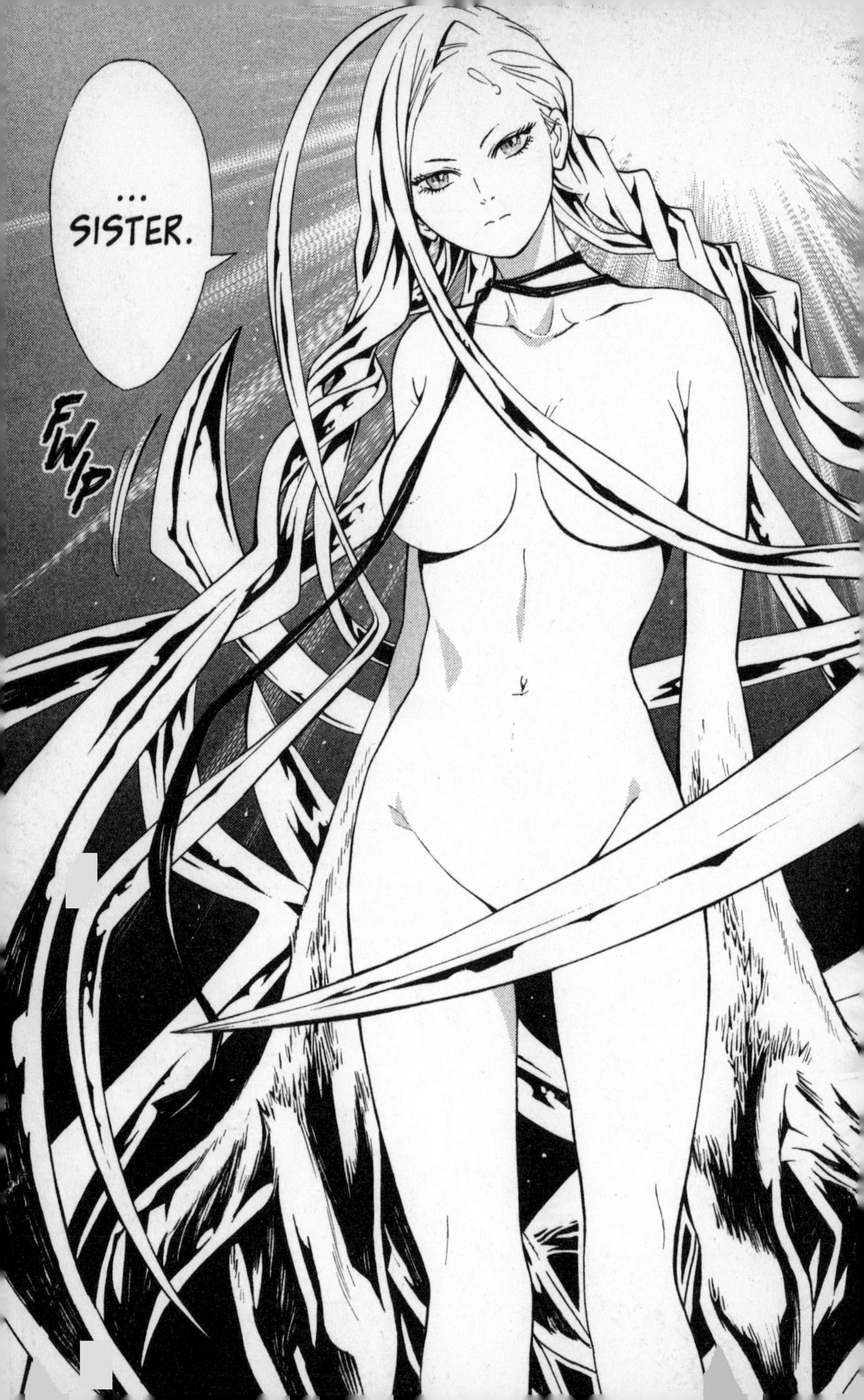
... SISTER.
FWIP

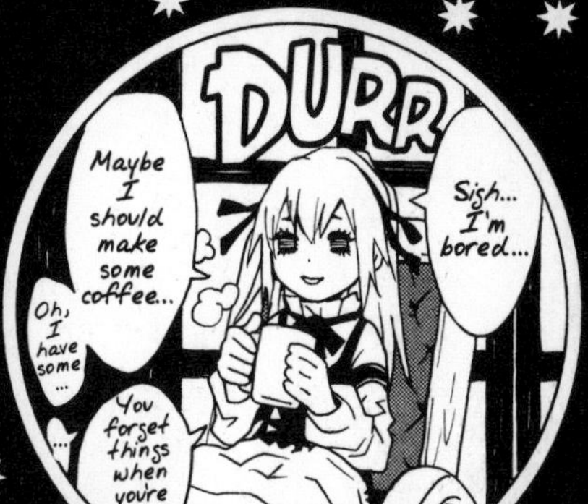
DURR
Sigh... I'm bored...
Maybe I should make some coffee...
Oh, I have some...
You forget things when you're bored.
...

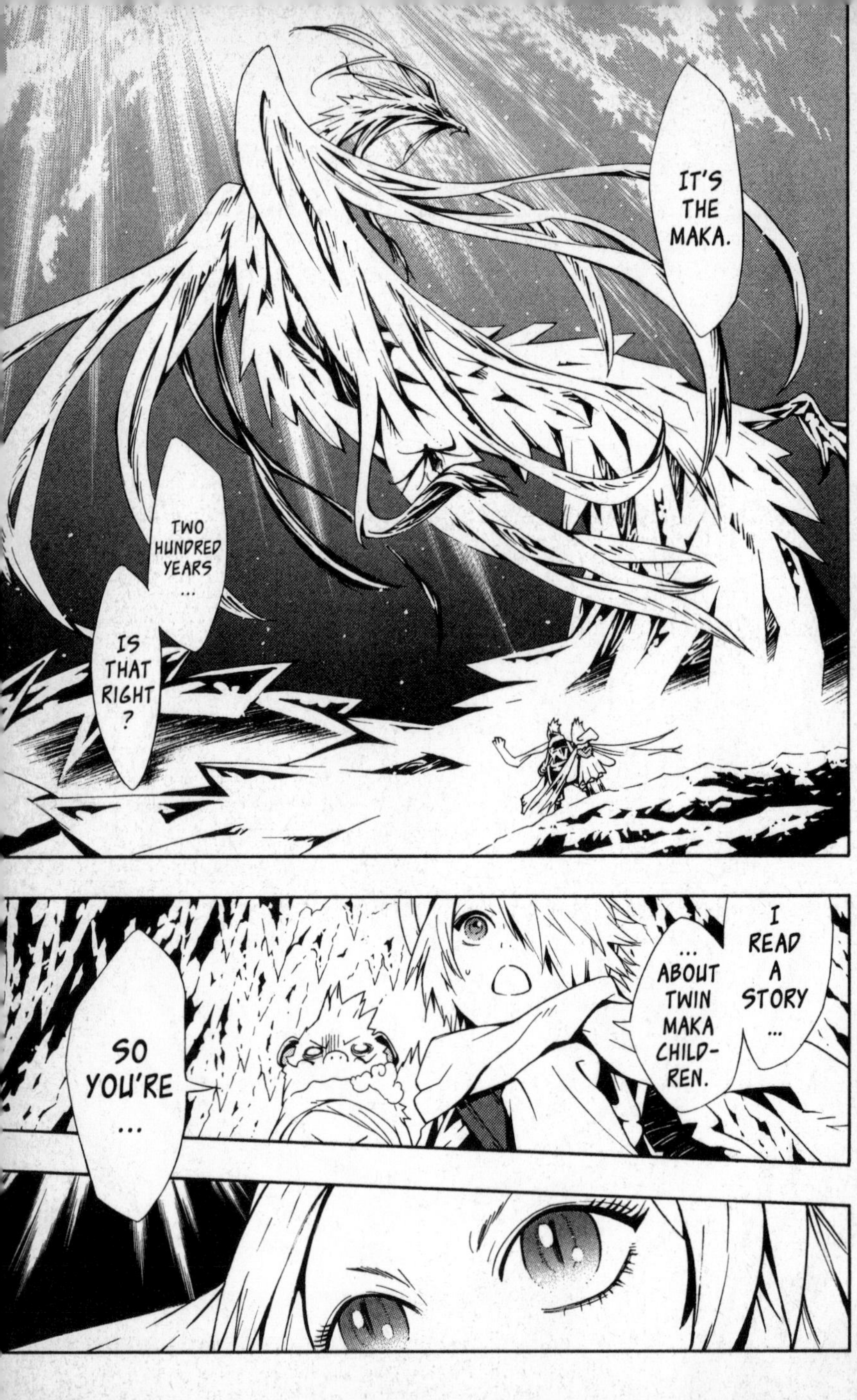
IT'S THE MAKA.
TWO HUNDRED YEARS ...
IS THAT RIGHT?
I READ A STORY ...
... ABOUT TWIN MAKA CHILD-REN.
SO YOU'RE ...

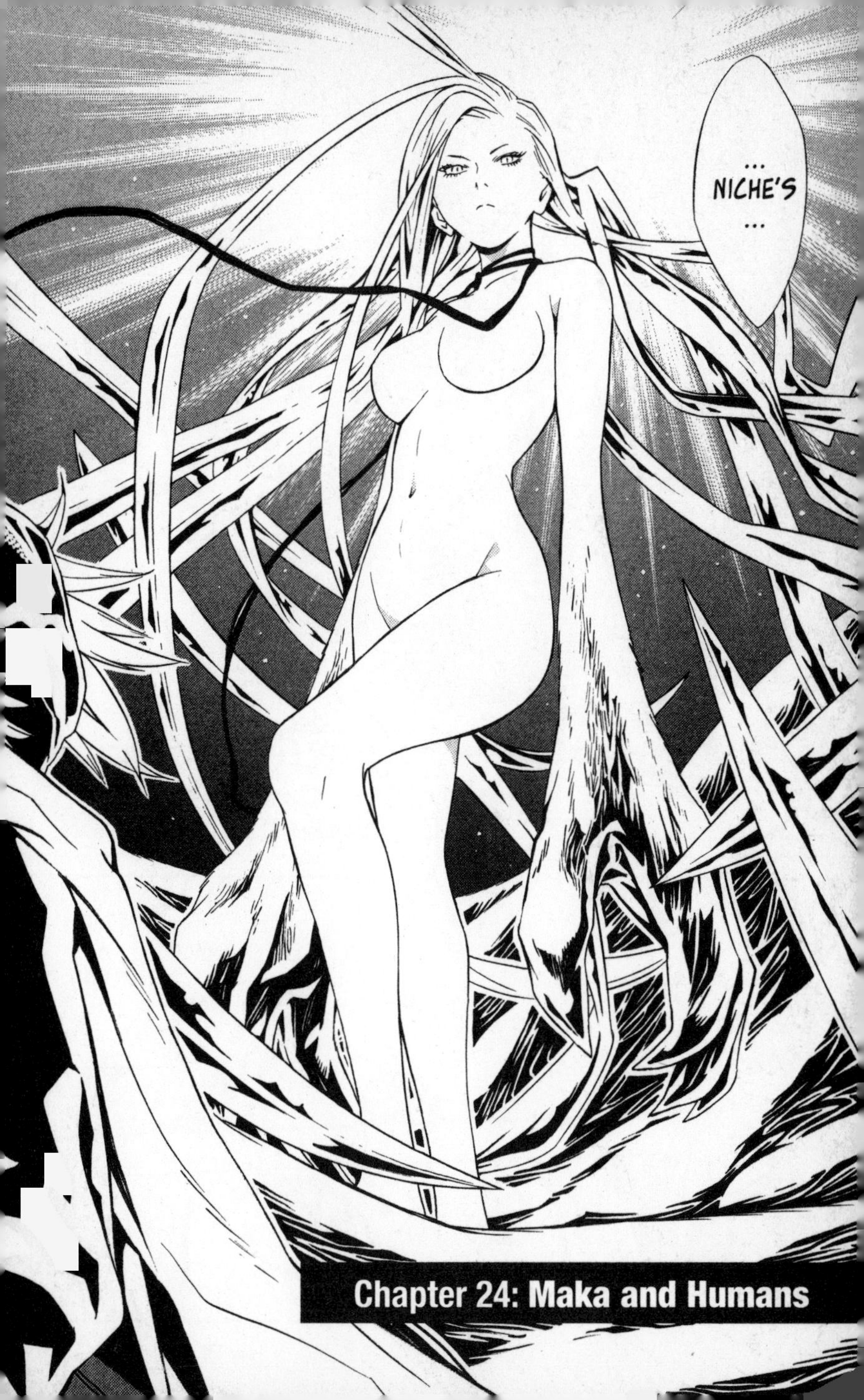
... NICHE'S ...

Chapter 24: Maka and Humans

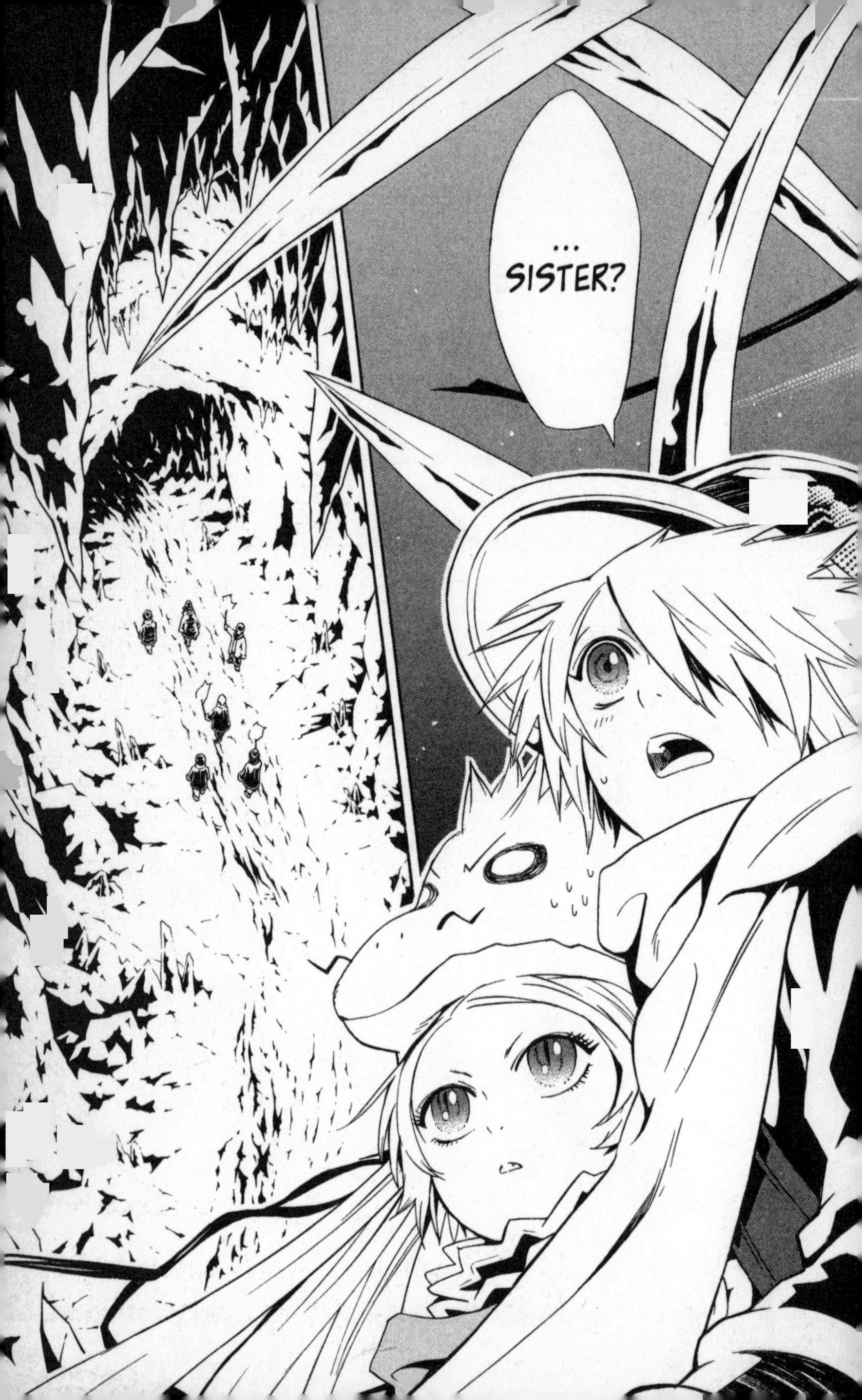
...
SISTER?

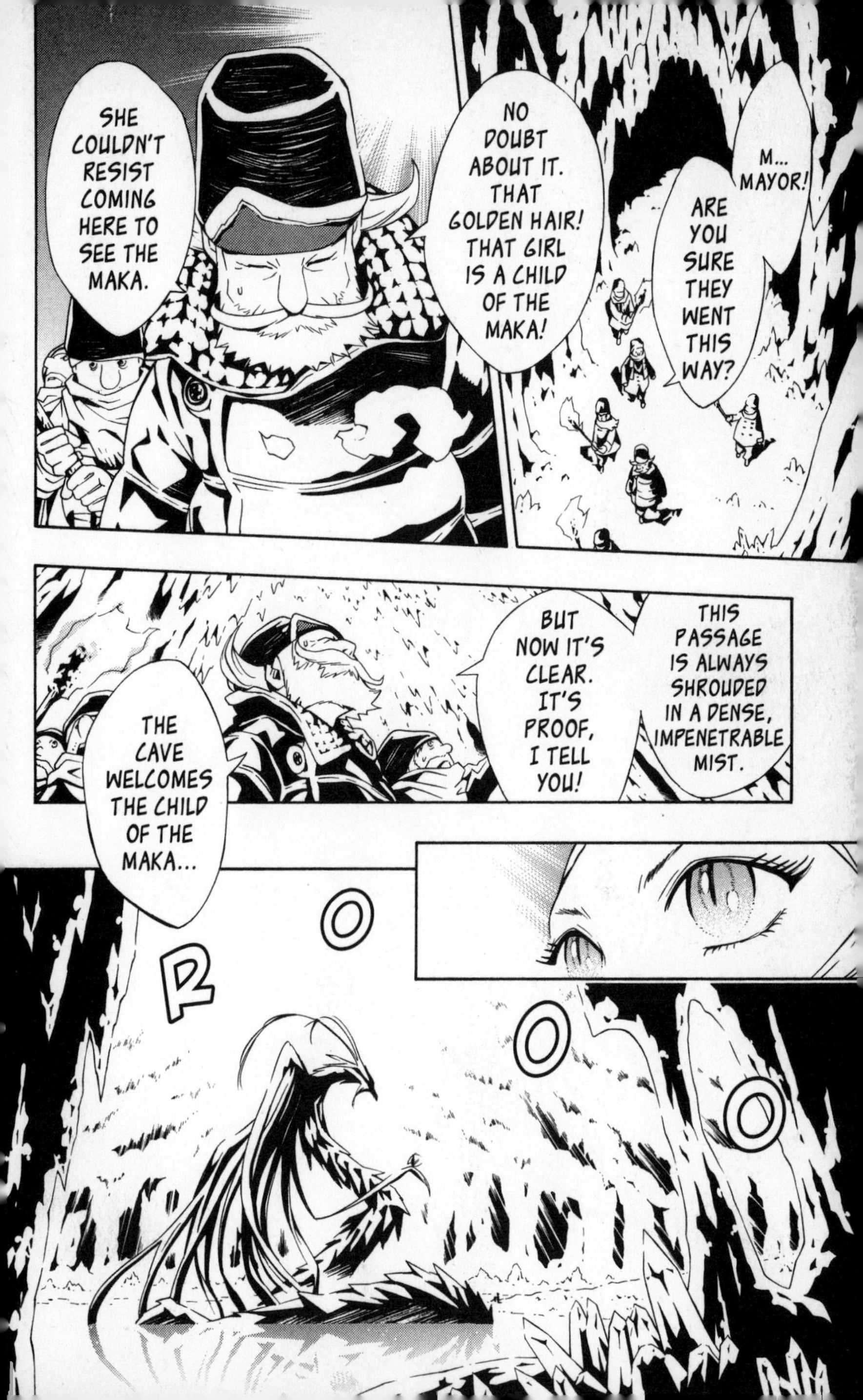
M... MAYOR!
ARE YOU SURE THEY WENT THIS WAY?
NO DOUBT ABOUT IT. THAT GOLDEN HAIR! THAT GIRL IS A CHILD OF THE MAKA!
SHE COULDN'T RESIST COMING HERE TO SEE THE MAKA.
THIS PASSAGE IS ALWAYS SHROUDED IN A DENSE, IMPENETRABLE MIST.
BUT NOW IT'S CLEAR. IT'S PROOF, I TELL YOU!
THE CAVE WELCOMES THE CHILD OF THE MAKA...
ROOO

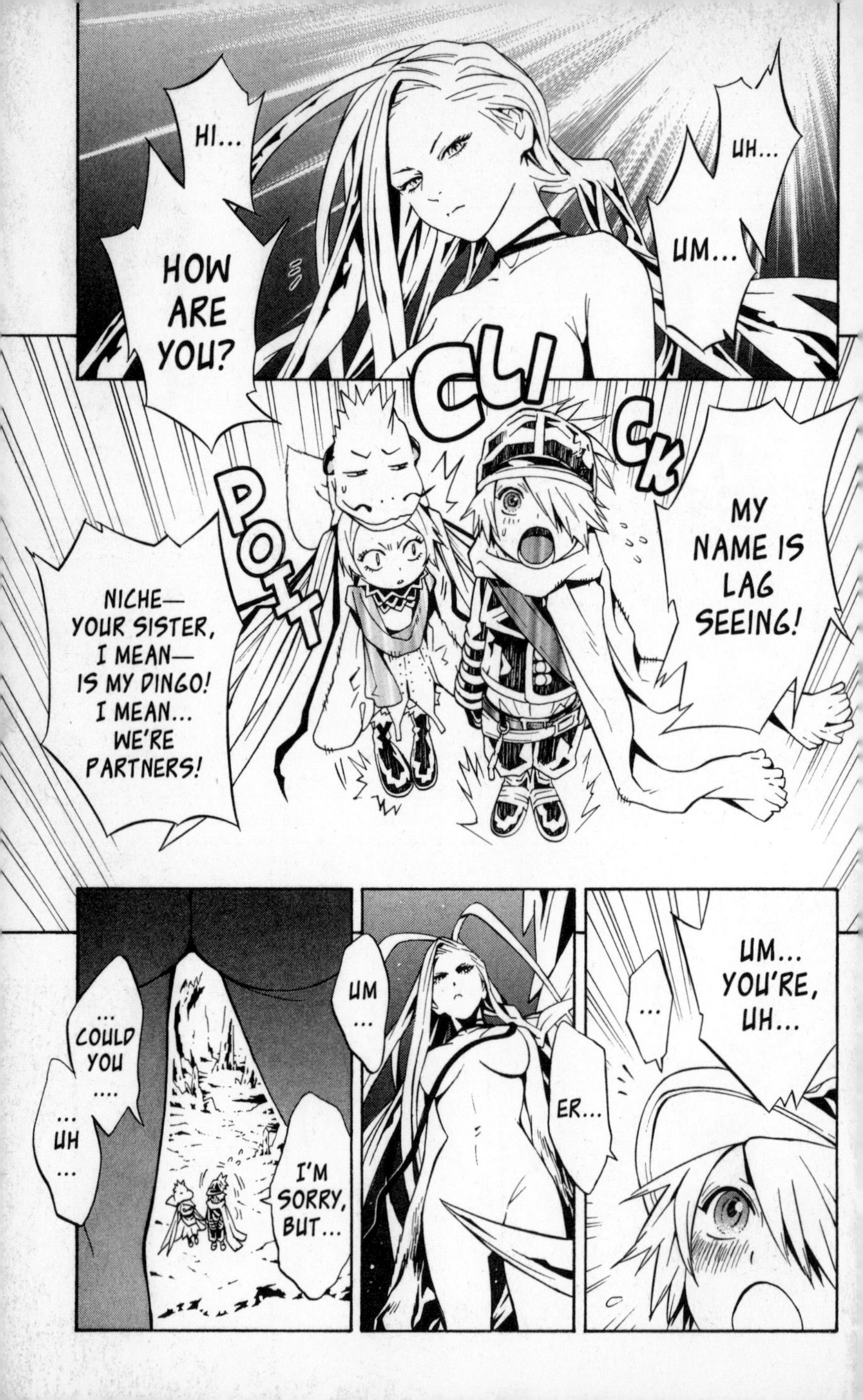
UH...
UM...
HI...
HOW ARE YOU?
CLICK
MY NAME IS LAG SEEING!
POIT
NICHE— YOUR SISTER, I MEAN— IS MY DINGO! I MEAN... WE'RE PARTNERS!
UM... YOU'RE, UH...
...
ER...
UM ...
I'M SORRY, BUT...
... COULD YOU ....
... UH ...

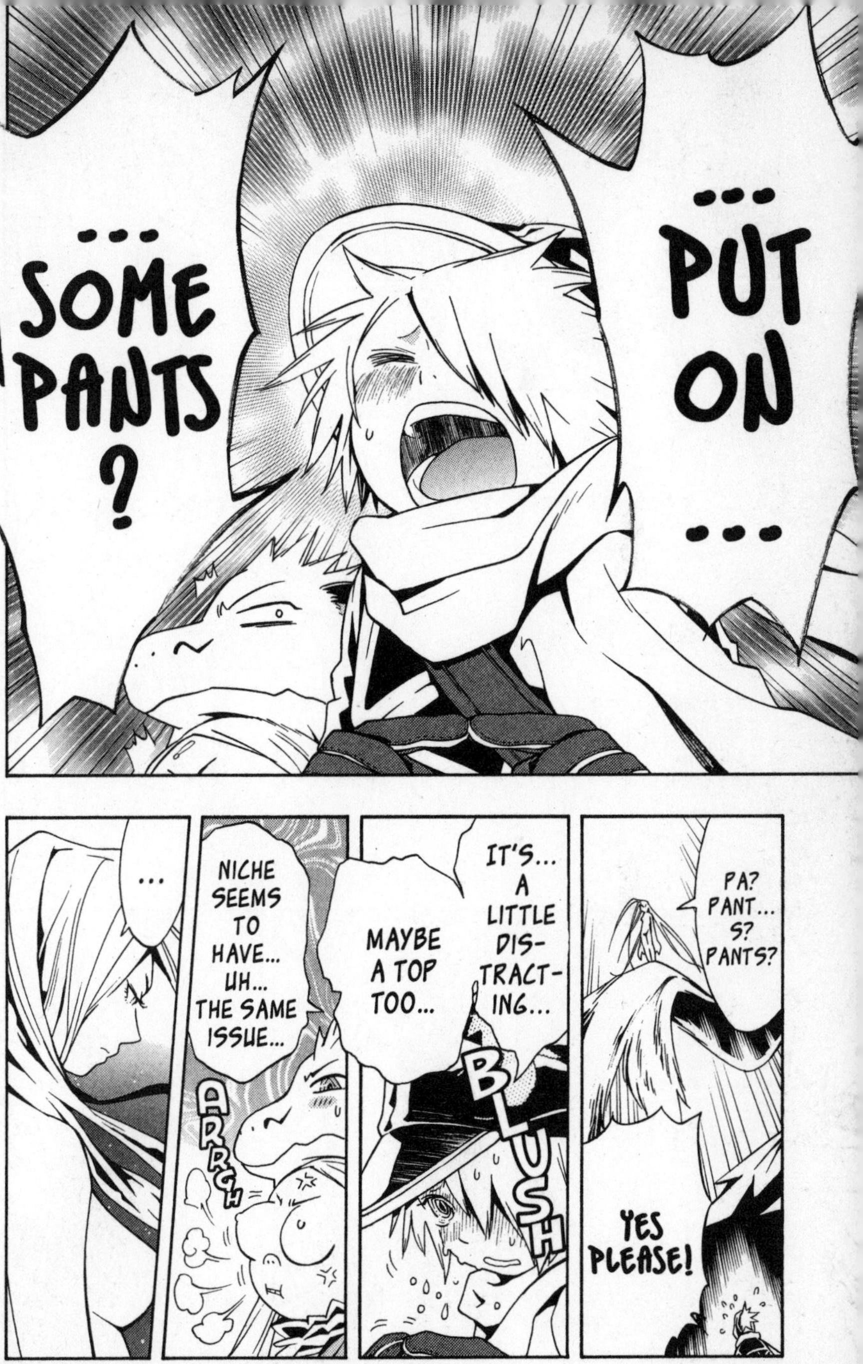
...PUT ON...
...SOME PANTS?
PA? PANT... S? PANTS?
YES PLEASE!
IT'S... A LITTLE DIS-TRACT-ING...
MAYBE A TOP TOO...
BLUSH
NICHE SEEMS TO HAVE... UH... THE SAME ISSUE...
ARRGH
...

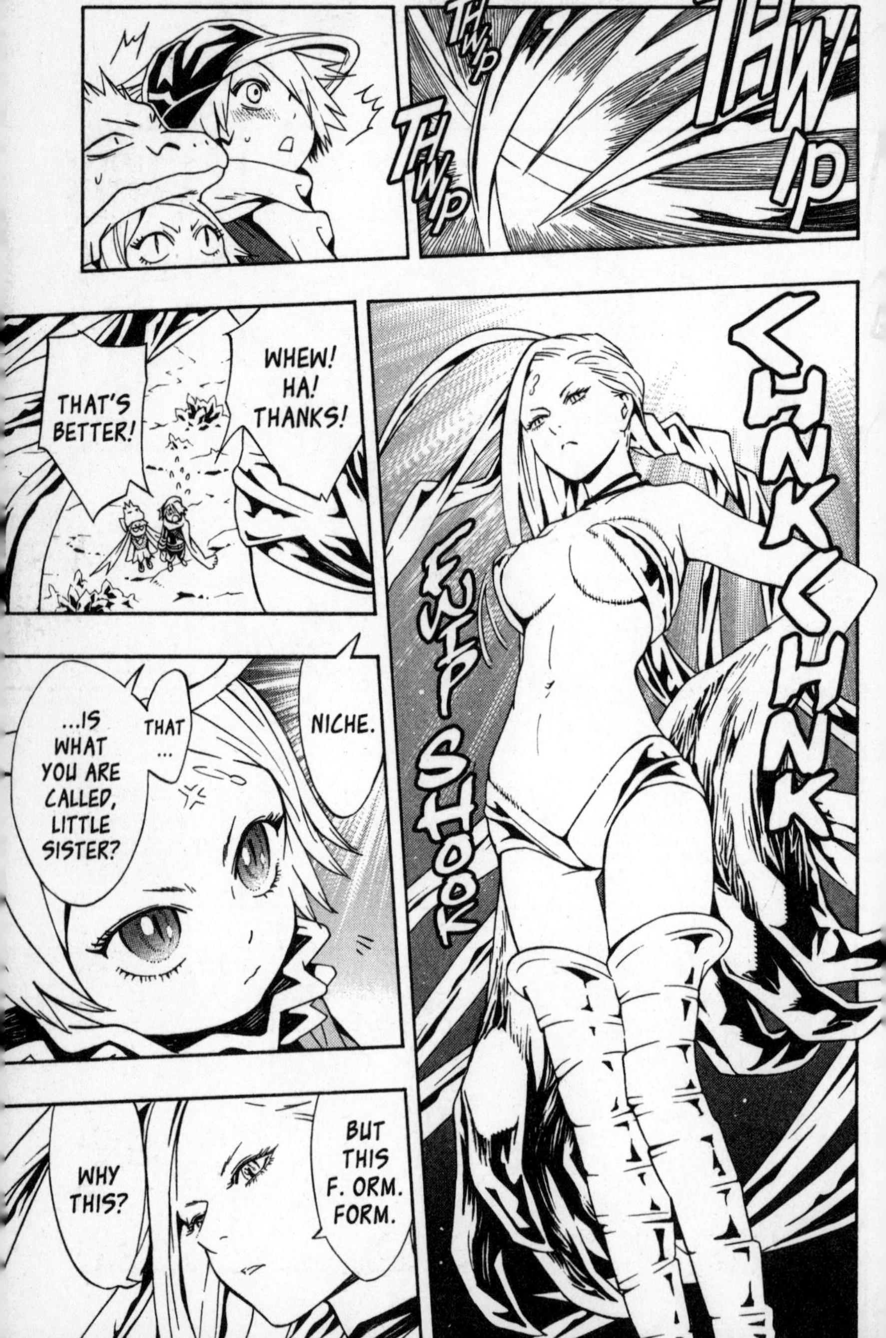
THWIP
THWP
THWP
CLUNK CLUNK
FLIP SHOOK
WHEW! HA! THANKS!
THAT'S BETTER!
NICHE.
THAT ...
...IS WHAT YOU ARE CALLED, LITTLE SISTER?
BUT THIS F. ORM. FORM.
WHY THIS?

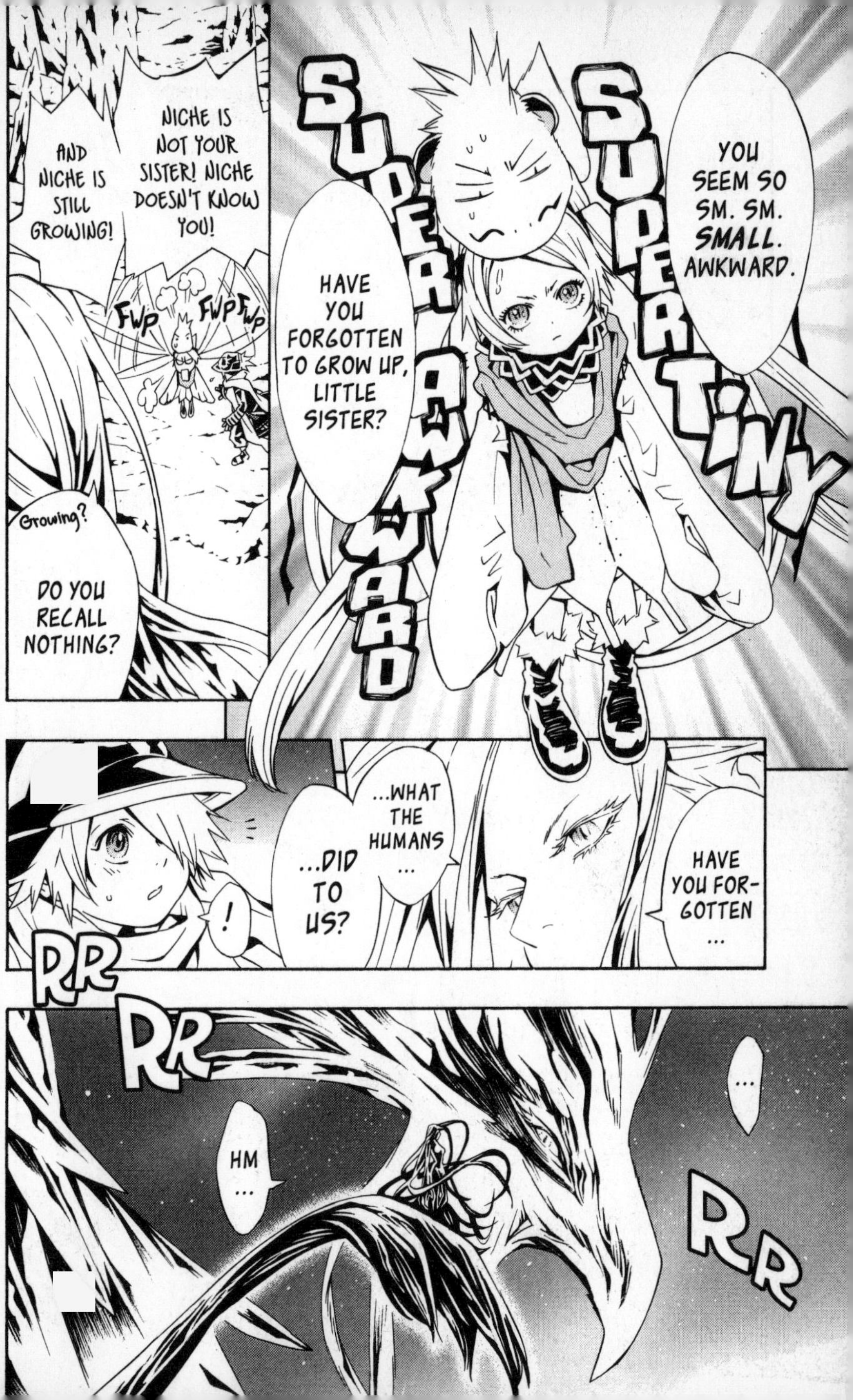

YOU SEEM SO SM. SM. SMALL. AWKWARD.
SUPER TINY
HAVE YOU FORGOTTEN TO GROW UP, LITTLE SISTER?
SUPER AWKWARD
NICHE IS NOT YOUR SISTER! NICHE DOESN'T KNOW YOU!
AND NICHE IS STILL GROWING!
FWP FWP FWP
Growing?
DO YOU RECALL NOTHING?
HAVE YOU FOR-GOTTEN ...
...WHAT THE HUMANS ...
...DID TO US?
!
RR
RR
...
HM ...
RR

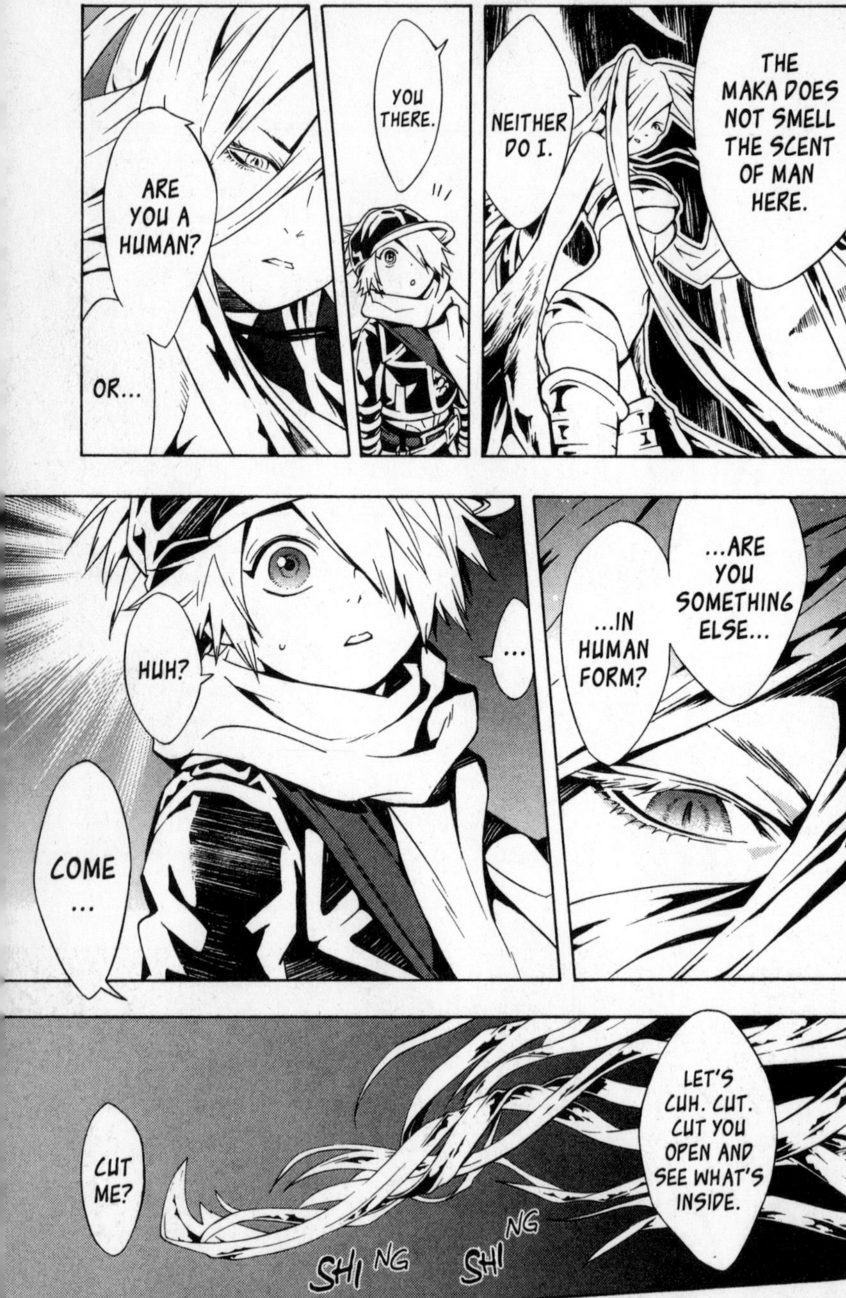
THE MAKA DOES NOT SMELL THE SCENT OF MAN HERE.
NEITHER DO I.
YOU THERE.
ARE YOU A HUMAN?
OR...
...ARE YOU SOMETHING ELSE...
...IN HUMAN FORM?
...
HUH?
COME ...
LET'S CUH. CUT. CUT YOU OPEN AND SEE WHAT'S INSIDE.
SHING
SHING
CUT ME?

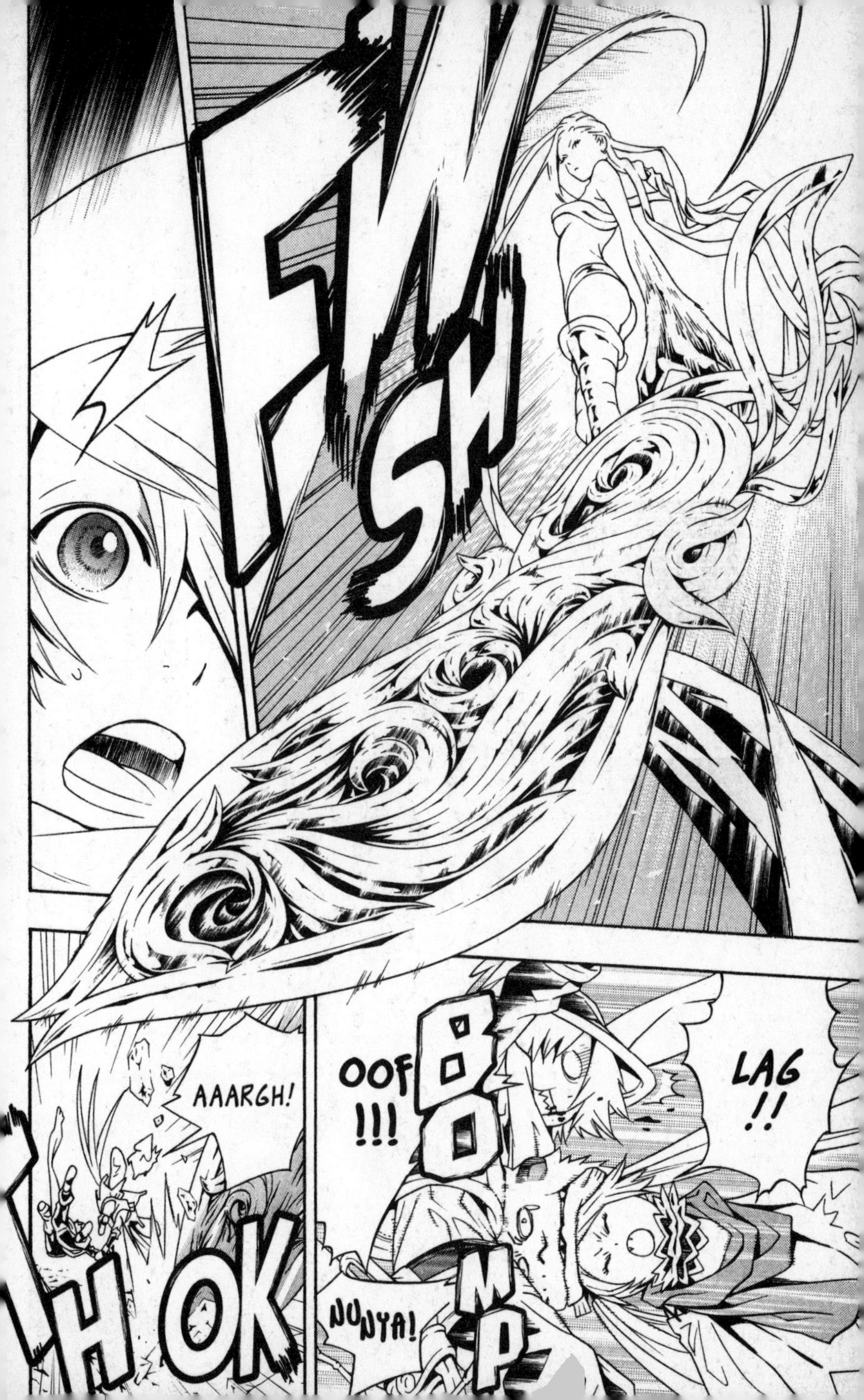
FLASH
LAG !!
BOMP
OOF !!!
NUNYA!
AAARGH!
CHOK

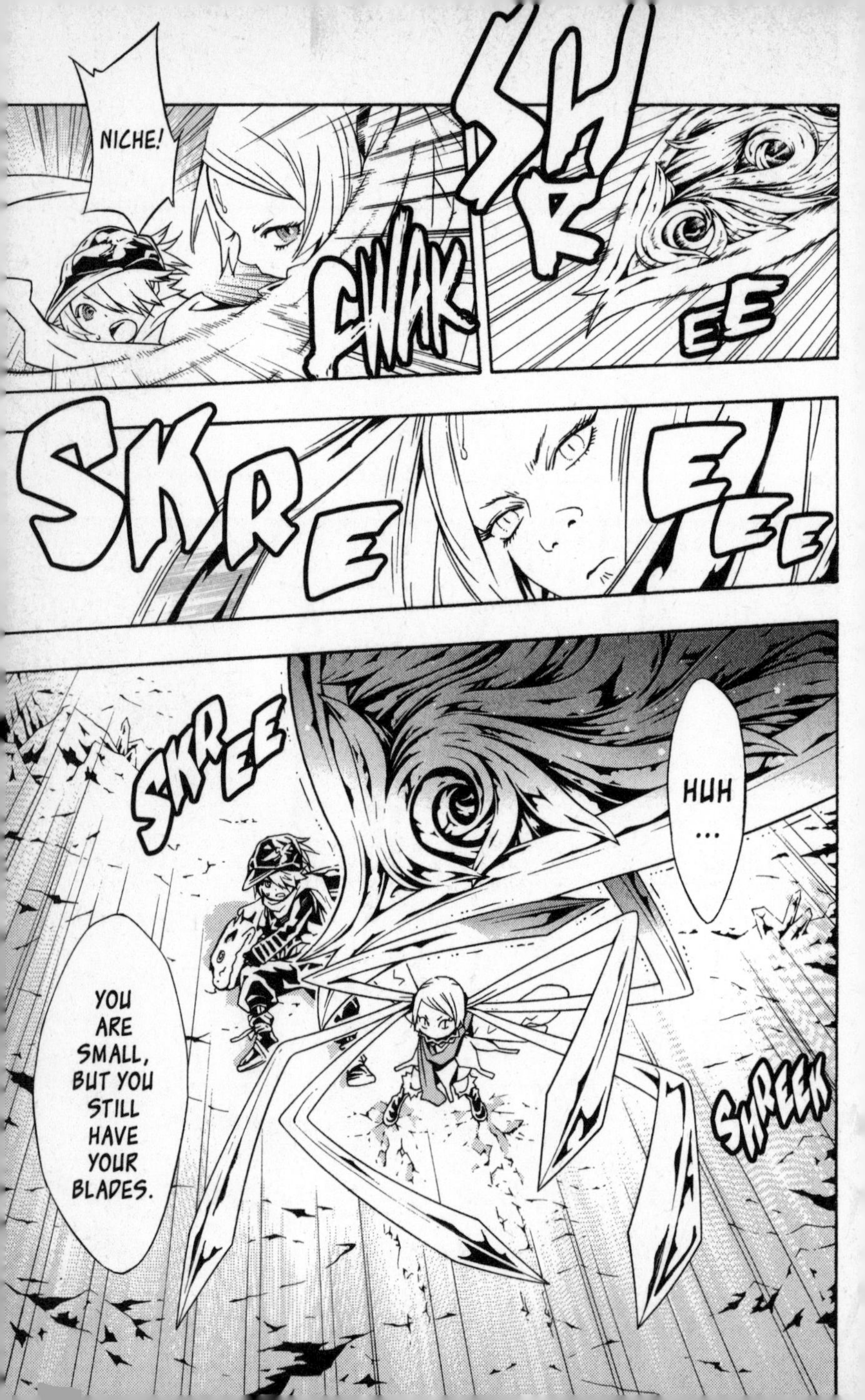
SHREE
CWAK
NICHE!
SKREEEE
HUH...
SKREE
SHREEK
YOU ARE SMALL, BUT YOU STILL HAVE YOUR BLADES.

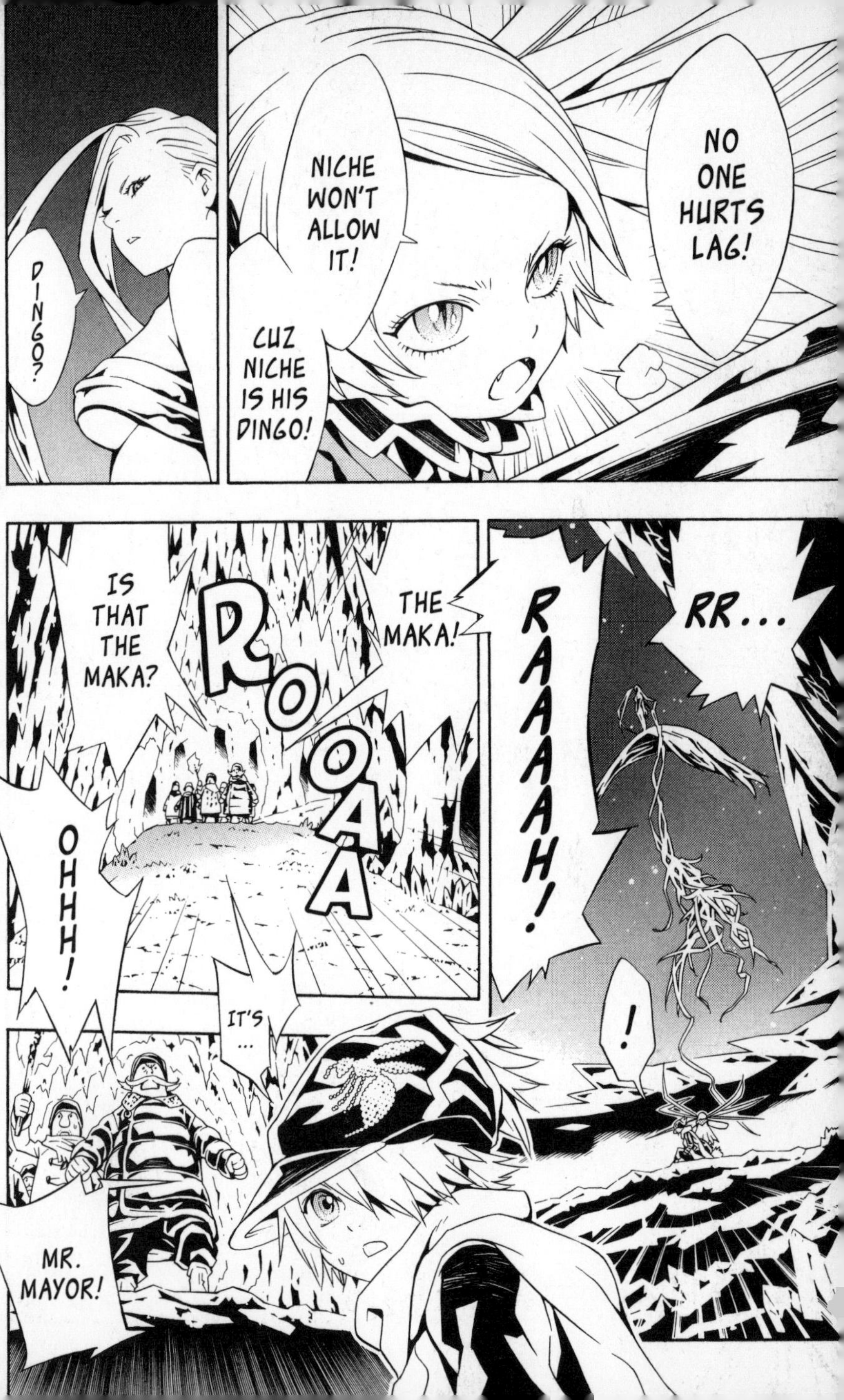
NO ONE HURTS LAG!
NICHE WON'T ALLOW IT!
CUZ NICHE IS HIS DINGO!
DINGO?
RR...
RAAAAAH!
THE MAKA!
ROOAA
IS THAT THE MAKA?
!
IT'S ...
OHHH!
MR. MAYOR!

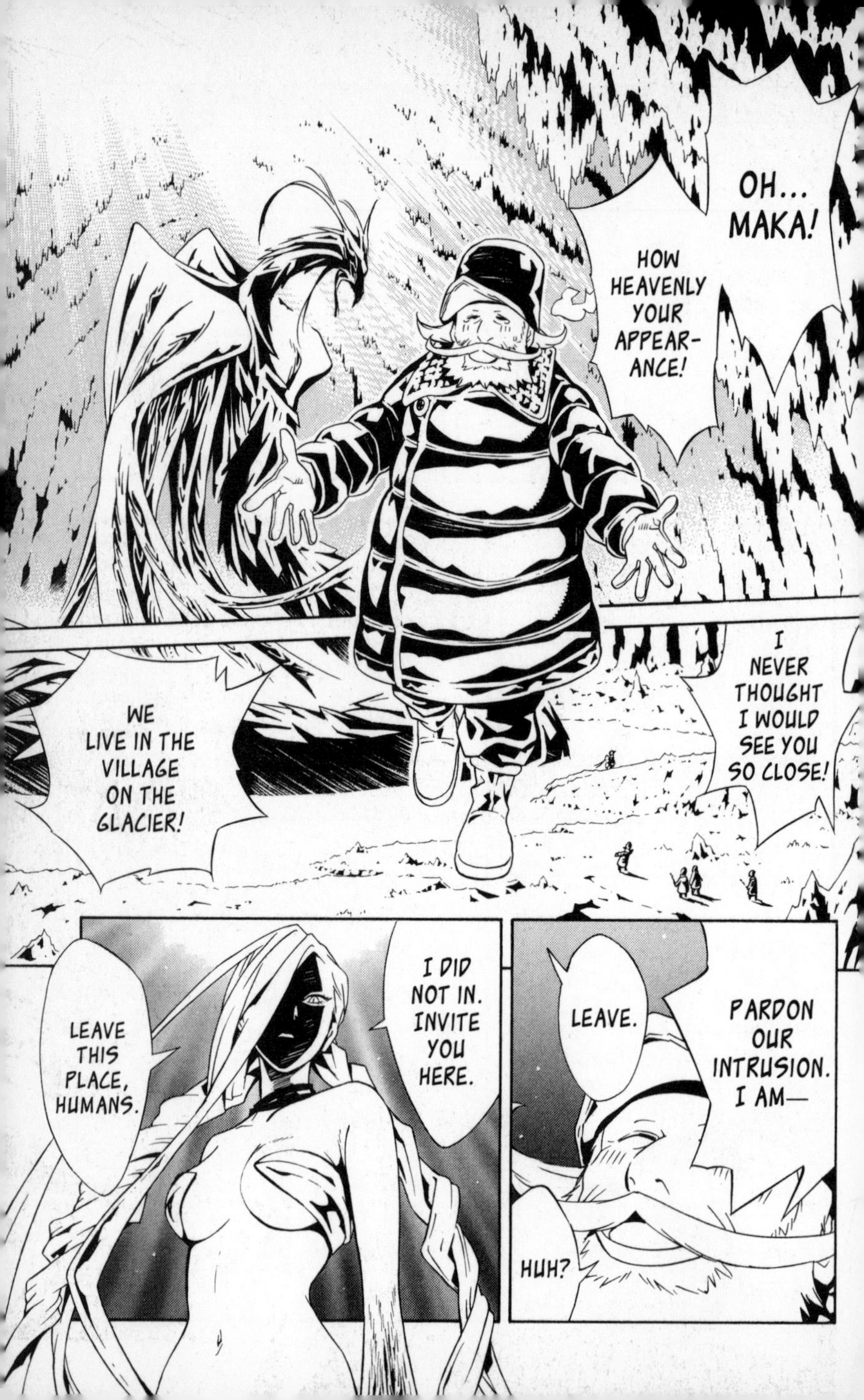
OH... MAKA!
HOW HEAVENLY YOUR APPEAR-ANCE!
I NEVER THOUGHT I WOULD SEE YOU SO CLOSE!
WE LIVE IN THE VILLAGE ON THE GLACIER!
PARDON OUR INTRUSION. I AM—
LEAVE.
HUH?
I DID NOT IN. INVITE YOU HERE.
LEAVE THIS PLACE, HUMANS.

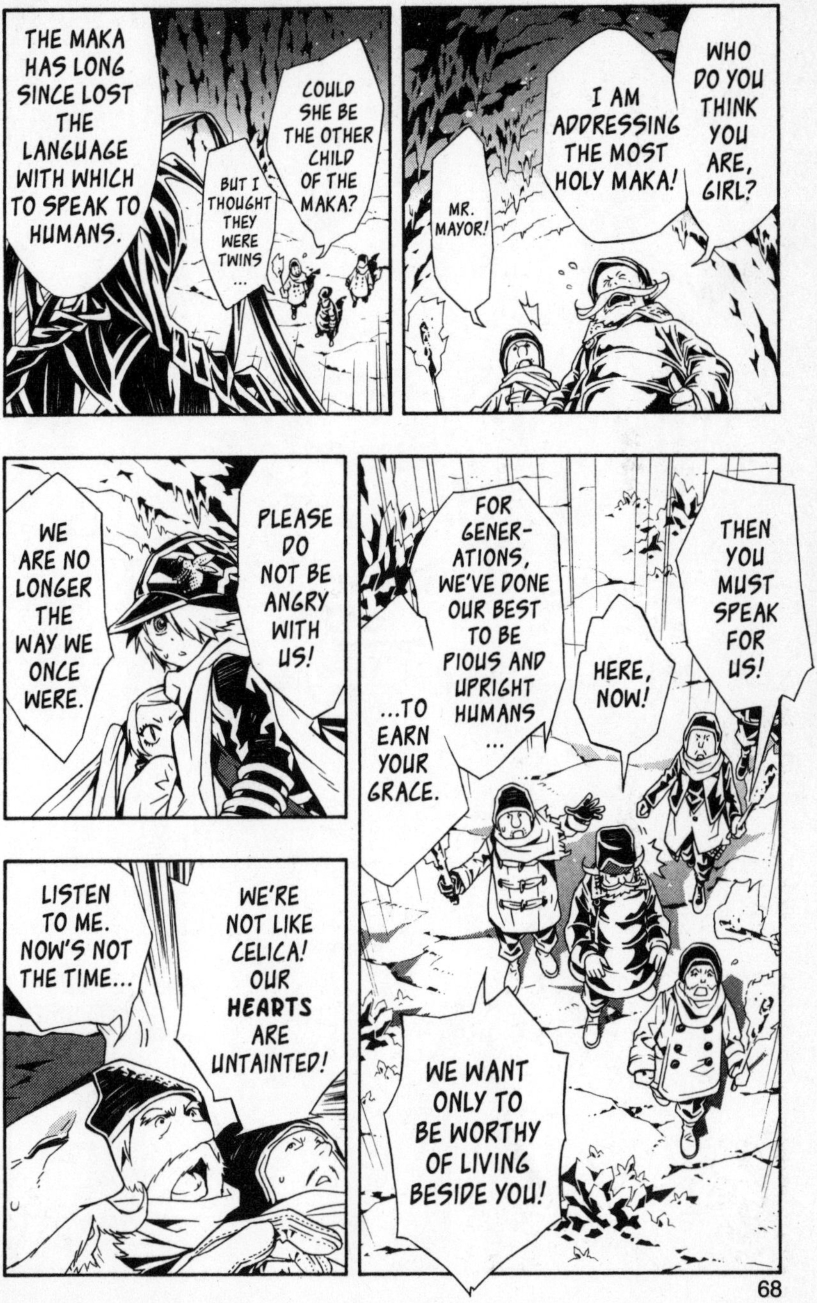
WHO DO YOU THINK YOU ARE, GIRL?
I AM ADDRESSING THE MOST HOLY MAKA!
MR. MAYOR!
COULD SHE BE THE OTHER CHILD OF THE MAKA?
BUT I THOUGHT THEY WERE TWINS...
THE MAKA HAS LONG SINCE LOST THE LANGUAGE WITH WHICH TO SPEAK TO HUMANS.
THEN YOU MUST SPEAK FOR US!
HERE, NOW!
FOR GENERATIONS, WE'VE DONE OUR BEST TO BE PIOUS AND UPRIGHT HUMANS...
...TO EARN YOUR GRACE.
WE WANT ONLY TO BE WORTHY OF LIVING BESIDE YOU!
PLEASE DO NOT BE ANGRY WITH US!
WE ARE NO LONGER THE WAY WE ONCE WERE.
WE'RE NOT LIKE CELICA! OUR **HEARTS** ARE UNTAINTED!
LISTEN TO ME. NOW'S NOT THE TIME...

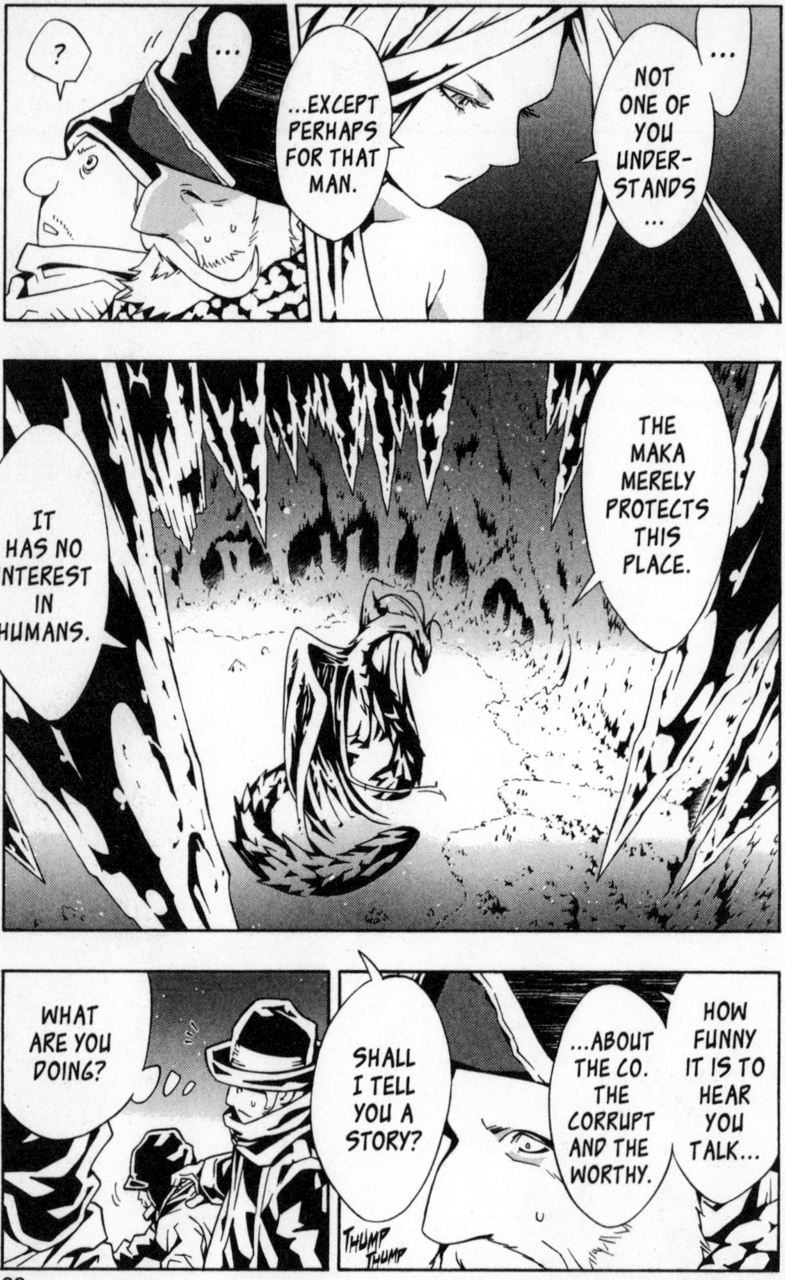
...
NOT ONE OF YOU UNDERSTANDS...
...EXCEPT PERHAPS FOR THAT MAN.
...
?
THE MAKA MERELY PROTECTS THIS PLACE.
IT HAS NO INTEREST IN HUMANS.
HOW FUNNY IT IS TO HEAR YOU TALK...
...ABOUT THE CO. THE CORRUPT AND THE WORTHY.
SHALL I TELL YOU A STORY?
THUMP THUMP
WHAT ARE YOU DOING?

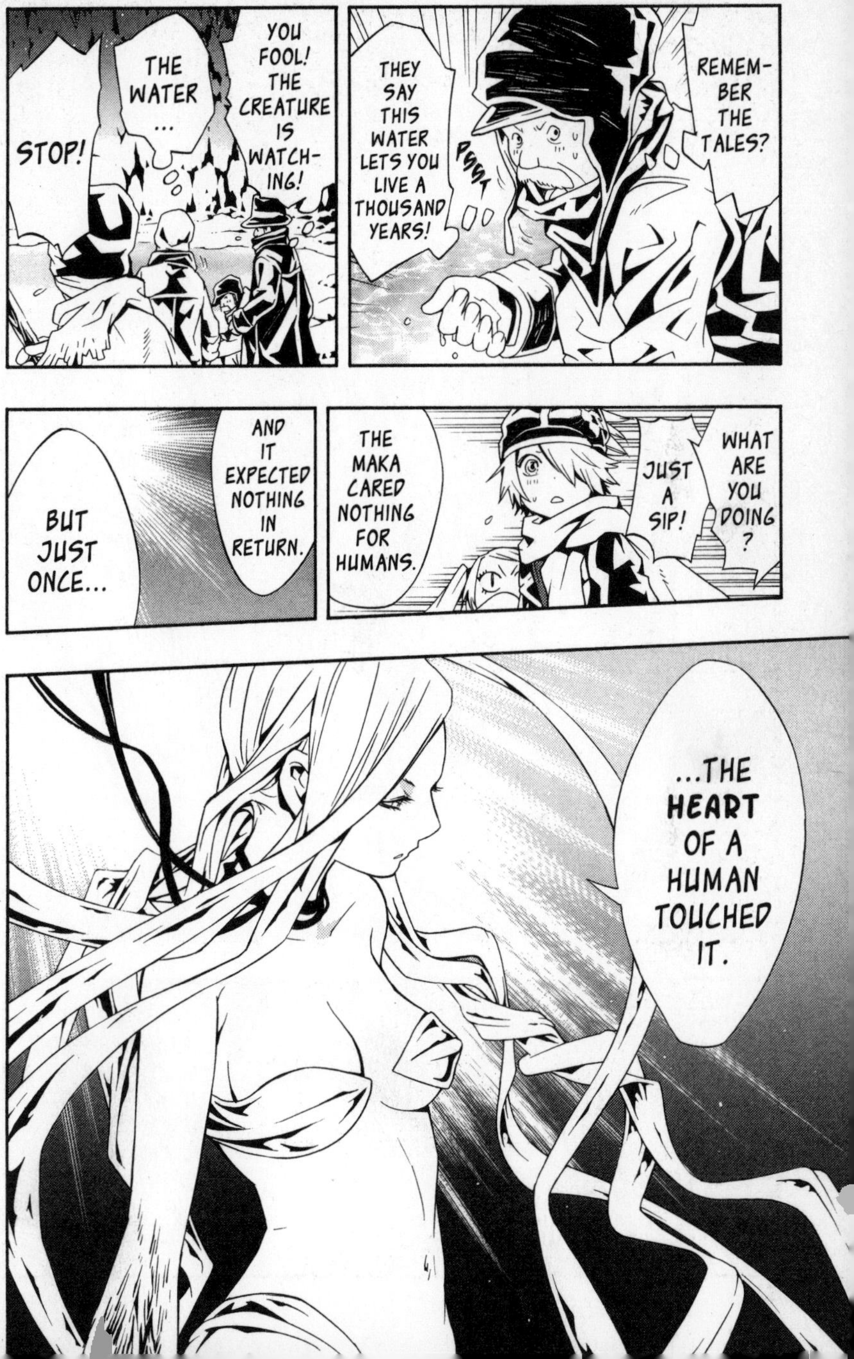
REMEMBER THE TALES?
THEY SAY THIS WATER LETS YOU LIVE A THOUSAND YEARS!
YOU FOOL! THE CREATURE IS WATCHING!
THE WATER...
STOP!
WHAT ARE YOU DOING?
JUST A SIP!
THE MAKA CARED NOTHING FOR HUMANS.
AND IT EXPECTED NOTHING IN RETURN.
BUT JUST ONCE...
...THE **HEART** OF A HUMAN TOUCHED IT.

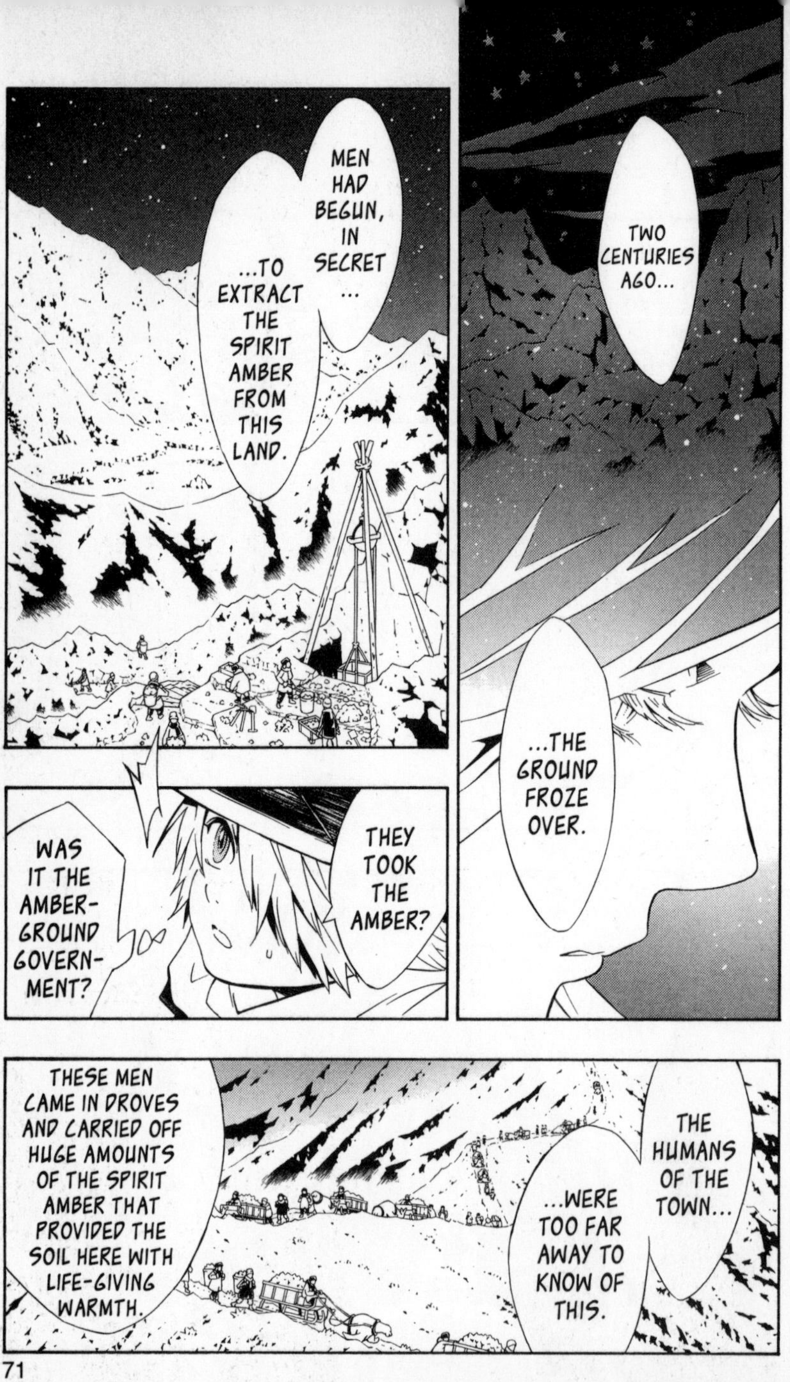

TWO CENTURIES AGO...
...THE GROUND FROZE OVER.
MEN HAD BEGUN, IN SECRET...
...TO EXTRACT THE SPIRIT AMBER FROM THIS LAND.
THEY TOOK THE AMBER?
WAS IT THE AMBER-GROUND GOVERNMENT?
THE HUMANS OF THE TOWN...
...WERE TOO FAR AWAY TO KNOW OF THIS.
THESE MEN CAME IN DROVES AND CARRIED OFF HUGE AMOUNTS OF THE SPIRIT AMBER THAT PROVIDED THE SOIL HERE WITH LIFE-GIVING WARMTH.

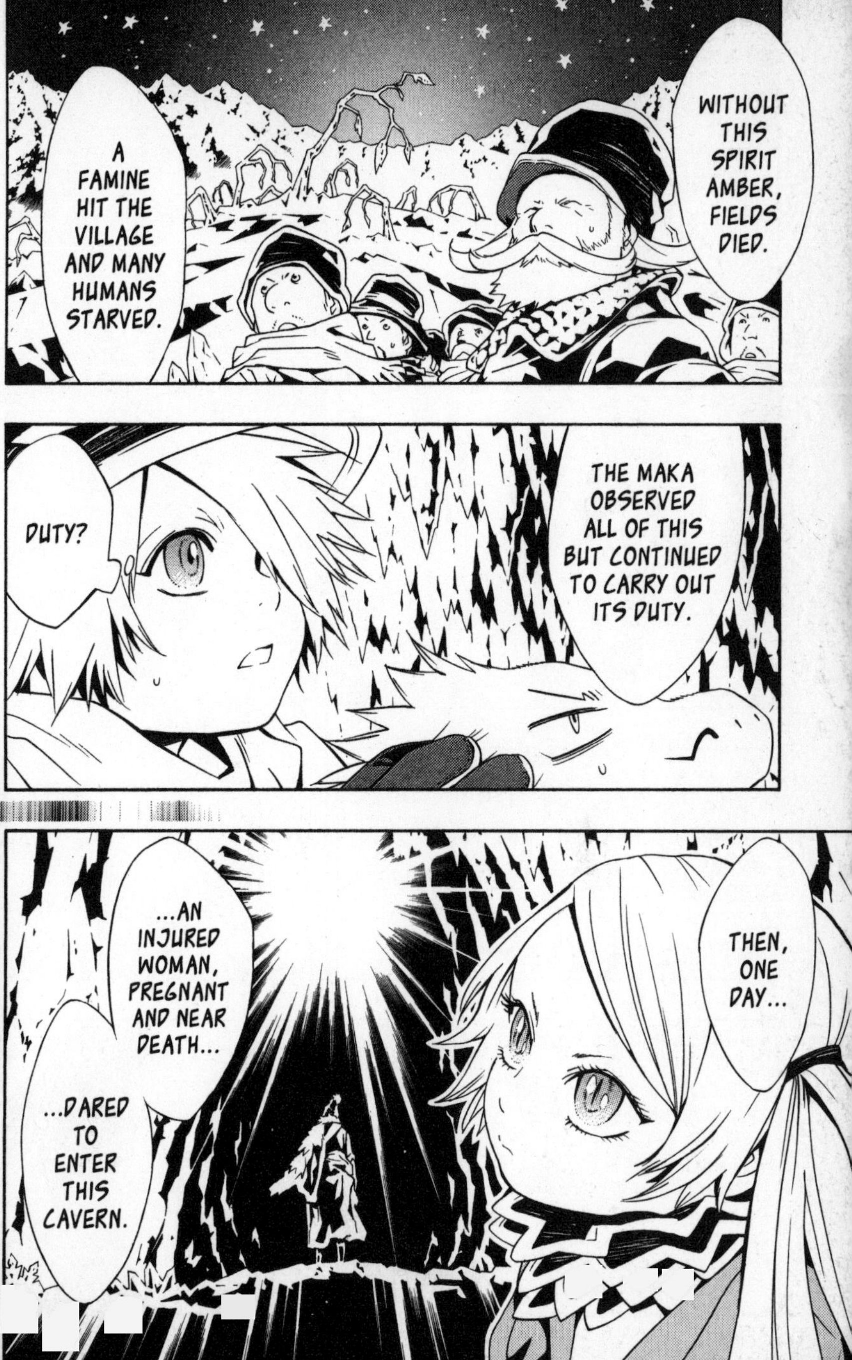
WITHOUT THIS SPIRIT AMBER, FIELDS DIED.
A FAMINE HIT THE VILLAGE AND MANY HUMANS STARVED.
THE MAKA OBSERVED ALL OF THIS BUT CONTINUED TO CARRY OUT ITS DUTY.
DUTY?
THEN, ONE DAY...
...AN INJURED WOMAN, PREGNANT AND NEAR DEATH...
...DARED TO ENTER THIS CAVERN.

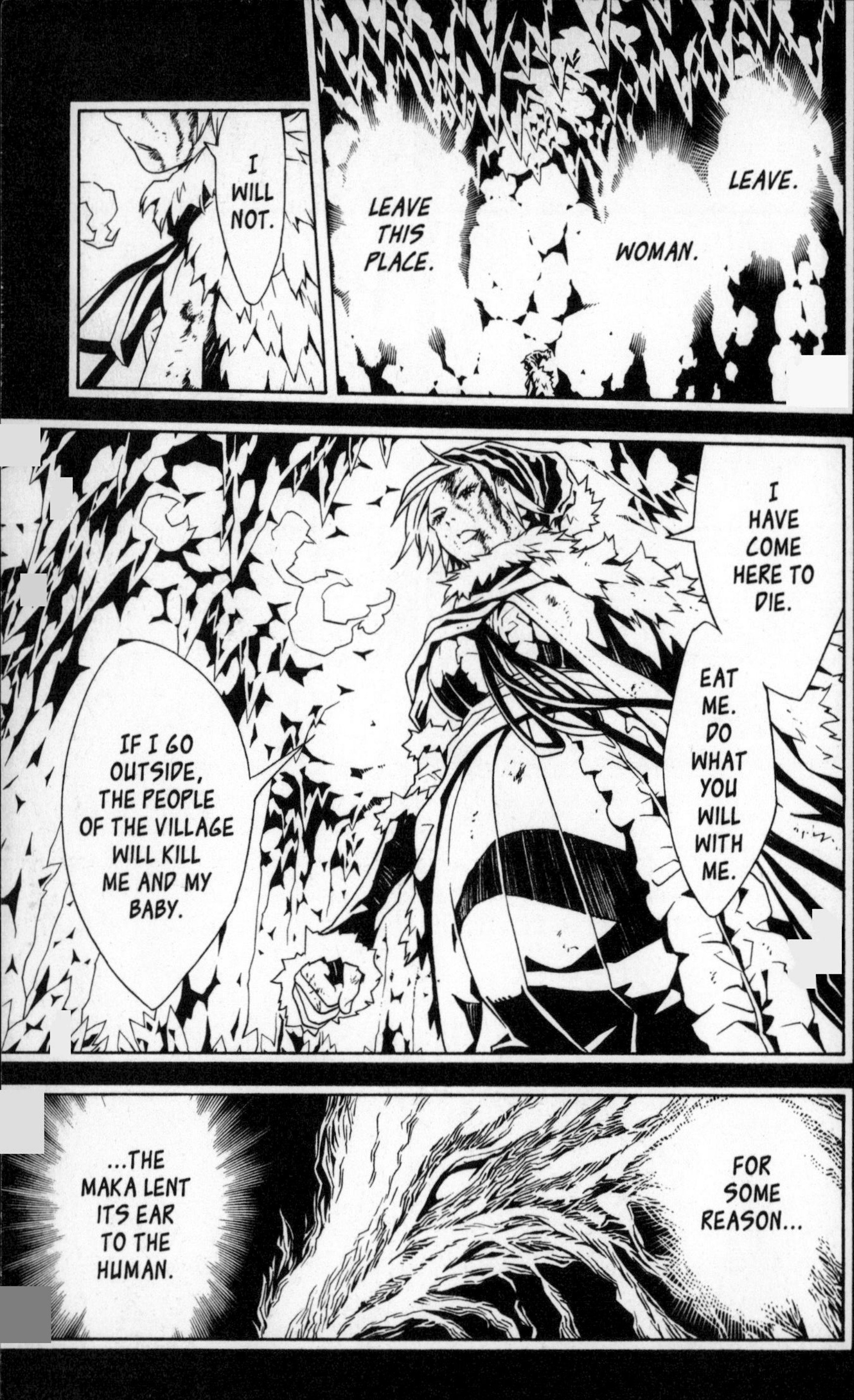
LEAVE.
WOMAN.
LEAVE THIS PLACE.
I WILL NOT.
I HAVE COME HERE TO DIE.
EAT ME. DO WHAT YOU WILL WITH ME.
IF I GO OUTSIDE, THE PEOPLE OF THE VILLAGE WILL KILL ME AND MY BABY.
FOR SOME REASON...
...THE MAKA LENT ITS EAR TO THE HUMAN.

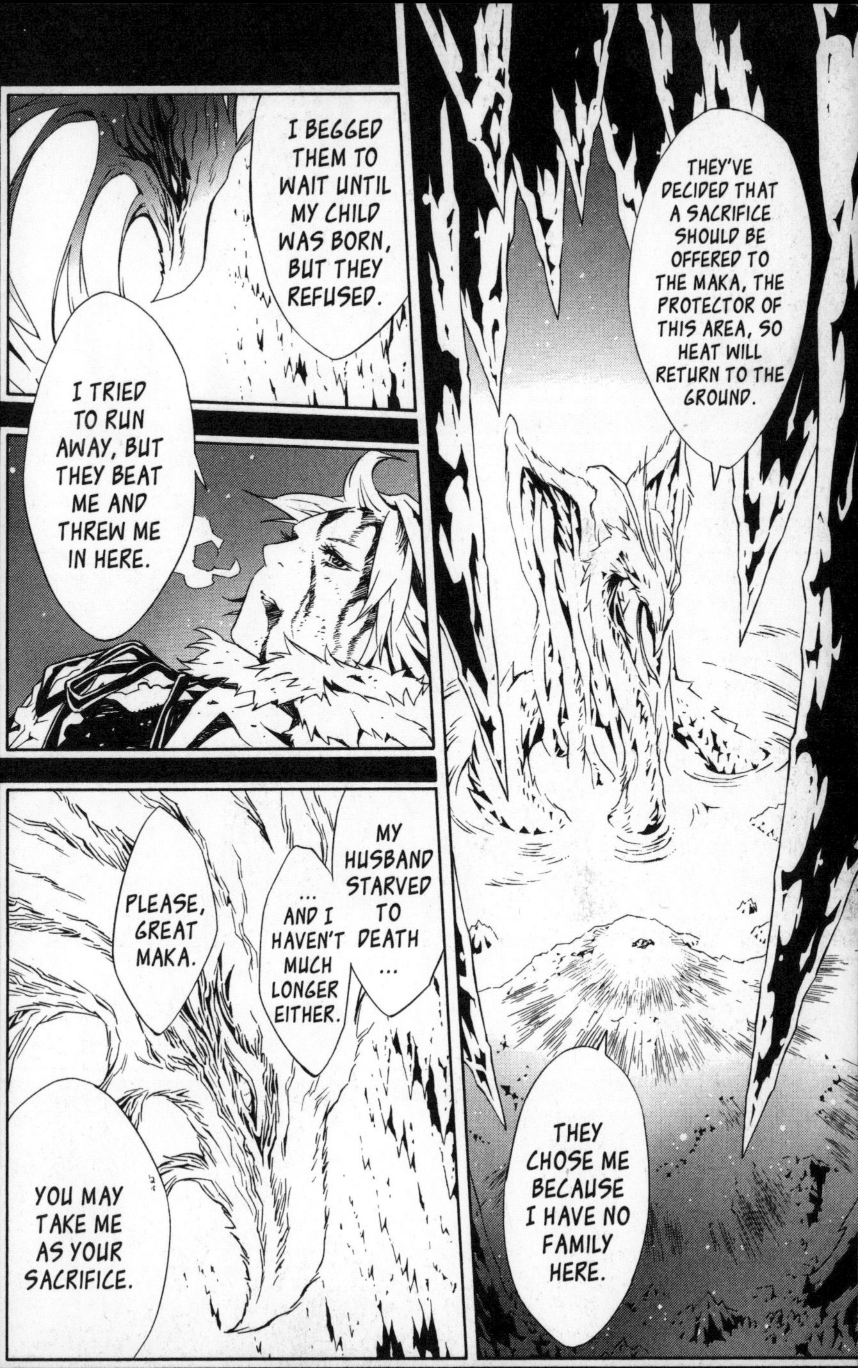
THEY'VE DECIDED THAT A SACRIFICE SHOULD BE OFFERED TO THE MAKA, THE PROTECTOR OF THIS AREA, SO HEAT WILL RETURN TO THE GROUND.
THEY CHOSE ME BECAUSE I HAVE NO FAMILY HERE.
I BEGGED THEM TO WAIT UNTIL MY CHILD WAS BORN, BUT THEY REFUSED.
I TRIED TO RUN AWAY, BUT THEY BEAT ME AND THREW ME IN HERE.
MY HUSBAND STARVED TO DEATH ...
... AND I HAVEN'T MUCH LONGER EITHER.
PLEASE, GREAT MAKA.
YOU MAY TAKE ME AS YOUR SACRIFICE.

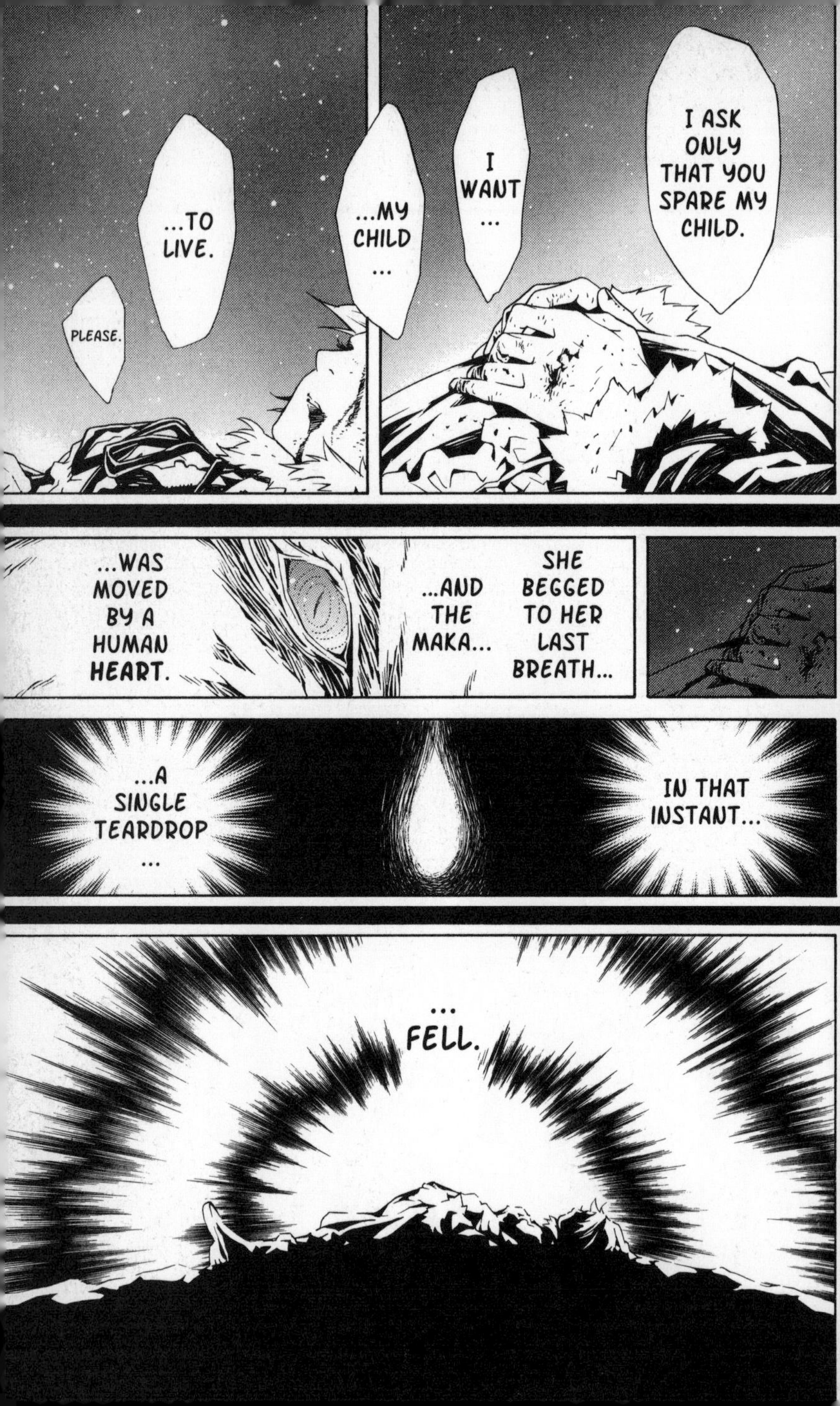
I ASK ONLY THAT YOU SPARE MY CHILD.
I WANT ...
...MY CHILD ...
...TO LIVE.
PLEASE.
SHE BEGGED TO HER LAST BREATH...
...AND THE MAKA...
...WAS MOVED BY A HUMAN HEART.
IN THAT INSTANT...
...A SINGLE TEARDROP ...
... FELL.

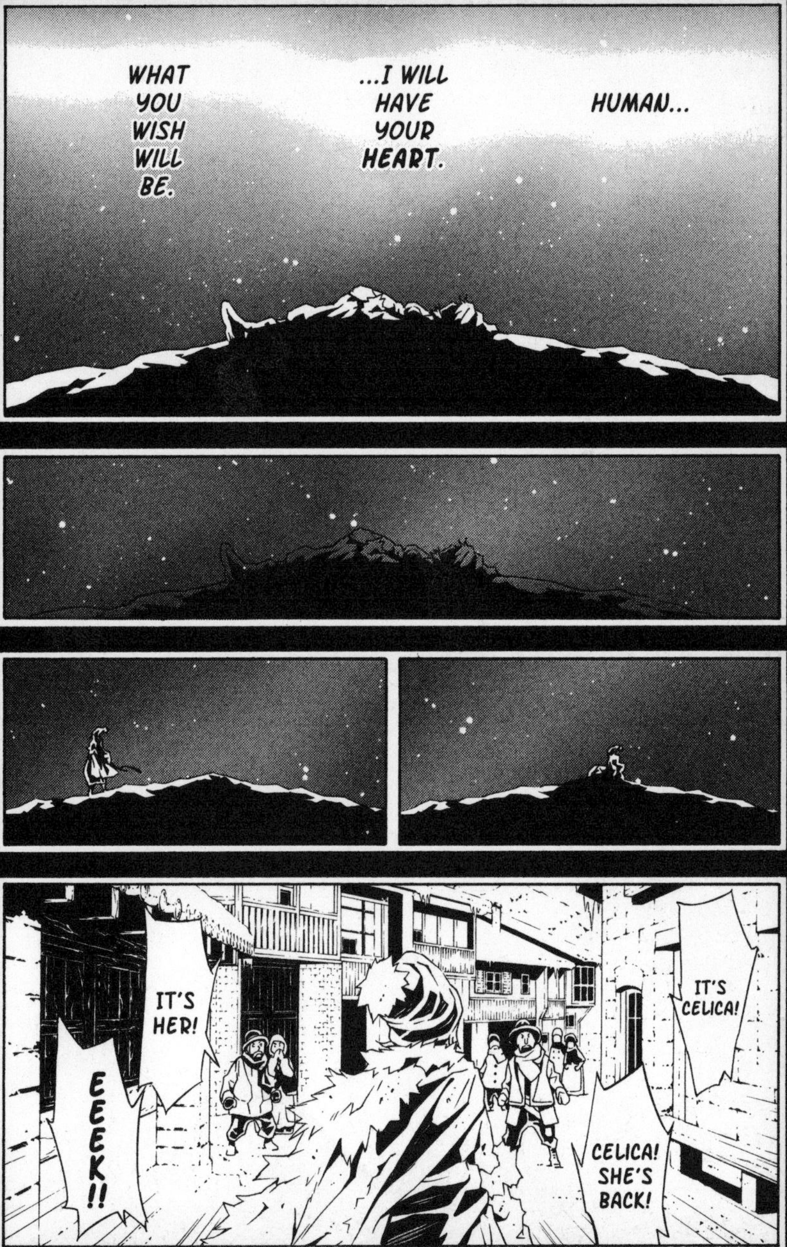
HUMAN...
...I WILL HAVE YOUR HEART.
WHAT YOU WISH WILL BE.
IT'S CELICA!
CELICA! SHE'S BACK!
IT'S HER!
EEEK!!

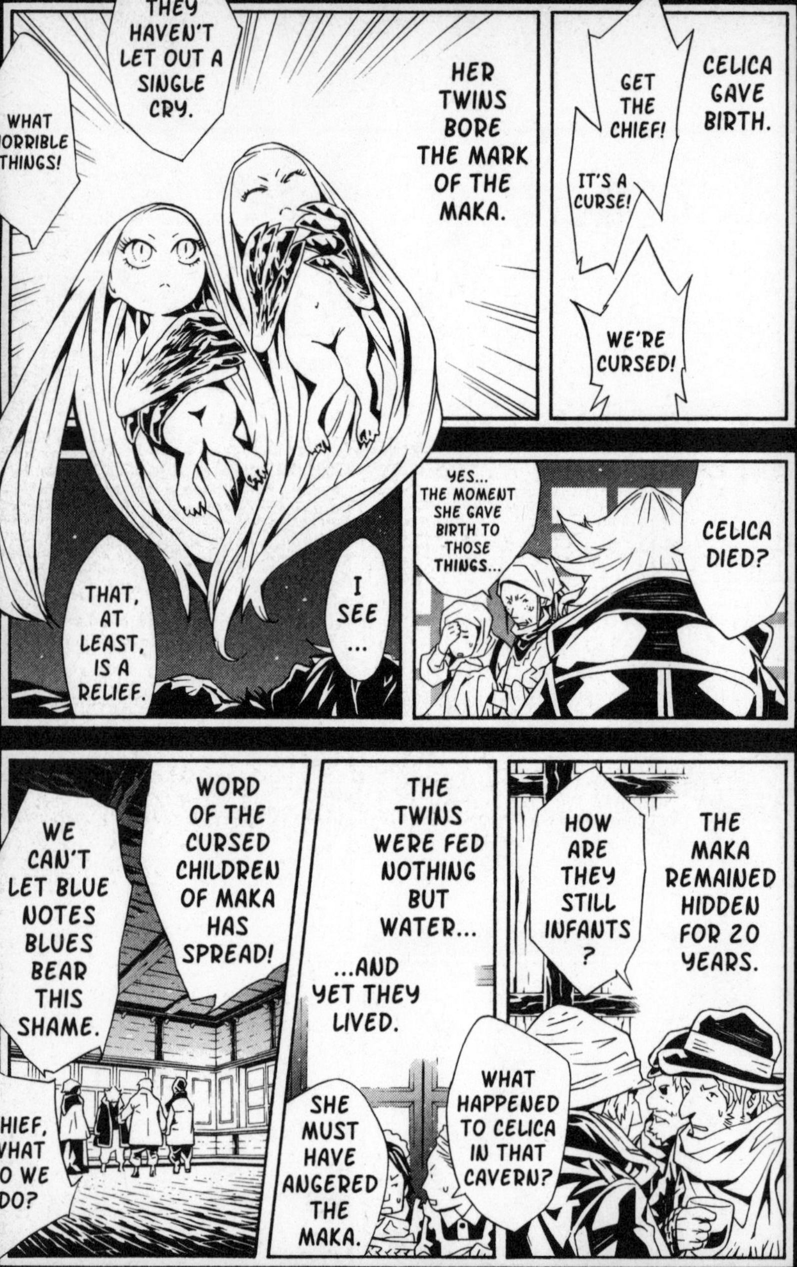
CELICA GAVE BIRTH.
GET THE CHIEF!
IT'S A CURSE!
WE'RE CURSED!
HER TWINS BORE THE MARK OF THE MAKA.
THEY HAVEN'T LET OUT A SINGLE CRY.
WHAT HORRIBLE THINGS!
CELICA DIED?
YES... THE MOMENT SHE GAVE BIRTH TO THOSE THINGS...
I SEE...
THAT, AT LEAST, IS A RELIEF.
THE MAKA REMAINED HIDDEN FOR 20 YEARS.
HOW ARE THEY STILL INFANTS?
WHAT HAPPENED TO CELICA IN THAT CAVERN?
SHE MUST HAVE ANGERED THE MAKA.
THE TWINS WERE FED NOTHING BUT WATER...
...AND YET THEY LIVED.
WORD OF THE CURSED CHILDREN OF MAKA HAS SPREAD!
WE CAN'T LET BLUE NOTES BLUES BEAR THIS SHAME.
CHIEF, WHAT DO WE DO?

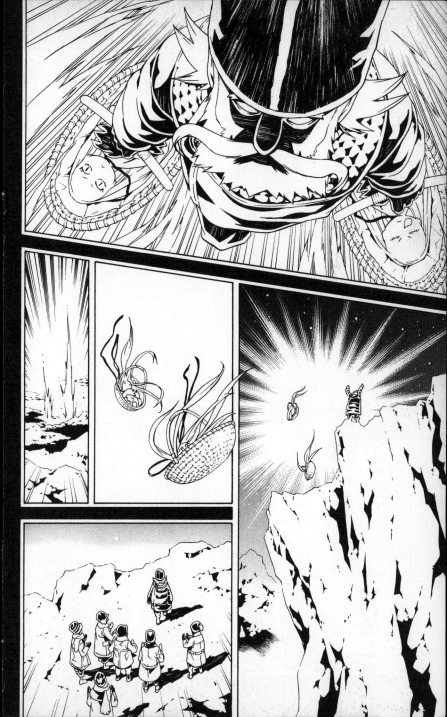

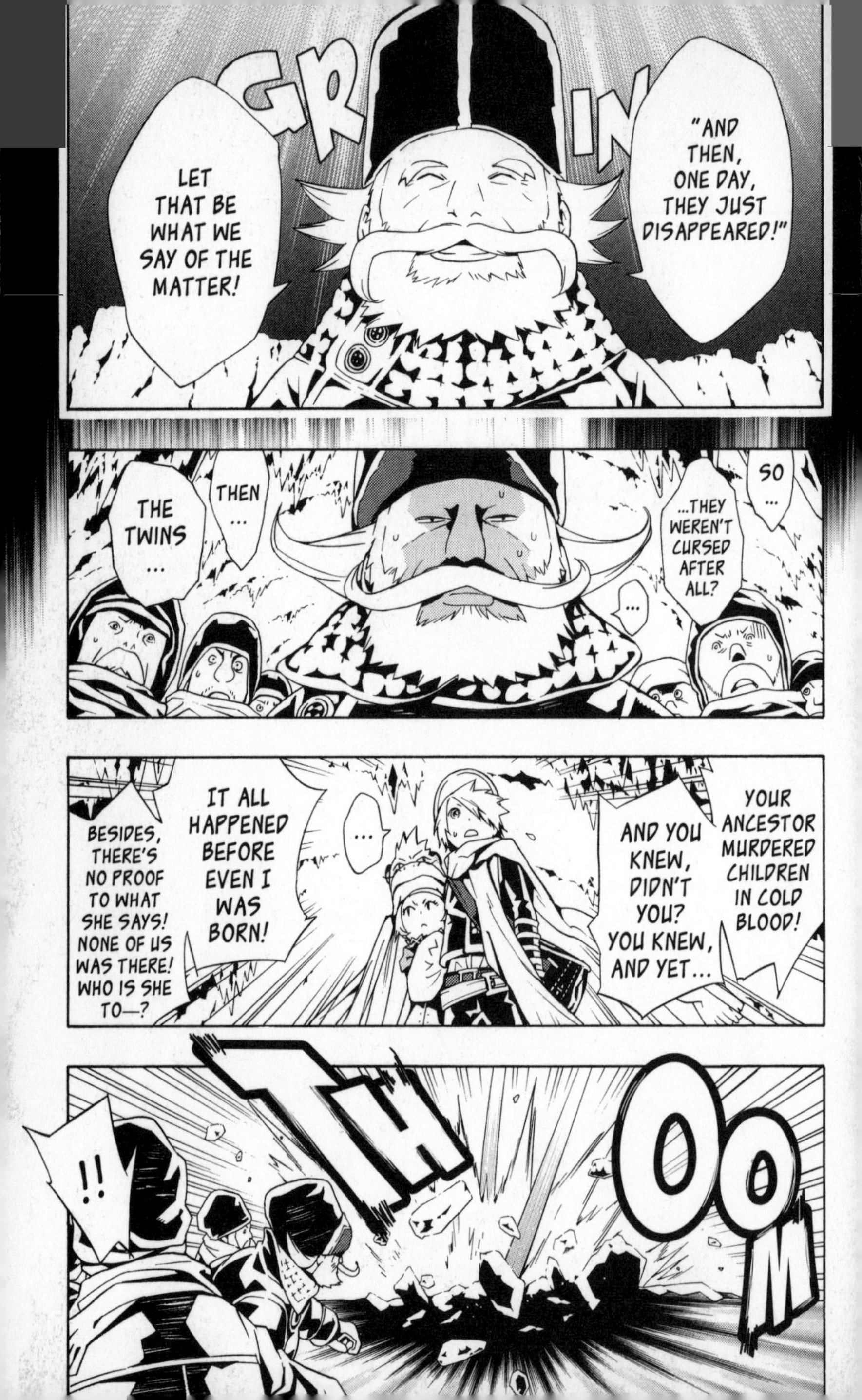
GRIN
"AND THEN, ONE DAY, THEY JUST DISAPPEARED!"
LET THAT BE WHAT WE SAY OF THE MATTER!
SO ...
...THEY WEREN'T CURSED AFTER ALL?
...
THEN ...
THE TWINS ...
YOUR ANCESTOR MURDERED CHILDREN IN COLD BLOOD!
AND YOU KNEW, DIDN'T YOU? YOU KNEW, AND YET...
...
IT ALL HAPPENED BEFORE EVEN I WAS BORN!
BESIDES, THERE'S NO PROOF TO WHAT SHE SAYS! NONE OF US WAS THERE! WHO IS SHE TO—?
THOOM
!!

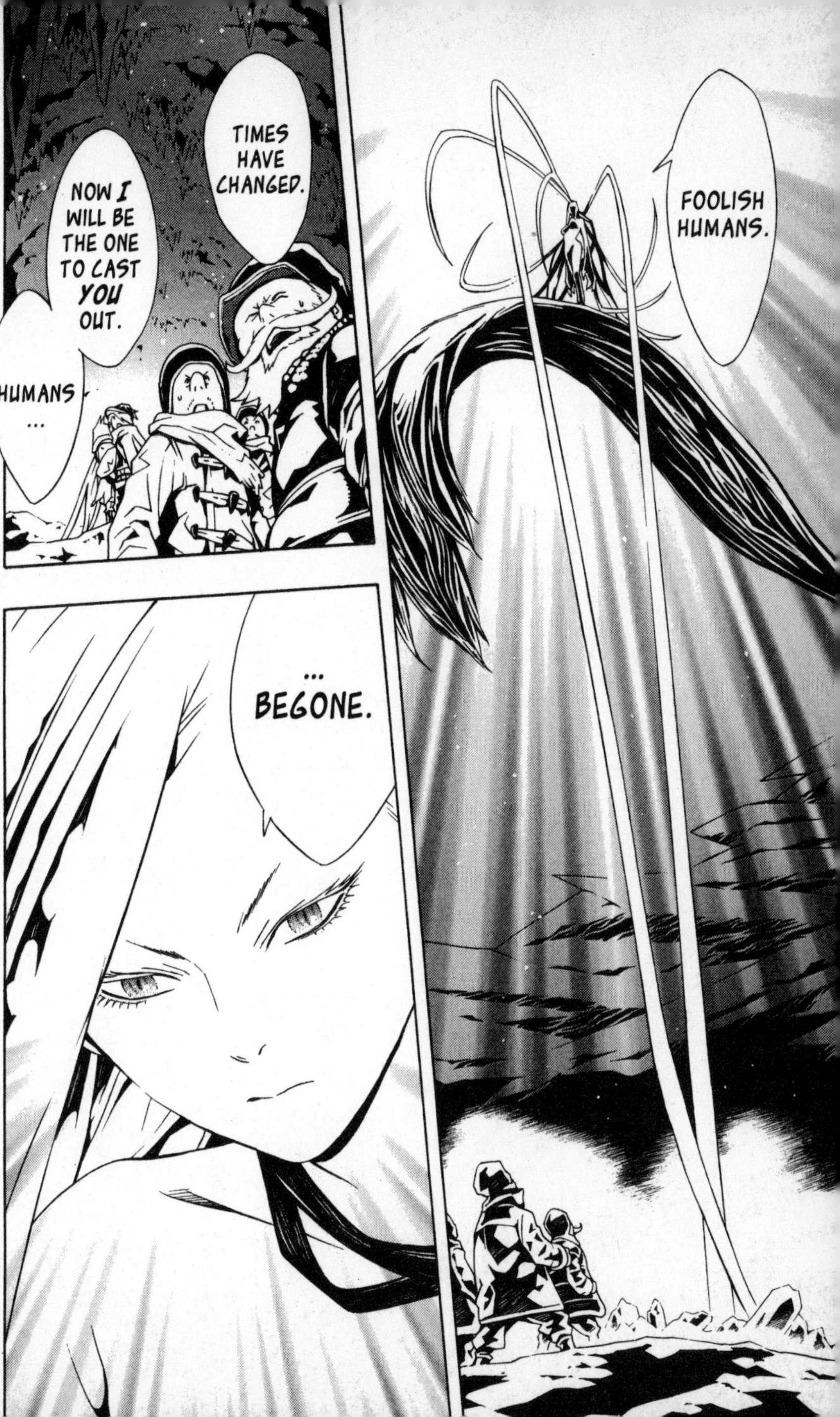
FOOLISH HUMANS.
TIMES HAVE CHANGED.
NOW I WILL BE THE ONE TO CAST YOU OUT.
HUMANS ...
... BEGONE.

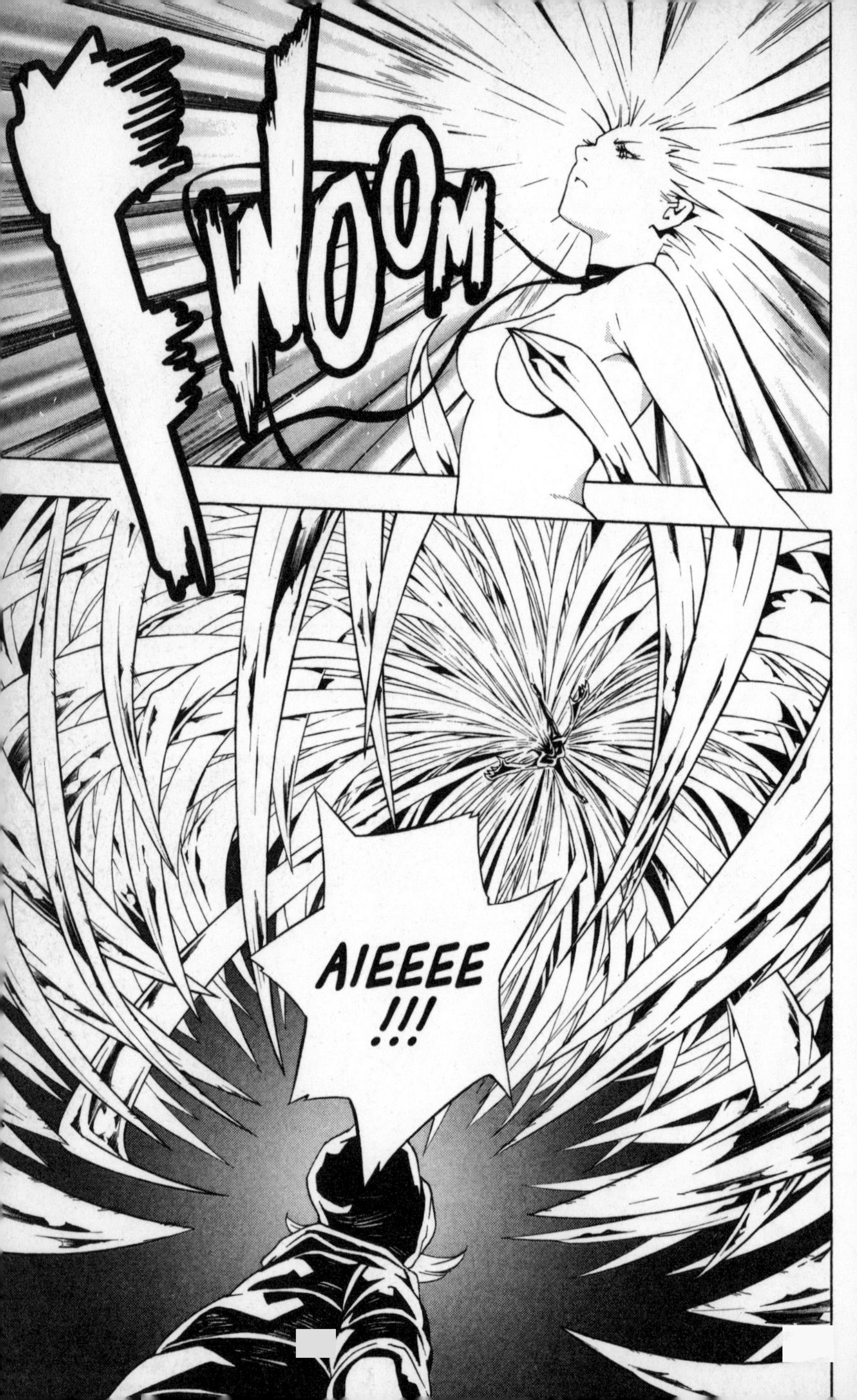
WOOM
AIEEEE !!!

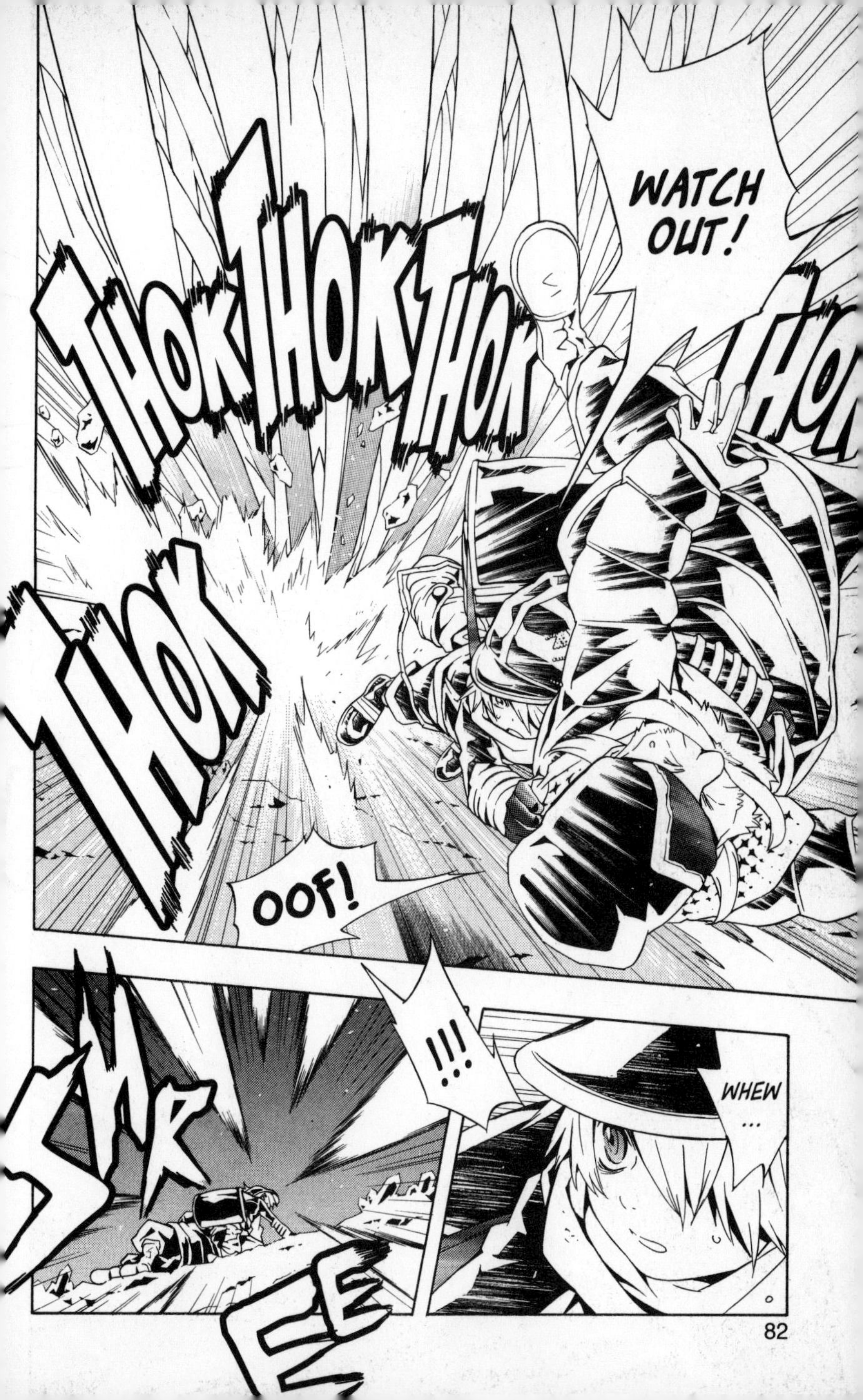
WATCH OUT!
THOK THOK THOK THOK
THOK
OOF!
WHEW ...
!!!

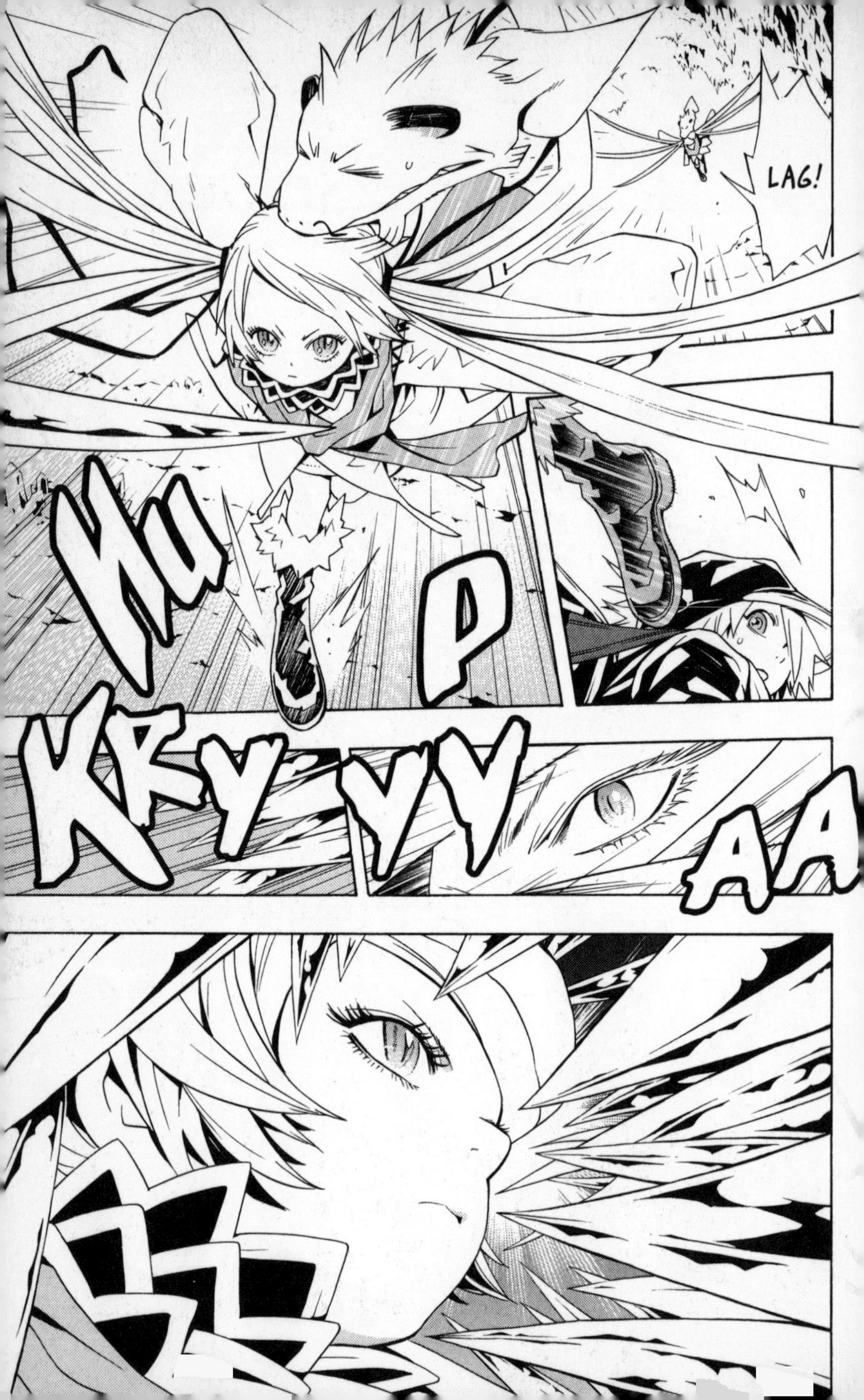
LAG!
HUP
KRYYYAA

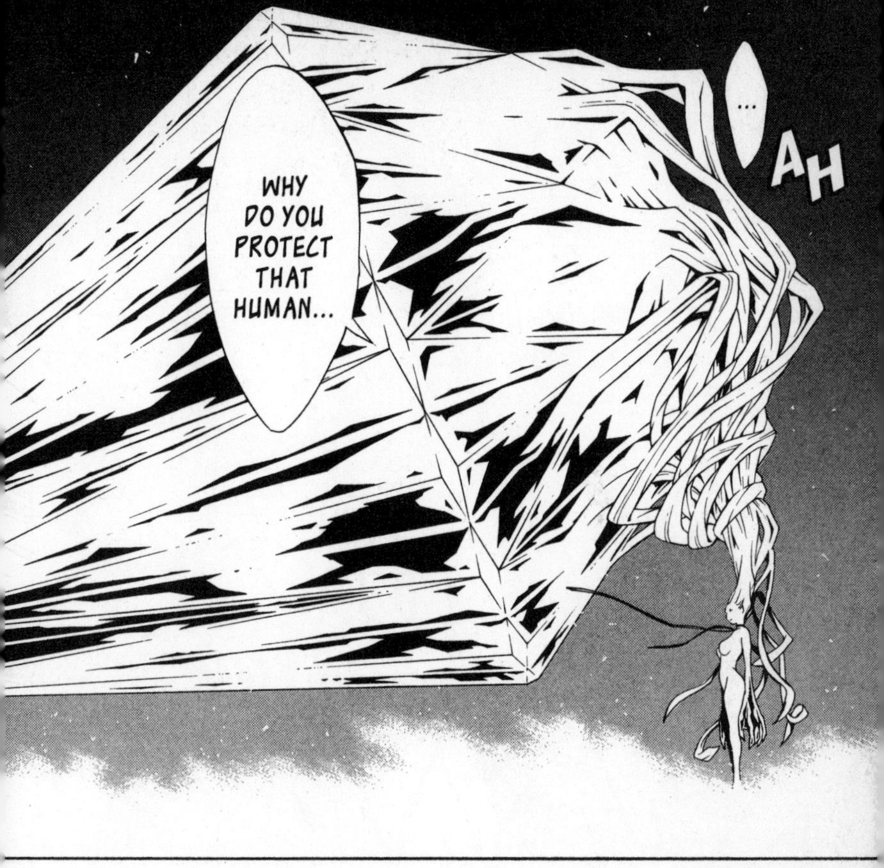
...
AH
WHY DO YOU PROTECT THAT HUMAN...
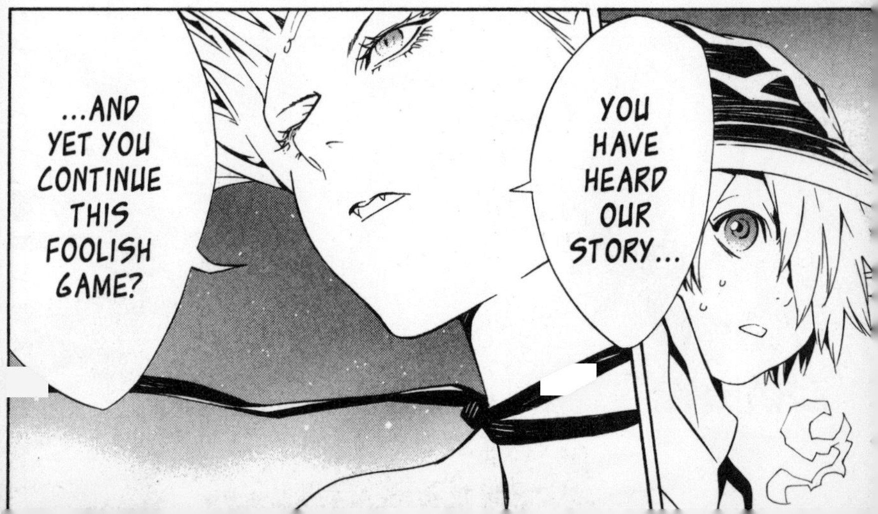
YOU HAVE HEARD OUR STORY...
...AND YET YOU CONTINUE THIS FOOLISH GAME?

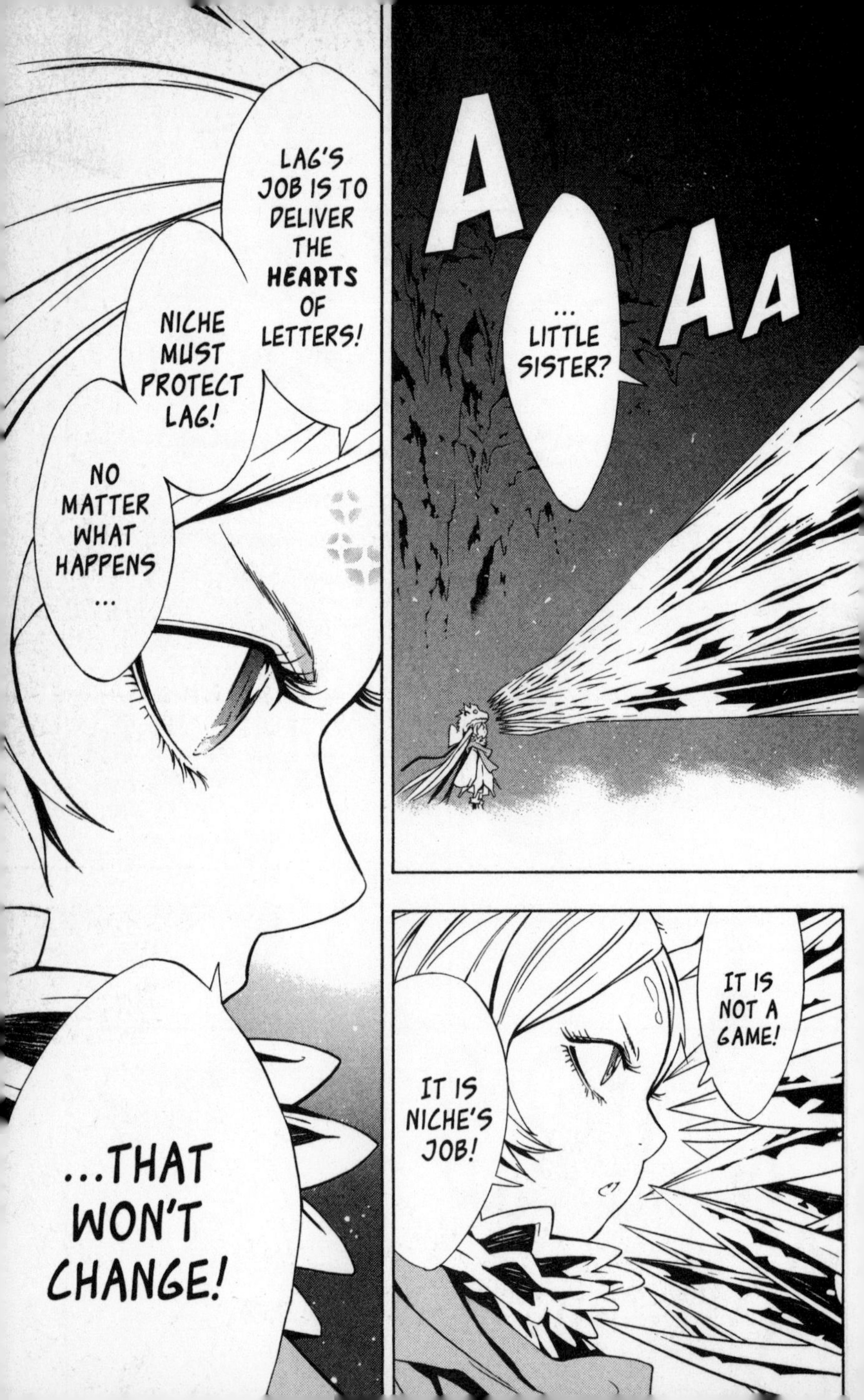

A AA
... LITTLE SISTER?
IT IS NOT A GAME!
IT IS NICHE'S JOB!
LAG'S JOB IS TO DELIVER THE HEARTS OF LETTERS!
NICHE MUST PROTECT LAG!
NO MATTER WHAT HAPPENS ...
...THAT WON'T CHANGE!

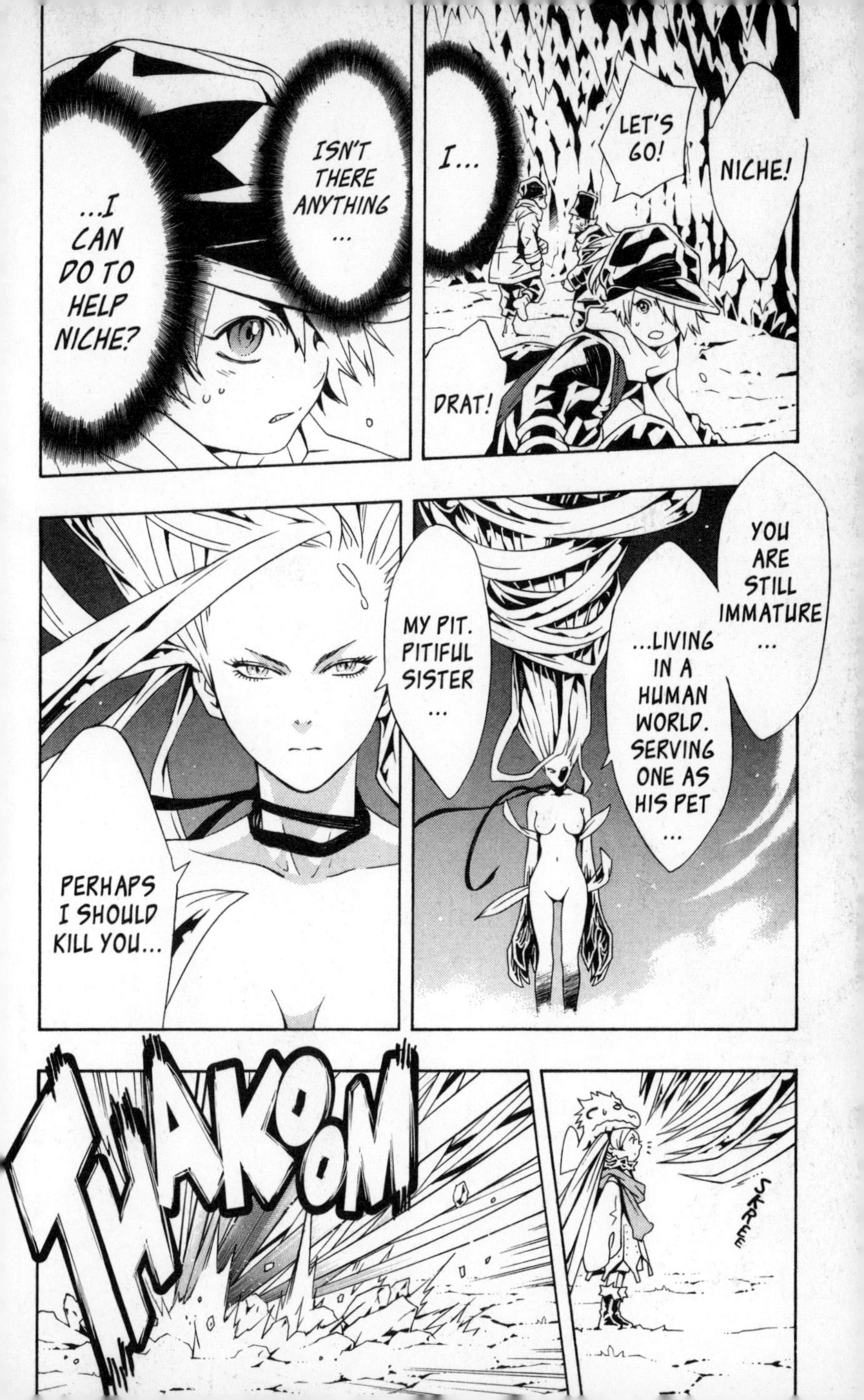
NICHE!
LET'S GO!
I...
DRAT!
ISN'T THERE ANYTHING ...
...I CAN DO TO HELP NICHE?
YOU ARE STILL IMMATURE ...
...LIVING IN A HUMAN WORLD. SERVING ONE AS HIS PET ...
MY PIT. PITIFUL SISTER ...
PERHAPS I SHOULD KILL YOU...
SKREE
THAKOOM

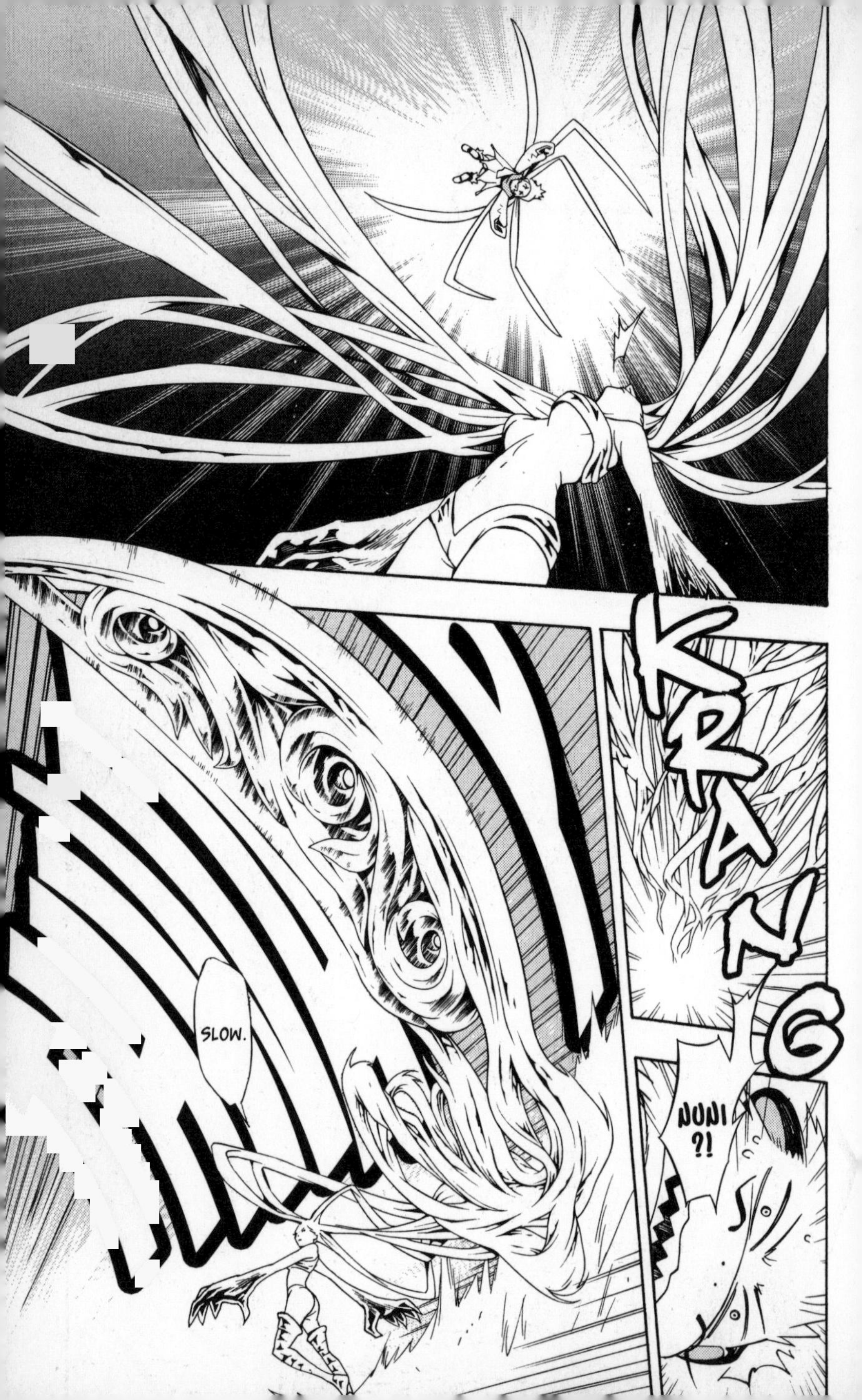
KRANG
NUNI ?!
SLOW.

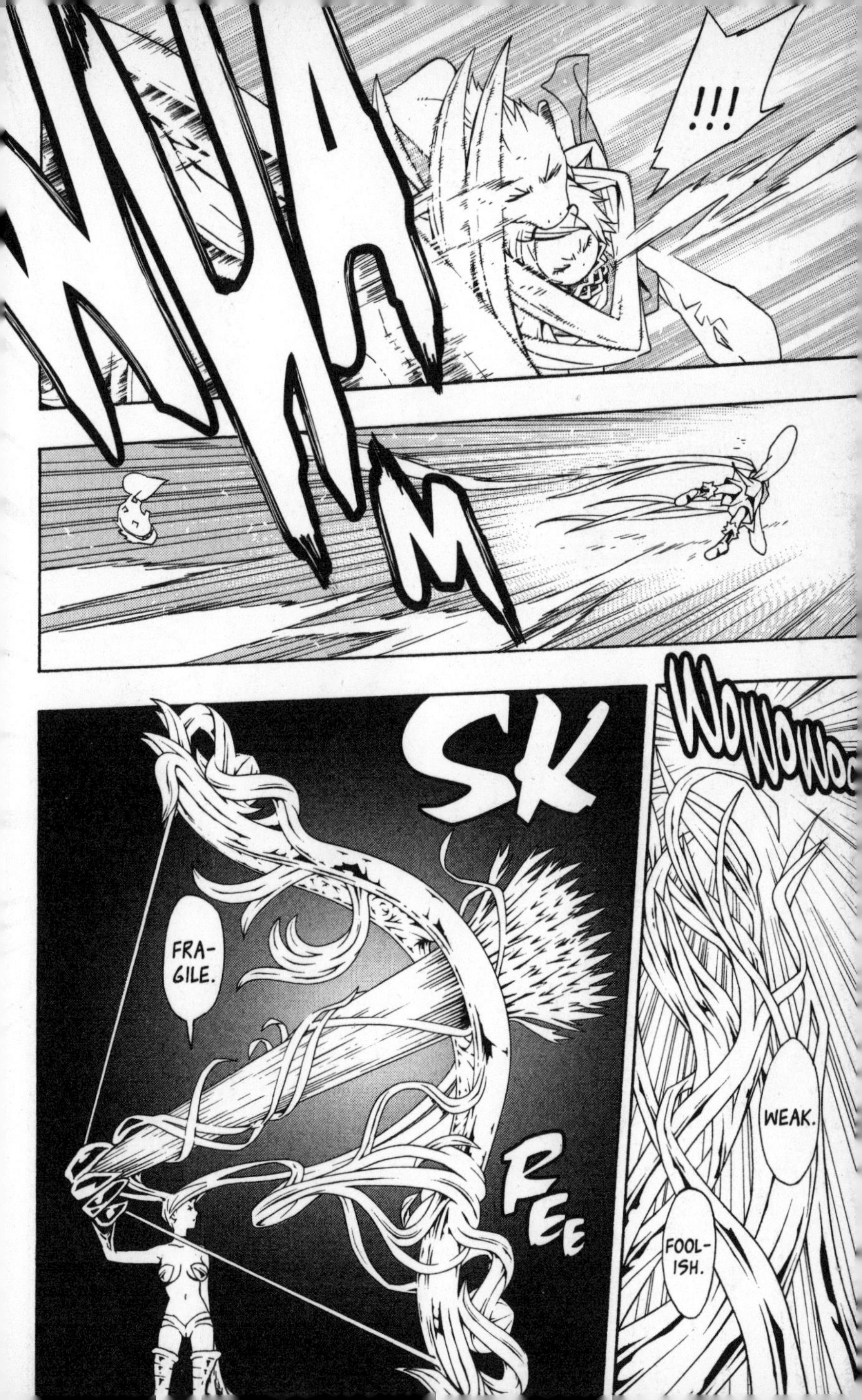
!!!
WHAM
WOWOWO
WEAK.
FOOL-ISH.
SK
REE
FRA-GILE.

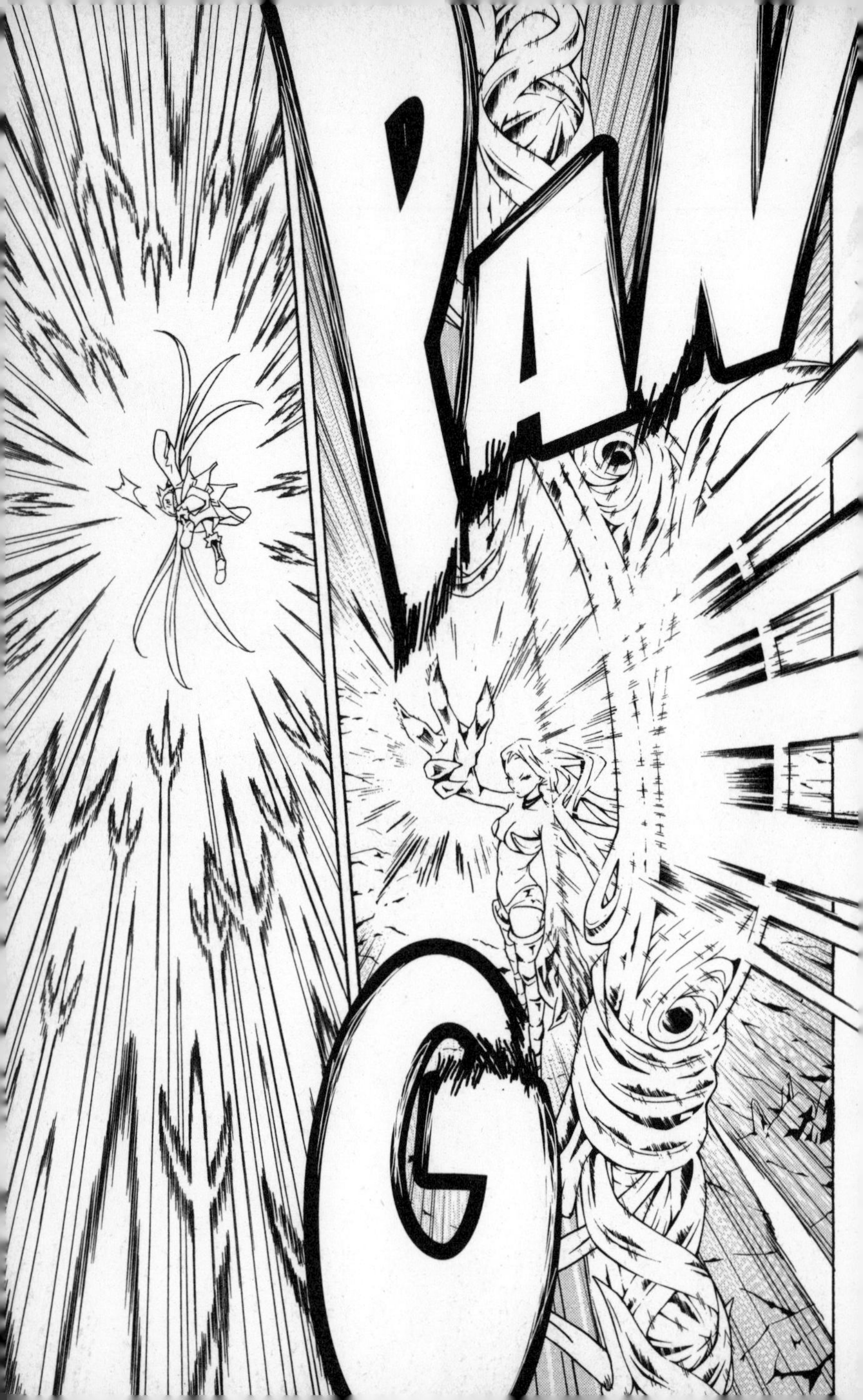

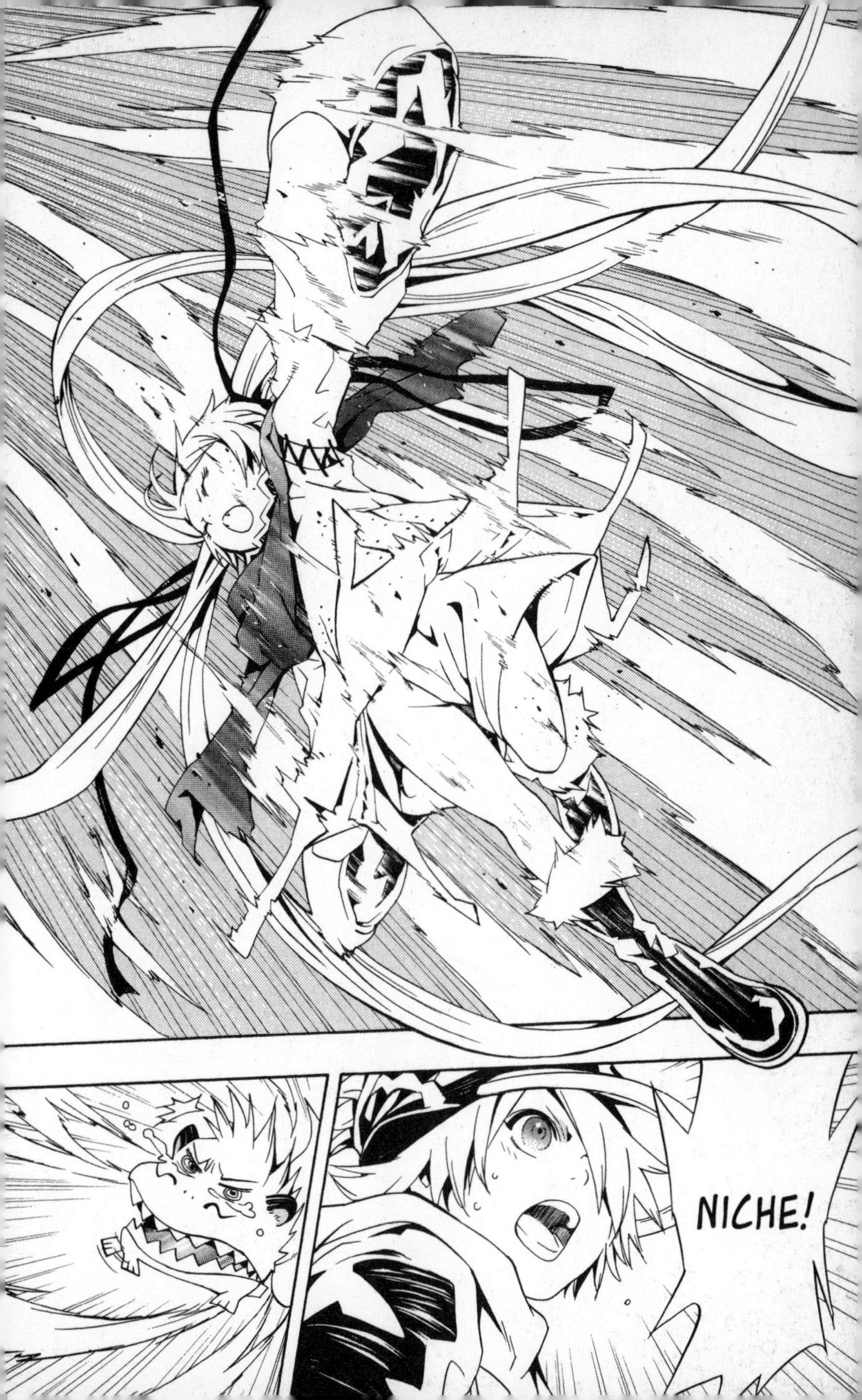
NICHE!

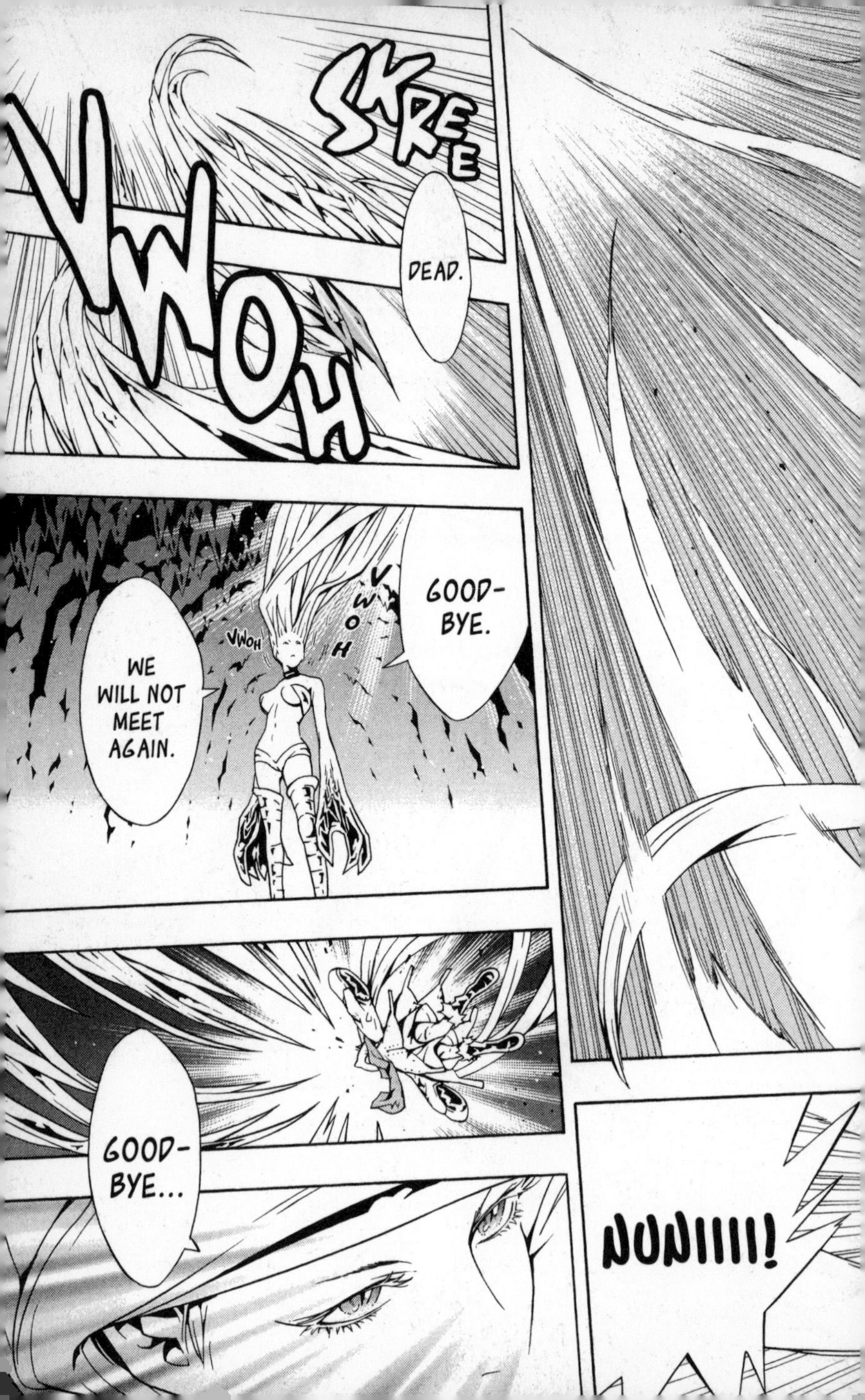
SKREE
VWOH
DEAD.
GOOD-BYE.
VWOH
VWOH
WE WILL NOT MEET AGAIN.
GOOD-BYE...
NUNIIII!

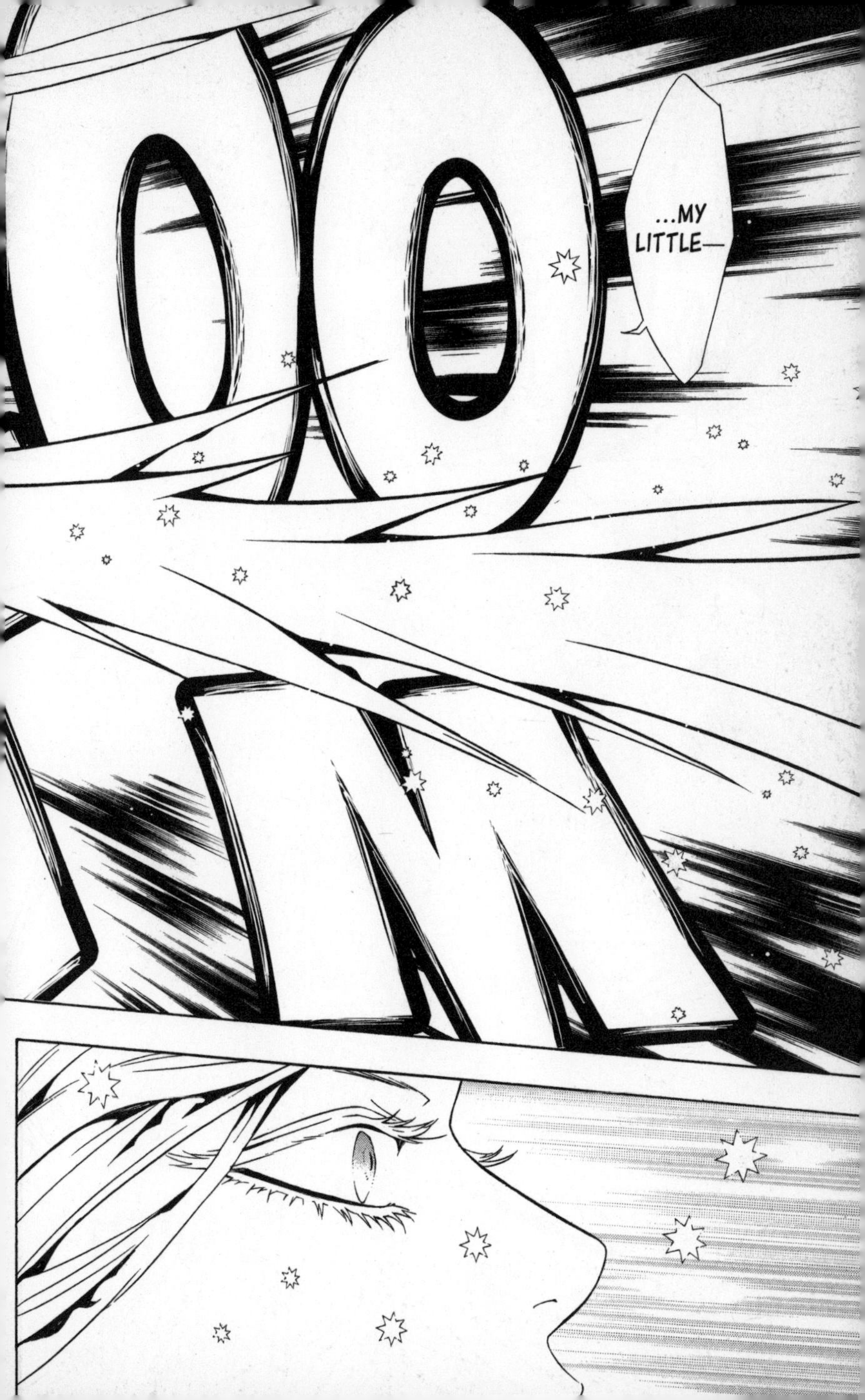
...MY LITTLE—

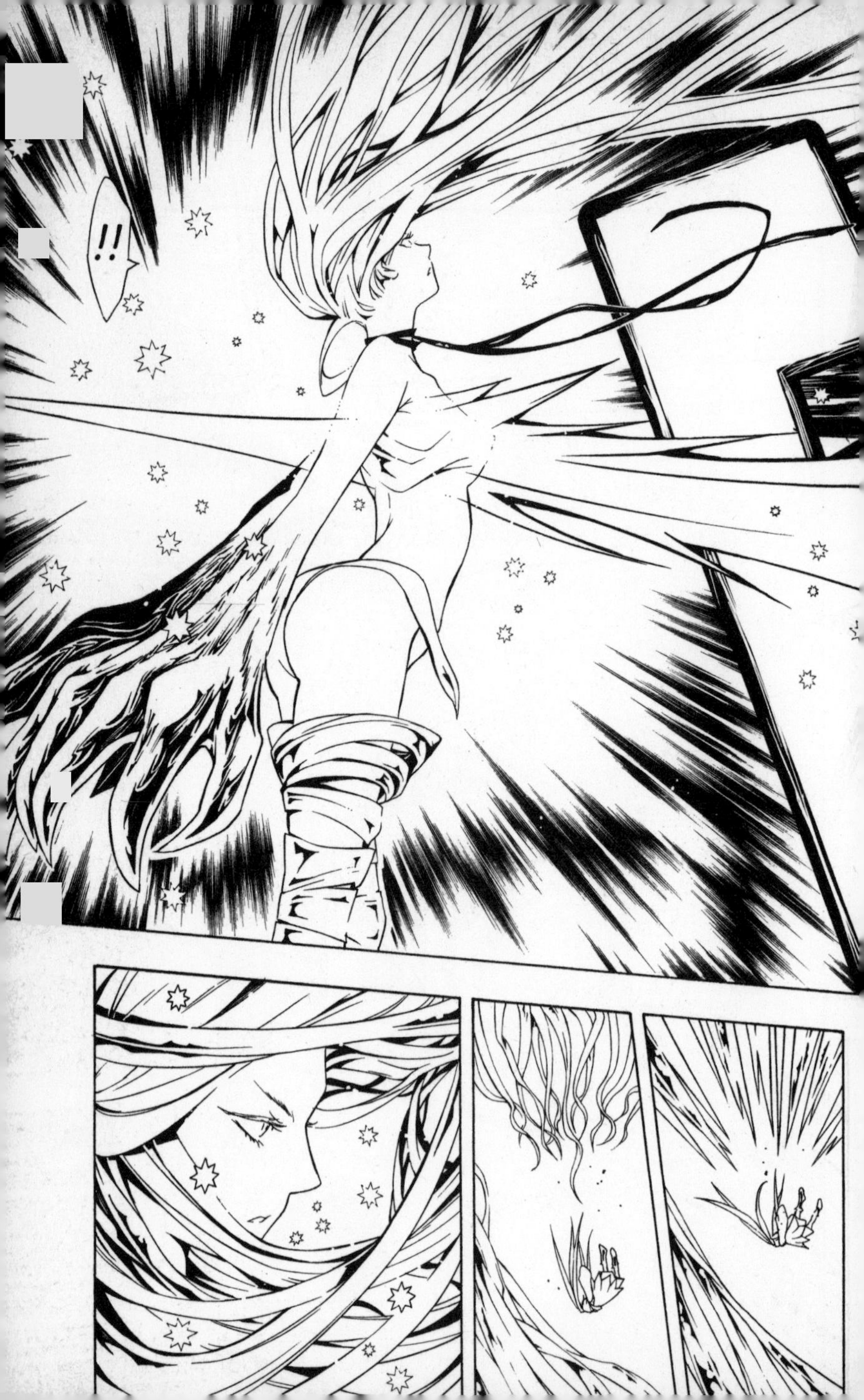
!!

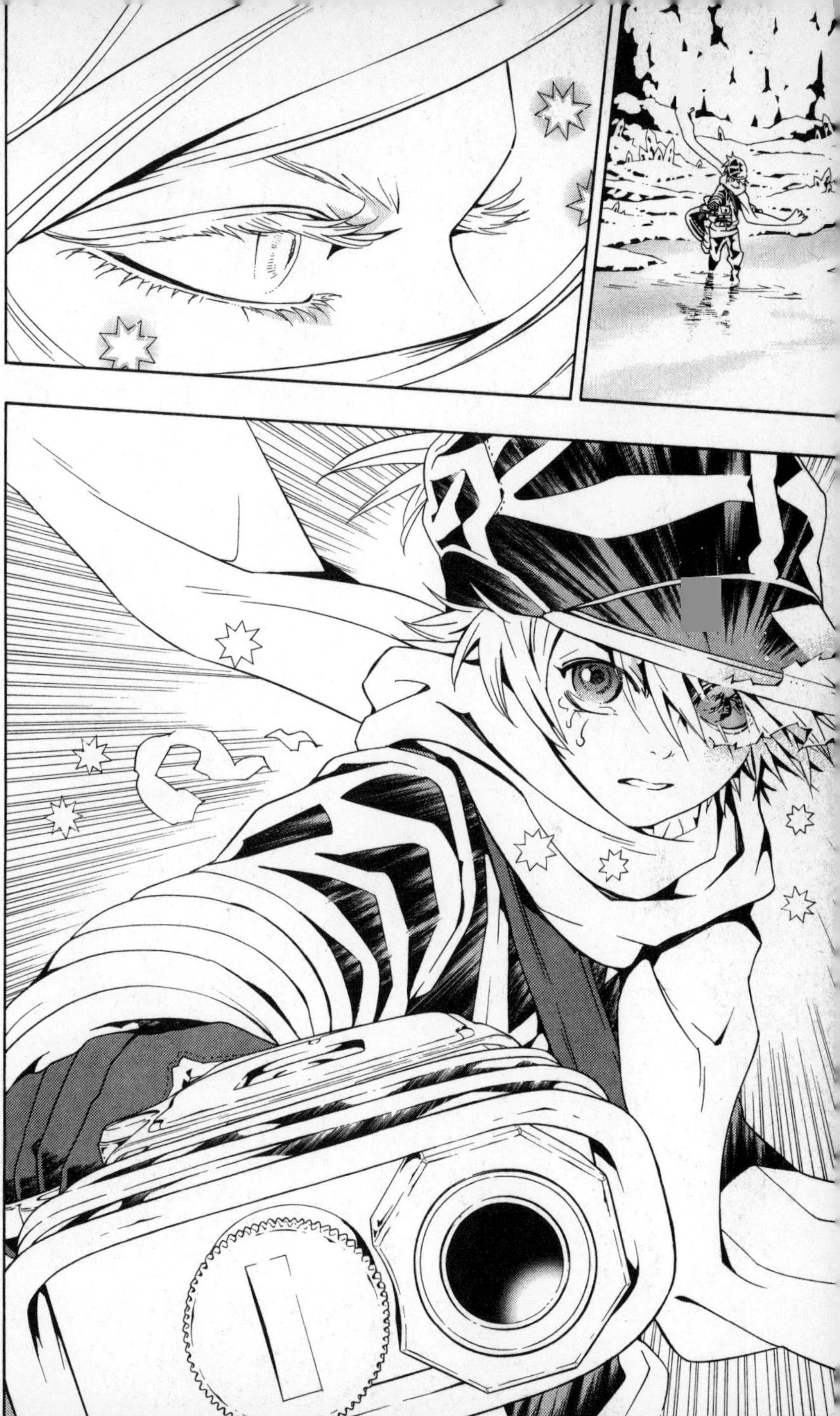

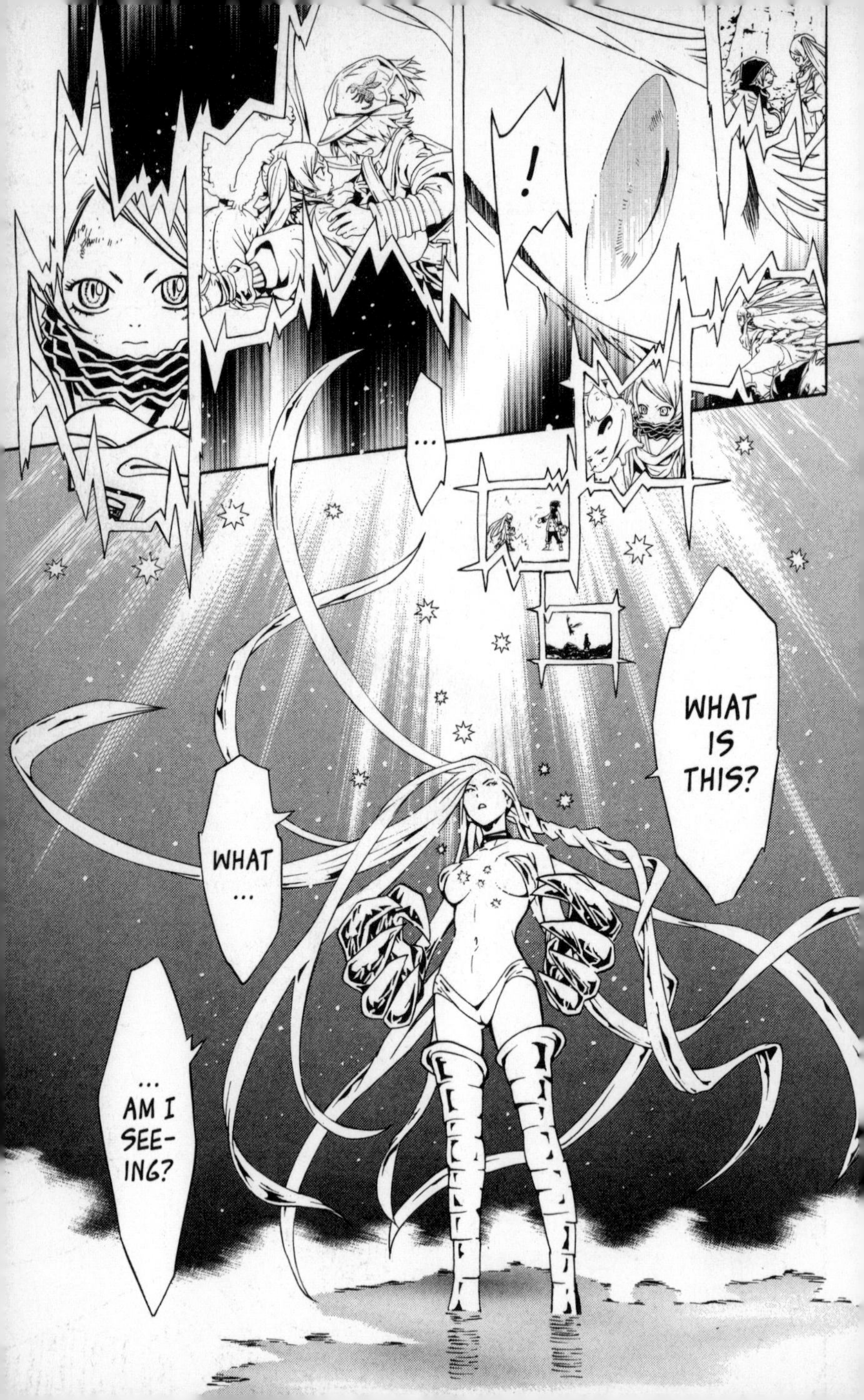
!
...
WHAT IS THIS?
WHAT ...
... AM I SEE-ING?

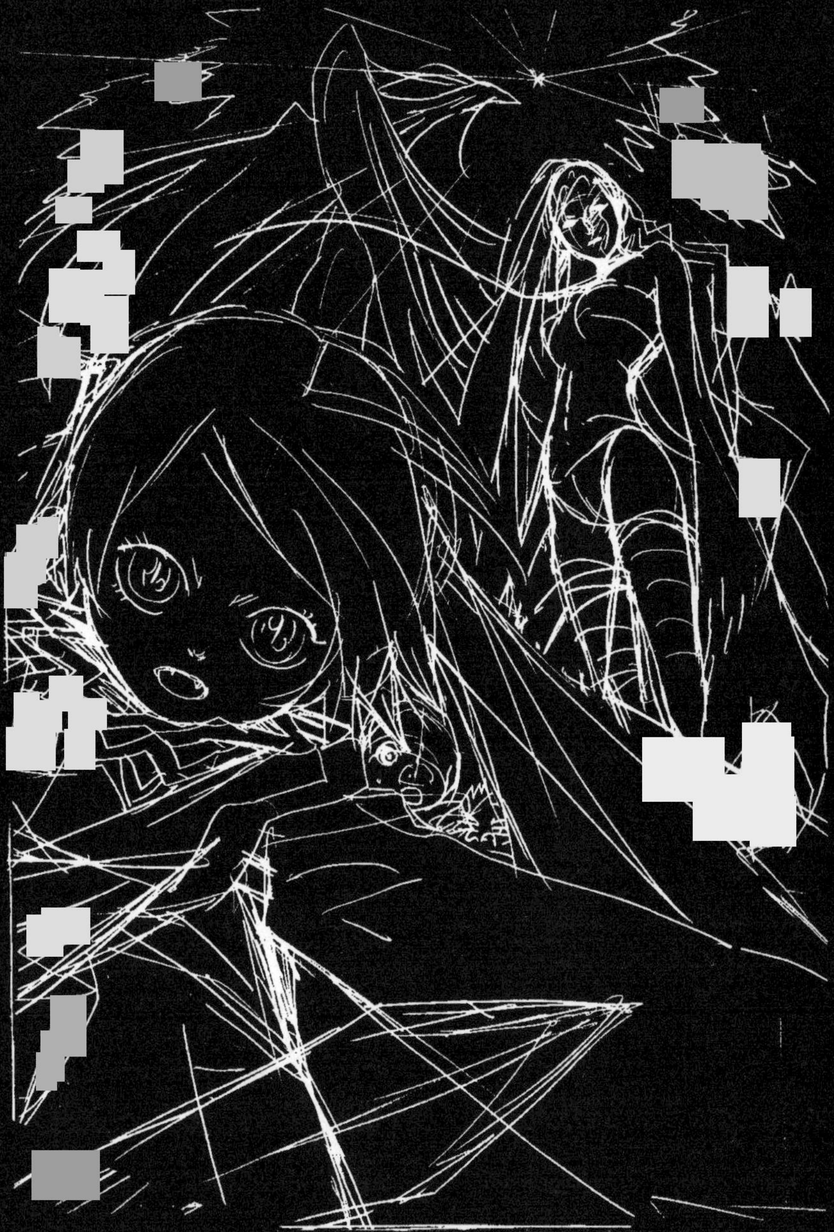

Rough sketch for the cover.

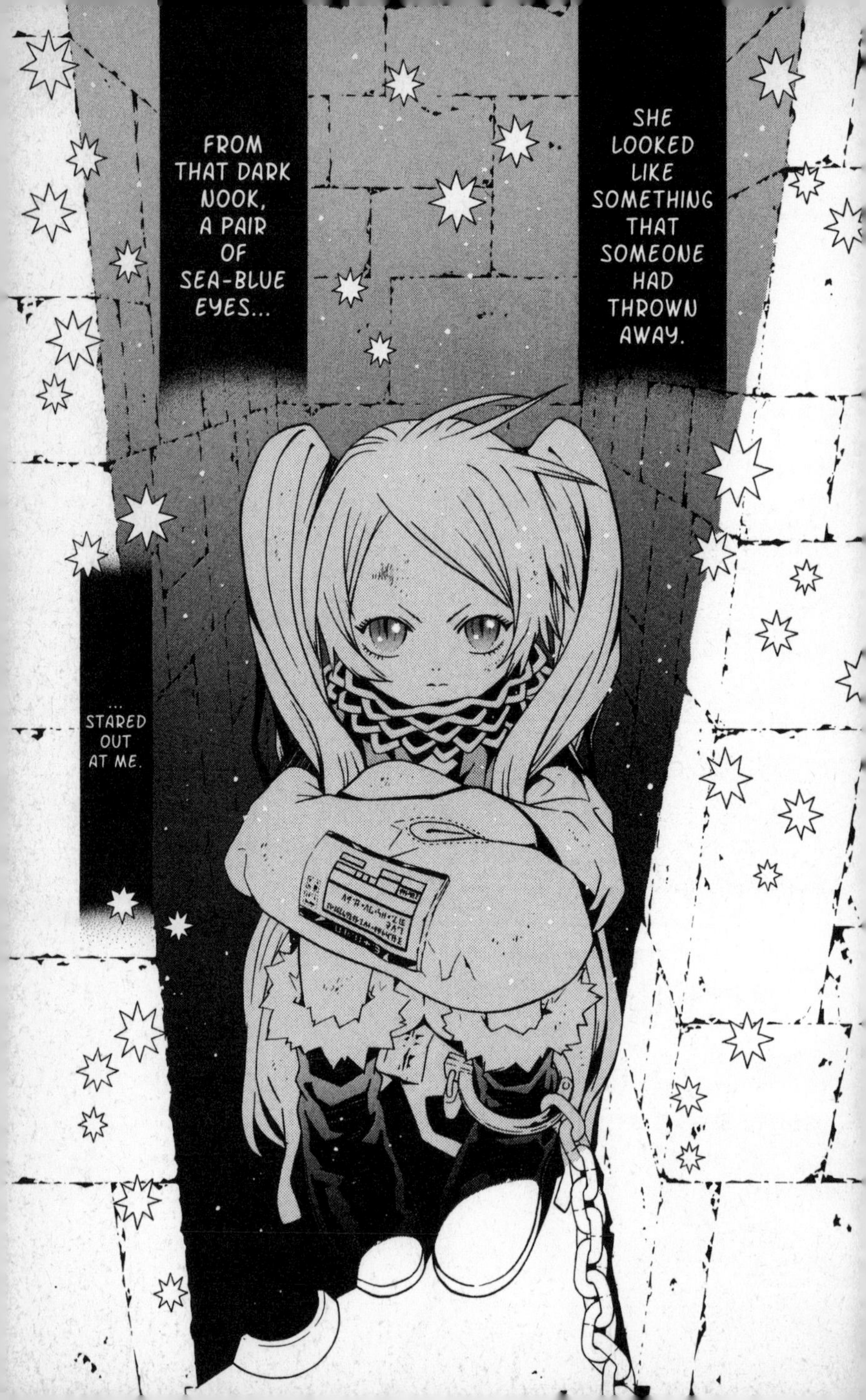
SHE LOOKED LIKE SOMETHING THAT SOMEONE HAD THROWN AWAY.
FROM THAT DARK NOOK, A PAIR OF SEA-BLUE EYES...
...STARED OUT AT ME.

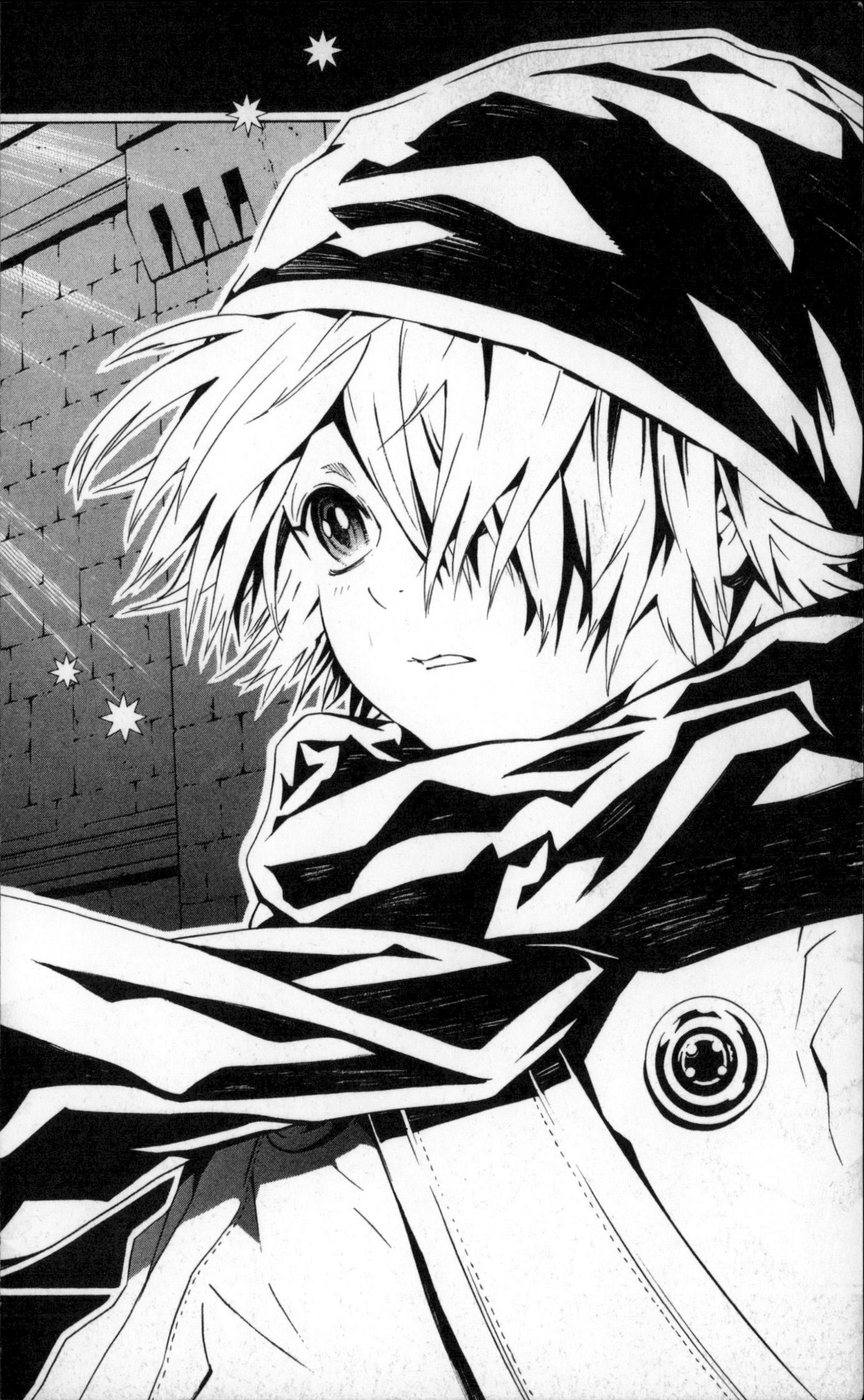

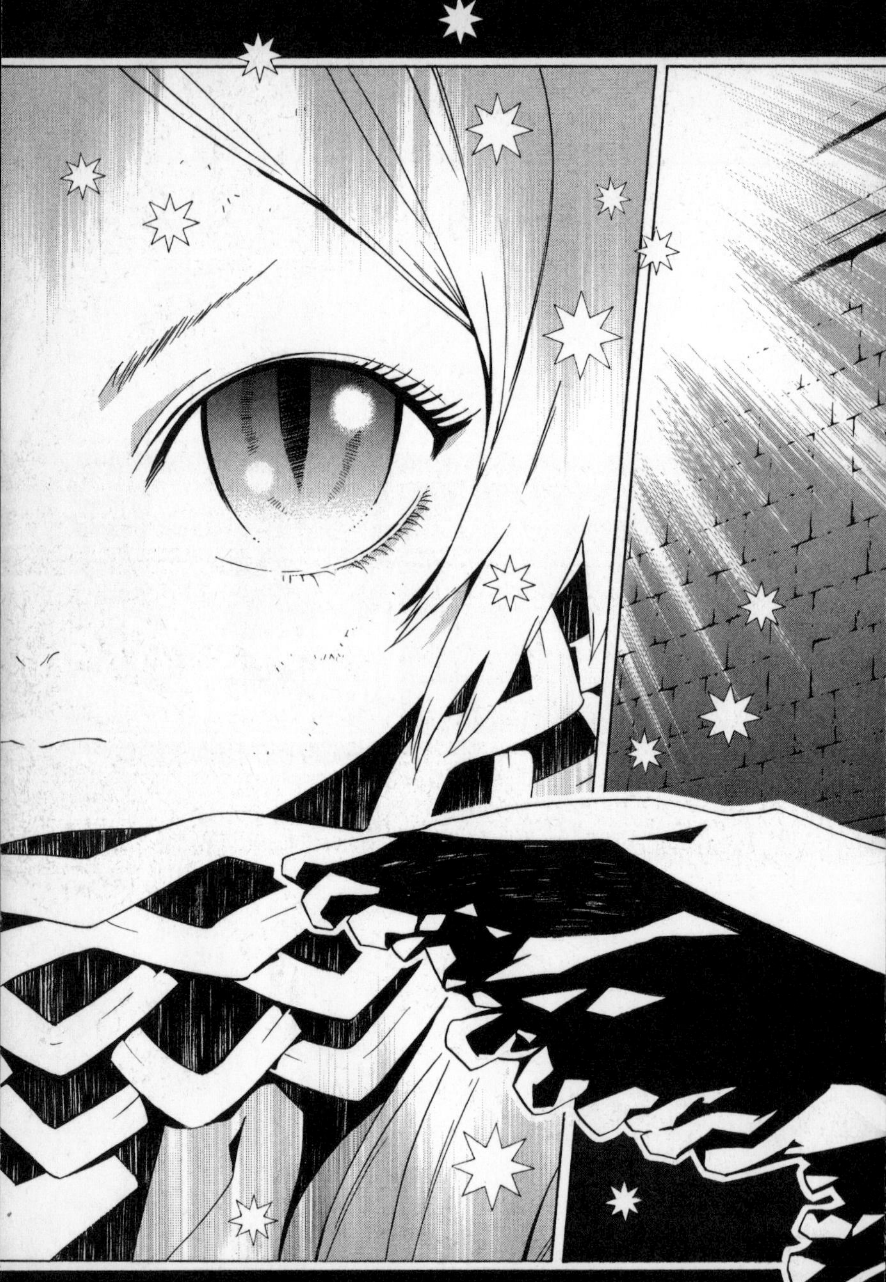

Chapter 25: All Alone for 200 Years

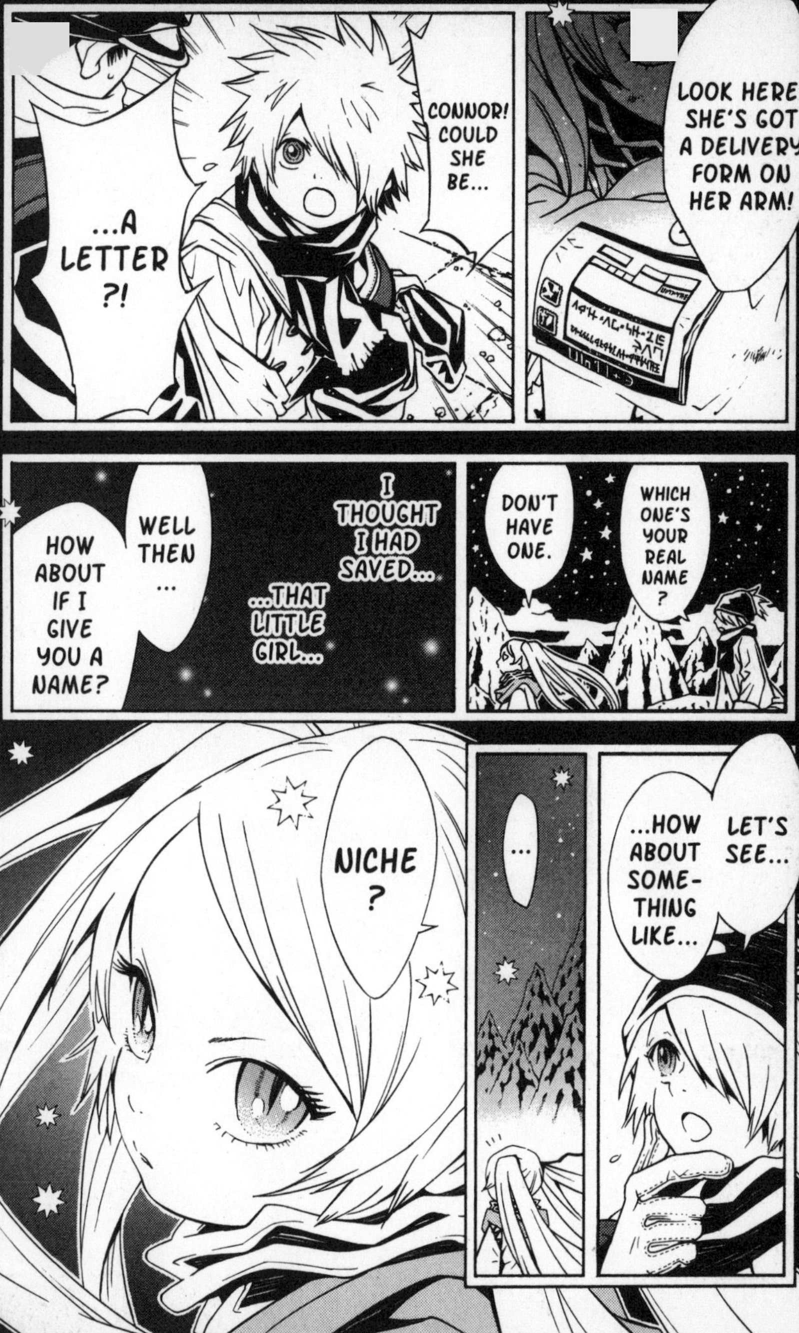

LOOK HERE! SHE'S GOT A DELIVERY FORM ON HER ARM!
CONNOR! COULD SHE BE...
...A LETTER?!
WHICH ONE'S YOUR REAL NAME?
DON'T HAVE ONE.
I THOUGHT I HAD SAVED...
...THAT LITTLE GIRL...
WELL THEN...
HOW ABOUT IF I GIVE YOU A NAME?
LET'S SEE...
...HOW ABOUT SOMETHING LIKE...
...
NICHE?

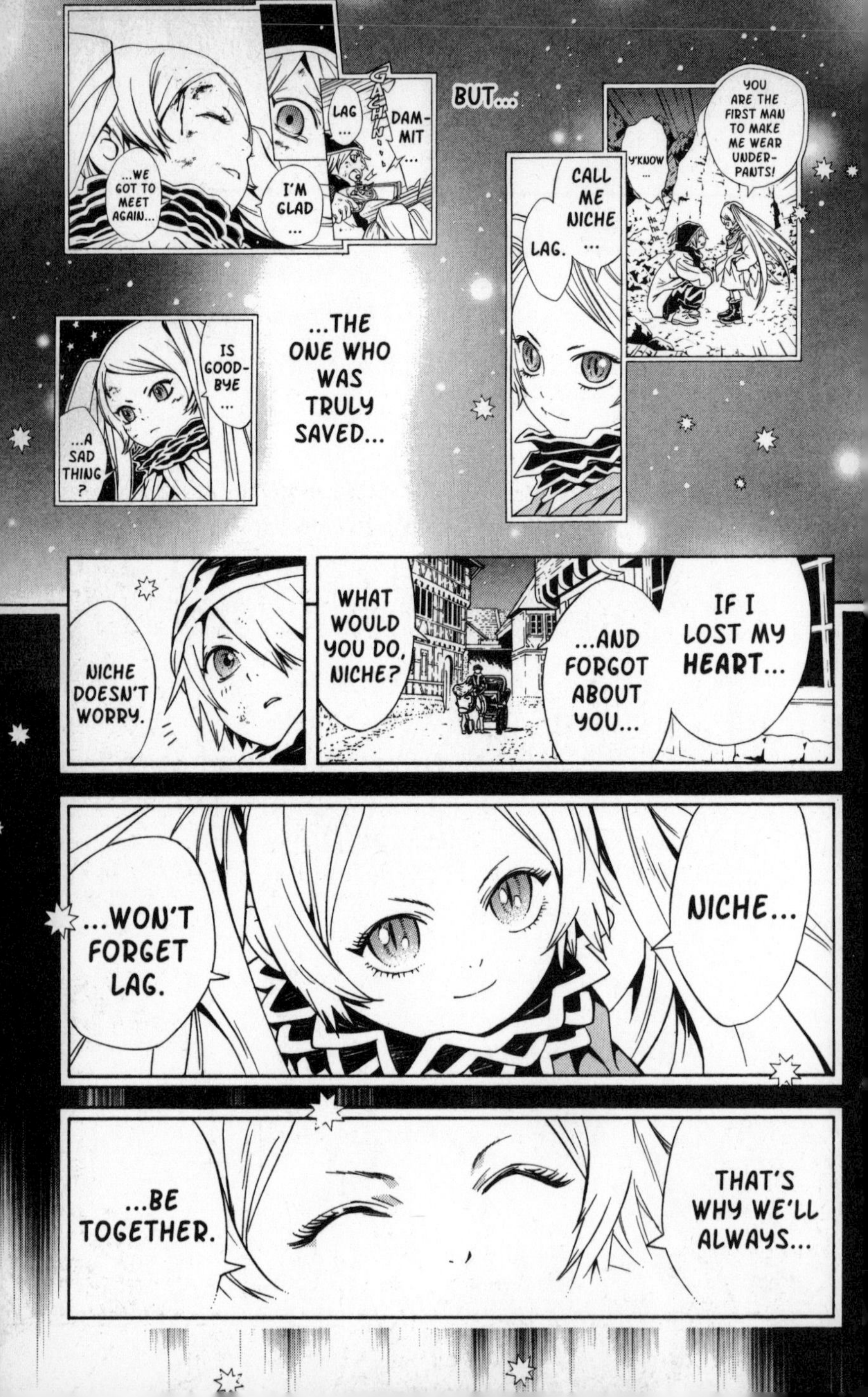
YOU ARE THE FIRST MAN TO MAKE ME WEAR UNDER-PANTS!
Ha ha ha
Y'KNOW...
CALL ME NICHE...
LAG.
BUT...
DAM-MIT...
GACHIN
LAG...
I'M GLAD...
...WE GOT TO MEET AGAIN...
...THE ONE WHO WAS TRULY SAVED...
IS GOOD-BYE...
...A SAD THING?
IF I LOST MY HEART...
...AND FORGOT ABOUT YOU...
WHAT WOULD YOU DO, NICHE?
NICHE DOESN'T WORRY.
NICHE...
...WON'T FORGET LAG.
THAT'S WHY WE'LL ALWAYS...
...BE TOGETHER.

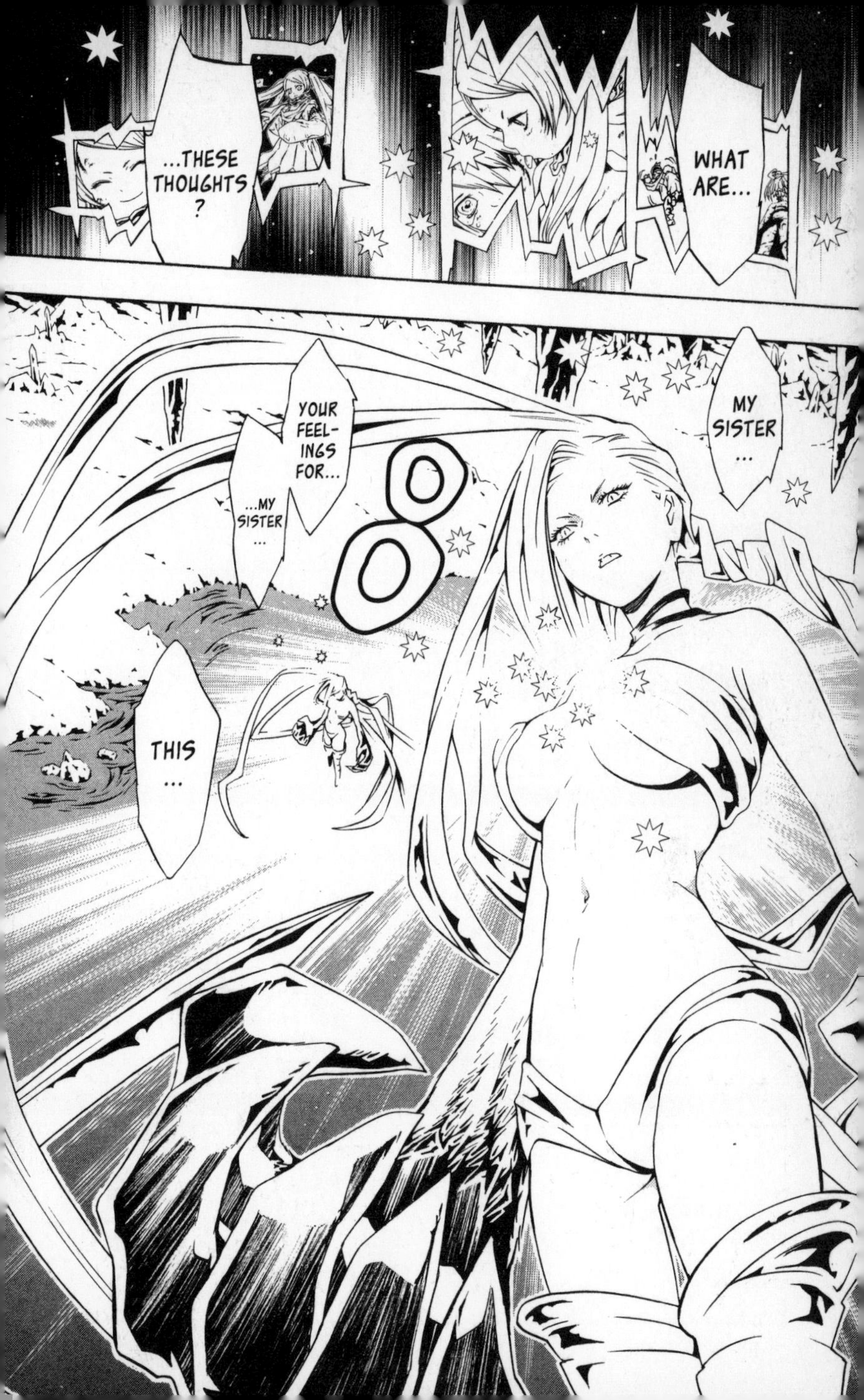
WHAT ARE...
...THESE THOUGHTS?
MY SISTER...
YOUR FEEL-INGS FOR...
...MY SISTER...
THIS...

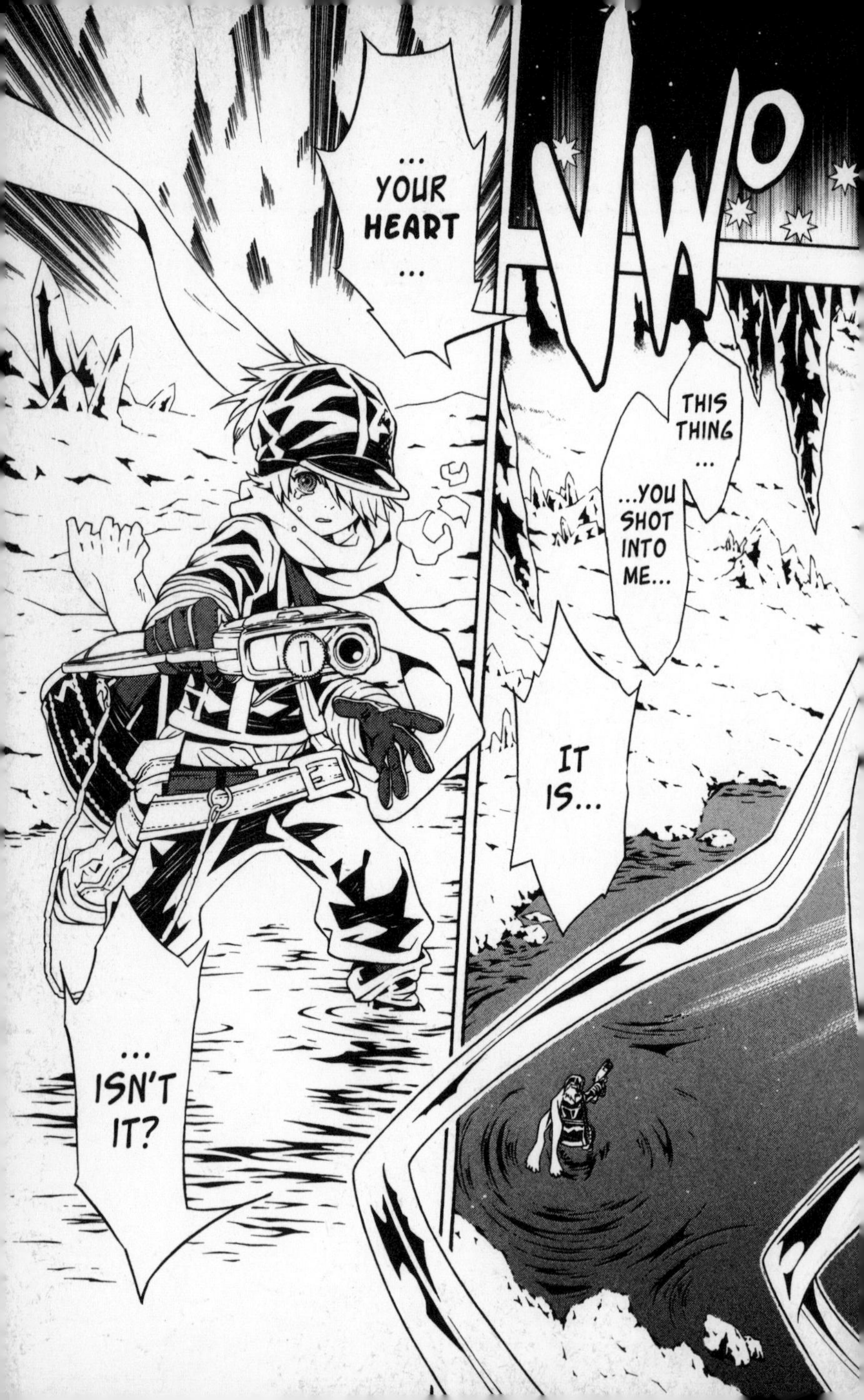
VWO
THIS THING ...
...YOU SHOT INTO ME...
IT IS...
... YOUR HEART ...
... ISN'T IT?

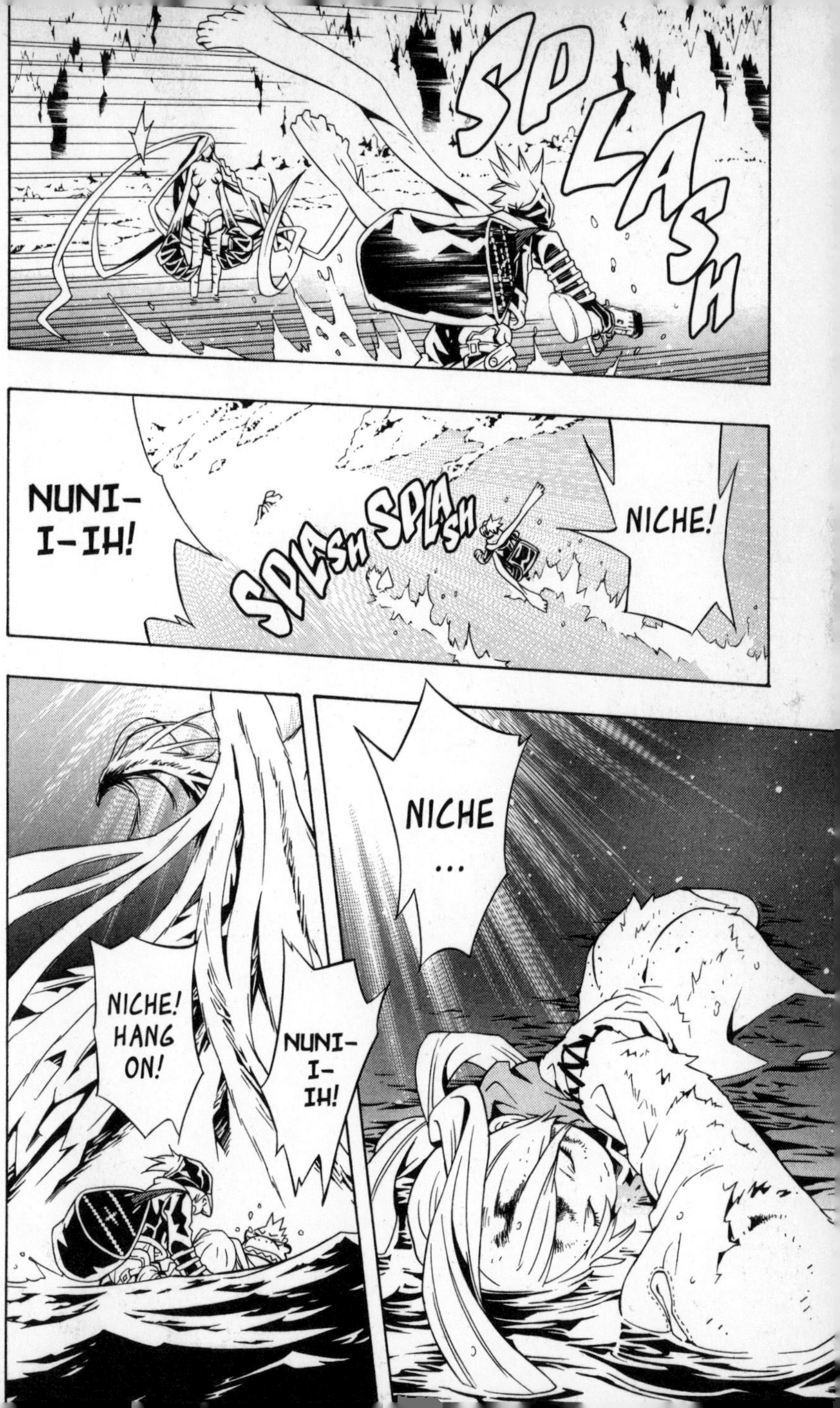
SPLASH
NICHE!
SPLASH SPLASH
NUNI-I-IH!
NICHE ...
NUNI-I-IH!
NICHE! HANG ON!

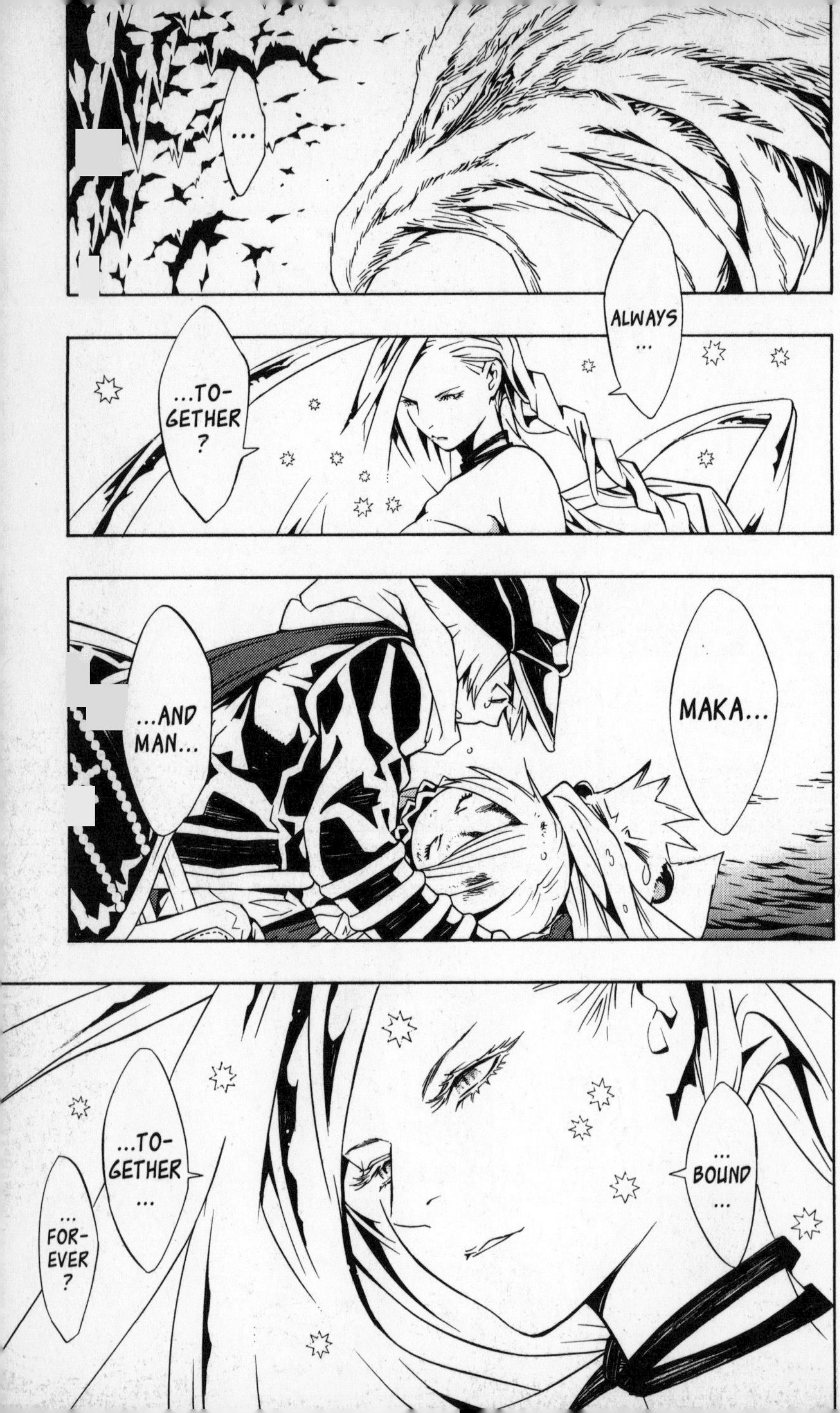
...
ALWAYS...
...TO-GETHER?
MAKA...
...AND MAN...
...BOUND...
...TO-GETHER...
...FOR-EVER?

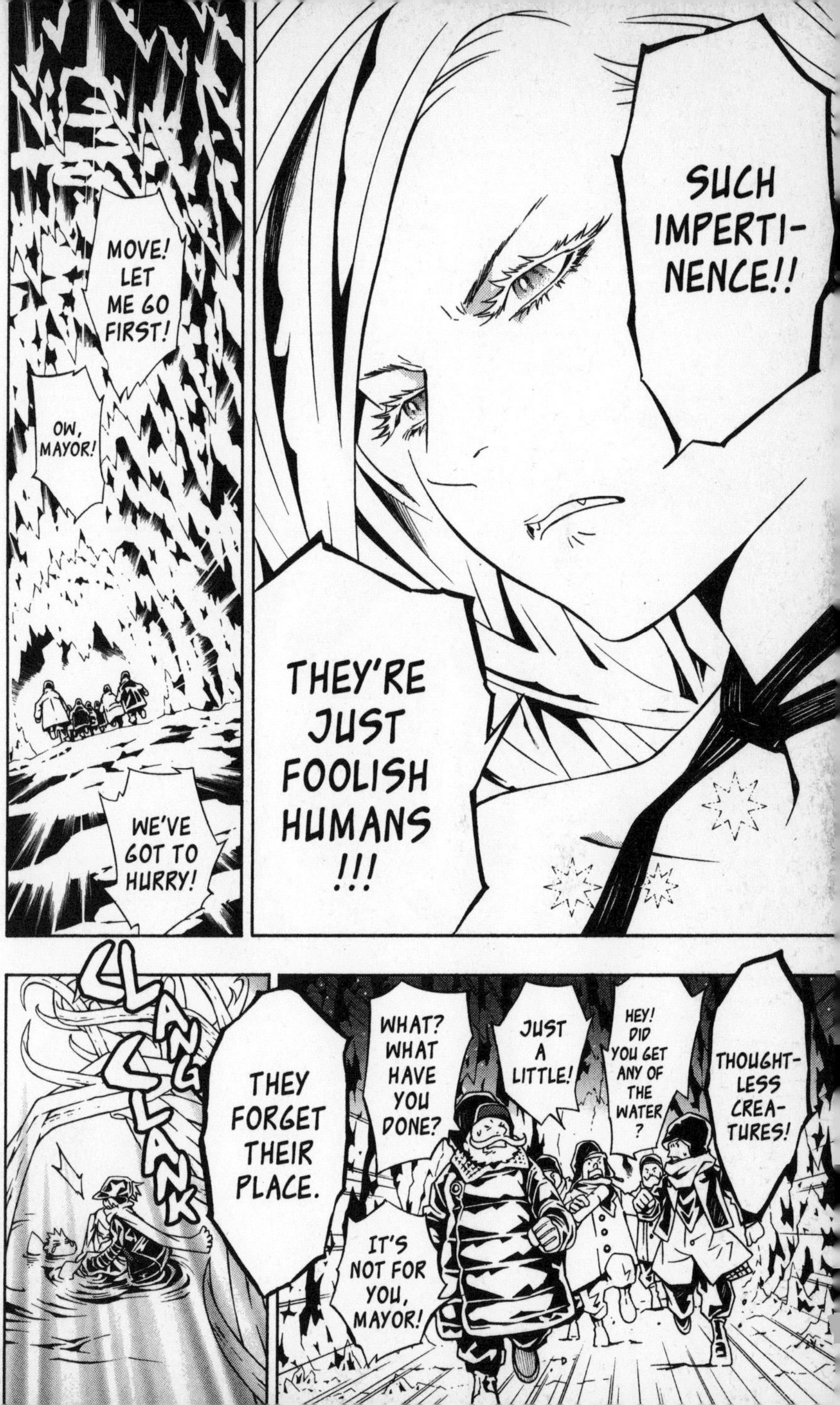
SUCH IMPERTINENCE!!
THEY'RE JUST FOOLISH HUMANS!!!
MOVE! LET ME GO FIRST!
OW, MAYOR!
WE'VE GOT TO HURRY!
THOUGHTLESS CREATURES!
HEY! DID YOU GET ANY OF THE WATER?
JUST A LITTLE!
WHAT? WHAT HAVE YOU DONE?
IT'S NOT FOR YOU, MAYOR!
THEY FORGET THEIR PLACE.
CLANG CLANK

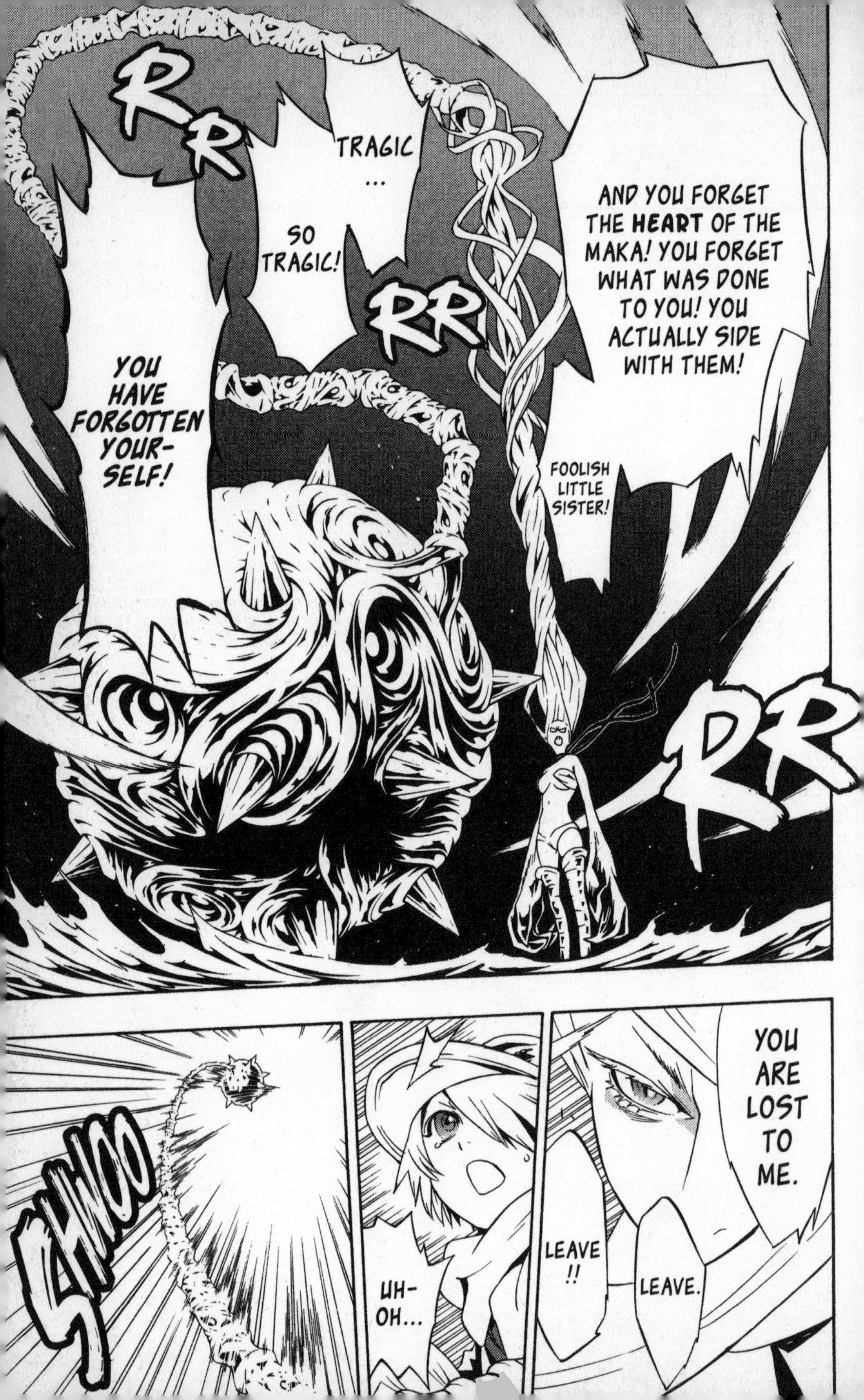
R
R
TRAGIC ...
SO TRAGIC!
RR
YOU HAVE FORGOTTEN YOUR-SELF!
AND YOU FORGET THE **HEART** OF THE MAKA! YOU FORGET WHAT WAS DONE TO YOU! YOU ACTUALLY SIDE WITH THEM!
FOOLISH LITTLE SISTER!
RR
YOU ARE LOST TO ME.
LEAVE.
LEAVE !!
UH-OH...
SHWOO

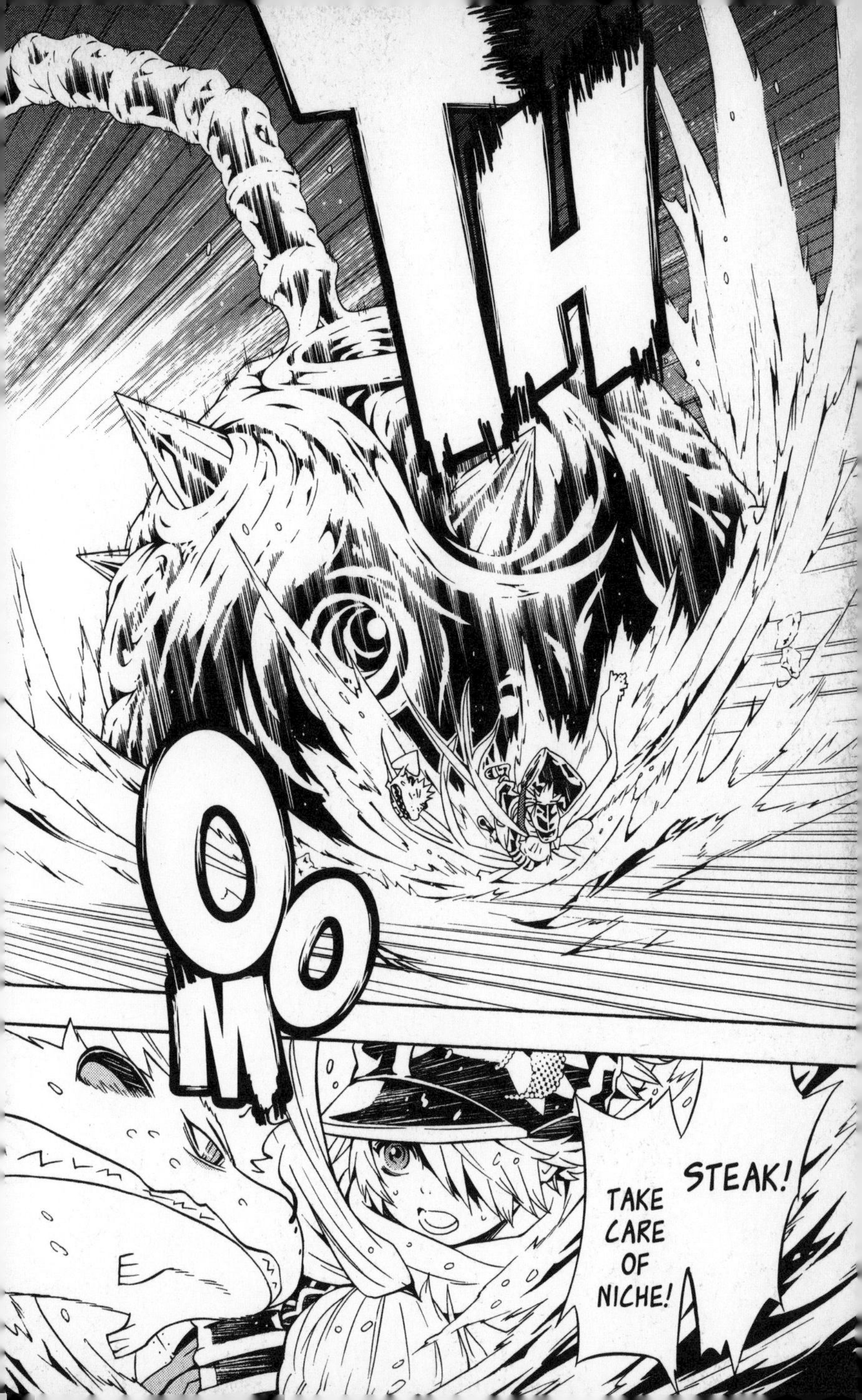
STEAK!
TAKE CARE OF NICHE!

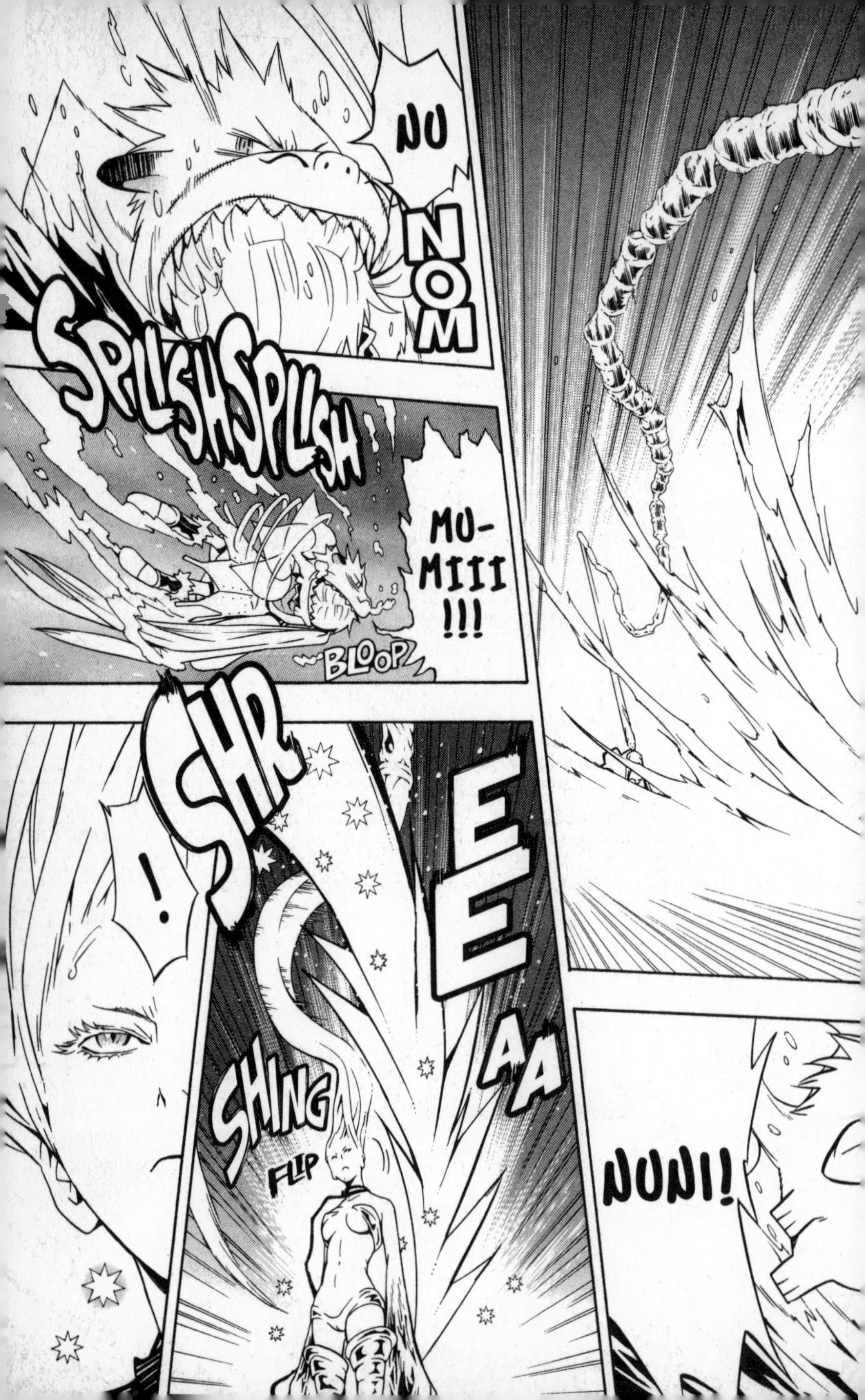
NU
NOM
SPLISHSPLISH
MU-MIII!!!
BLOOP
NUNI!
SHR
EEEAA
SHING
FLIP
!

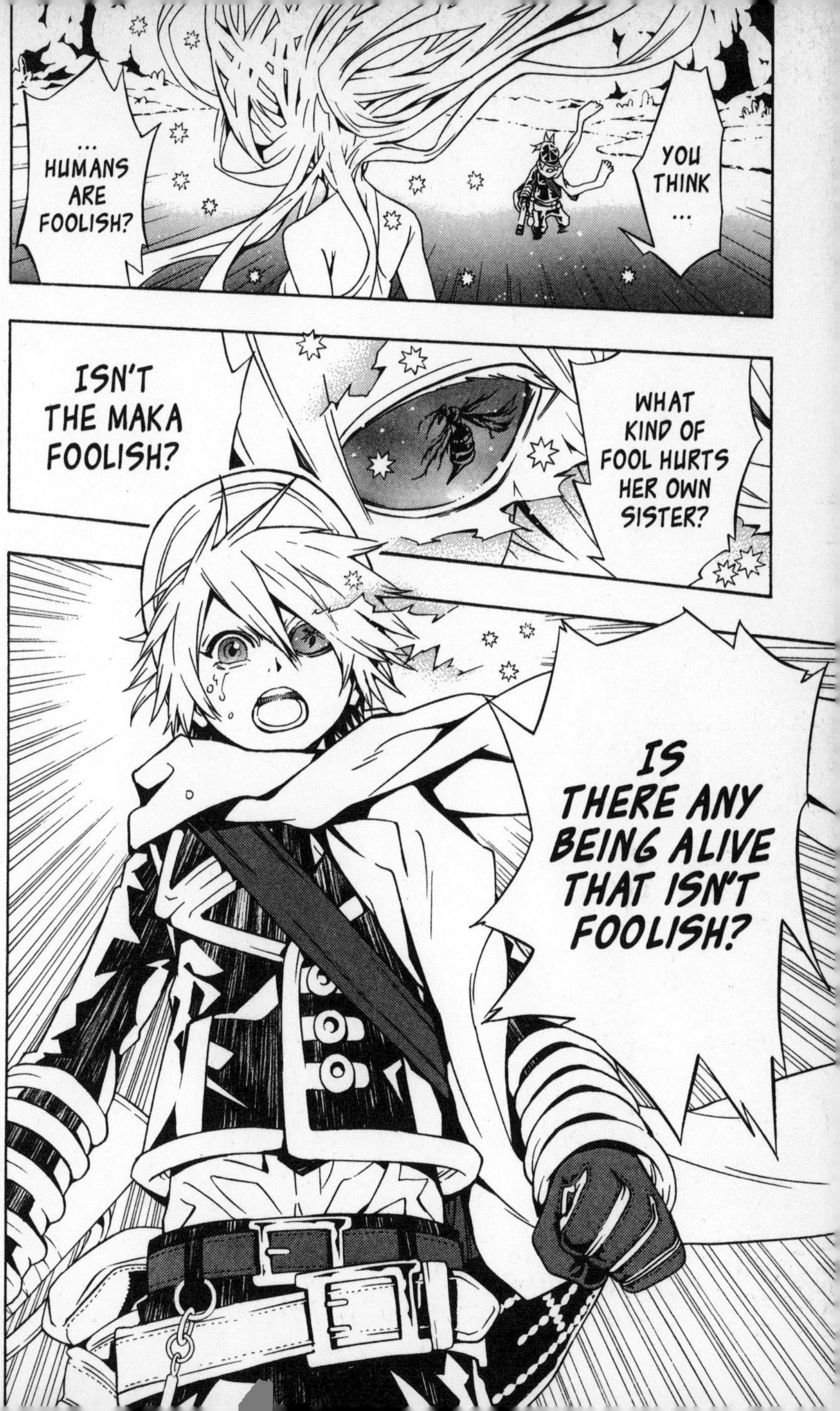
YOU THINK ...
... HUMANS ARE FOOLISH?
WHAT KIND OF FOOL HURTS HER OWN SISTER?
ISN'T THE MAKA FOOLISH?
IS THERE ANY BEING ALIVE THAT ISN'T FOOLISH?

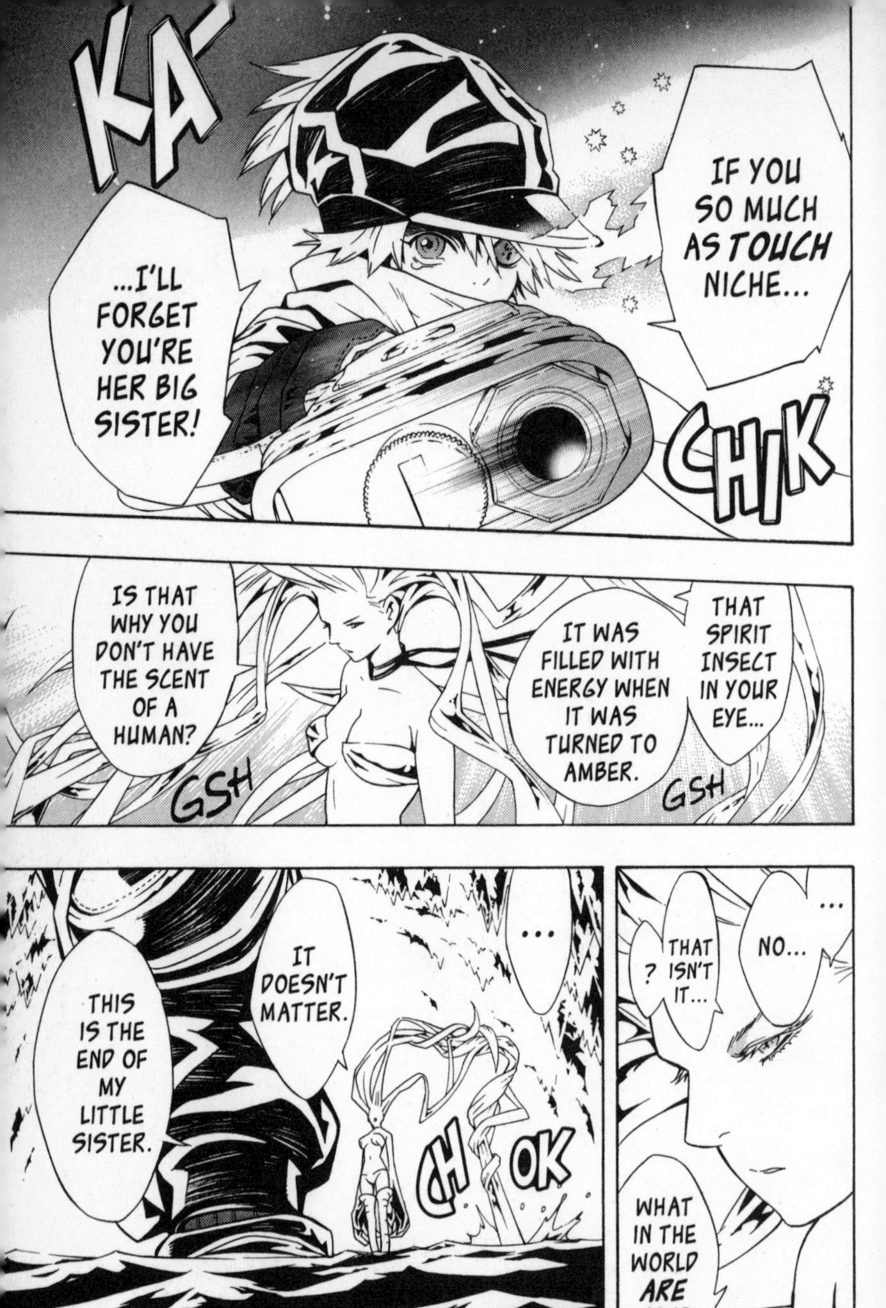
IF YOU SO MUCH AS TOUCH NICHE...
KA'
...I'LL FORGET YOU'RE HER BIG SISTER!
CHIK
THAT SPIRIT INSECT IN YOUR EYE...
IT WAS FILLED WITH ENERGY WHEN IT WAS TURNED TO AMBER.
GSH
IS THAT WHY YOU DON'T HAVE THE SCENT OF A HUMAN?
GSH
...
NO...
THAT ISN'T IT...
?
WHAT IN THE WORLD ARE YOU?
...
IT DOESN'T MATTER.
THIS IS THE END OF MY LITTLE SISTER.
CHOK

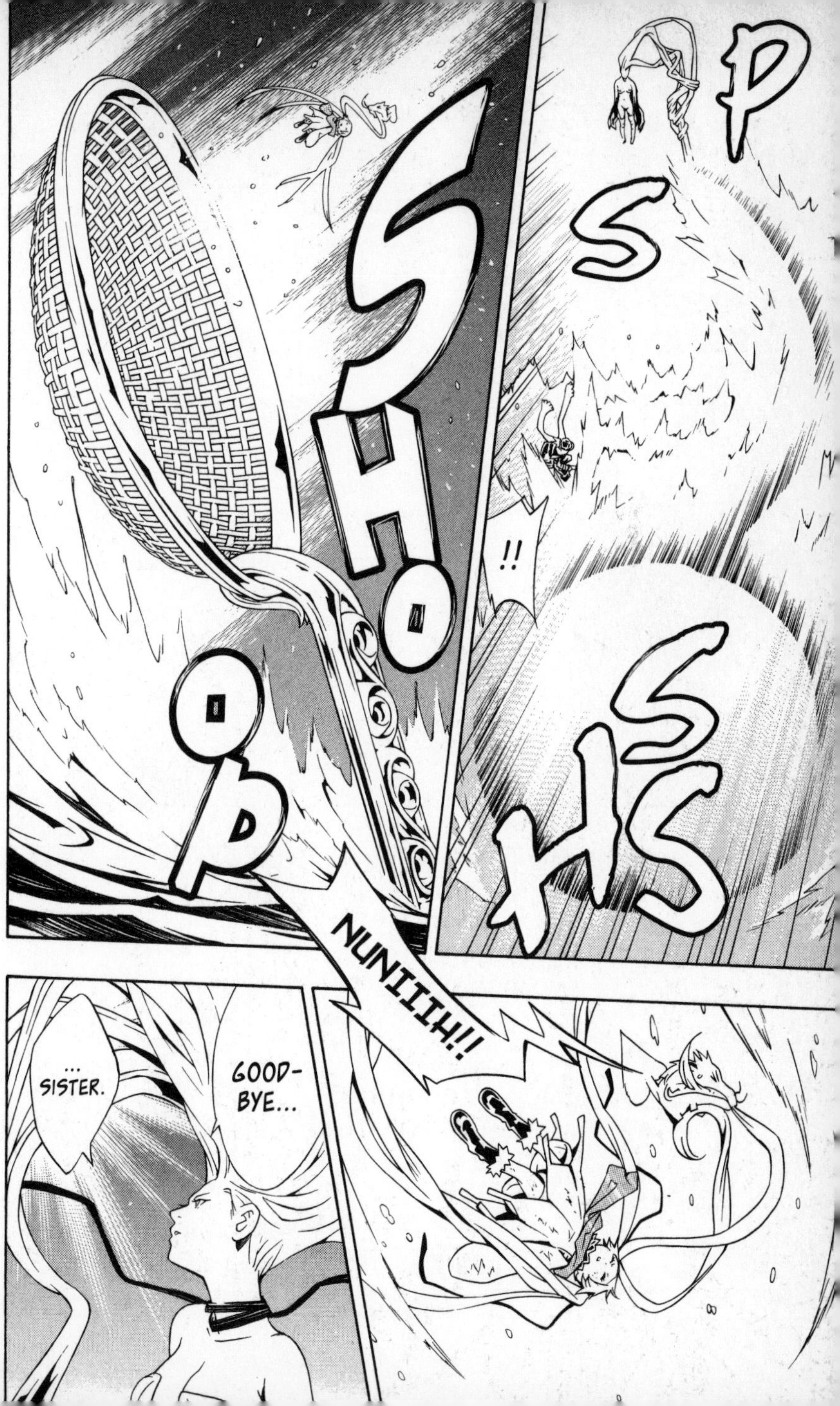

!!
SHOOP
NUNIIIH!!
GOOD-BYE...
...SISTER.

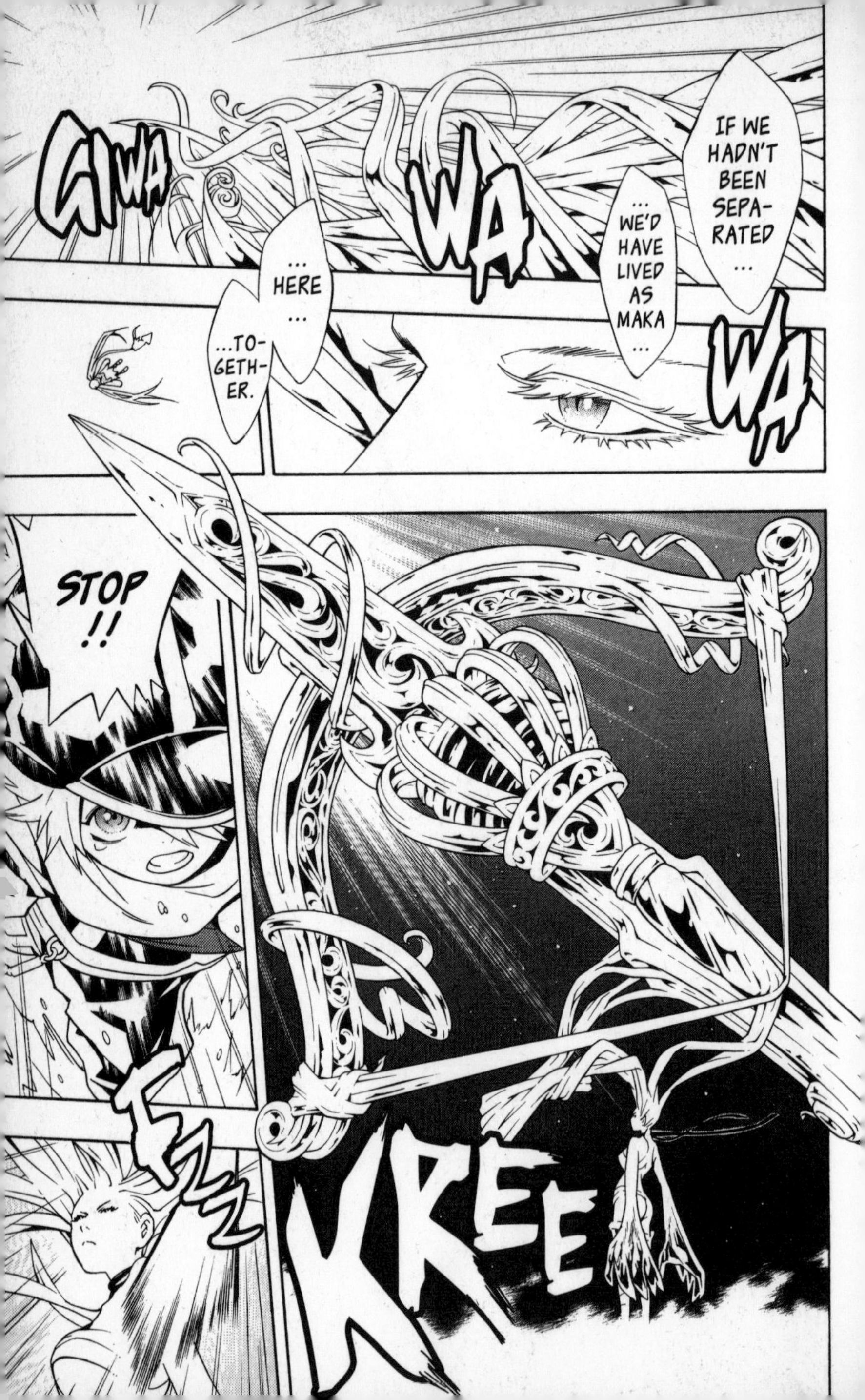
IF WE HADN'T BEEN SEPARATED...
...WE'D HAVE LIVED AS MAKA...
GIWA
WA
WA
...HERE...
...TOGETHER.
STOP!!
KREE

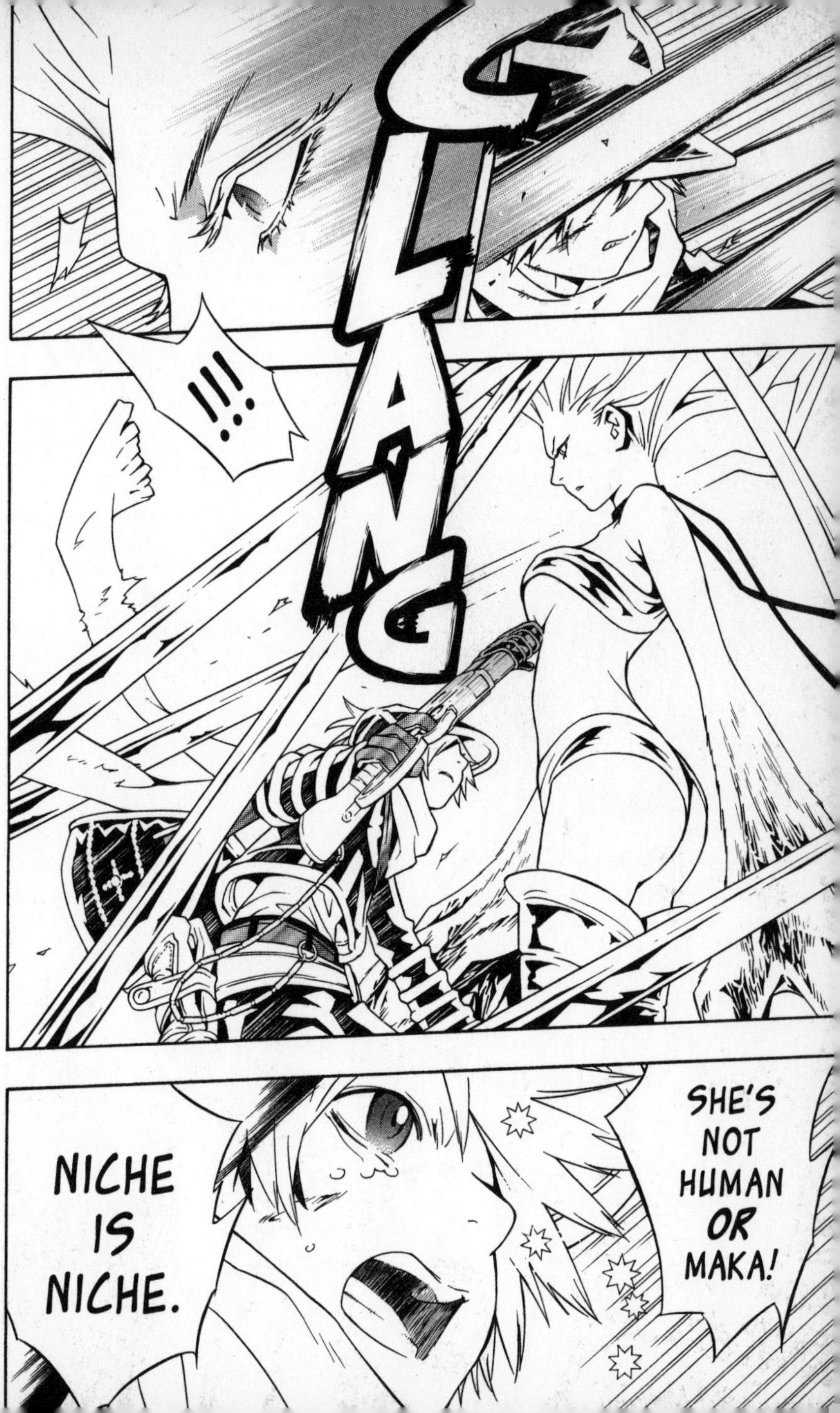
CLANG
!!!
SHE'S NOT HUMAN OR MAKA!
NICHE IS NICHE.

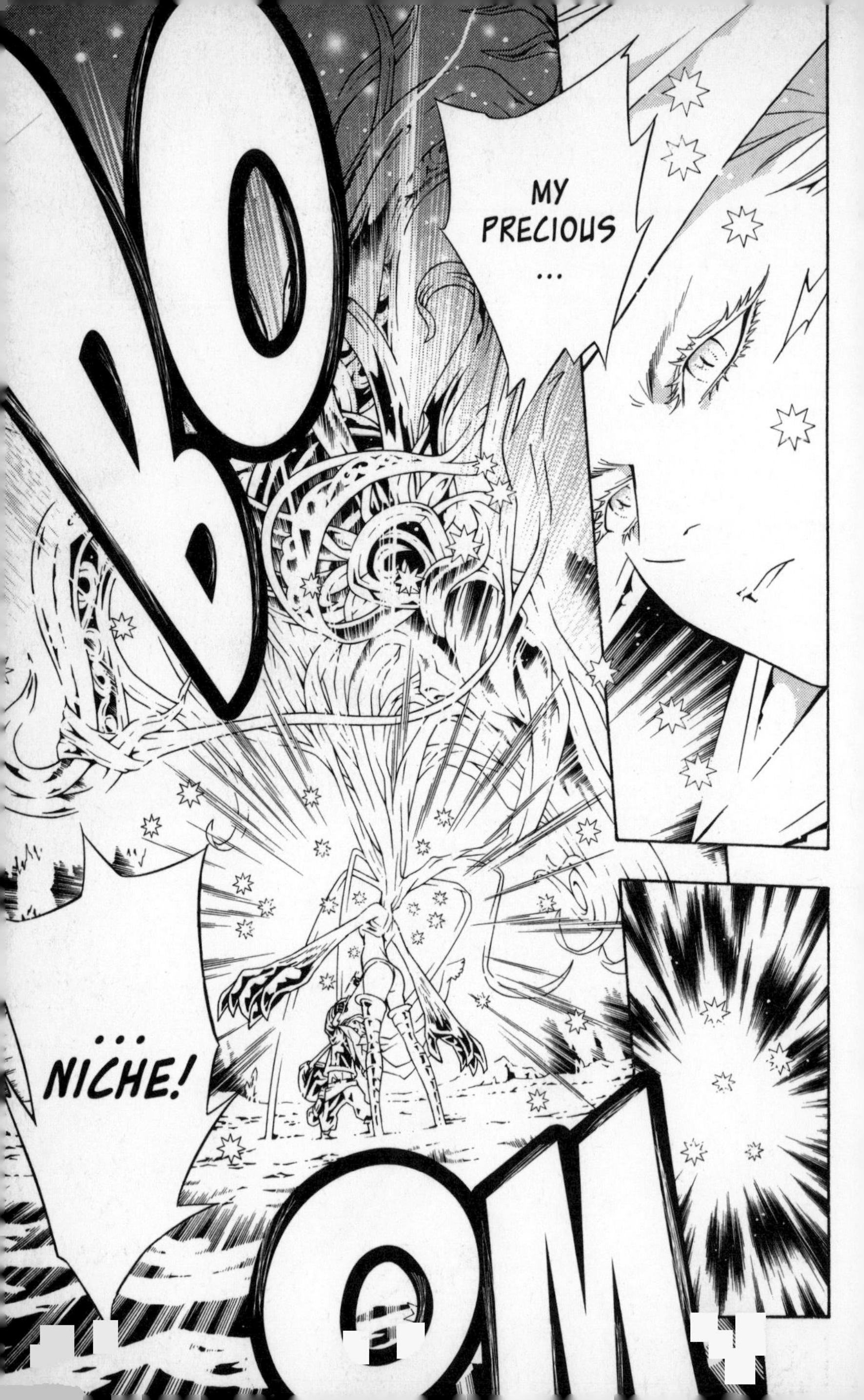
MY PRECIOUS ...
... NICHE!

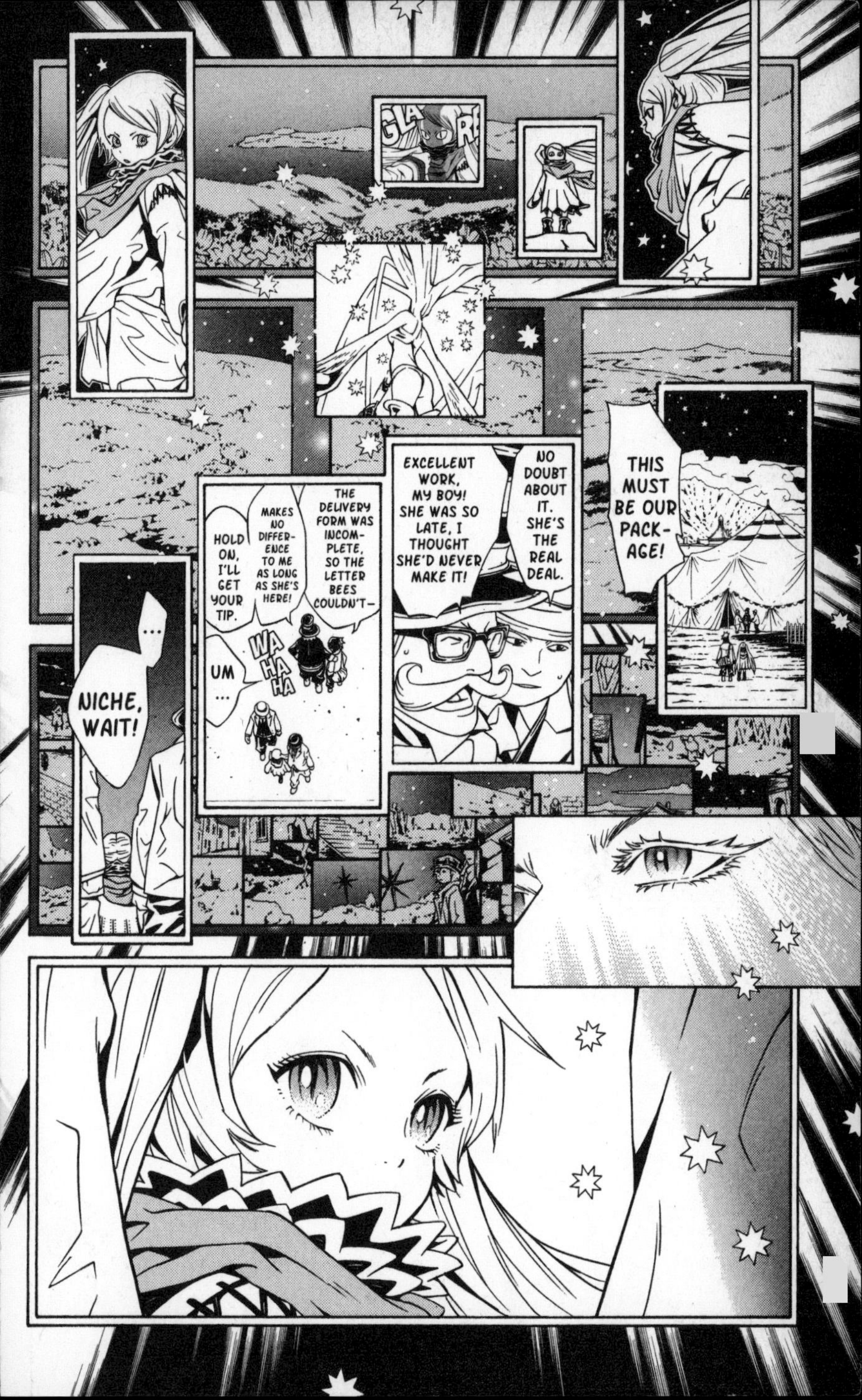
GLARE
THIS MUST BE OUR PACKAGE!
NO DOUBT ABOUT IT. SHE'S THE REAL DEAL.
EXCELLENT WORK, MY BOY! SHE WAS SO LATE, I THOUGHT SHE'D NEVER MAKE IT!
THE DELIVERY FORM WAS INCOMPLETE, SO THE LETTER BEES COULDN'T–
MAKES NO DIFFERENCE TO ME AS LONG AS SHE'S HERE!
HOLD ON, I'LL GET YOUR TIP.
WA HA HA
UM ...
...
NICHE, WAIT!

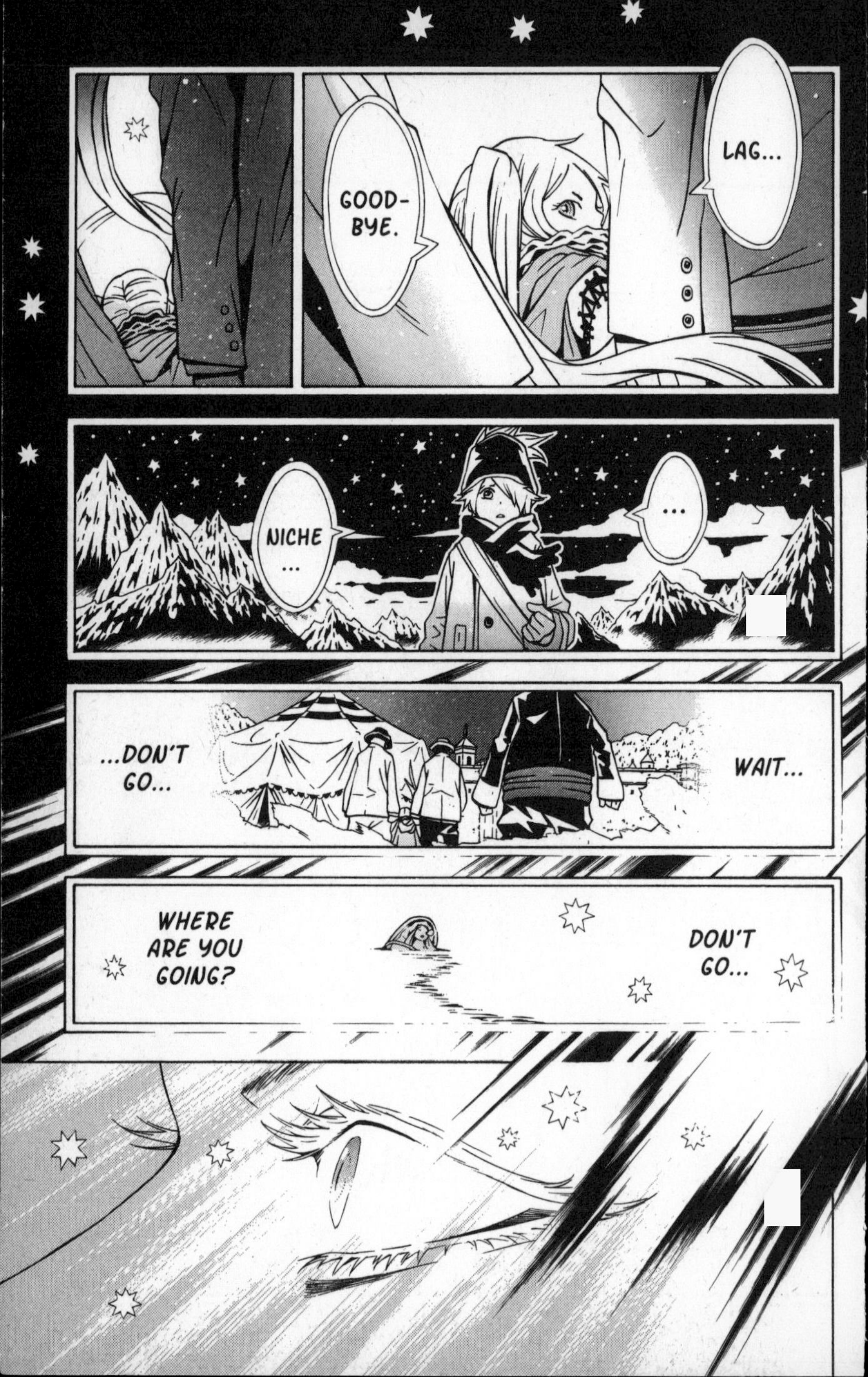
LAG...
GOOD-BYE.
...
NICHE ...
WAIT...
...DON'T GO...
DON'T GO...
WHERE ARE YOU GOING?

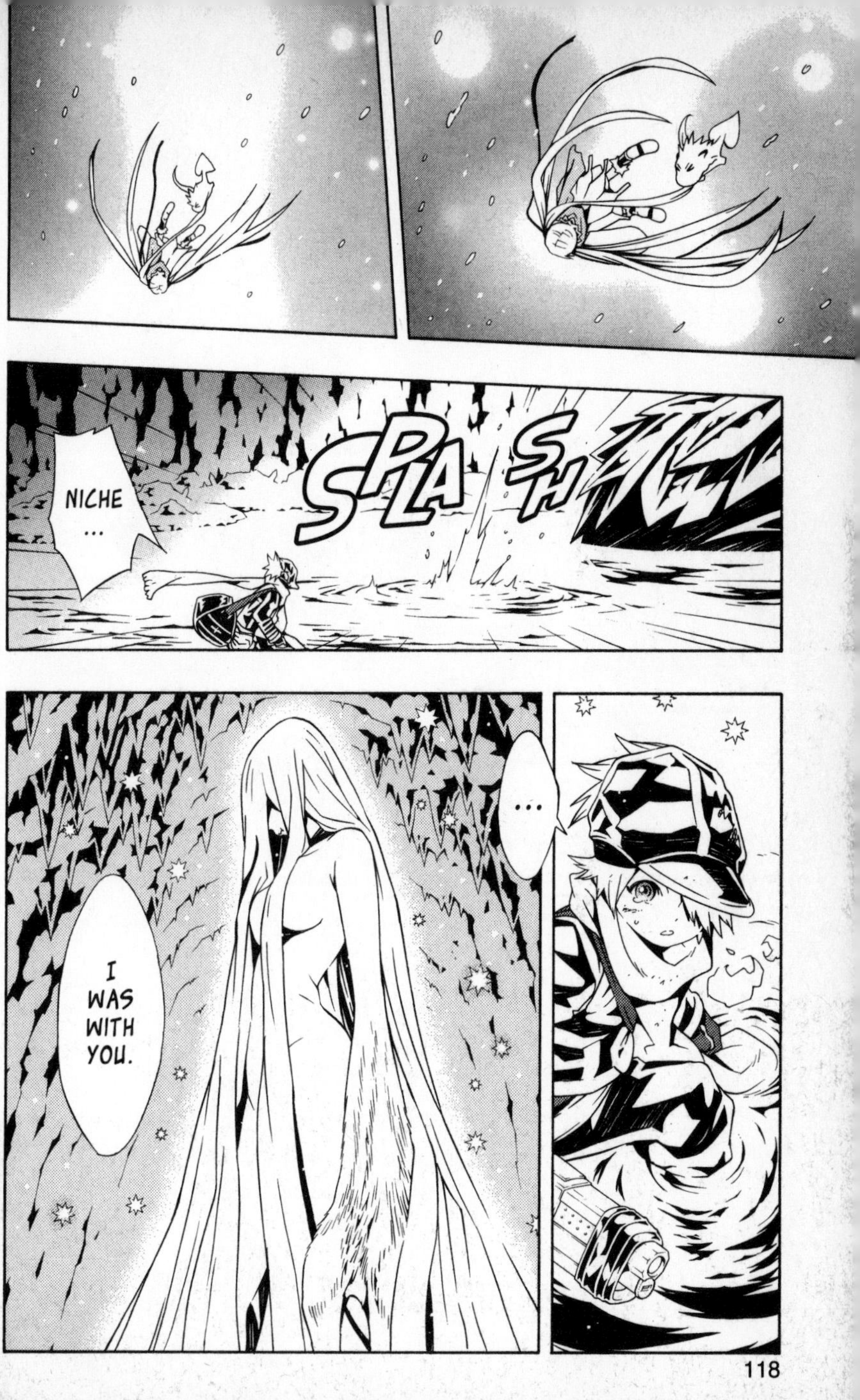
SPLASH
NICHE ...
...
I WAS WITH YOU.

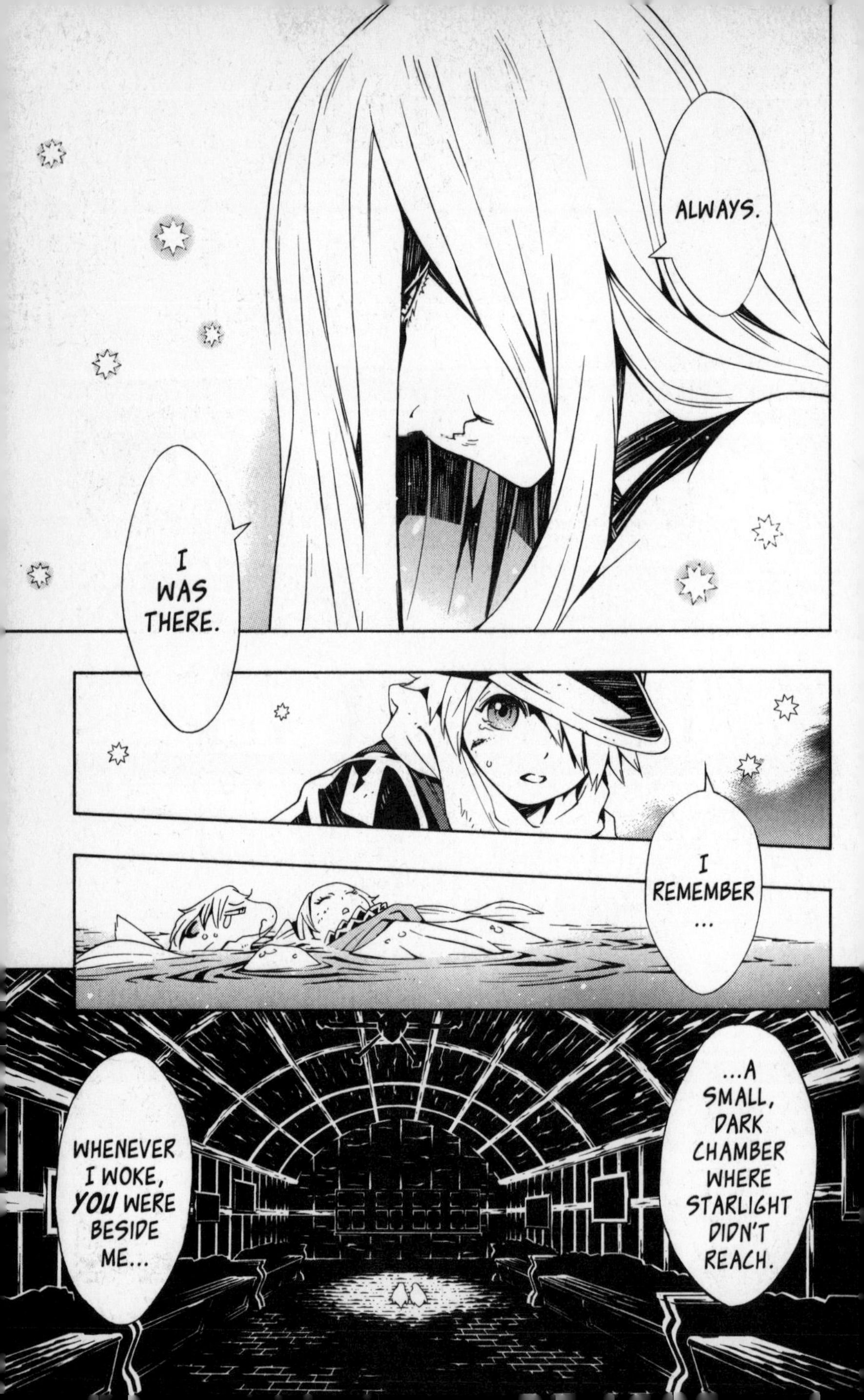
ALWAYS.
I WAS THERE.
I REMEMBER...
...A SMALL, DARK CHAMBER WHERE STARLIGHT DIDN'T REACH.
WHENEVER I WOKE, *YOU* WERE BESIDE ME...

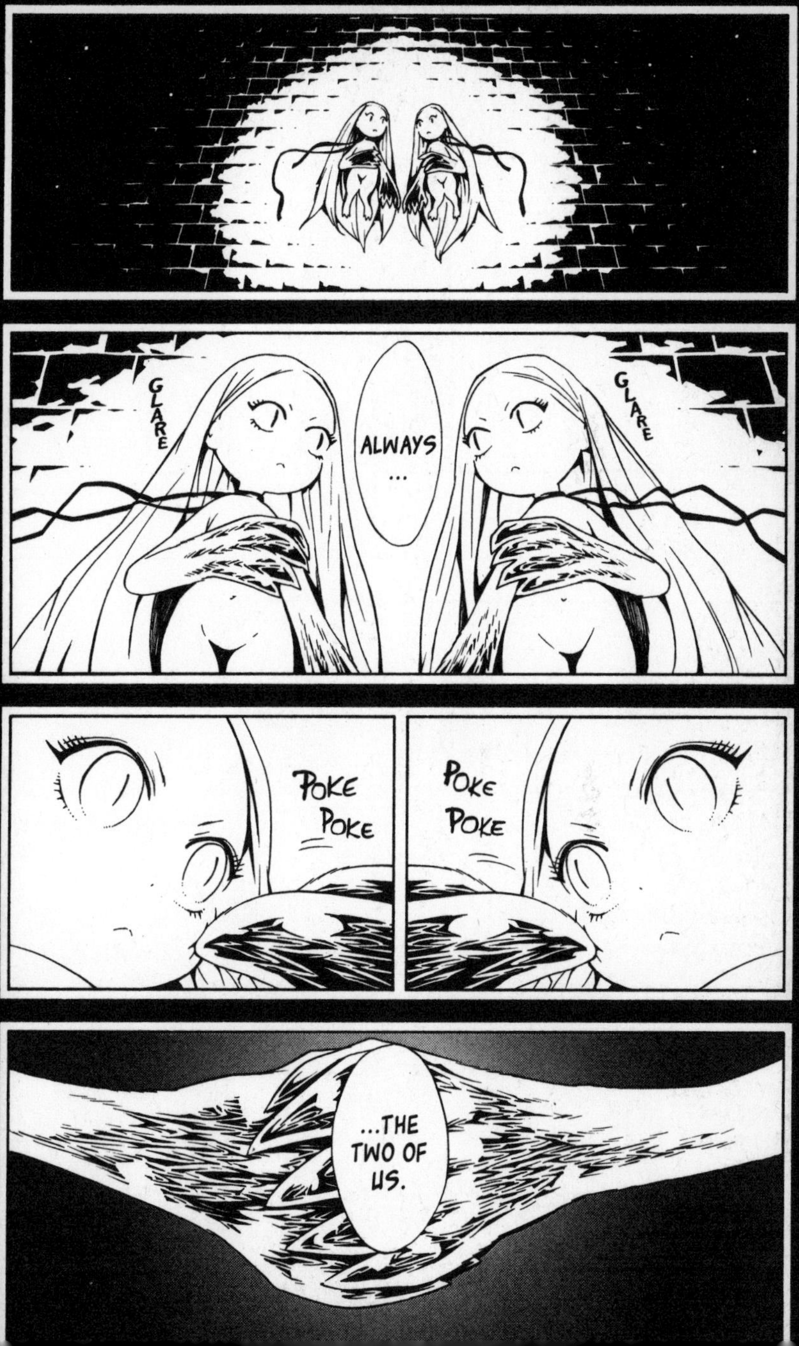
GLARE
ALWAYS...
GLARE
POKE POKE
POKE POKE
...THE TWO OF US.

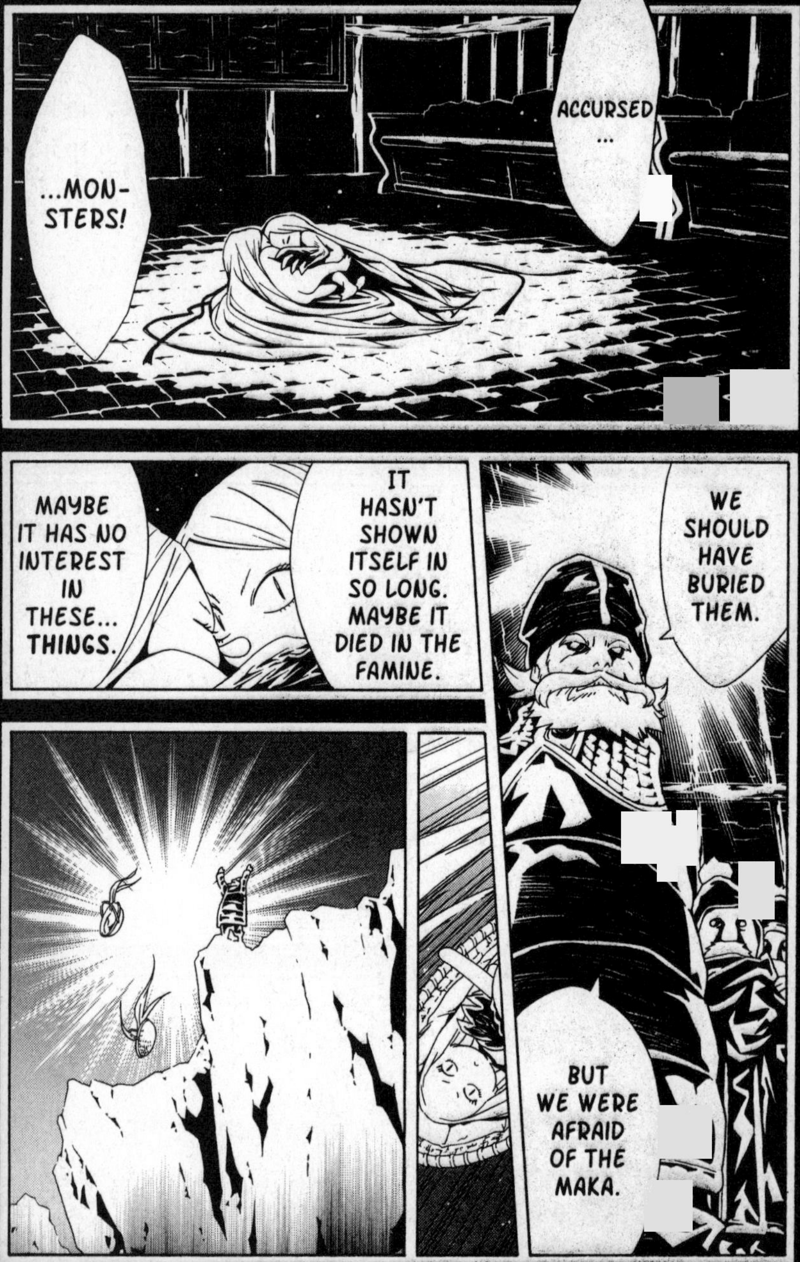
ACCURSED ...
...MON-STERS!
WE SHOULD HAVE BURIED THEM.
BUT WE WERE AFRAID OF THE MAKA.
IT HASN'T SHOWN ITSELF IN SO LONG. MAYBE IT DIED IN THE FAMINE.
MAYBE IT HAS NO INTEREST IN THESE... THINGS.

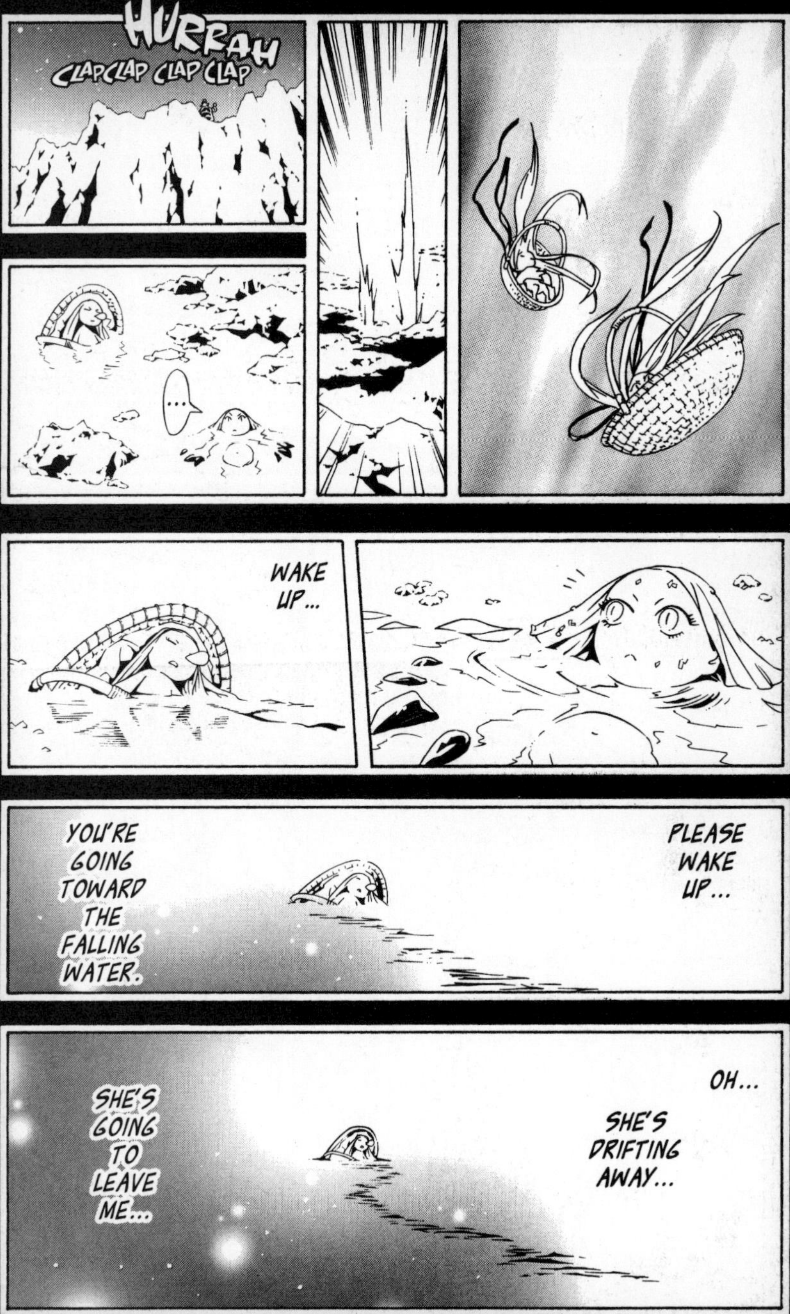
HURRAH
CLAPCLAP CLAP CLAP
...
WAKE UP...
PLEASE WAKE UP...
YOU'RE GOING TOWARD THE FALLING WATER.
OH...
SHE'S DRIFTING AWAY...
SHE'S GOING TO LEAVE ME...

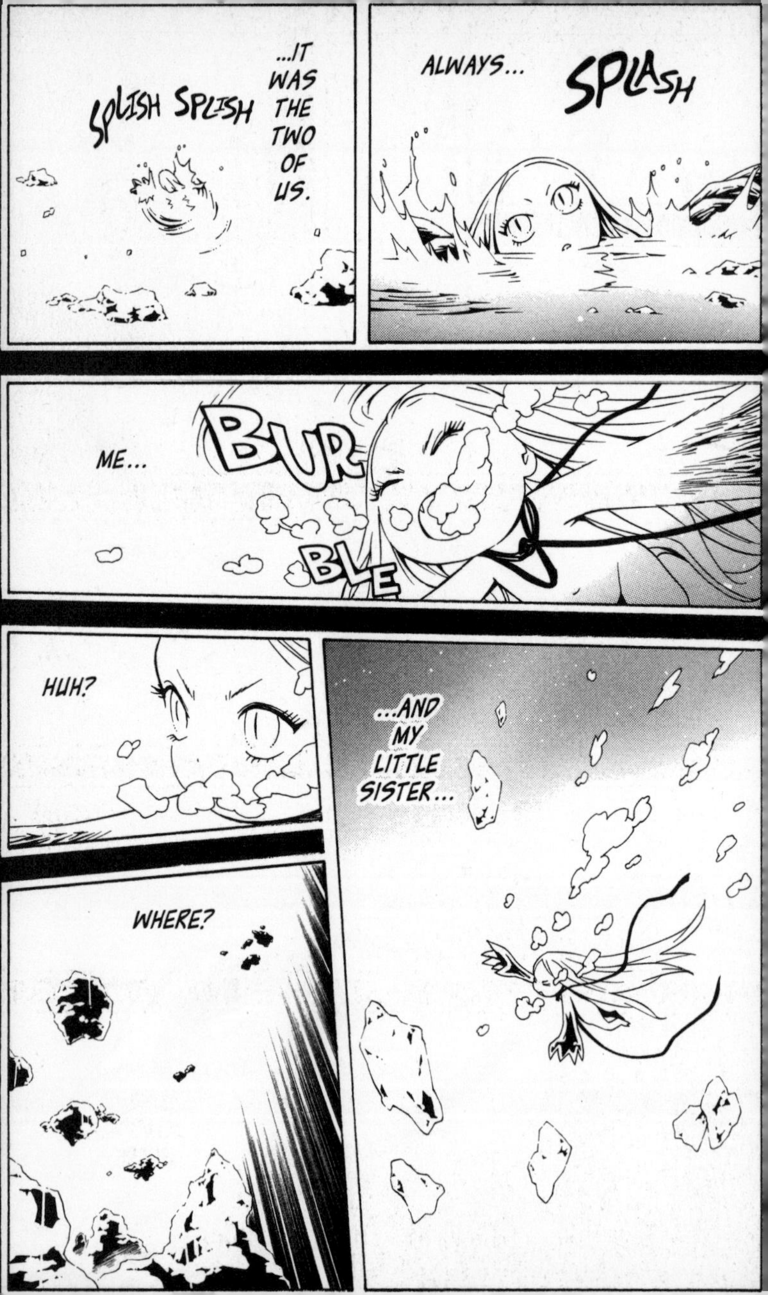
SPLASH
ALWAYS...
...IT WAS THE TWO OF US.
SPLISH SPLISH
BURBLE
ME...
...AND MY LITTLE SISTER...
HUH?
WHERE?

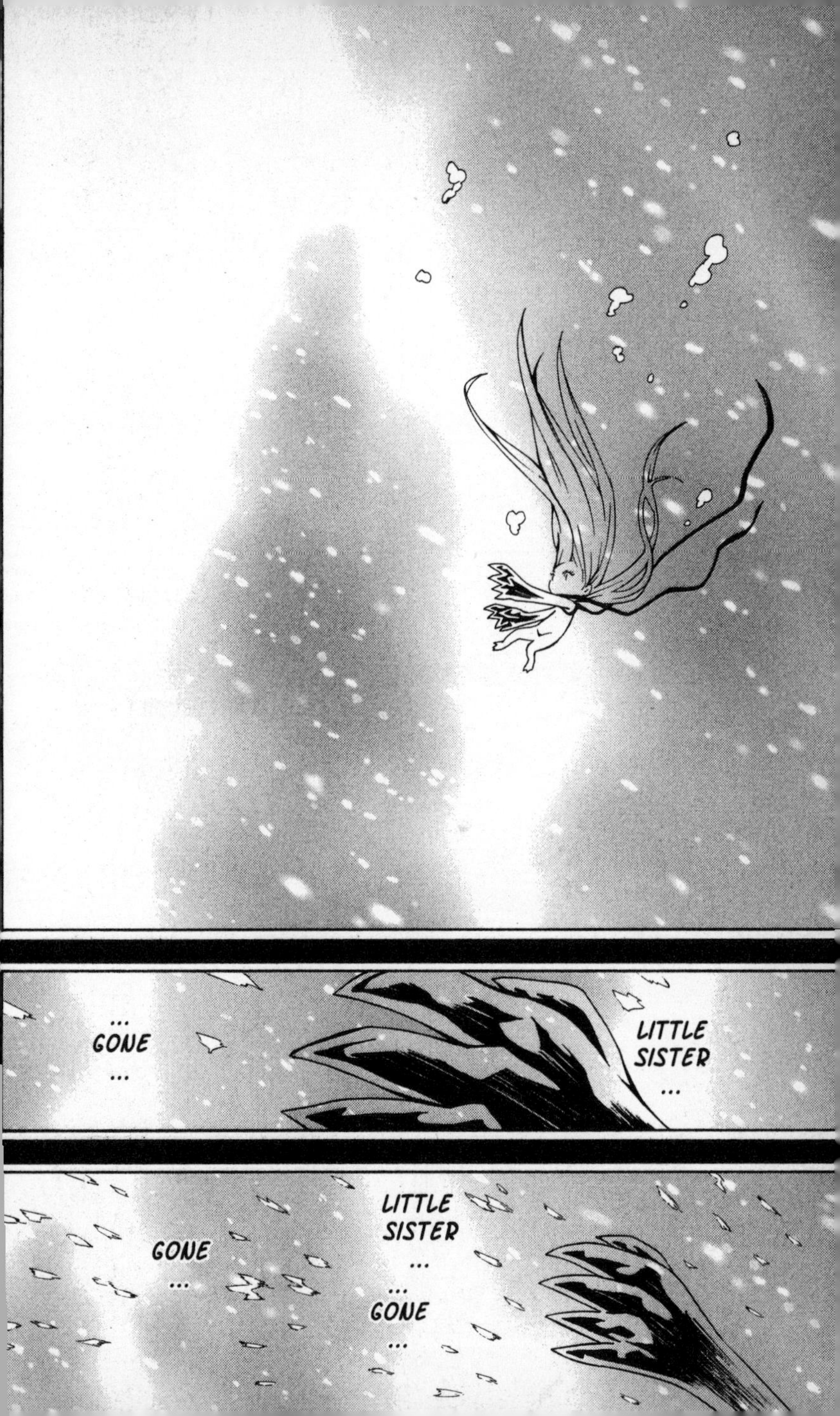

LITTLE SISTER ...
... GONE ...
LITTLE SISTER ...
... GONE ...
GONE ...

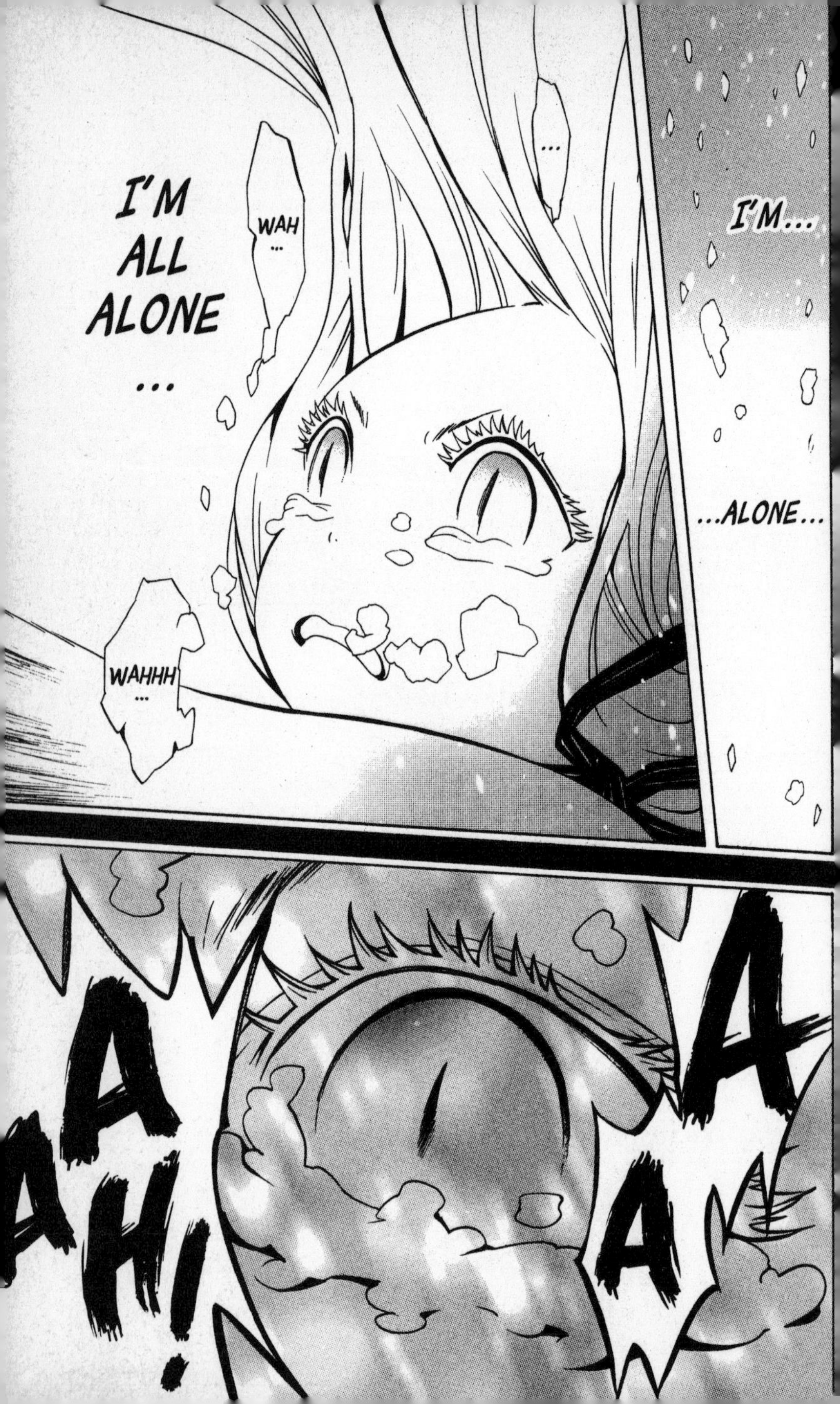

I'M...
...ALONE...
...
WAH ...
I'M ALL ALONE ...
WAHHH ...
AAA
AAH!

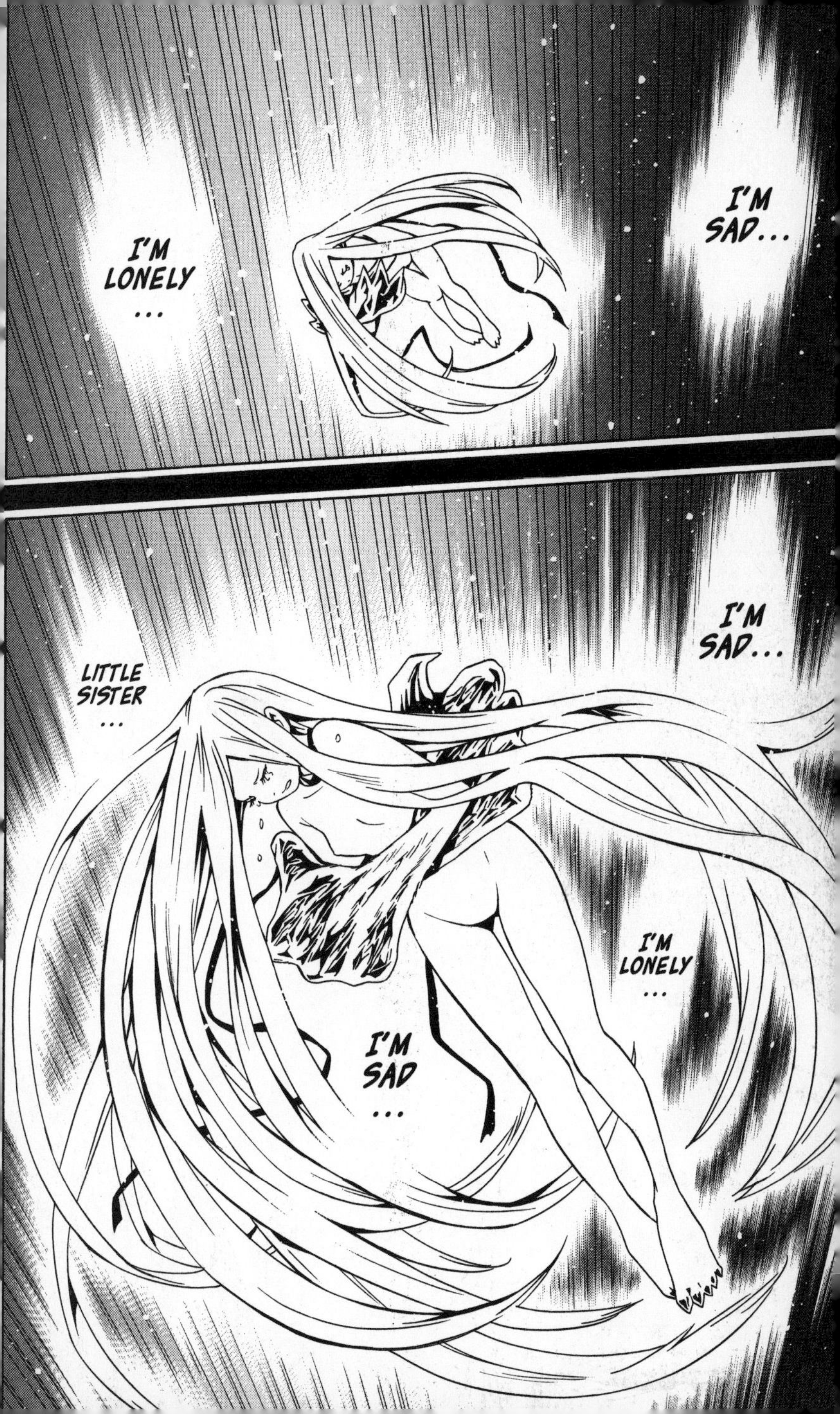
I'M SAD...
I'M LONELY...
I'M SAD...
LITTLE SISTER...
I'M LONELY...
I'M SAD...

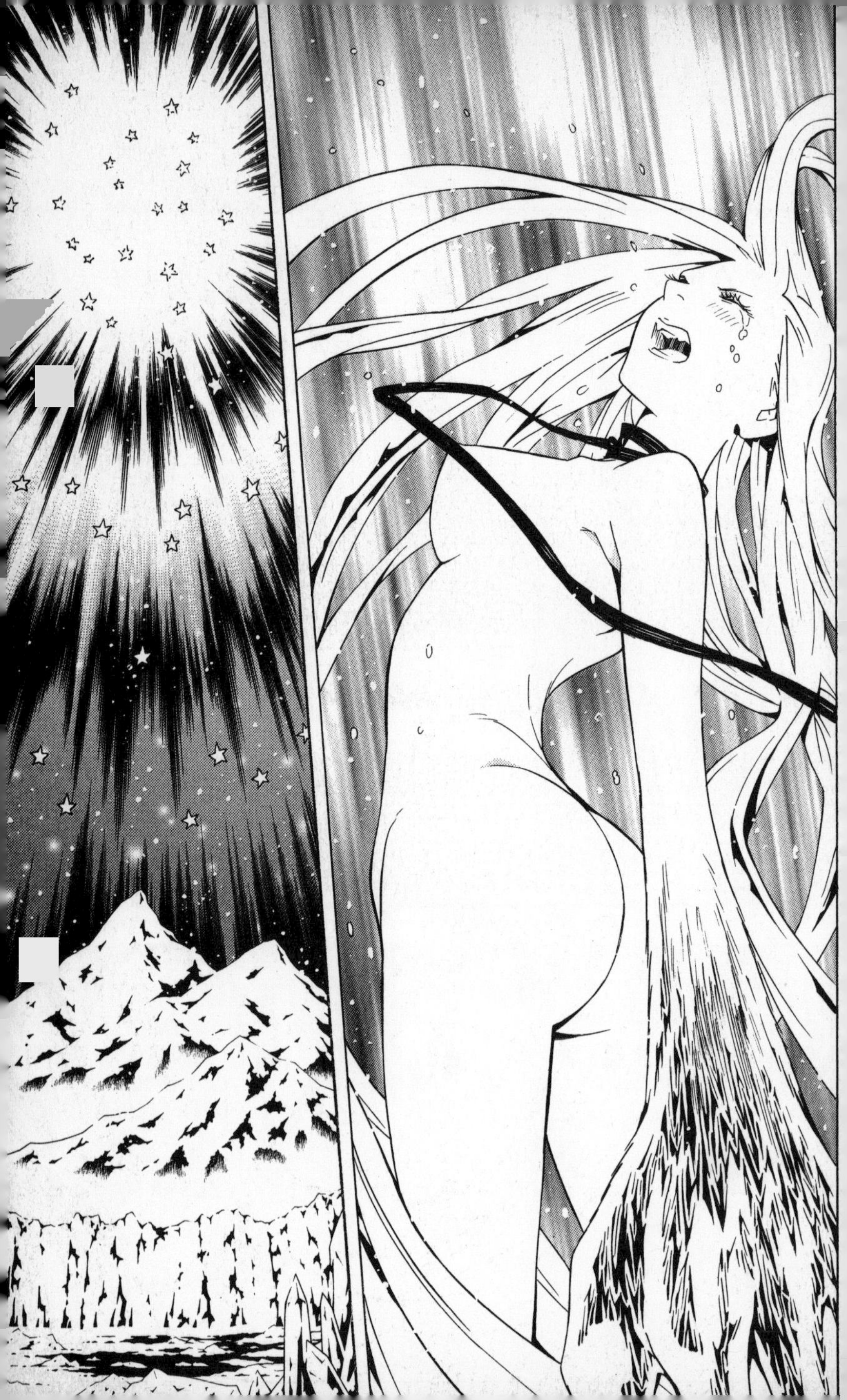

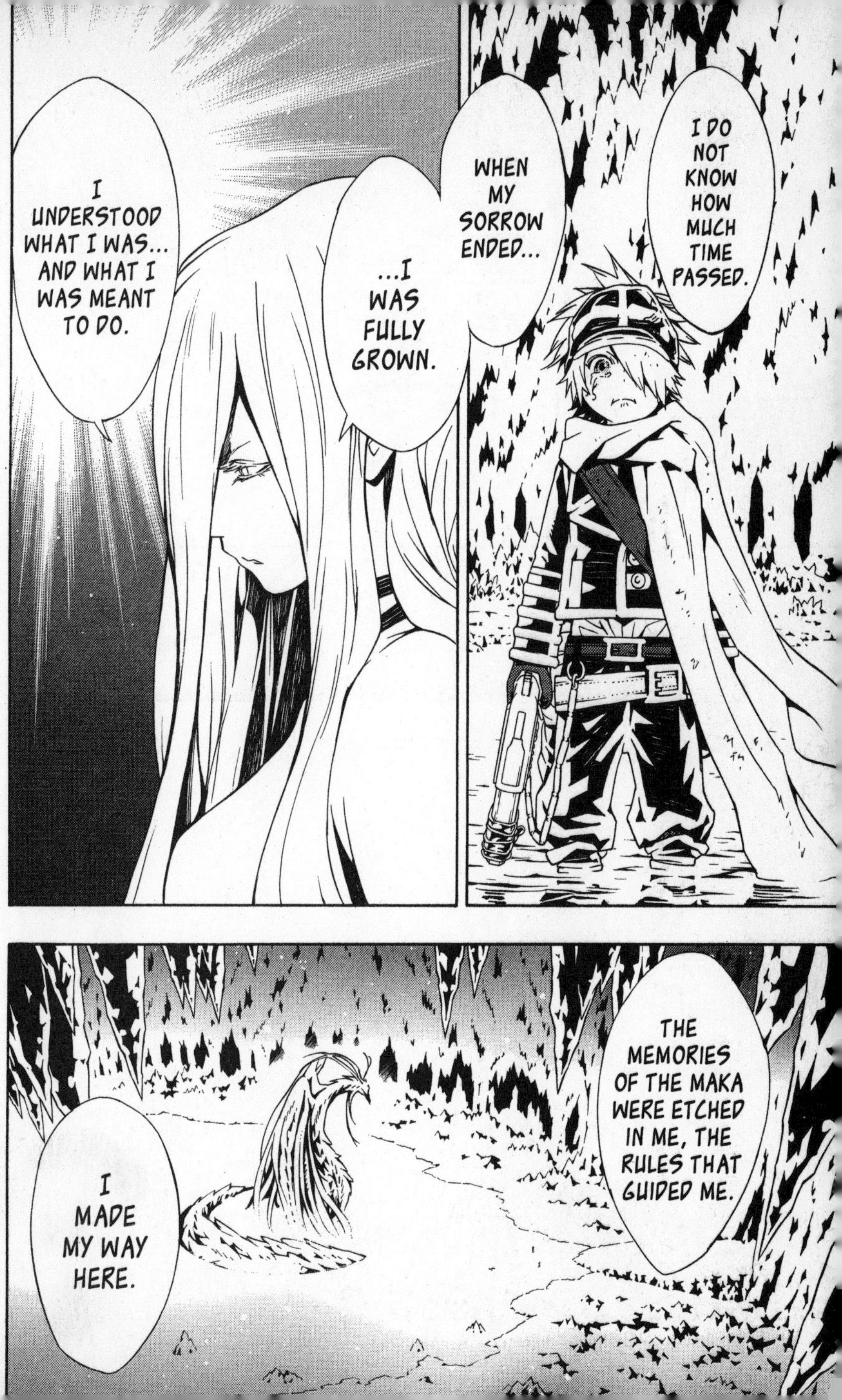

I DO NOT KNOW HOW MUCH TIME PASSED.
WHEN MY SORROW ENDED...
...I WAS FULLY GROWN.
I UNDERSTOOD WHAT I WAS... AND WHAT I WAS MEANT TO DO.
THE MEMORIES OF THE MAKA WERE ETCHED IN ME, THE RULES THAT GUIDED ME.
I MADE MY WAY HERE.

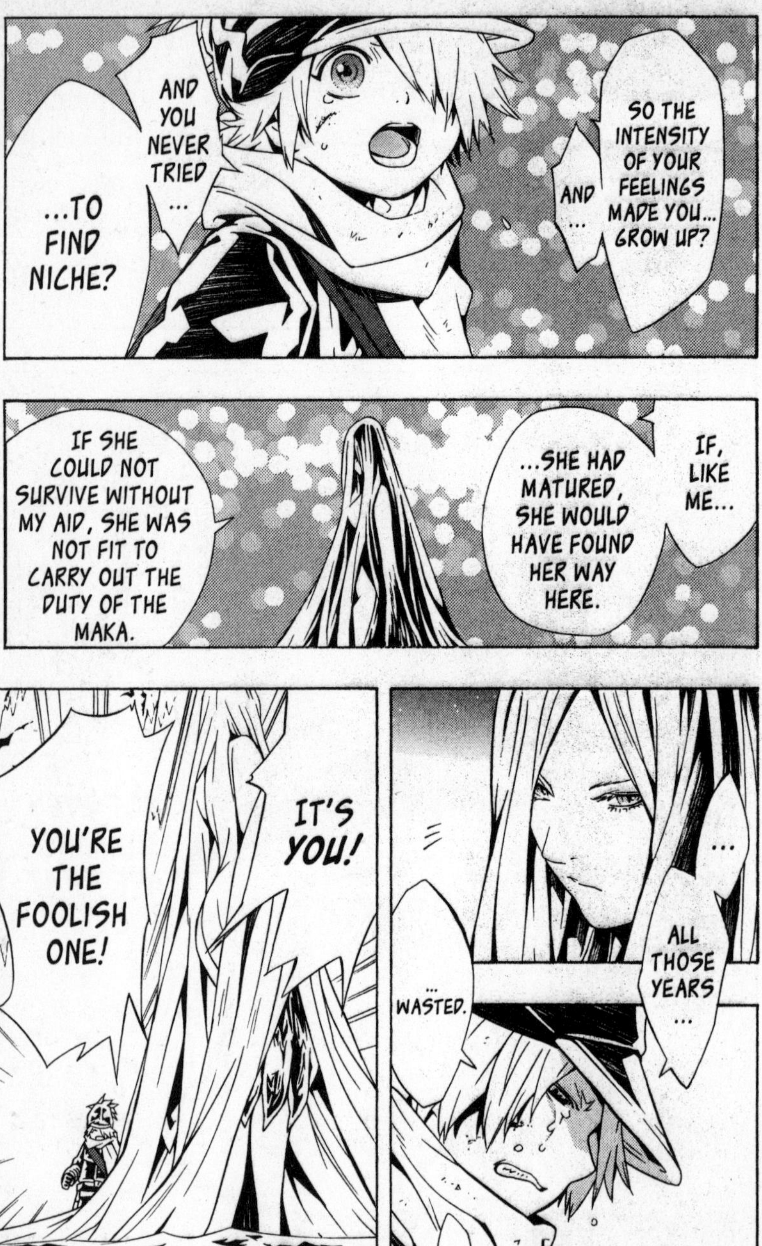

SO THE INTENSITY OF YOUR FEELINGS MADE YOU... GROW UP?
AND...
AND YOU NEVER TRIED...
...TO FIND NICHE?
IF, LIKE ME...
...SHE HAD MATURED, SHE WOULD HAVE FOUND HER WAY HERE.
IF SHE COULD NOT SURVIVE WITHOUT MY AID, SHE WAS NOT FIT TO CARRY OUT THE DUTY OF THE MAKA.
...
ALL THOSE YEARS...
...WASTED.
...
IT'S YOU!
YOU'RE THE FOOLISH ONE!

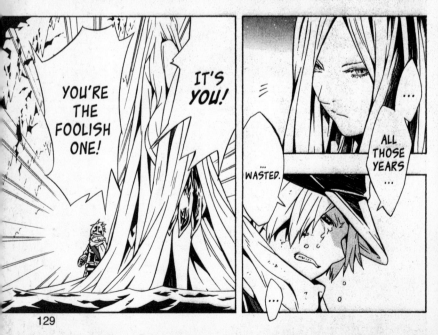

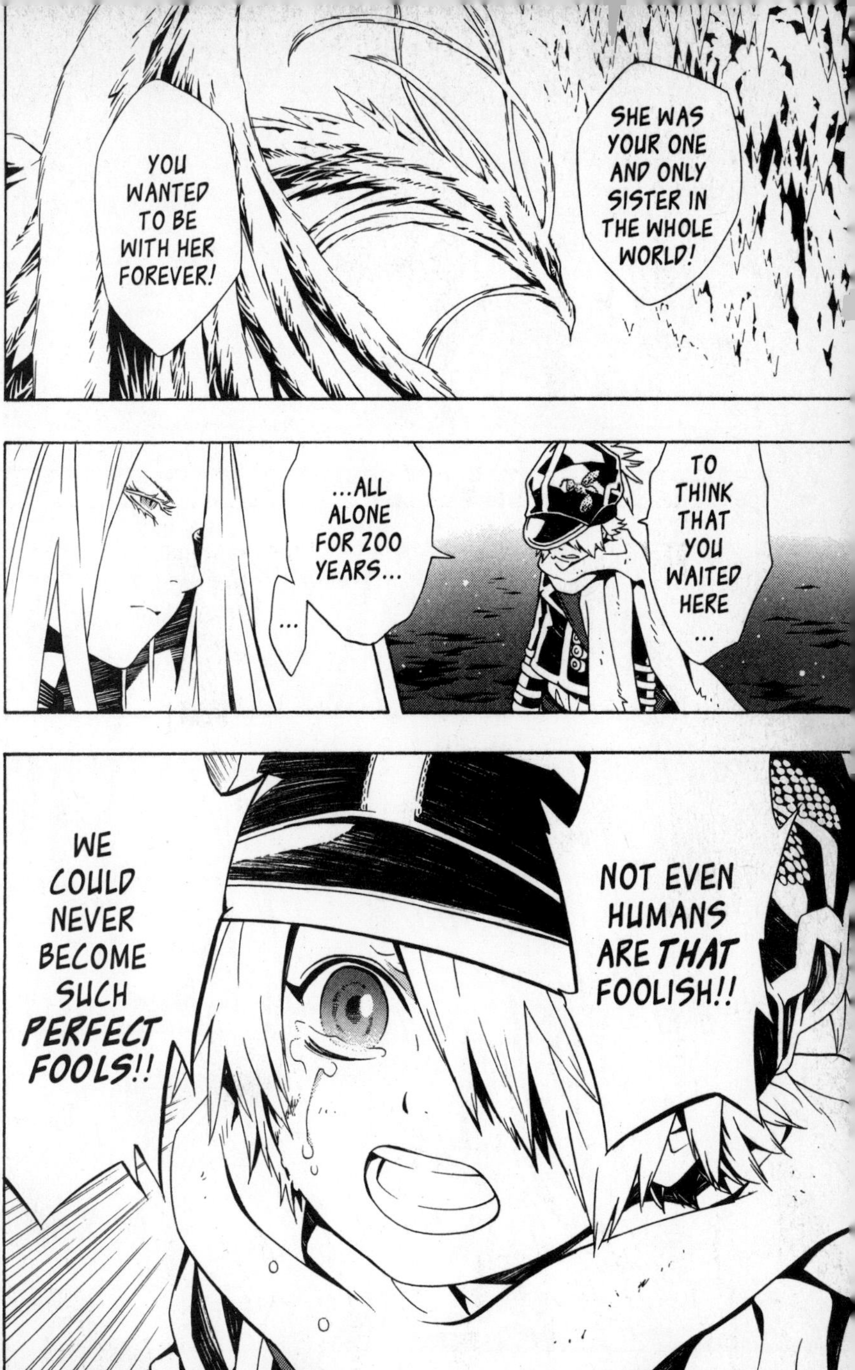
SHE WAS YOUR ONE AND ONLY SISTER IN THE WHOLE WORLD!
YOU WANTED TO BE WITH HER FOREVER!
TO THINK THAT YOU WAITED HERE...
...ALL ALONE FOR 200 YEARS...
...
NOT EVEN HUMANS ARE *THAT* FOOLISH!!
WE COULD NEVER BECOME SUCH *PERFECT FOOLS*!!

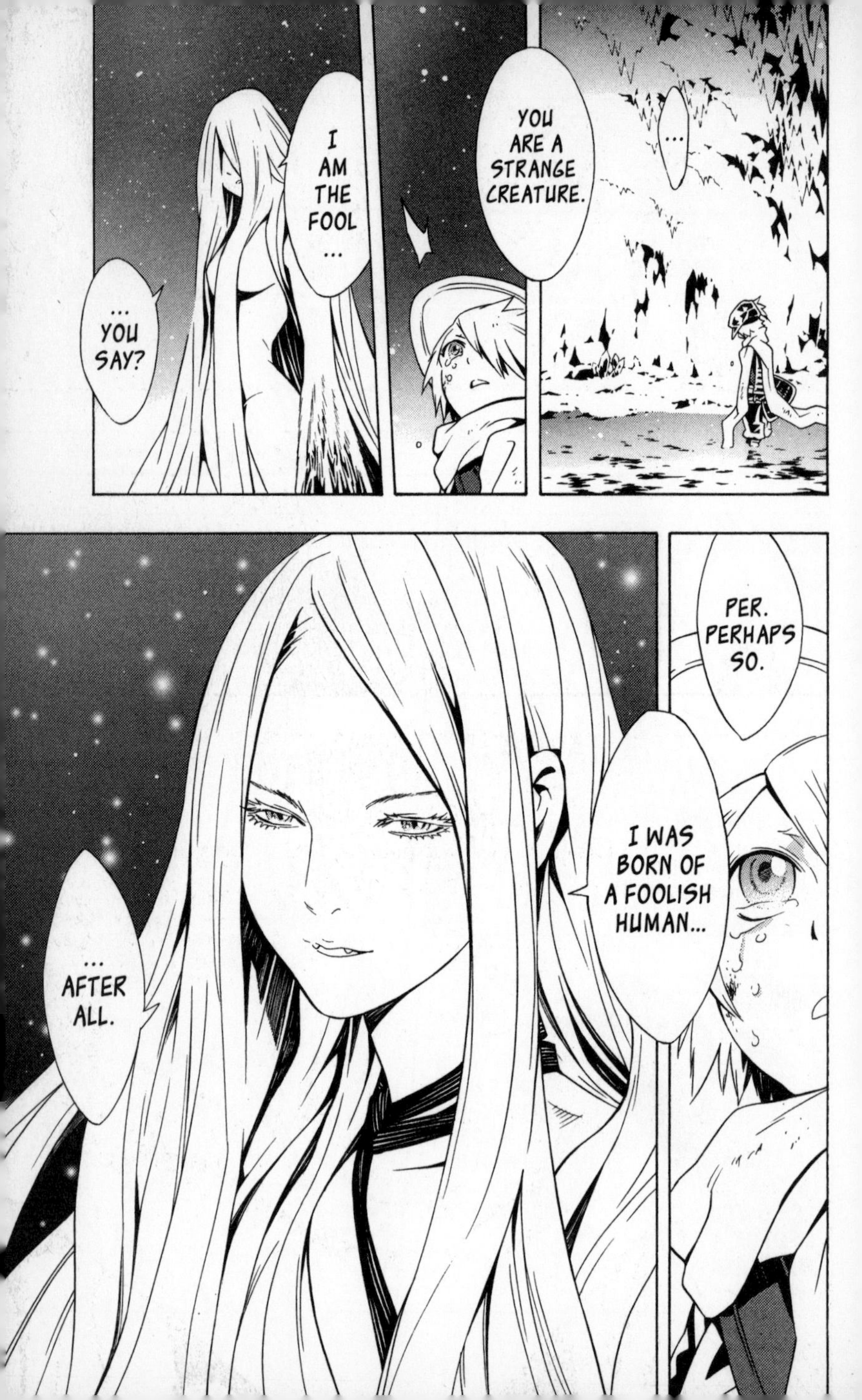
...
YOU ARE A STRANGE CREATURE.
I AM THE FOOL...
...YOU SAY?
PER. PERHAPS SO.
I WAS BORN OF A FOOLISH HUMAN...
...AFTER ALL.

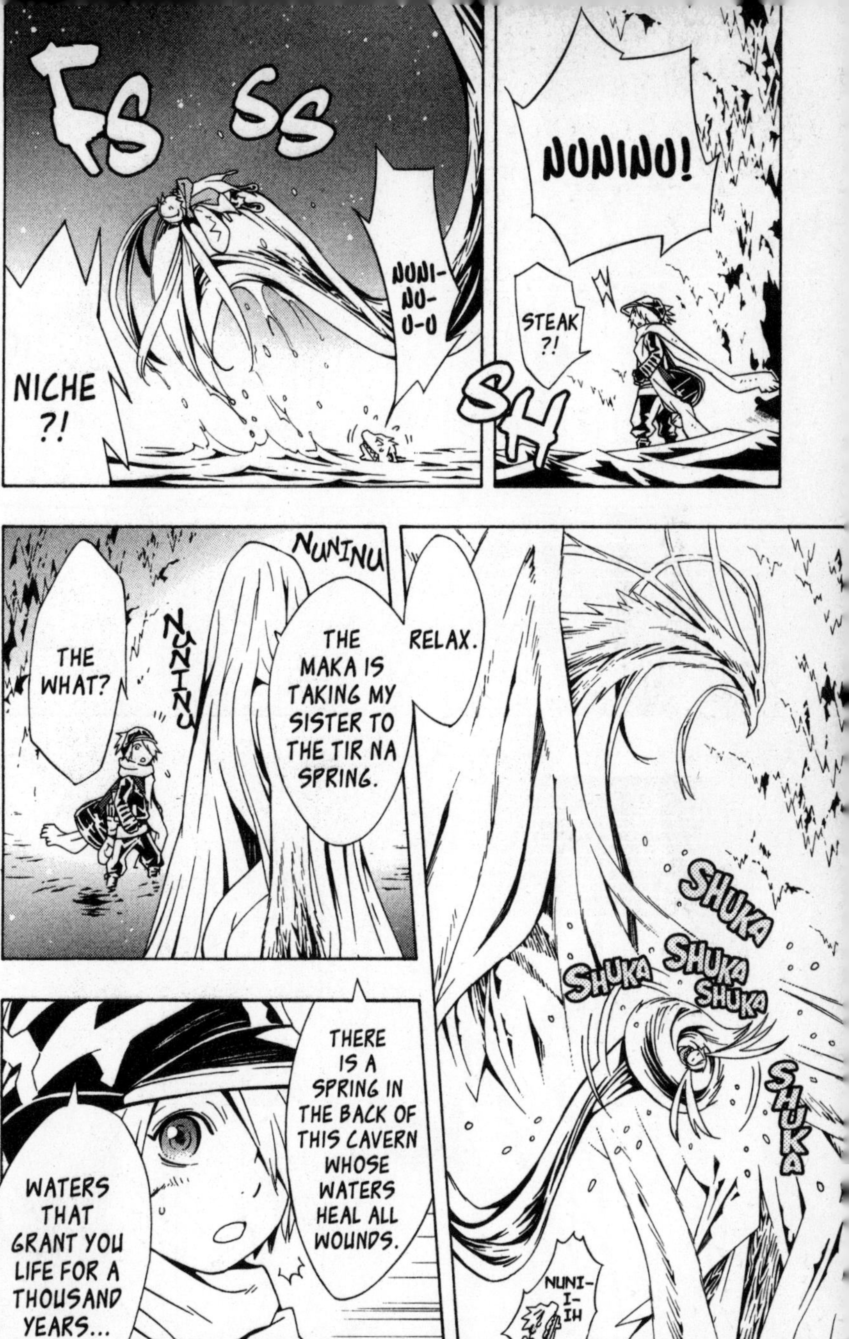
NUNINU!
STEAK ?!
SH
TSSS
NUNI-NU-U-U
NICHE ?!
RELAX.
SHUKA
SHUKA SHUKA
SHUKA
SHUKA
NUNI-I-IH
NUNINU
THE MAKA IS TAKING MY SISTER TO THE TIR NA SPRING.
THE WHAT?
NUNINU
THERE IS A SPRING IN THE BACK OF THIS CAVERN WHOSE WATERS HEAL ALL WOUNDS.
WATERS THAT GRANT YOU LIFE FOR A THOUSAND YEARS...

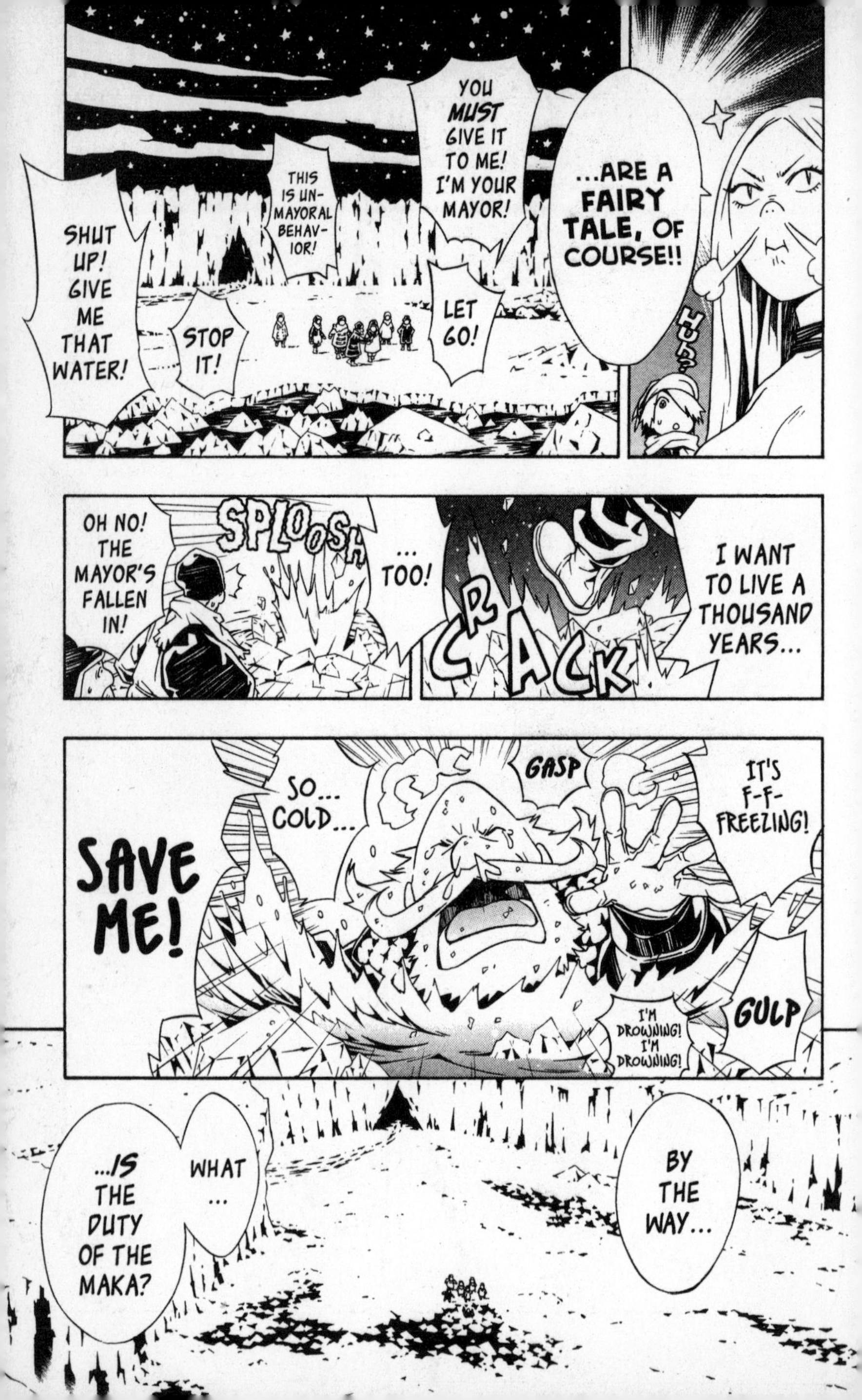
...ARE A FAIRY TALE, OF COURSE!!
HUH?
YOU MUST GIVE IT TO ME! I'M YOUR MAYOR!
THIS IS UN-MAYORAL BEHAVIOR!
LET GO!
STOP IT!
SHUT UP! GIVE ME THAT WATER!
I WANT TO LIVE A THOUSAND YEARS...
CRACK
...TOO!
SPLOOSH
OH NO! THE MAYOR'S FALLEN IN!
IT'S F-F-FREEZING!
GASP
SO... COLD...
SAVE ME!
GULP
I'M DROWNING! I'M DROWNING!
BY THE WAY...
WHAT...
...IS THE DUTY OF THE MAKA?

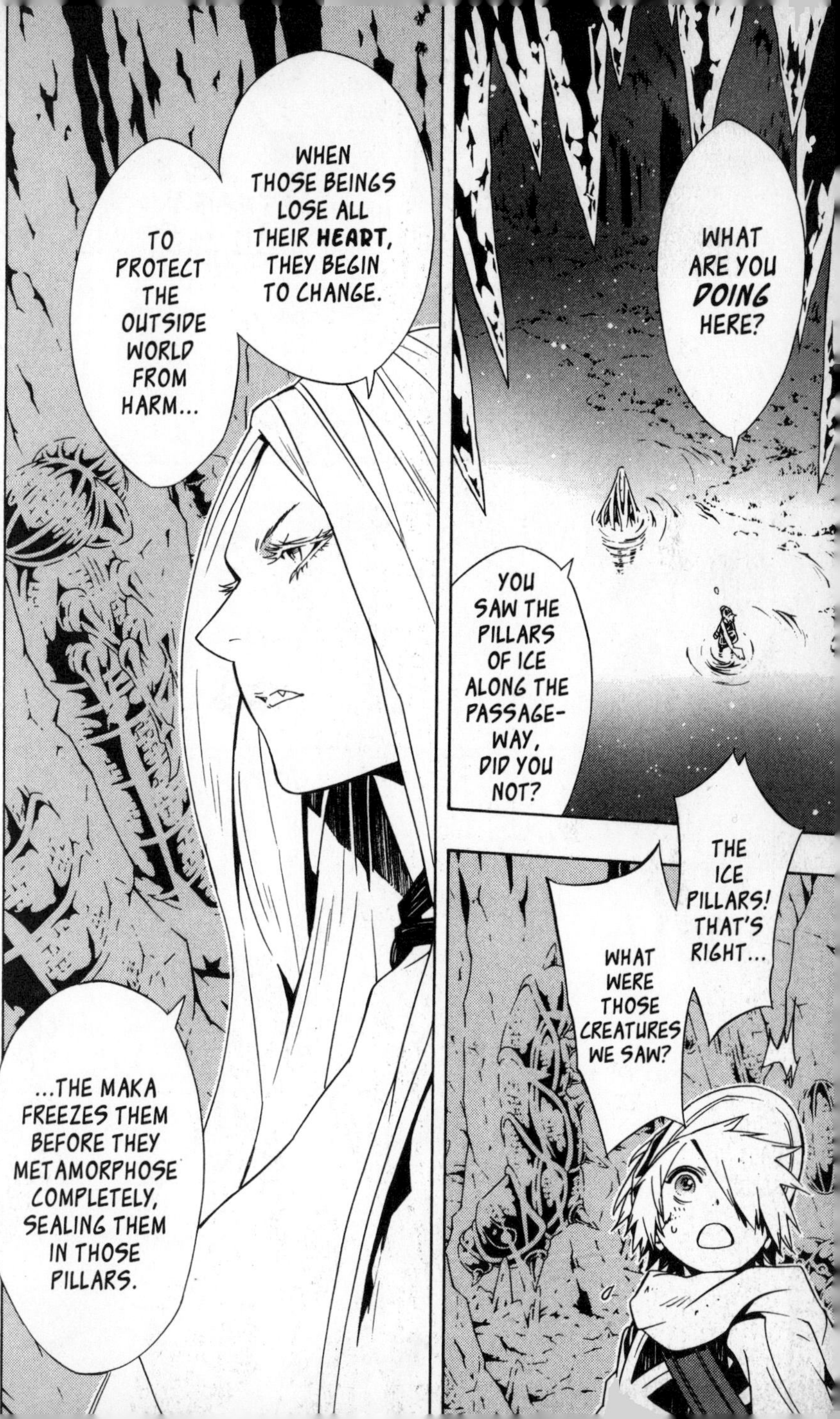
WHAT ARE YOU *DOING* HERE?
YOU SAW THE PILLARS OF ICE ALONG THE PASSAGE-WAY, DID YOU NOT?
THE ICE PILLARS! THAT'S RIGHT...
WHAT WERE THOSE CREATURES WE SAW?
WHEN THOSE BEINGS LOSE ALL THEIR **HEART**, THEY BEGIN TO CHANGE.
TO PROTECT THE OUTSIDE WORLD FROM HARM...
...THE MAKA FREEZES THEM BEFORE THEY METAMORPHOSE COMPLETELY, SEALING THEM IN THOSE PILLARS.

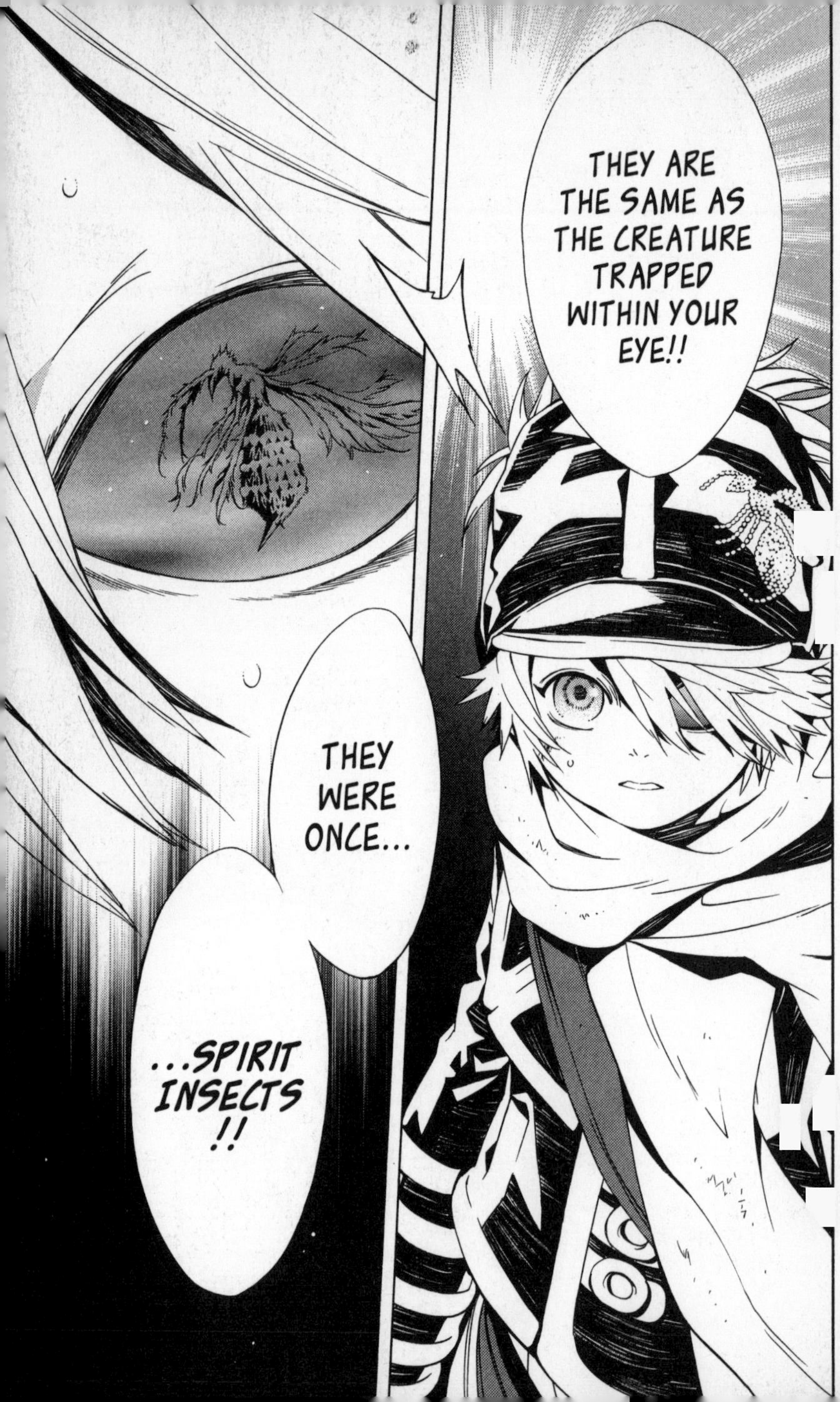
THEY ARE THE SAME AS THE CREATURE TRAPPED WITHIN YOUR EYE!!
THEY WERE ONCE...
...SPIRIT INSECTS!!

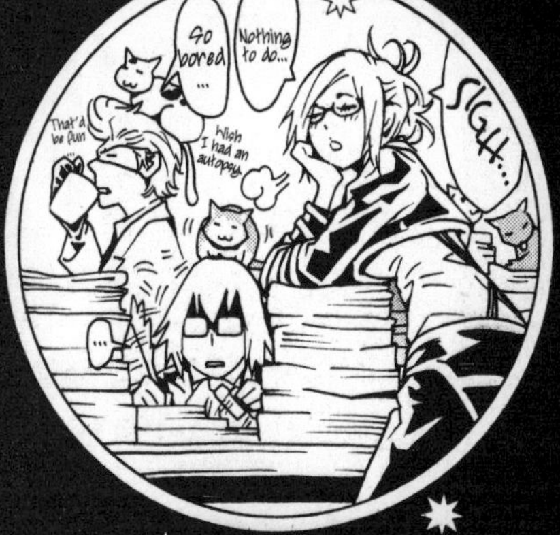
SIGH...
Nothing to do...
So bored ...
Wish I had an autopsy.
That'd be fun ...
...

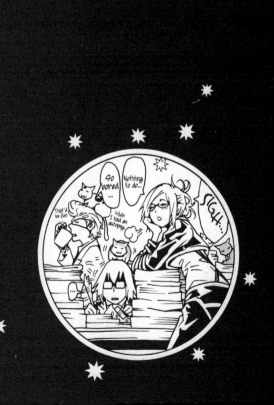

Chapter 26: Garden of Spirits

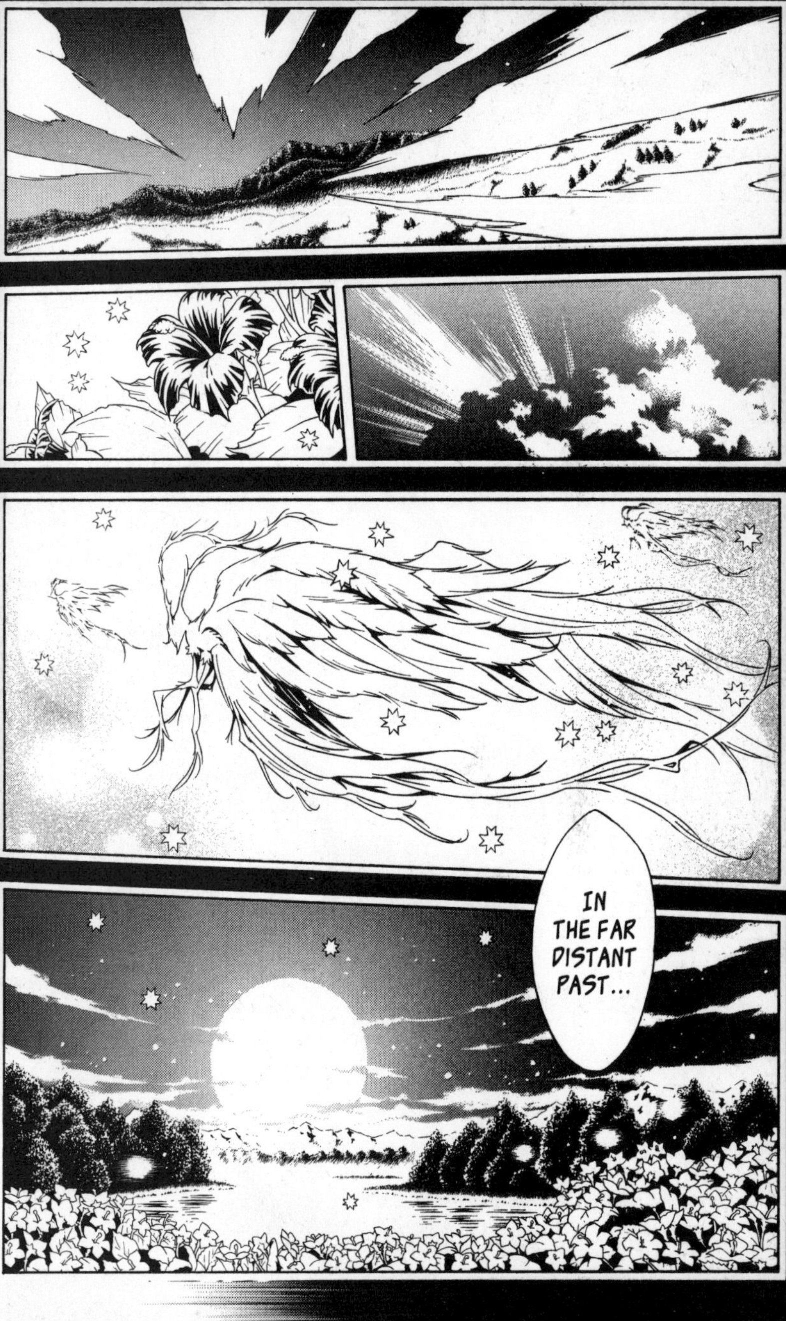
IN THE FAR DISTANT PAST...

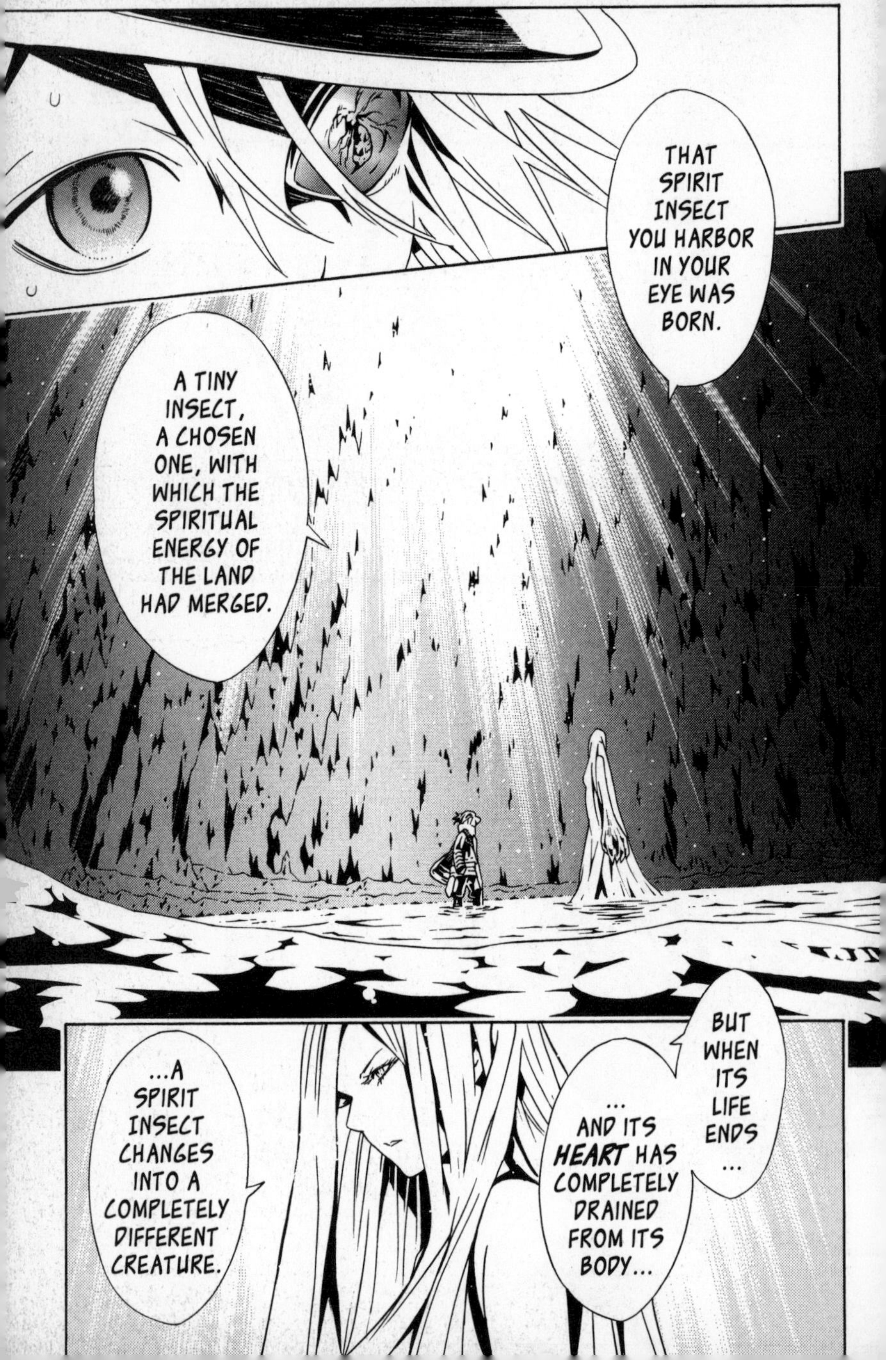
THAT SPIRIT INSECT YOU HARBOR IN YOUR EYE WAS BORN.
A TINY INSECT, A CHOSEN ONE, WITH WHICH THE SPIRITUAL ENERGY OF THE LAND HAD MERGED.
BUT WHEN ITS LIFE ENDS...
...AND ITS **HEART** HAS COMPLETELY DRAINED FROM ITS BODY...
...A SPIRIT INSECT CHANGES INTO A COMPLETELY DIFFERENT CREATURE.

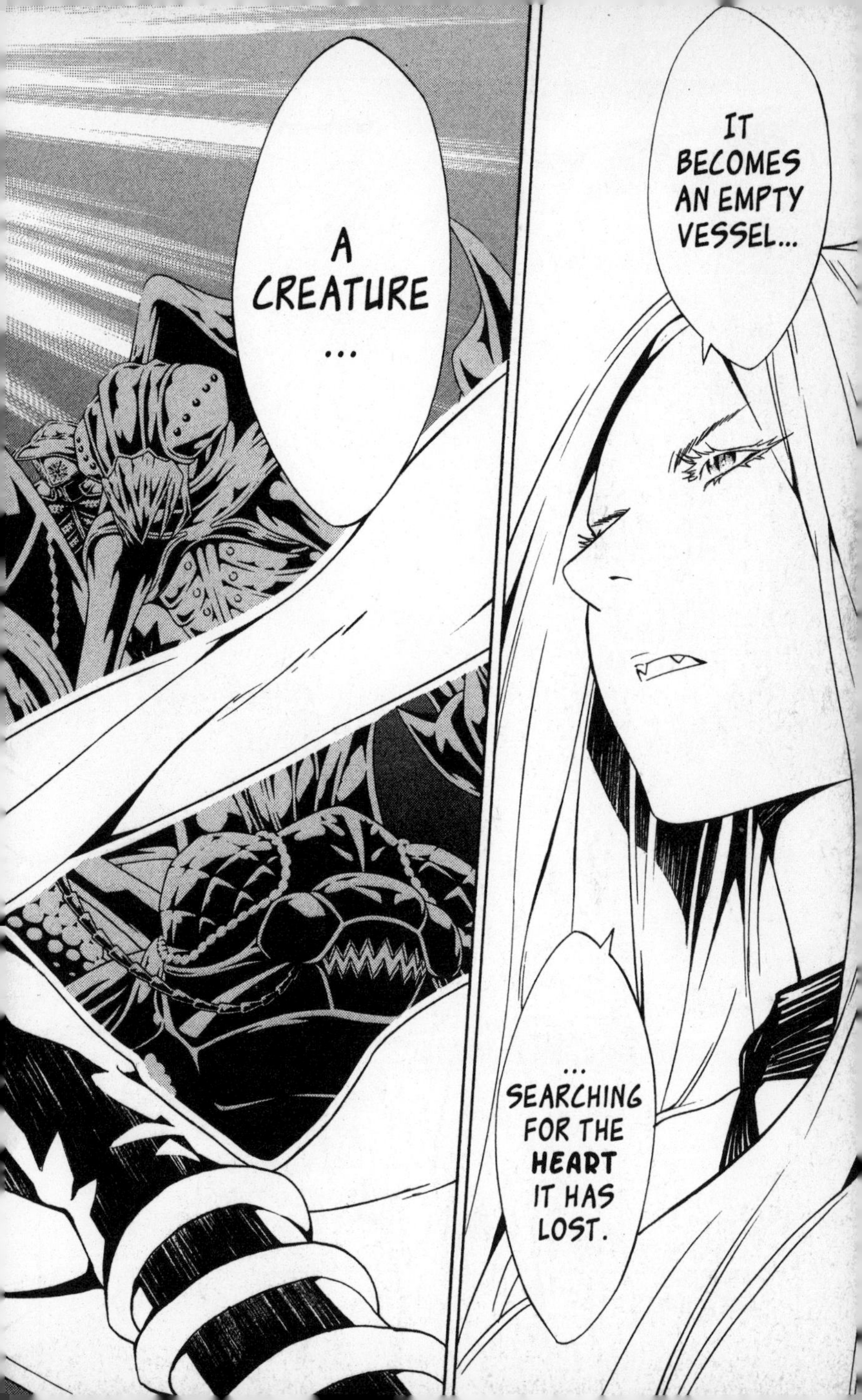
IT BECOMES AN EMPTY VESSEL...
... SEARCHING FOR THE **HEART** IT HAS LOST.
A CREATURE ...

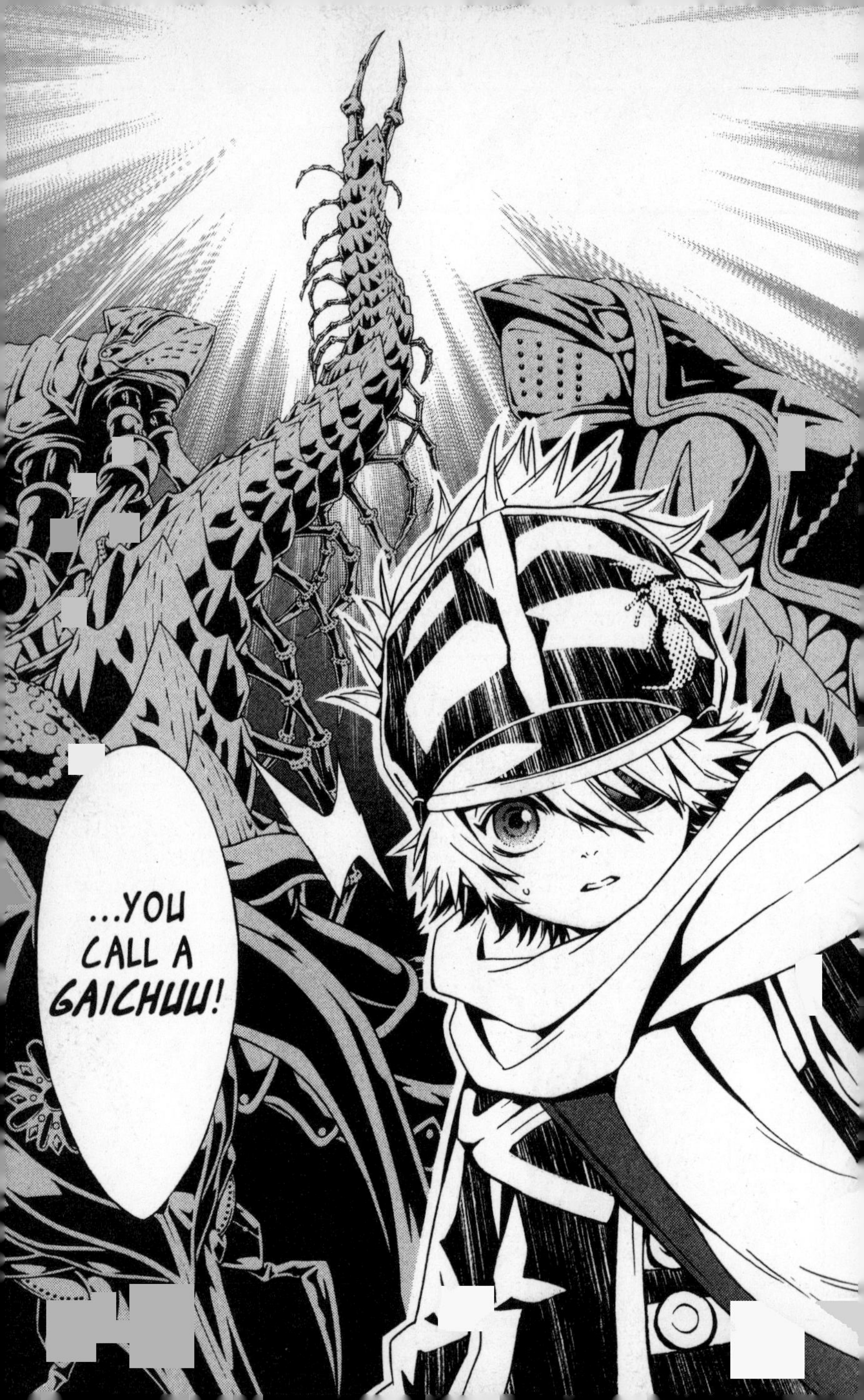
...YOU CALL A GAICHUU!

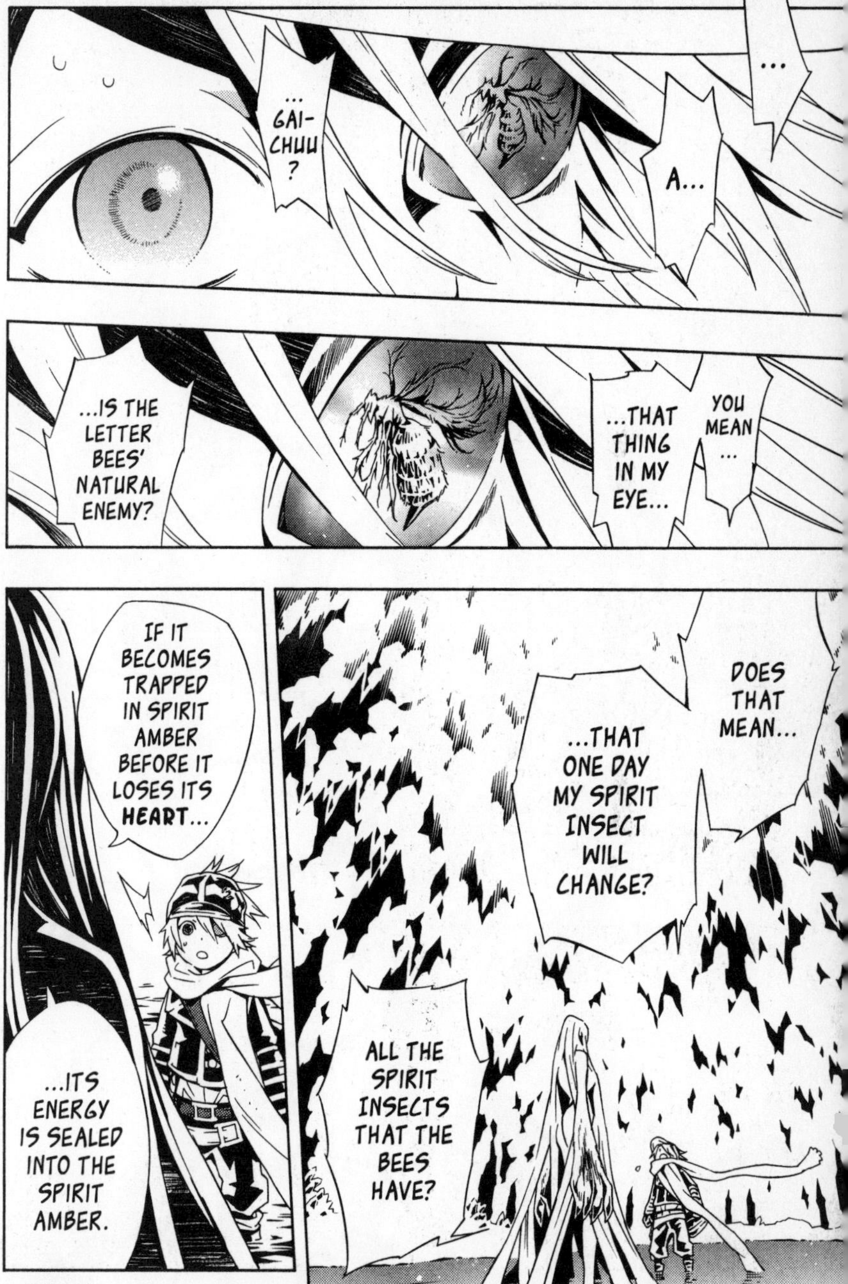
...
A...
...GAI-CHUU?
YOU MEAN...
...THAT THING IN MY EYE...
...IS THE LETTER BEES' NATURAL ENEMY?
DOES THAT MEAN...
...THAT ONE DAY MY SPIRIT INSECT WILL CHANGE?
ALL THE SPIRIT INSECTS THAT THE BEES HAVE?
IF IT BECOMES TRAPPED IN SPIRIT AMBER BEFORE IT LOSES ITS HEART...
...ITS ENERGY IS SEALED INTO THE SPIRIT AMBER.

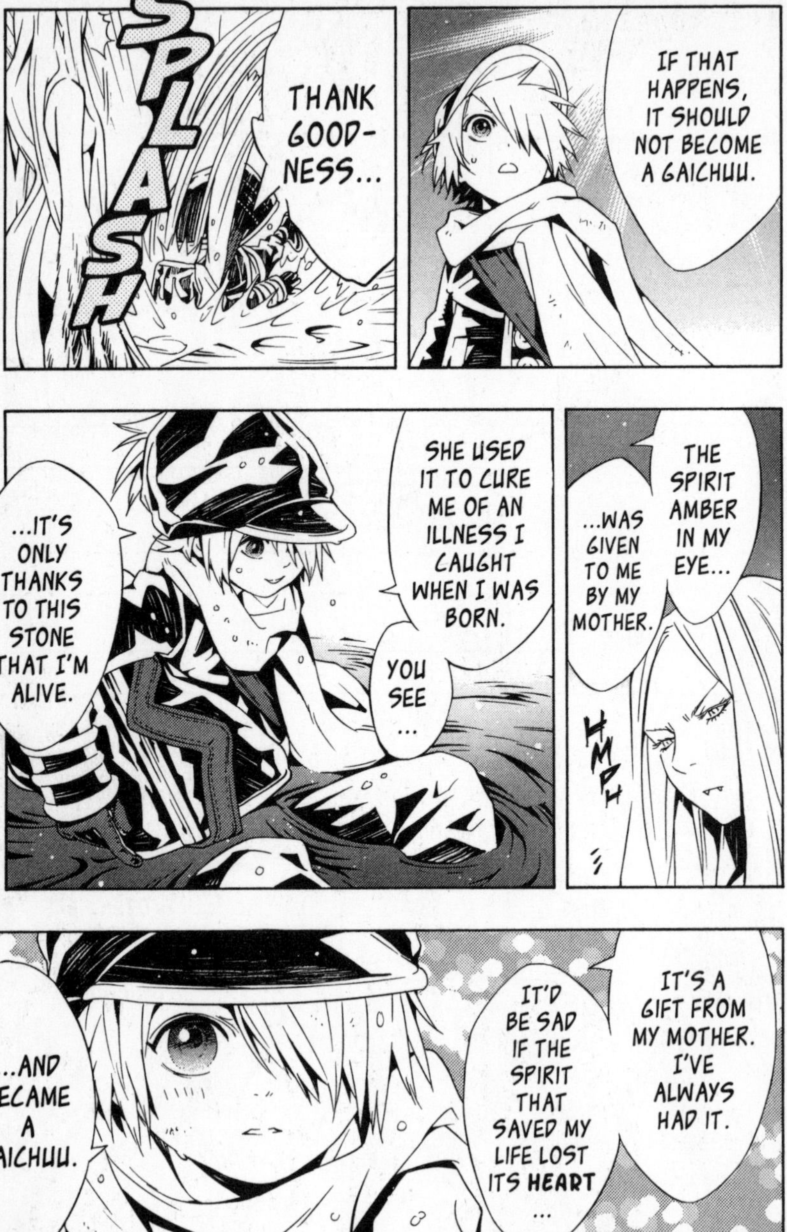
IF THAT HAPPENS, IT SHOULD NOT BECOME A GAICHUU.
THANK GOODNESS...
SPLASH
THE SPIRIT AMBER IN MY EYE...
...WAS GIVEN TO ME BY MY MOTHER.
HMPH
SHE USED IT TO CURE ME OF AN ILLNESS I CAUGHT WHEN I WAS BORN.
YOU SEE...
...IT'S ONLY THANKS TO THIS STONE THAT I'M ALIVE.
IT'S A GIFT FROM MY MOTHER. I'VE ALWAYS HAD IT.
IT'D BE SAD IF THE SPIRIT THAT SAVED MY LIFE LOST ITS **HEART**...
...AND BECAME A GAICHUU.

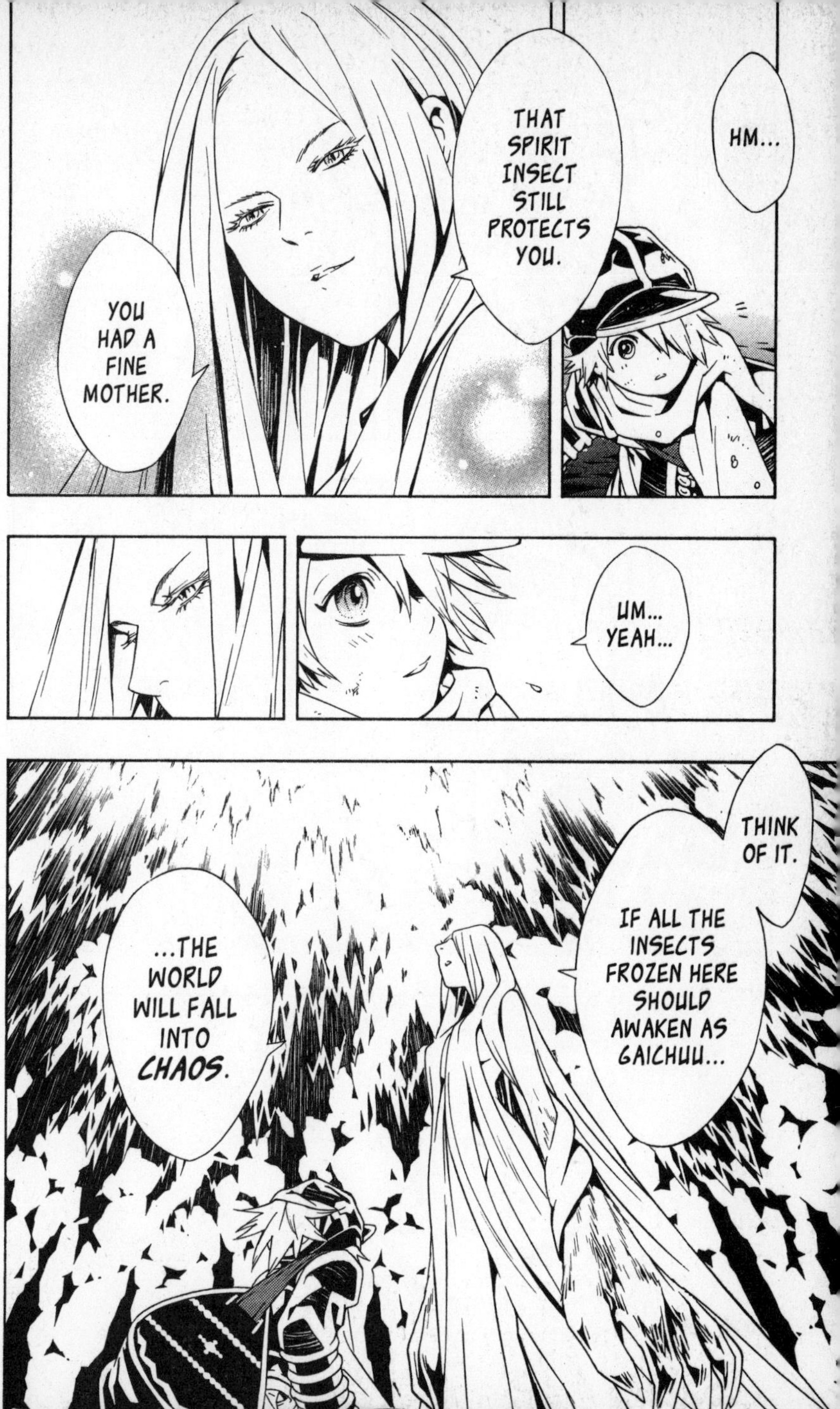
HM...
THAT SPIRIT INSECT STILL PROTECTS YOU.
YOU HAD A FINE MOTHER.
UM... YEAH...
THINK OF IT.
IF ALL THE INSECTS FROZEN HERE SHOULD AWAKEN AS GAICHUU...
...THE WORLD WILL FALL INTO *CHAOS*.

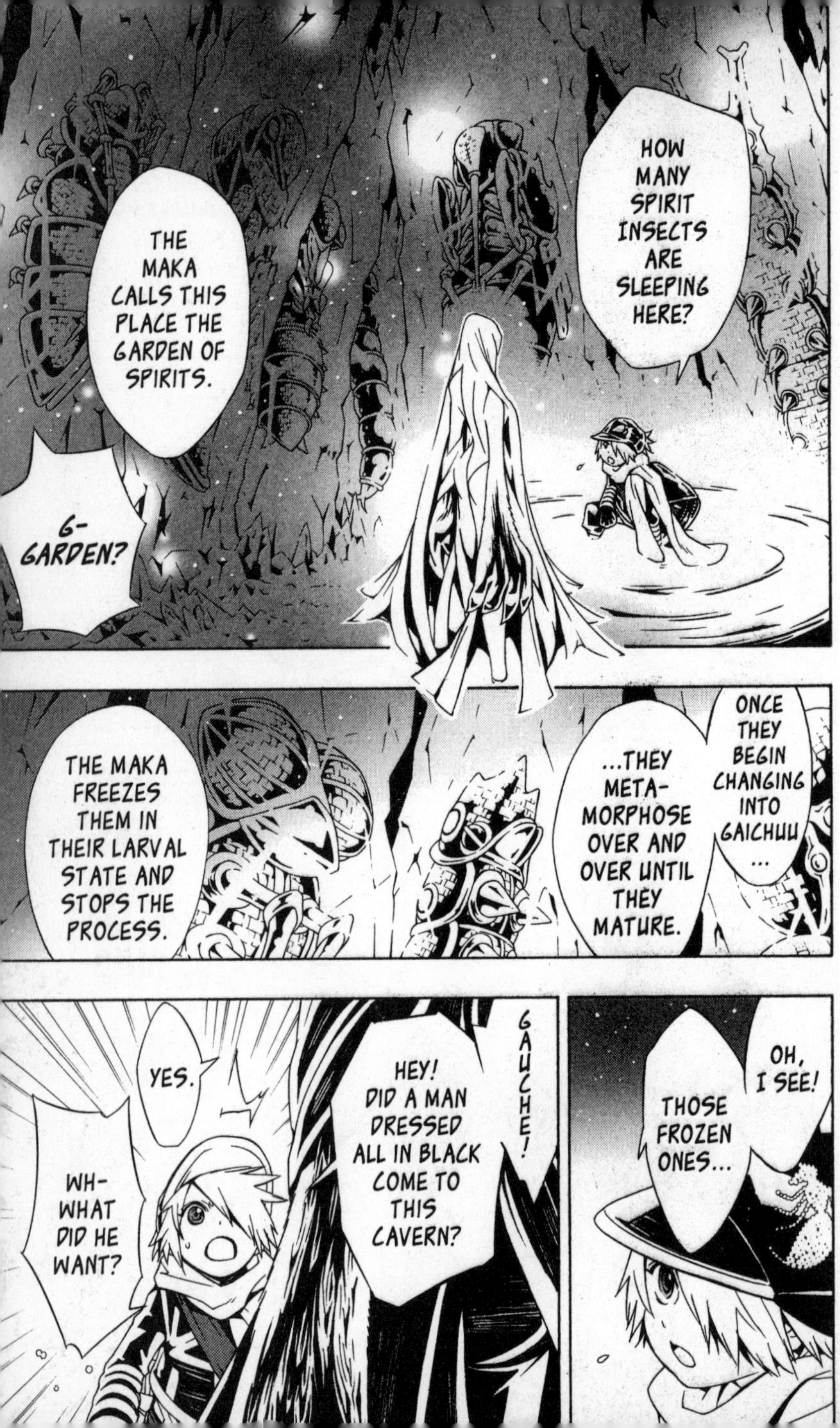
HOW MANY SPIRIT INSECTS ARE SLEEPING HERE?
THE MAKA CALLS THIS PLACE THE GARDEN OF SPIRITS.
G-GARDEN?
ONCE THEY BEGIN CHANGING INTO GAICHUU...
...THEY META-MORPHOSE OVER AND OVER UNTIL THEY MATURE.
THE MAKA FREEZES THEM IN THEIR LARVAL STATE AND STOPS THE PROCESS.
OH, I SEE!
THOSE FROZEN ONES...
GAUCHE!
HEY! DID A MAN DRESSED ALL IN BLACK COME TO THIS CAVERN?
YES.
WH-WHAT DID HE WANT?

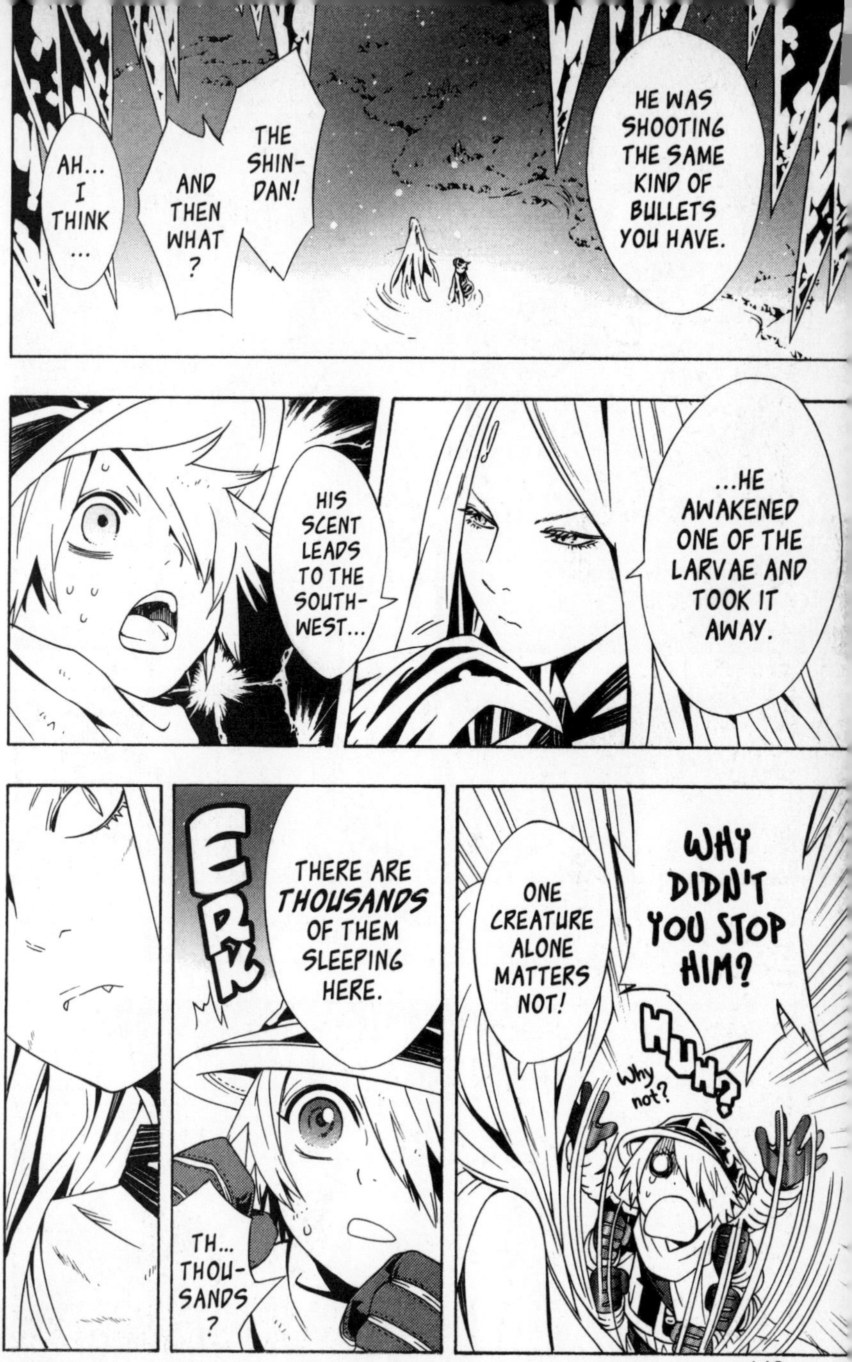
HE WAS SHOOTING THE SAME KIND OF BULLETS YOU HAVE.
THE SHIN-DAN!
AND THEN WHAT?
AH... I THINK...
...HE AWAKENED ONE OF THE LARVAE AND TOOK IT AWAY.
HIS SCENT LEADS TO THE SOUTH-WEST...
WHY DIDN'T YOU STOP HIM?
ONE CREATURE ALONE MATTERS NOT!
HUH?
Why not?
THERE ARE THOUSANDS OF THEM SLEEPING HERE.
ERK
TH... THOU-SANDS?

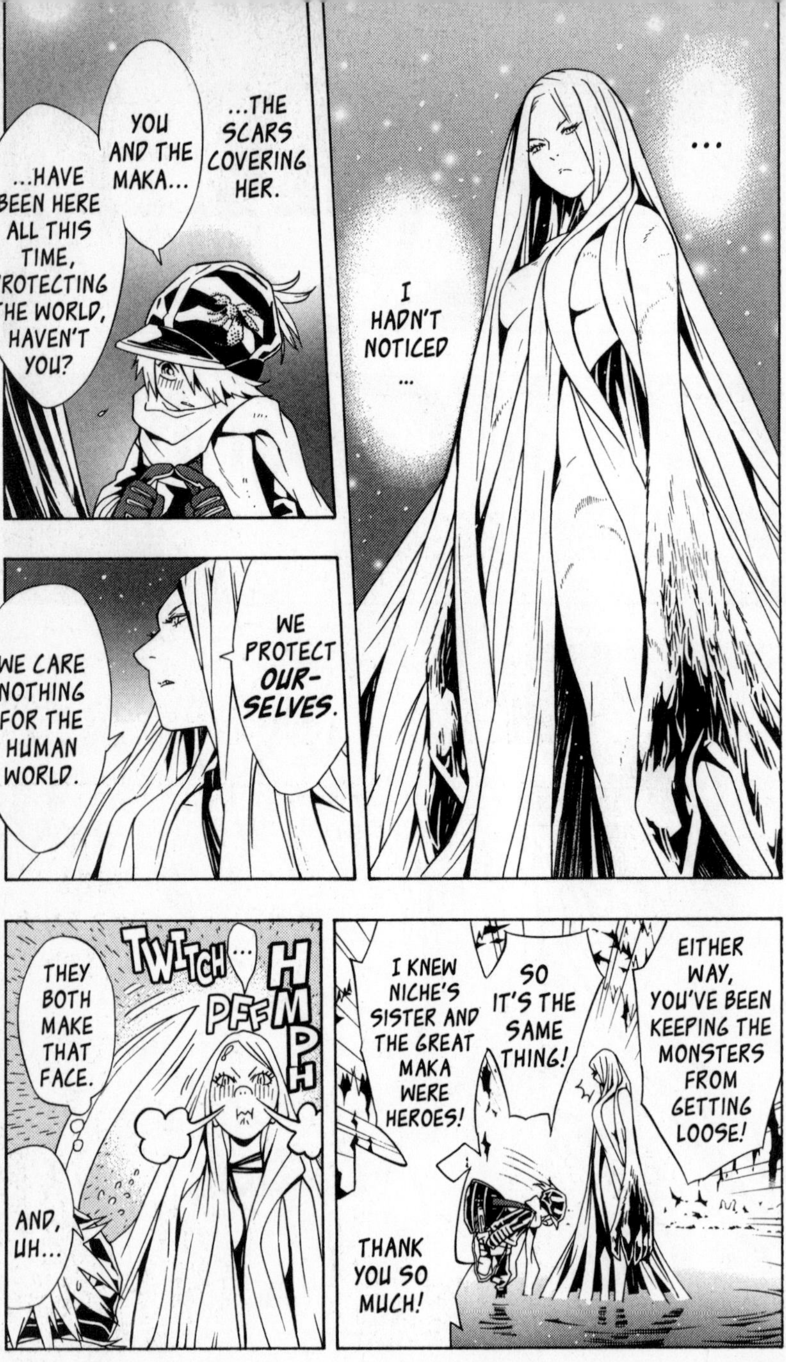
...
I HADN'T NOTICED ...
...THE SCARS COVERING HER.
YOU AND THE MAKA...
...HAVE BEEN HERE ALL THIS TIME, PROTECTING THE WORLD, HAVEN'T YOU?
WE PROTECT OURSELVES.
WE CARE NOTHING FOR THE HUMAN WORLD.
EITHER WAY, YOU'VE BEEN KEEPING THE MONSTERS FROM GETTING LOOSE!
SO IT'S THE SAME THING!
I KNEW NICHE'S SISTER AND THE GREAT MAKA WERE HEROES!
THANK YOU SO MUCH!
HMPH
TWITCH
...
PFF
THEY BOTH MAKE THAT FACE.
AND, UH...

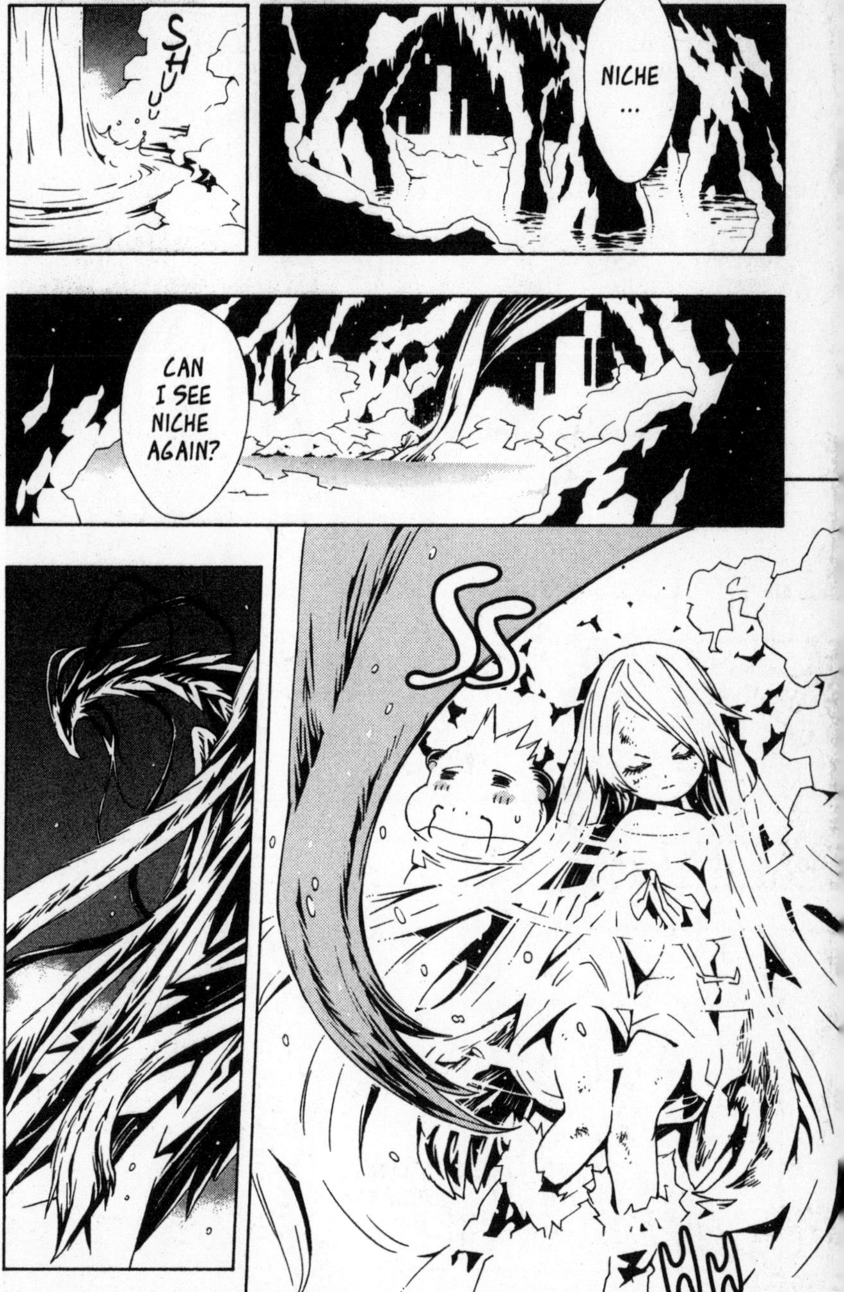
NICHE ...
SHUUU
CAN I SEE NICHE AGAIN?
SS
HH

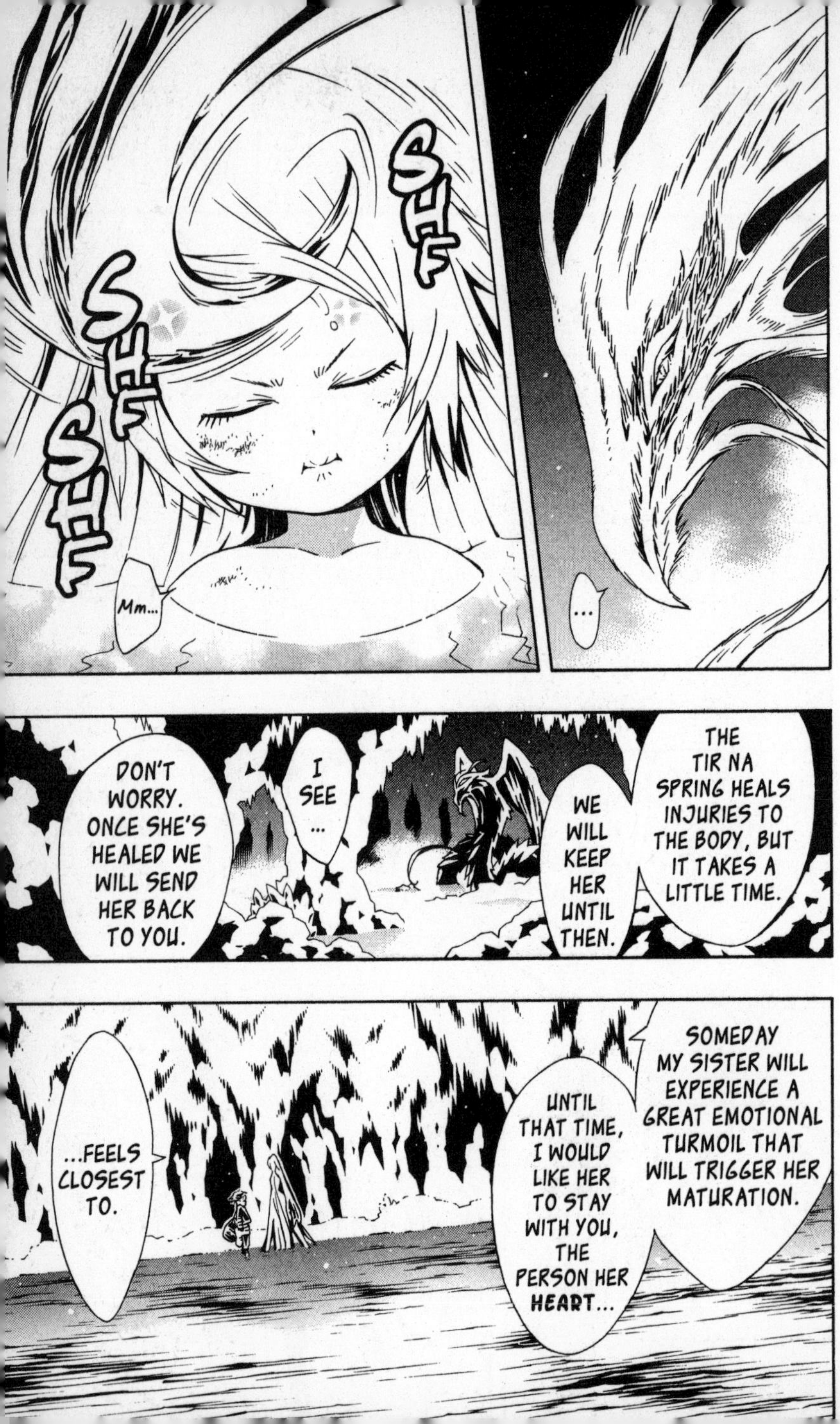
...
SHF
SHF
SHF
Mm...
THE TIR NA SPRING HEALS INJURIES TO THE BODY, BUT IT TAKES A LITTLE TIME.
WE WILL KEEP HER UNTIL THEN.
I SEE...
DON'T WORRY. ONCE SHE'S HEALED WE WILL SEND HER BACK TO YOU.
SOMEDAY MY SISTER WILL EXPERIENCE A GREAT EMOTIONAL TURMOIL THAT WILL TRIGGER HER MATURATION.
UNTIL THAT TIME, I WOULD LIKE HER TO STAY WITH YOU, THE PERSON HER HEART...
...FEELS CLOSEST TO.

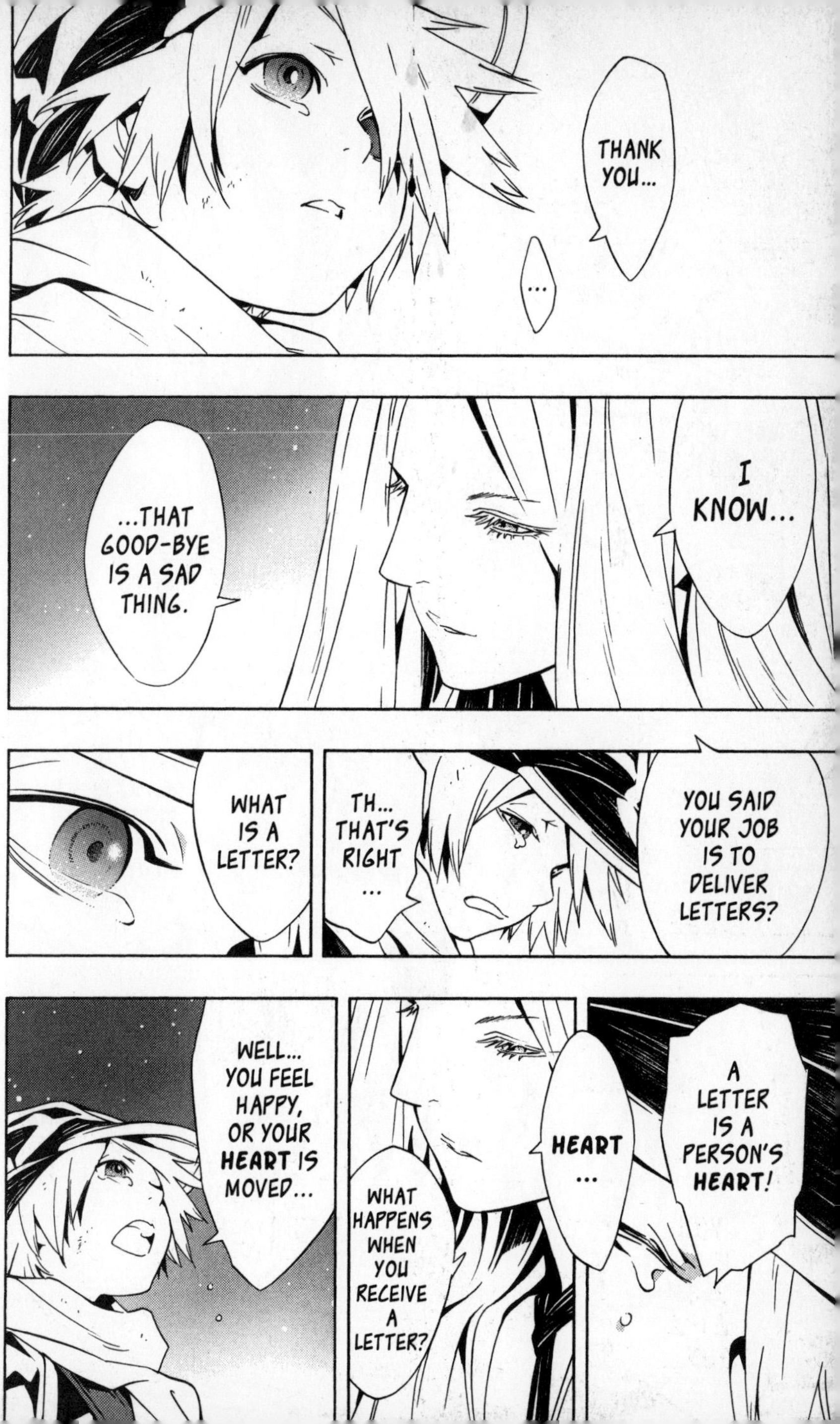
THANK YOU...
...
I KNOW...
...THAT GOOD-BYE IS A SAD THING.
YOU SAID YOUR JOB IS TO DELIVER LETTERS?
TH... THAT'S RIGHT ...
WHAT IS A LETTER?
A LETTER IS A PERSON'S **HEART**!
HEART ...
WHAT HAPPENS WHEN YOU RECEIVE A LETTER?
WELL... YOU FEEL HAPPY, OR YOUR **HEART** IS MOVED...

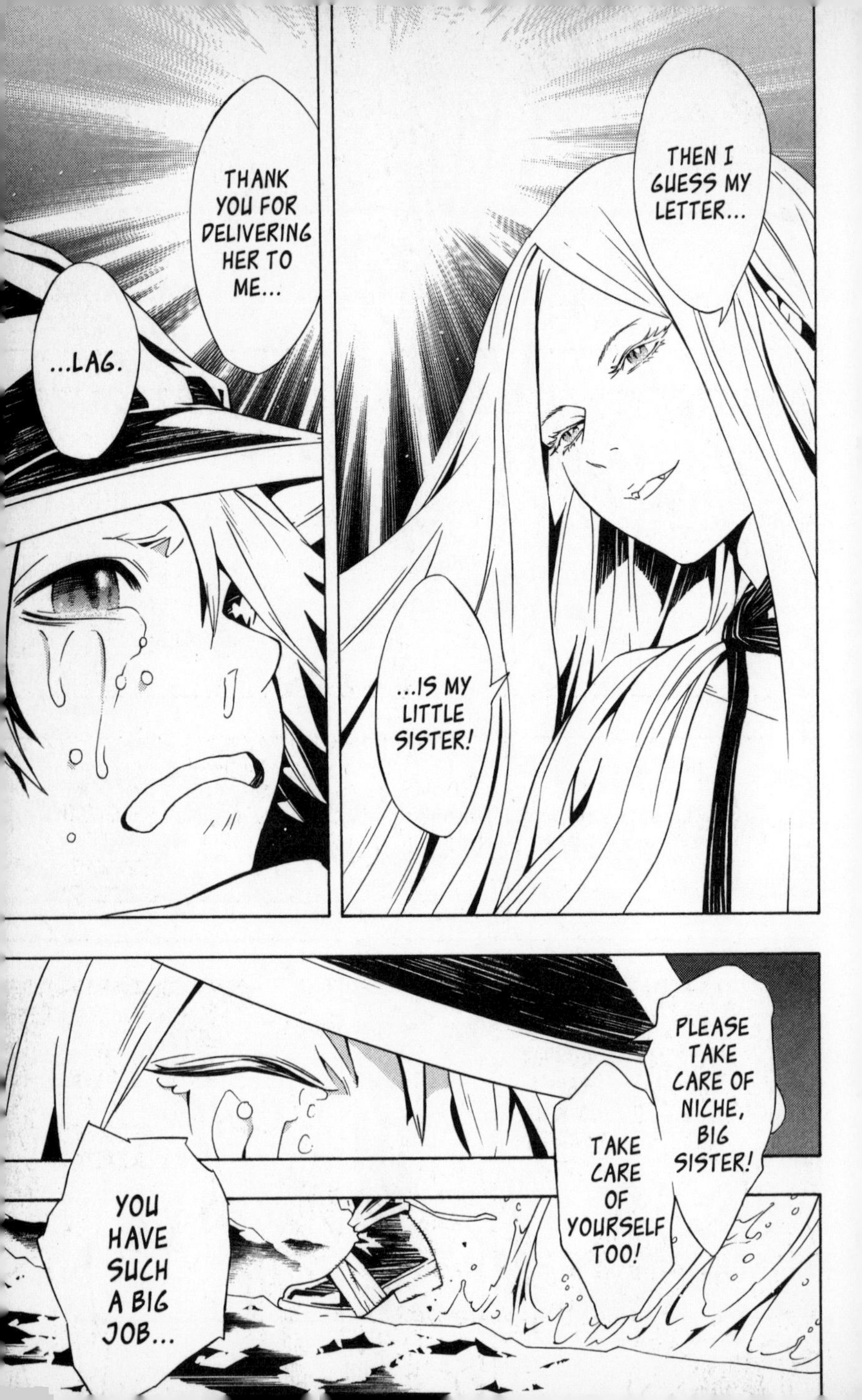
THEN I GUESS MY LETTER...
...IS MY LITTLE SISTER!
THANK YOU FOR DELIVERING HER TO ME...
...LAG.
PLEASE TAKE CARE OF NICHE, BIG SISTER!
TAKE CARE OF YOURSELF TOO!
YOU HAVE SUCH A BIG JOB...

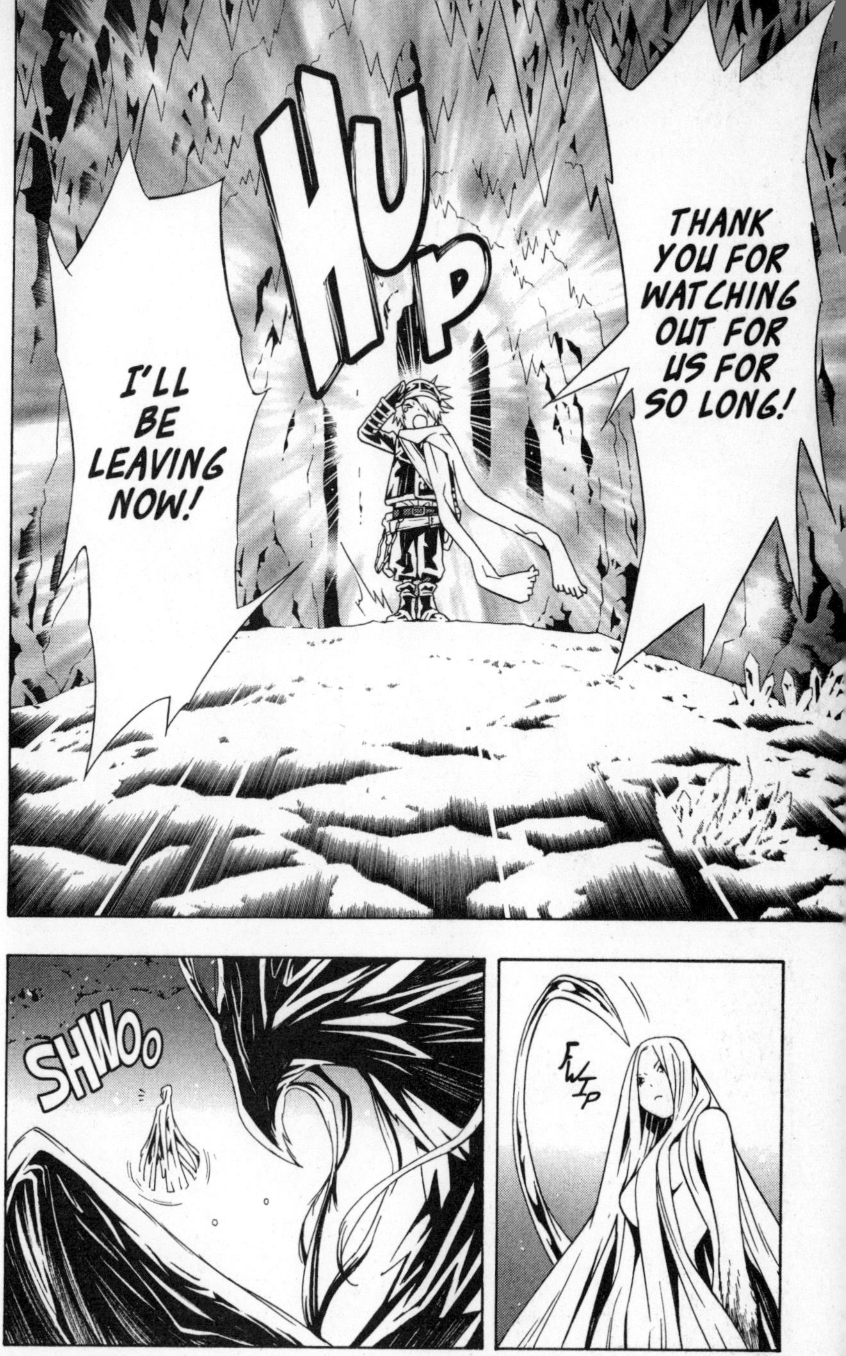
THANK YOU FOR WATCHING OUT FOR US FOR SO LONG!
HUP
I'LL BE LEAVING NOW!
FWIP
SHWOO

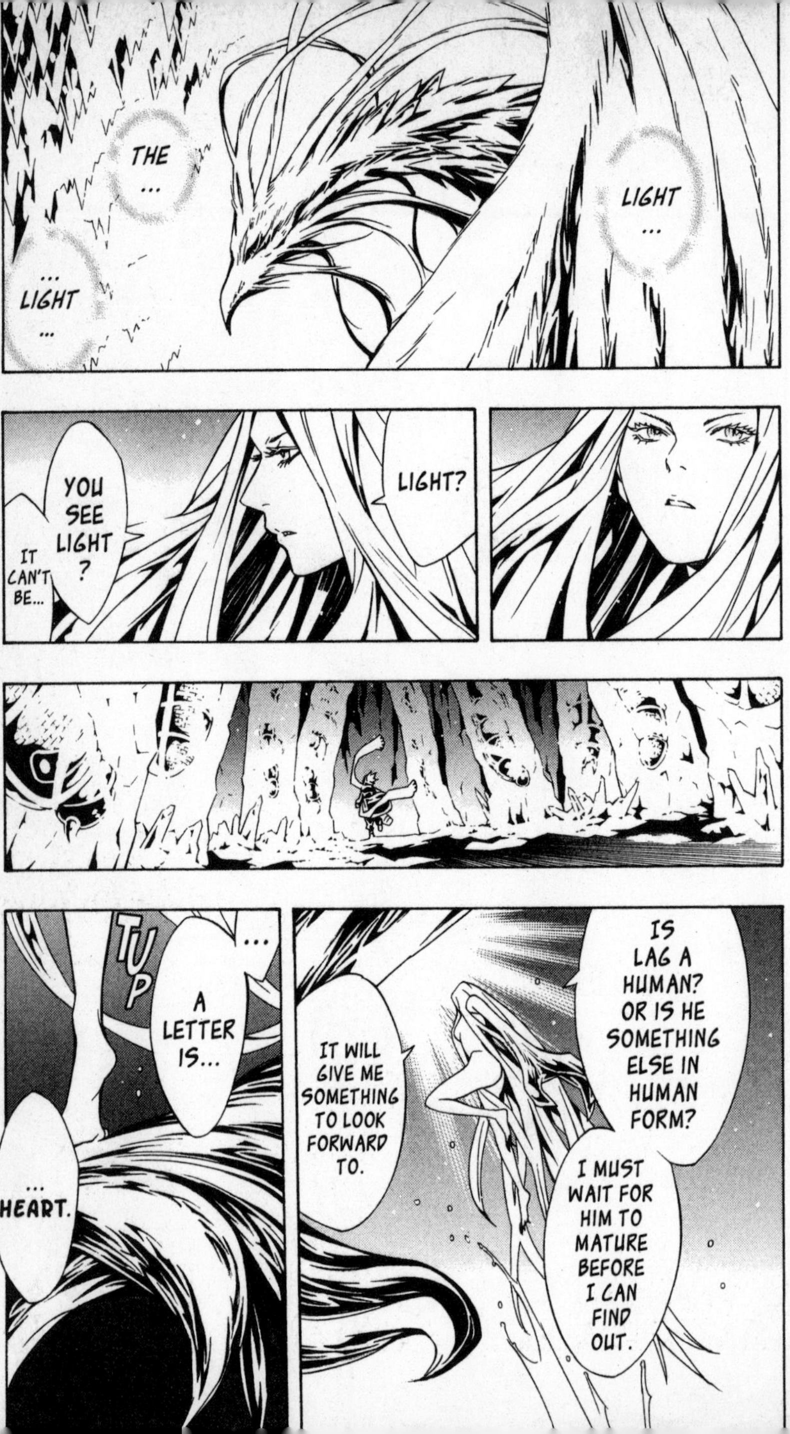
LIGHT ...
THE ...
... LIGHT ...
LIGHT?
YOU SEE LIGHT?
IT CAN'T BE...
IS LAG A HUMAN? OR IS HE SOMETHING ELSE IN HUMAN FORM?
I MUST WAIT FOR HIM TO MATURE BEFORE I CAN FIND OUT.
IT WILL GIVE ME SOMETHING TO LOOK FORWARD TO.
...
TUP
A LETTER IS...
... HEART.

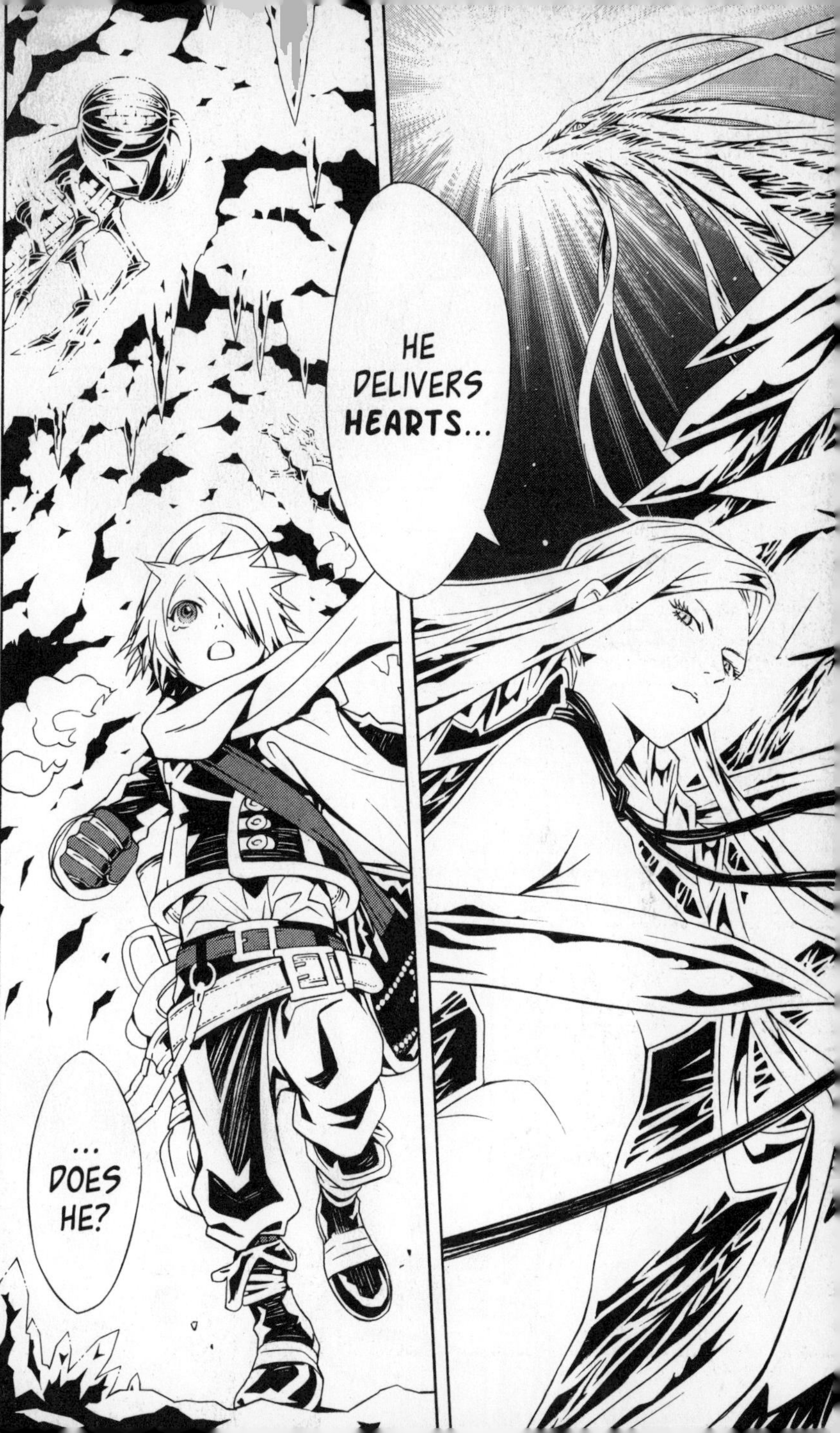
HE DELIVERS HEARTS...
...DOES HE?

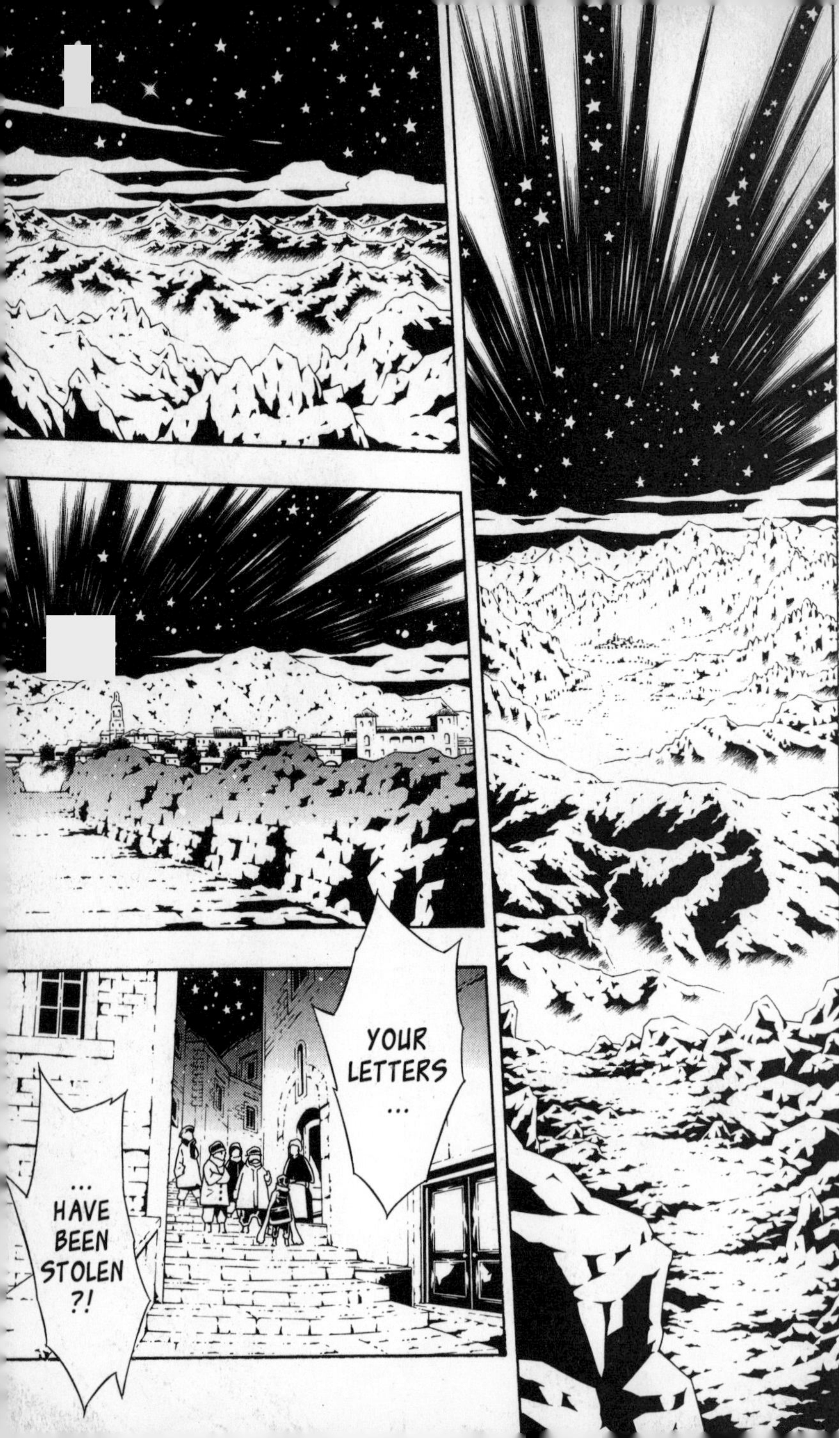
YOUR LETTERS ...
... HAVE BEEN STOLEN ?!

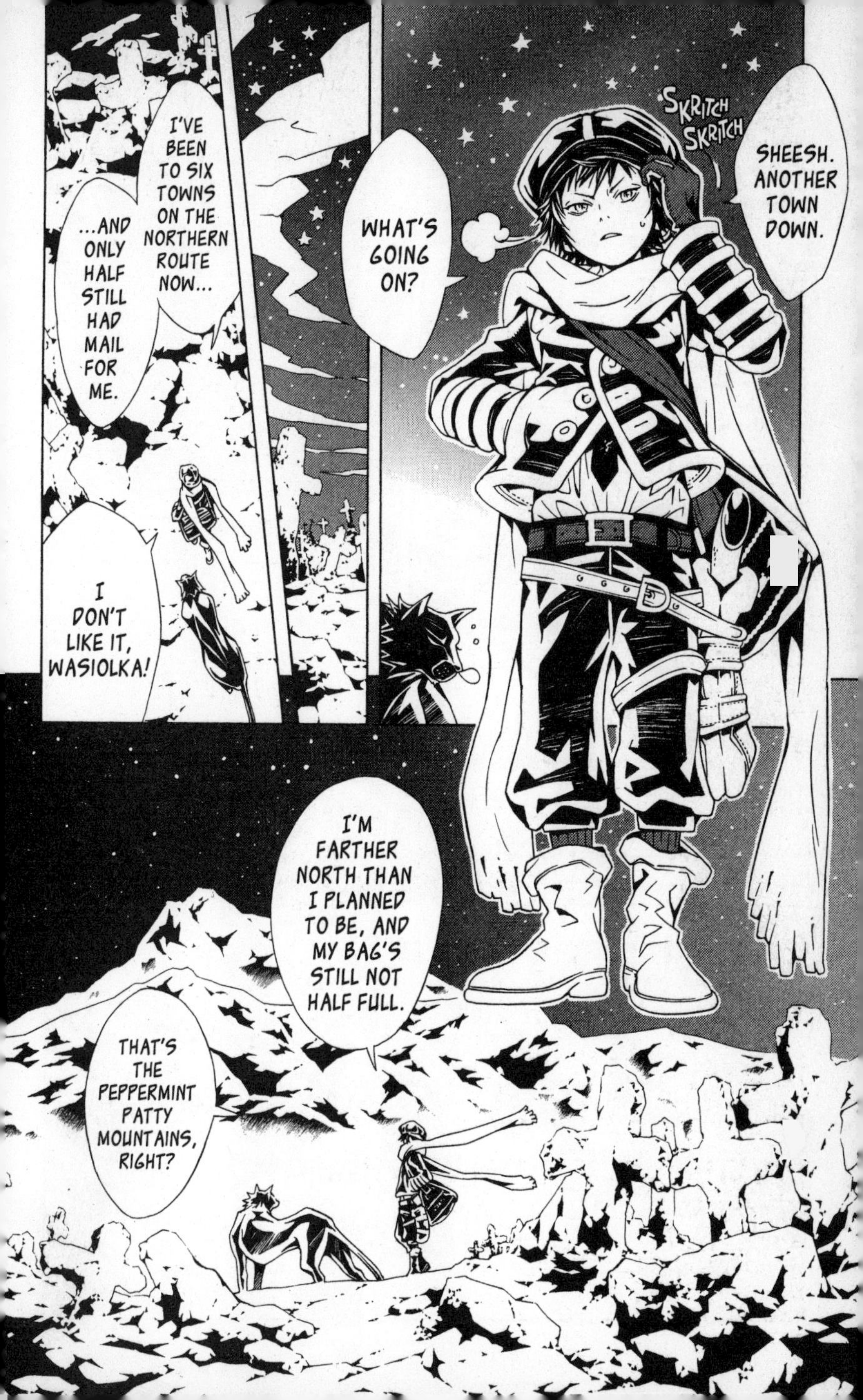
SKRITCH SKRITCH
SHEESH. ANOTHER TOWN DOWN.
WHAT'S GOING ON?
I'VE BEEN TO SIX TOWNS ON THE NORTHERN ROUTE NOW...
...AND ONLY HALF STILL HAD MAIL FOR ME.
I DON'T LIKE IT, WASIOLKA!
I'M FARTHER NORTH THAN I PLANNED TO BE, AND MY BAG'S STILL NOT HALF FULL.
THAT'S THE PEPPERMINT PATTY MOUNTAINS, RIGHT?

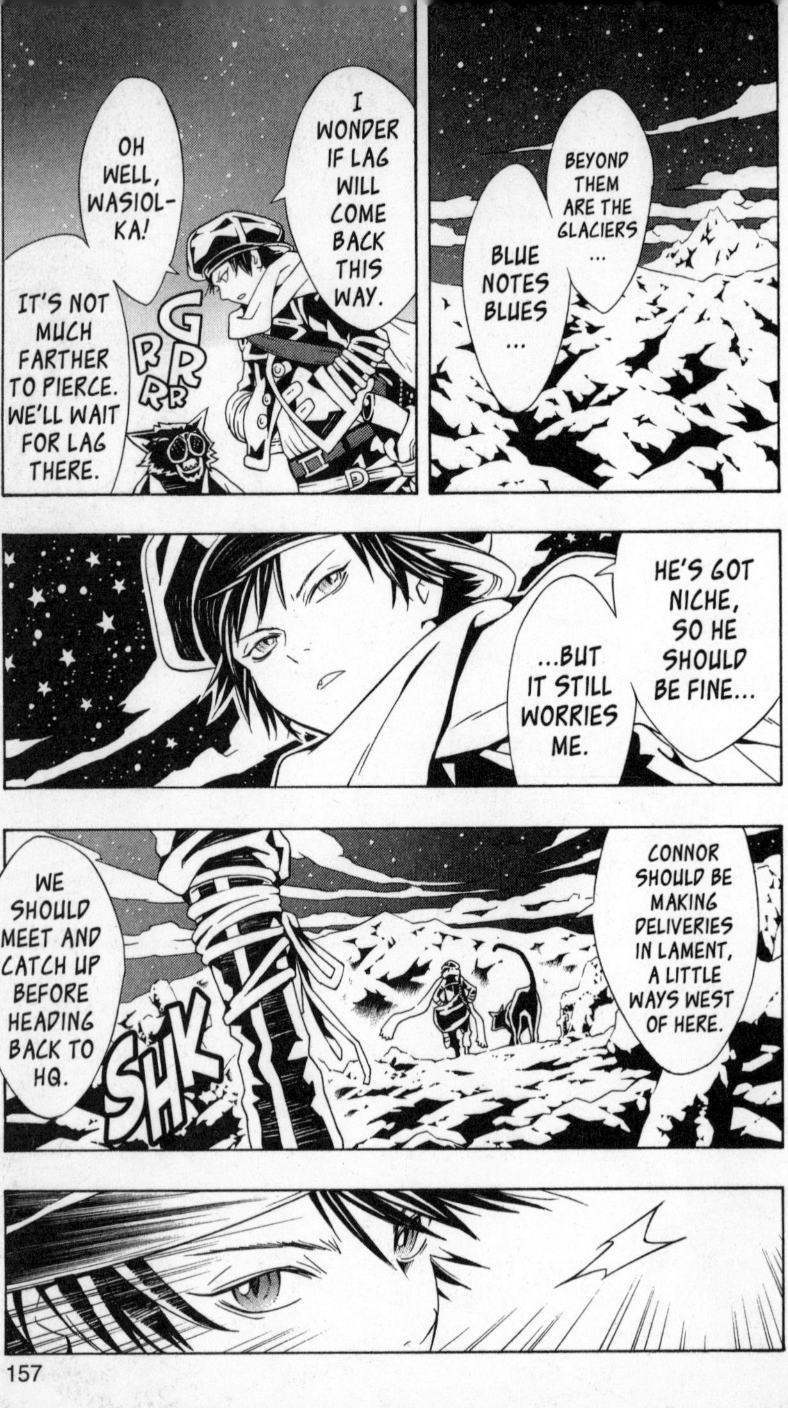
BEYOND THEM ARE THE GLACIERS ...
BLUE NOTES BLUES ...
I WONDER IF LAG WILL COME BACK THIS WAY.
OH WELL, WASIOL-KA!
GRRRR
IT'S NOT MUCH FARTHER TO PIERCE. WE'LL WAIT FOR LAG THERE.
HE'S GOT NICHE, SO HE SHOULD BE FINE...
...BUT IT STILL WORRIES ME.
CONNOR SHOULD BE MAKING DELIVERIES IN LAMENT, A LITTLE WAYS WEST OF HERE.
SHK
WE SHOULD MEET AND CATCH UP BEFORE HEADING BACK TO HQ.

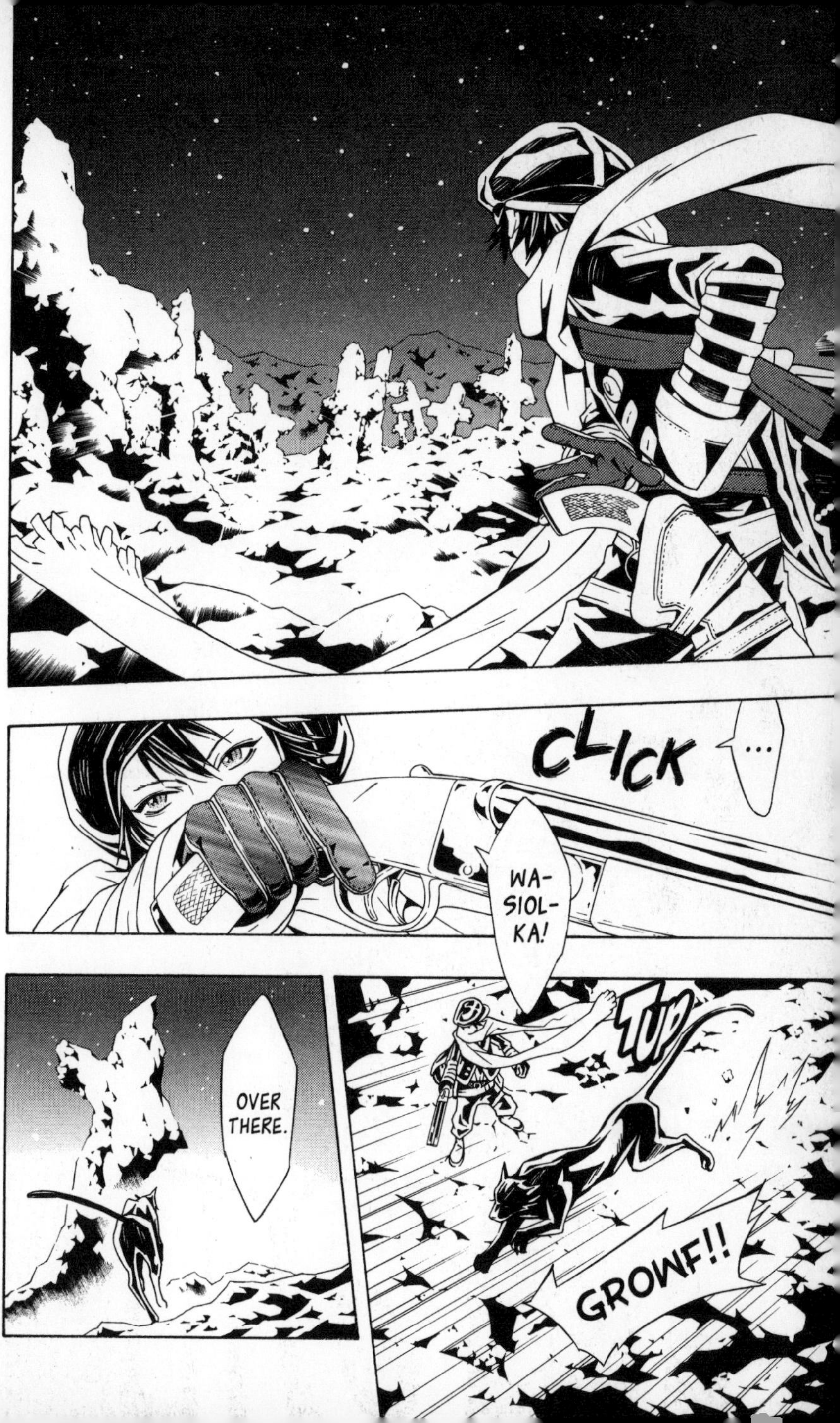
...
CLICK
WA-SIOLKA!
TUP
GROWF!!
OVER THERE.

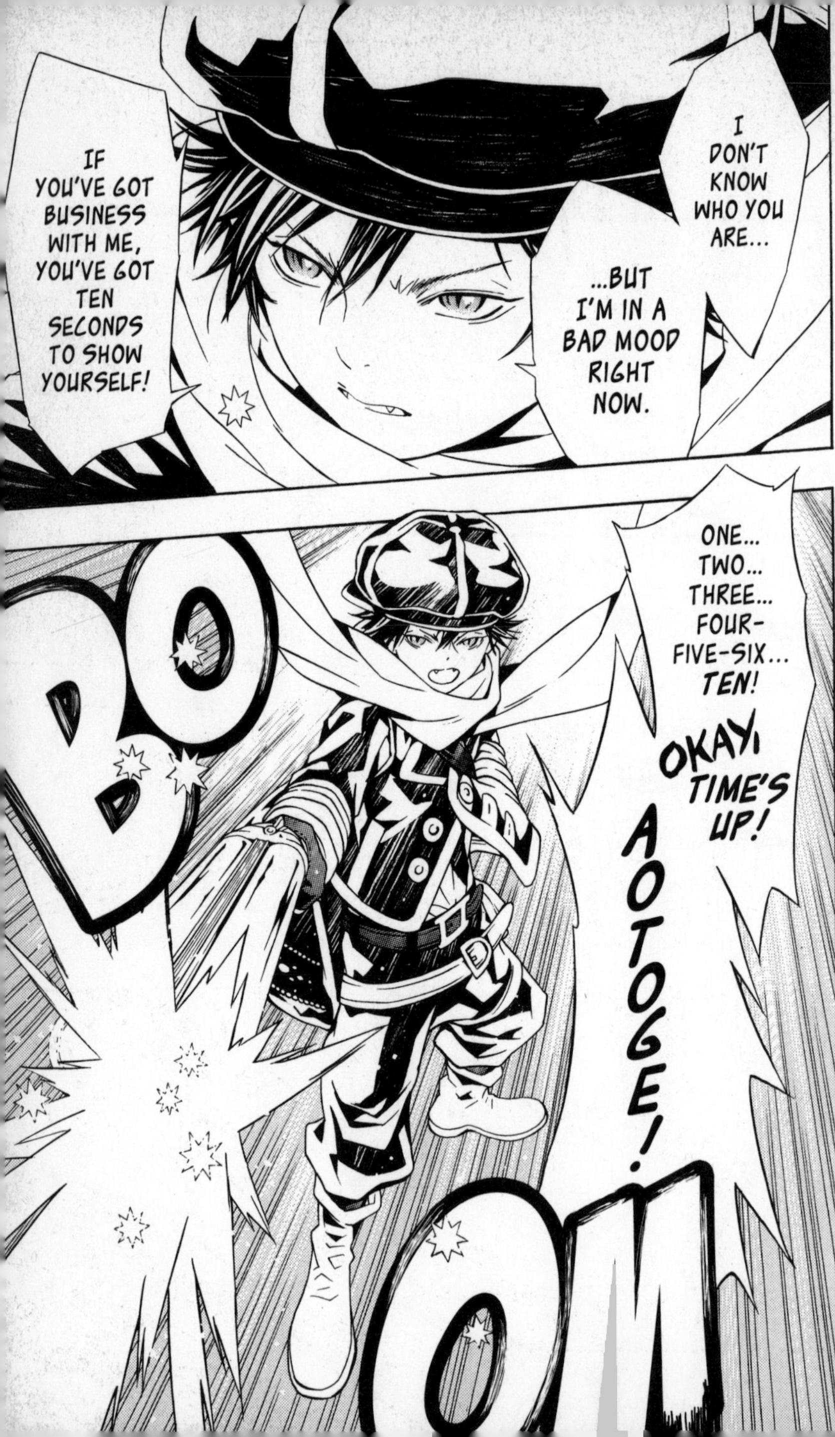
I DON'T KNOW WHO YOU ARE...
...BUT I'M IN A BAD MOOD RIGHT NOW.
IF YOU'VE GOT BUSINESS WITH ME, YOU'VE GOT TEN SECONDS TO SHOW YOURSELF!
ONE... TWO... THREE... FOUR-FIVE-SIX... TEN!
OKAY, TIME'S UP!
AOTOGE!
BOOM

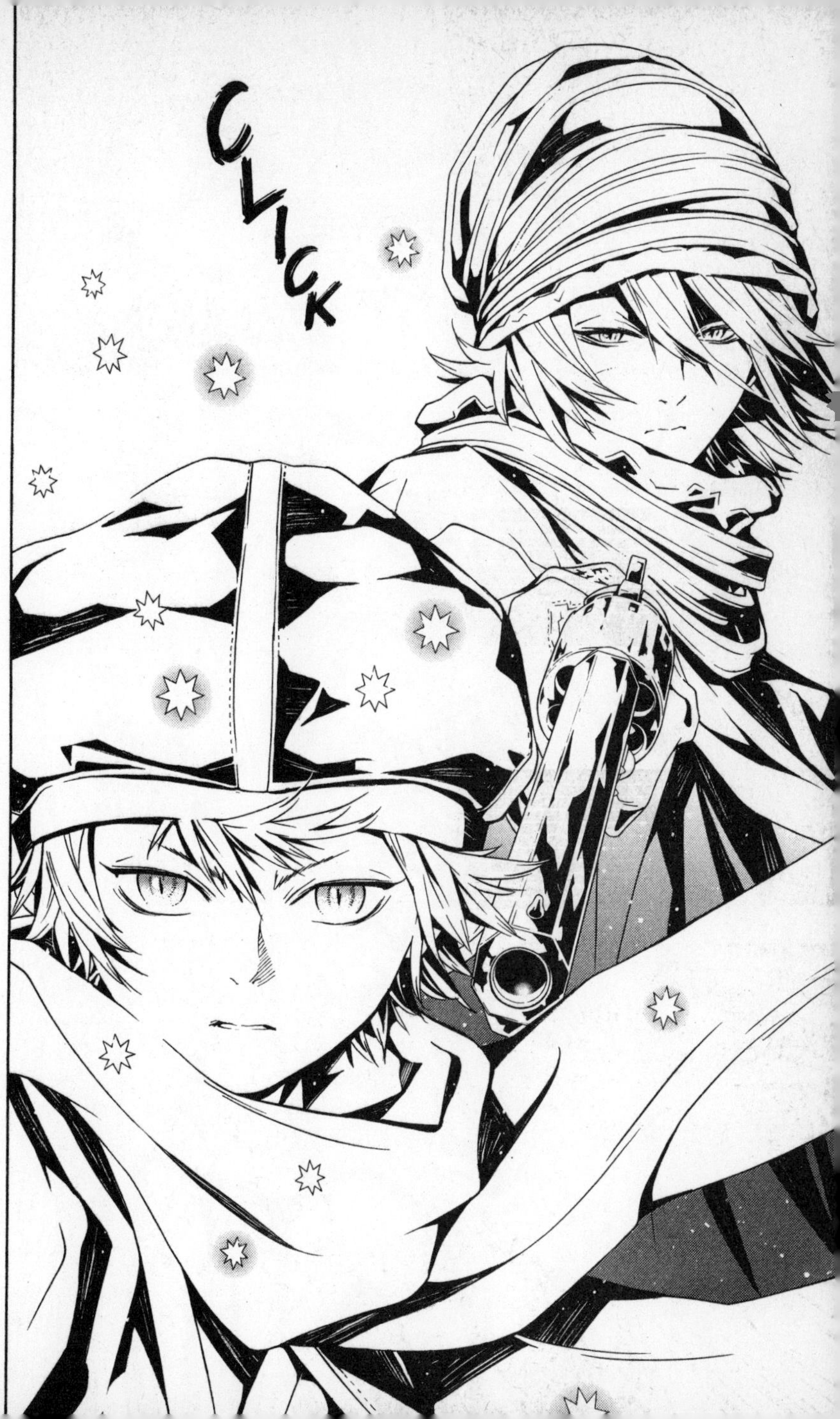
CLICK

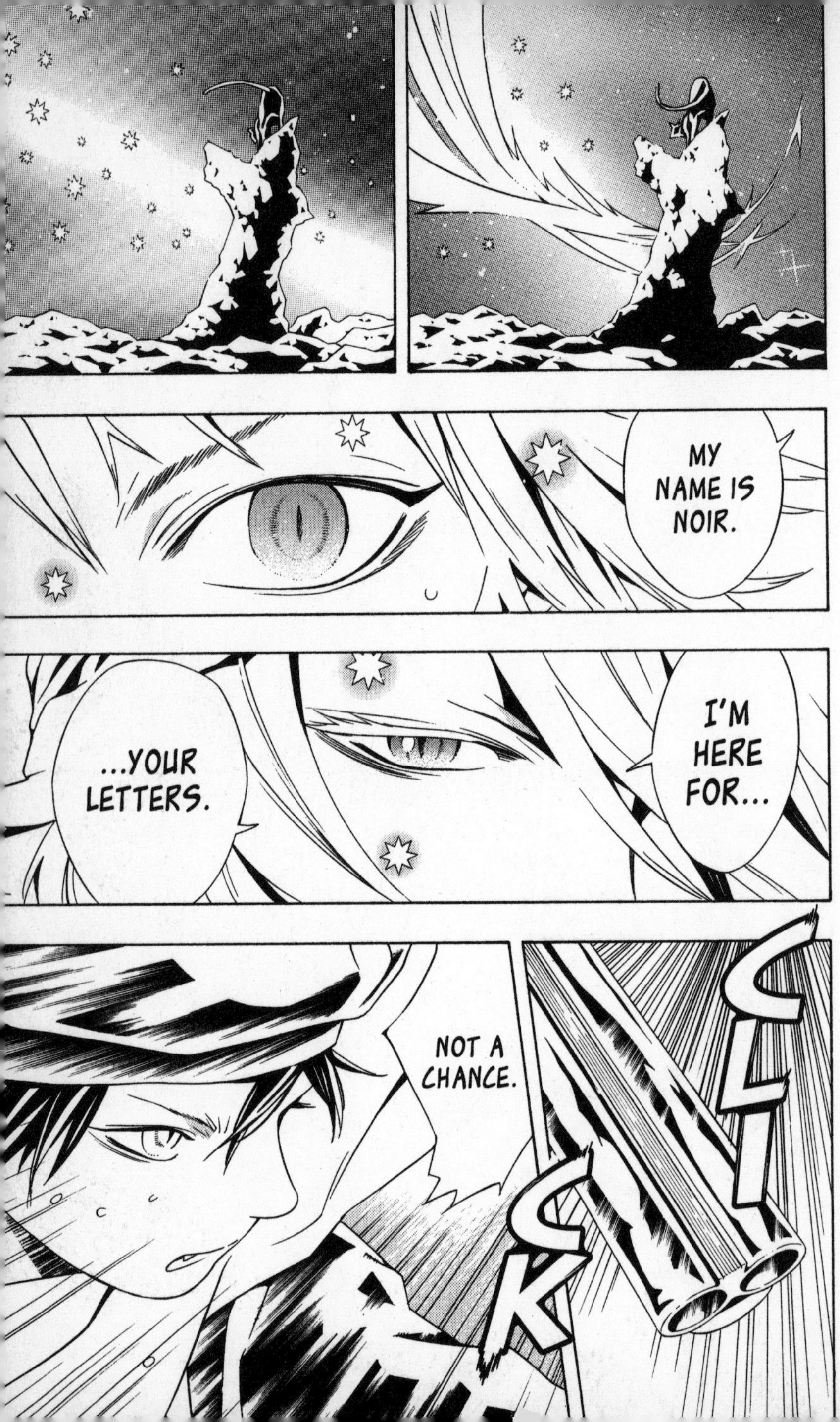
MY NAME IS NOIR.
I'M HERE FOR...
...YOUR LETTERS.
CLICK
NOT A CHANCE.